DATE DUE

Women and the Workplace

The Implications
of Occupational Segregation

Women and the Workplace

The Implications of Occupational Segregation

Edited by Martha Blaxall
and Barbara Reagan

The University of Chicago Press
Chicago and London

Based on a conference on occupational segregation held May 21–23, 1975. Sponsored by the Committee on the Status of Women in the Economics Profession, American Economic Association, with the Center for Research on Women in Higher Education and the Professions, Wellesley College. This volume originally appeared as a supplement to the Spring 1976 issue of *Signs: Journal of Women in Culture and Society* (Volume 1, Number 3, Part 2).

The University of Chicago Press, Chicago 60637
The University of Chicago Press, Ltd., London

Library of Congress Cataloging in Publication Data
Main entry under title:

Women and the workplace.

"Expanded version of the proceedings of a workshop conference on occupational segregation held
in May 1975 . . . jointly sponsored by the American
Economic Association Committee on the Status of
Women in the Economics Profession (CSWEP) and the
Center for Research on Women in Higher Education and
the Professions at Wellesley College."
"Originally appeared as a supplement to the Spring
1976 issue of Signs: journal of women in culture
and society."
Includes index.
1. Women—Employment—Congresses. 2. Discrimi-
nation in employment—Congresses. 3. Sex discrimi-
nation against women—Congresses. I. Blaxall,
Martha. II. Regan, Barbara Benton, 1920-
HD6052.W56 1976   331.4   76-10536
ISBN 0-226-05821-2
ISBN 0-226-05822-0 pbk.

Contents

Preface

Martha Blaxall and Barbara B. Reagan

The papers and comments in this volume represent an expanded version of the proceedings of a workshop conference on occupational segregation held in May 1975. Funded by the Carnegie Corporation of New York, it was jointly sponsored by the American Economic Association Committee on the Status of Women in the Economics Profession (CSWEP) and the Center for Research on Women in Higher Education and the Professions at Wellesley College.

CSWEP has an explicit charge to collect and analyze data relevant to the status of women economists in particular and to further theoretical and applied research related to the status of women in general. It feels that it is vital for professional associations to undertake research that might help to build a solid foundation for policy prescriptions related to the reappraisal of women's place in society. In addition, CSWEP wished to make a contribution to International Women's Year on a topic central to women in American society. Occupational segregation is such a subject. No improvement in women's economic standing can be realized unless it is diminished and the forces behind it understood.

The workshop conference had two major objectives: (1) to analyze occupational segregation as an interlocking set of institutions with sociological, psychological, and economic aspects and with deep historical roots; and (2) to consider what policy changes might be needed to achieve a society free from denial of job opportunities on the basis of sex. To accomplish these ends, economic analyses of labor market phenomena were accompanied by work from other disciplines in the social sciences. Within the several disciplines, a multiplicity of points of view were sought and obtained.

The many persons who contributed to the planning and execution of the conference and to the publication of this volume are too numerous for individual acknowledgment. We are grateful for all of their contributions. Particular mention is due to all the CSWEP members who designed, planned, and participated in the conference;[1] to the staff of the Center for Research on Women in Higher Education and the Professions, especially Carolyn Elliott, director, and Bronwen Haddad, conference coordinator. Finally, we would like to thank all those who participated in the conference as paper presenters, discussants, observers, or guests. Their work made possible the publication of this volume.

National Academy of Sciences (Blaxall)
Southern Methodist University (Reagan)

1. Barbara B. Reagan, Chair, Southern Methodist University; Walter Adams, Michigan State University; Carolyn Shaw Bell, Wellesley College; Martha Blaxall, National Academy of Sciences; Francine Blau, University of Illinois at Urbana-Champaign; Kenneth Boulding, University of Colorado; Collette Moser, Michigan State University; Myra Strober, Stanford University; Phyllis Wallace, Massachusetts Institute of Technology; Florence Weiss, National Economic Research Associates; and Robert Aaron Gordon, ex-officio as president of the American Economic Association.

INTRODUCTION

Occupational Segregation in International Women's Year

Barbara B. Reagan and Martha Blaxall

That something is wrong with women's position in today's world is now evident to many. Women tend to be segregated into certain "female" occupations. Almost universally, their work is less valued than work done by men. In labor markets women are often paid less than men for work that is recognizably equal. Even more commonly, women's jobs are given different job descriptions and titles so that the equivalent nature of similar jobs for women and men is masked and the lower pay for women rationalized.[1] In some cases, occupational segregation by sex denies employment opportunities to men who wish to enter such fields as nursing, grade school teaching, or secretarial work. Eradication of sexism would benefit such males. But the preponderant effect of sexism in labor markets is denial of opportunity to women with the skills and ability to contribute more to production than they are permitted to do under present conditions.

Why should this be so? Some economists argue that women get lower pay for similar work and, to some extent, are occupationally segregated by sex because of a combination of factors such as (1) women are less efficient than men in a given job; (2) they have lower skills, which may be related to lower investment in human capital (less formal education and/or less on-the-job training); (3) they have higher turnover rates;

1. Both Martha Griffiths and Winn Newman in this volume refer to specific examples in their experience where women have deliberately been paid less than men for the same work.

1

and (4) they are relatively immobile. Finally, some people argue that women may have less attachment to the labor force than men. Such explanations, focusing on real or imagined deficiencies of women, often also assume competitive models of labor markets. Another set of explanations of the lower valuation of women's work focuses on the monopsony aspects of labor markets, which permit employers to implement their distaste for hiring women and/or their perception that male workers do not want female co-workers or supervisors. The residual difference in pay between men and women that may be attributable to sexism, after accounting for other appropriate differences in various types of labor markets, is currently being subjected to economic analysis.[2] The answers are not yet on the table.

What is now clear is that, even if equal pay for equal work in the real sense is achieved, equality of opportunity will not occur simultaneously. This is because occupational segregation of the sexes results from the interaction of a well-entrenched and complex set of institutions that perpetuates the inferior position of women in the labor market, since all pressures within society, be they familial, legal, economic, cultural, or historical, tend to reinforce and support occupational segregation. All social and behavioral science disciplines must be used for a complete analysis of the key questions. Even a new discipline, "dimorphics," may be necessary, according to Kenneth Boulding, to permit us to shed our traditional habits of thinking about occupational segregation and target our research efforts more precisely at those elements which perpetuate the current unequal system.

No agreement was reached at the Wellesley conference on defining occupational segregation—or desegregation—in quantitative terms. However, Martha Griffiths provided fact after fact illustrating that women receive an unequal share of the benefits in the labor force due to the discrimination they suffer under the "justification" that men, not women, are the breadwinners. In fact, she points out, many women are breadwinners—two-thirds of all women workers are single, divorced, widowed, separated, or with husbands earning less than $7,000 per year. If society wishes to give equal treatment to "breadwinners," then women should have the same opportunities as men in the labor market. We can no longer afford occupational segregation, the former congresswoman concluded.

That these issues are also beginning to be seen worldwide as an important topic is shown in the preliminary working papers and later deliberations of the United Nation's World Conference of International Women's Year in Mexico City in June 1975. The main theme of the conference was equality, development, and peace. Patricia Hutar, head

2. See Francine D. Blau and Carol L. Jusenius, "Economists' Approaches to Sex Segregation in the Labor Market: An Appraisal," in this volume, for a survey of economists' explanations of occupational segregation.

of the United States delegation, called for greater equality for women in her official address to the conference: "We hope that from this conference men will gain a vision of a more just society in which a new equality for women and participation by them will mean a more varied and equitable sharing, to the benefit of men as well as women."[3] Furthermore, the provisional agenda of the *World Plan of Action* called for equal pay for equal work[4] and an end to occupational segregation by sex. "Special efforts should be made to foster positive attitudes towards the employment of women, irrespective of marital status, among employers and workers and among women and men in society at large, and to eliminate obstacles based on sex-typed divisions of labour."[5]

One of the results of the World Conference was to recognize the deep-seated as well as the pervasive nature of the problem by calling for a decade of effort to end sexism in occupational segregation. In order to accomplish this, the way in which sexism and our social institutions mutually reinforce each other must be identified and understood.

Thus, for the conference at Wellesley, CSWEP commissioned three papers and a major comment by the session chair to look at the social and institutional structures which maintain occupational segregation by sex. Jean Lipman-Blumen suggests a conceptual framework for understanding how we have arrived at a world that is widely segregated by sex. Judith Long Laws analyzes women's work aspiration and the way role relationships are used to control, inhibit, or support behavior. She concludes that work orientations of women have been constrained by role relationships that give precedence to the sex role. This, then, is one of the current determinants of a woman's work motivation and aspiration.

3. Address by Mrs. Patricia Hutar, head, United States delegation to World Conference of International Women's Year, June 20, 1975, p. 8.

4. Through the work of the International Labor Organization, eighty-one member countries had ratified, by November 1974, the Equal Remuneration Convention (1951), which calls for equal pay for work of equal value. This refers to rates of remuneration established without sex discrimination. See International Labor Office, *Equality of Opportunity and Treatment for Women Workers*, Report 8 (Geneva, 1974), p. 100.

The World Plan of Action drafted for the United Nations World Conference of International Women's Year used the phrase "equal pay for equal work." Many of the countries, including the delegation from the United States, and trade union representatives on delegations or among official observers worked to get the wording of the World Plan of Action changed to "equal pay for work of equal value," as in the ILO Convention. The New Zealand delegation opposed the change of wording in a press conference held on June 27, 1975 because they feared that, given the general undervaluation of women's work, this too would be used against women. The New Zealand delegation preferred a phrase such as "equal rate for the job." (New Zealand is one of several countries, including the United States, which has not ratified the ILO Convention but does accept and implement the principle. See p. 33 of publication cited above.) The final version of the World Plan of Action in some places changed the draft wording of "equal pay for equal work" to "equality in conditions of employment, including remuneration, regardless of marital status."

5. *World Plan of Action*, Item 11 of the Provisional Agenda, E/Con F. 66/5, p. 18.

Similarly, Margaret J. Gates, in her paper on occupational segregation and the law, concludes that though legislation and the legal system have seldom created occupational segregation, they have often reinforced it. Only in the past five to ten years have legal remedies to break down gender-related barriers in the work force been devised. At the same time, she notes, "the legal profession has remained male dominated."

Constantina Safilios-Rothschild discusses the marginality of women in the labor market, analyzing it in terms of its linkage with the family system and suggesting that structural changes in the occupational and family systems must be made to accommodate the equal occupational status of husbands and wives. Her discussion of the model of the USSR and the Eastern European societies and the resulting strains and oppression is particularly interesting in view of the position of the official delegations of these countries at the plenary sessions of the World Conference of International Women's Year. They strongly recognized the importance of eliminating discrimination against women but consistently denied that sexism exists in the USSR and the Eastern European countries. Gail Warshofsky Lapidus in her comparative paper on the United States and the Soviet Union concludes, "the Soviet experience seems to suggest that, contrary to earlier expectations shaped by Marxian theory, economic participation does not, in and of itself, guarantee equality of status and authority for women."

Ideas about the historical roots of occupational segregation were also explored at the conference. Heidi Hartmann deals with the interrelation and mutual accommodation of capitalism and patriarchy throughout history and across cultures from the viewpoint of an economic historian. From the viewpoint of a sociologist, Elise Boulding looks at familial constraints on women's work roles beginning with hunting and gathering societies, with emphasis on Western cultures. She sees women's role as a triple one of breeder-feeder-producer. However, the woman's producer role is differentiated from the male producer role. In commenting on these papers from the point of view of the developing nations, Hanna Papanek observes that "occupational segregation must be studied on an internationally comparative basis," so that those nations which are just beginning to industrialize can learn from the experience that the industrialized countries have had with respect to segregating women in the marketplace. She notes that it is not surprising that many of the new opportunities for women in these developing countries have tended to be in occupations where "traditional men's jobs" have turned into "women's occupations" with relatively low wages.

Three papers deal with the economic dimensions of occupational segregation. They focus almost entirely upon the U.S. labor market. Francine Blau and Carol Jusenius discuss the limited utility of neoclassical (traditional) economic theory for understanding the causes of sex segregation and the need to incorporate further institutional hypotheses—including overcrowding into women's occupations—into the mainstream of economic thinking about discrimination. Isabel Sawhill demonstrates the way in which sex segregation and the lower value associated with women's work tend to contribute to the poverty status of many female-headed families. Marianne Ferber and Helen Lowry further demonstrate the economic costs associated with sex segregation. Discrimination can help to explain women's inferior position in the labor force directly and indirectly as women adapt to the inferior labor market opportunities they find open to them. Higher unemployment for women is one result. In an Appendix, Myra Strober and Barbara B. Reagan analyze the occupational segregation by sex within the occupation of economist with respect to field specialization and suggest a path model of field choice for women economists. In commenting on these papers, David Gordon points out that none of the orthodox economic theories really permits the kind of analysis that is likely to lead to real improvement in employment conditions for women. To remove the inequality in the current economic and social division of labor, Gordon sees only one course of action—the overthrow of capitalism—although he recognizes that even this condition is not sufficient.

The six panelists offering policy recommendations for alternative courses of action offer nothing as radical as David Gordon's solution. Policy prescriptions range from enforcement of existing discrimination laws to more realistic counseling practices if women are to be prepared to fit into the kinds of technological opportunities which will be available in the labor market in ten years' time. There was no consensus that women's position in the labor market would rapidly improve, but there was overwhelming agreement that the struggle for more equality and better opportunity would have to continue at an intensive level if existing gains were to be maintained.

In her perceptive summary, Myra Strober admits that the conference did not adequately address policy issues. She calls for another series of conferences to explore policy alternatives to eliminate occupational segregation. The absence of occupational segregation can mean the equal distribution of men and women among occupations. It can also mean the freedom to elect any occupation one desires regardless of sex, race, or other characteristics.

We hope that the sharing of our deliberations will help others to further analyze the causes of occupational segregation and develop policy alternatives to achieve a society free from denial of job opportunities on the basis of sex.

Southern Methodist University (Reagan)
National Academy of Sciences (Blaxall)

Can We Still Afford Occupational Segregation? Some Remarks

Martha W. Griffiths

As of October 30, 1974, there were 33 million women working in the civilian labor force, women of all ages, of every race and ethnic group, single, married, divorced, and widowed. Although these women represented 37 percent of the total labor force, they were employed largely in teaching, health, and clerical occupations. A substantial majority of women workers—58 percent—were married and living with their husbands. More than 50 percent of all married women have been employed outside the home since 1972.

The more education a woman has, the more likely she is to be in the labor force. Seventy percent of all women workers in 1972 had at least a high school education, and one in eight was a college graduate. Although these women, on the average, are as well educated as men, there is a difference in the distribution of men and women in the labor force by occupational category and median income. For example, 7 percent of men workers and 35 percent of women workers are employed as clerical personnel. Despite the larger numbers of women, however, the median income for a female college graduate was only $5,551; for men in the same occupation, median earnings were $8,617. Although 14 percent of both male and female workers were in the professional and technical fields in 1972, the median income that year was $11,806 for male college graduates, but only $7,878 for women. Although I shall not dwell on this, it is clear that America is deprived of half its resources when a woman is denied a good job or a policymaking position. And the personal toll on the woman is enormous. One of the illuminating books on this subject is *Women and Madness* by Phyllis Chesler.[1]

The argument which men have used to claim the best jobs and the

---

1. Phyllis Chesler, *Women and Madness* (New York: Doubleday & Co., 1972).

most pay invokes traditional male and female stereotypes: men are breadwinners and women are wives or widows; men provide necessary incomes for their families, but women do not; women and families are supported by men, not women. The prevailing view in Congress is that every woman is born to a rich father who gives her in marriage to a rich husband, who in turn thoughtfully dies ahead of her, leaving her well provided not only with money but also with tender, loving sons.

Using this stereotype, society flagrantly and severely discriminates against women in the labor force, despite the fact that society's attitudes toward women are based on myths rather than reality. For example, many women are now rearing children without any financial assistance from their husbands. Families with a female head are increasing in our society. Divorce and separation are forcing many women without wage-earning skills into the primary support role for themselves and their children. Unless a woman has adequate alimony or other sources of income, she faces financial difficulty in this role. Yet, in divorce actions, 50 percent of the women involved do not receive alimony or child support, and for the other 50 percent who do have such court orders, the median payment is approximately $1,300 per year. The preliminary version of a report that I requested from the General Accounting Office before I left Congress found that the combined average monthly income of women and children receiving both welfare benefits and earned income in 1975 was sometimes less than $300 a month, whereas the median income of the man who had abandoned them was about $800 a month. These data are derived from an analysis of 1,700 cases that were specifically selected to represent a national sample.

This report did not consider wives who were not on welfare. Many of these latter women are divorced and supporting two to four children with incomes from jobs which pay from $5,000 to $7,000 per year. The median annual wage for a woman-headed family is $5,116, and with these earnings the woman must pay the costs of child care while she is absent from the home. In many cases the husbands of these women contribute nothing to the families' support. Even if the court decrees that the husband pay a substantial sum of money for the support of the children, a woman can rarely find a lawyer who will initiate legal proceedings for her until thousands of dollars are due and the lawyer determines that the husband is in a position to pay the uncollected amounts.

Thus, while men have been given jobs, high pay, and preferential promotion on the supposition that they are supporting wives and children, the facts show that this supposition is not true in a large percentage of cases. However, if the breadwinner argument is applied in fact rather than in theory, women can no longer be denied the right to the education, the jobs, the pay, and the promotions which have traditionally gone to men. If women are in reality the providers, then they should have the benefit of the law on their side. Nevertheless, despite recent gains, the facts are that women are still confined to low-paying jobs by virtue of their educational level, the type of career counseling they receive, and society's unwillingness to accept the real reasons why women work.

Women work because of economic need, just as men do. Two-thirds of all women workers are either single, divorced, widowed, or separated or have husbands who earn less than $7,000 per year. Working wives employed full time contribute almost two-fifths of their families' incomes, and in many cases these earnings make the difference between a middle- and a low-income standard of living.

Despite these facts policymakers continue to ignore the real role which women play in the labor force. When Willard Wirtz appeared before the House Ways and Means Committee to speak on unemployment compensation as secretary of labor, he explained that the unemployment situation was not as bad as one might think, because there were many "secondary workers" counted in those statistics. I asked Mr. Wirtz, "Since you are the secretary of labor, and since secondary workers probably have secondary rights, just who are the secondary workers?" Well, there was some hemming and hawing and scuffling about, and of course it turned out that they were women and children. So I said, "Well, I think when you come before this committee as the secretary of labor, you should have an objective definition of secondary workers, because I think the secretary of labor should treat all workers alike. Therefore I would like to make a suggestion for a definition of a secondary worker. The primary worker is the one who buys the children's clothes, the groceries, and pays for the music lessons and the books; and the secondary worker is the one who buys the fishing tackle, the outboard motors, and the booze."

No satisfactory response was made by the secretary, but shortly after the hearing that day, a young man came up to me and said, "Mrs. Griffiths, when you made that suggestion to the secretary, I personally felt I had been hit in the stomach. My children are now all in school, and on Monday my wife is going back to work. I wasn't paying much attention to the secretary, but as he was talking I was thinking to myself, when my wife goes back to work, we will buy an outboard motor."

The facts are that women experience rates of unemployment substantially greater than those of men, and over time the ratio of female unemployment to male unemployment has risen. The exception is during this current recession, when for some reason women have not been as badly hit as men. The greater proportion of women in service jobs may help to explain this situation. Yet those women who are able to find jobs work primarily in "women's" occupations.

Although the median school years completed is the same for both women and men in the labor force, women with the same educational

background as men generally have different jobs, with less pay, a e was some cases fewer and less costly fringe benefits. Let us look at the Male pational segregation first. Among college graduates sometimes 6,955, subtle difference in work location or title will indicate the subordina of a female employee. For example, a few years back *Time* magazine, earn- only men as reporters; women were hired as research assistants, de ivate their comparable or even higher educational credentials. Women w pa- there to supply men with the facts, which the men were then assigne rity write into stories. The male reporters had offices or desks by the v the dows, while the female research assistants were seated in the cente sion the room.   een

In addition to special privilege or choice office location, the tr ons ment of male employees is different from that of female employee other ways. During my years in Congress, it was brought to my atten men that one of the General Motors plants in my district was hiring me pen- the category of "receivers of shipped goods." Women were in the nthly gory of "shippers." According to union regulations, receivers coul men. be suspended, no matter what kinds of mistakes they made or what h, but of infractions of company rules they committed. Yet the shipper nount. were all women, could be suspended for a day or two for any erro ffering on the job. Although the required experience and the job dutie ot un- very similar for shippers and receivers, the women who worked age for pers received from two to three dollars an hour less than the me ress of worked as receivers. When I questioned the union about this pr they explained that the men had to lift heavy weights on the jo t the received more money because of this requirement. However, my for a band was then negotiating contracts for management, and he infor em- me that men were not required to lift any heavy object in any la off organized plant anywhere in the city of Detroit. Forklift trucks w ds, generally employed for this purpose, and when they were not u pt a several men would work as a group to lift the heavy object.   be

In early 1964 the union president of a large Detroit industry c to my office with a woman employee who had been a neighbor of mi rtly one time. This woman was having problems on the job, and in the co ady of the discussion she asked the union president about the differe ging between union wage rates for men and women. He acknowledge has differences but said that "men will never hit the bricks to raise s in women's pay."   39

Later that year, or early the next, that company needed to lay op- some workers, and under the rules of the 1964 Civil Rights Act, wo or- with little seniority were laid off, and men were bumped into their p er tions. One of these men wrote me a letter objecting to the two-dol is per-hour pay cut which accompanied his new job. I suggested t vith discuss this matter with his union president, since I had been inf , this earlier that the union was not supporting increased pay for "wo g-or-other," and the machine spelled out "rhododendron" as the correct flower. In the future highly skilled people will be needed to operate these machines. Clearly women will have tremendous opportunities in these fields if they obtain the necessary level of technical knowledge.

Another area which is discriminatory against women is that of tax legislation. Under current tax laws, a husband or wife who inherits the other's property must pay inheritance taxes; a church or another charity receiving the same bequest does not have to pay such taxes. All of this proves, of course, that churches and charities are organized, and wives are not.

It is also important to understand that a woman in the home has no "economic value" in this country. She is not in the tax structure, and unpaid household work is not counted in the gross national product. Despite manpower projections, there is little evidence of change in male and female enrollment patterns in vocational-technical education over the last five years. The repercussions of the energy crisis are probably being felt first and hardest among those most recently hired in the labor force—women and minorities. What effect a decreasing birthrate may have on the gross national product and the unemployment rate is not now known. But these trends suggest that underutilization of women will continue to be a problem unless plans are implemented now to expand women's opportunities in technical, trade, and industrial apprenticeship programs leading to higher-paying opportunities in which there is a growing demand for skilled workers, male and female.

Because women have been found to show the same skill aptitudes and abilities as men, they should be encouraged to train in and enter nontraditional fields as well as the more traditional ones. We cannot as a nation afford occupational segregation. We cannot afford to let the vast potential of half this nation go to waste. We must have improved student-counseling programs to go hand in hand with expanded employment and educational opportunities. And we must ensure that the legal remedies to combat occupational discrimination in hiring and promotional practices are known and readily available to women who need them.

Dollar for dollar, a woman's paycheck or pension seldom stretches as far as a man's. Credit is far less accessible to a woman. Single women have more trouble in getting credit than single men, and divorced women frequently cannot get credit at all. In many cases a woman on welfare is able to obtain credit or necessary home appliances much more easily than a woman who is working on a low salary, despite the fact that welfare benefits could never be garnisheed by a creditor, should the woman not make her payment. We must realize that the traditional stereotypes and the belief that only men are the breadwinners who provide the necessary funds for their families are no longer true in our modern society.

When a male breadwinner abdicates his responsibility, it is most likely that the woman will assume his wage-earning role in an effort to maintain a home for her children, regardless of any help she may obtain from their father. But in order to assume that role, she must be adequately prepared for work and get paid for it at the same rate as the man sitting next to her performing the same job, whether in an office, a factory, a hospital, a university, or wherever. Society can no longer afford occupational segregation, for women *are* breadwinners and play an equal role with men. Thus, in my judgment, we shall have to begin to live on a one-to-one, equal basis, and there is no more time to wait.

Farmington Hills, Michigan

THE SOCIAL INSTITUTIONS OF OCCUPATIONAL SEGREGATION

Toward a Homosocial Theory of Sex Roles: An Explanation of the Sex Segregation of Social Institutions

Jean Lipman-Blumen

Occupational segregation of women is a major reflection of the generalized segregation that characterizes all aspects of Western social life. It is the visible sign of a massive institutional substructure on which we are most likely to founder unless we are able to find a way around it. Two of the papers in this section deal with macrosociological segregation patterns that link different institutional sectors of society: Safilios-Rothschild addresses the question of sex segregation in the articulation between the institutions of the family and the occupational world; Gates explicates the ways in which the legal institutions buttress the segregation of the domestic and occupational domains. The Laws paper, operating on a different level of analysis, looks at different theoretical approaches to women's segregated involvement in the labor force.

All three of these papers discuss the segregated social context in which we live, a context that is the end result of a complex web of historical factors. Here we shall explore briefly a conceptual framework for understanding how we have arrived at this world so segregated at work, at home, in politics, and in recreation. This framework provides

I am indebted beyond measure to Dr. Jessie Bernard who critiqued an earlier version of this paper and whose many conversations with me have helped me to sharpen my own ideas and whose insights have opened new vistas to me. Dr. Harold Leavitt, in a similar way, helped me to clarify my thinking about many of the issues discussed in this paper.

an "organizing hypothesis" that allows us to bring together in some coherent way seemingly unrelated and even contradictory bits and pieces of evidence from many areas, including the domains of child development, sociology, politics, and economics. It is what we shall call a "homosocial theory of sex roles." It is meant to be, as we have suggested elsewhere,[1] a theory of the middle range[2] which attempts to explain a limited range of social phenomena.

Homosociality and Sex Roles

First, we shall define "homosocial" as the seeking, enjoyment, and/or preference for the company of the same sex. It is distinguished from "homosexual" in that it does not *necessarily* involve (although it may under certain circumstances) an explicitly erotic sexual interaction between members of the same sex.

The basic premise of this homosocial view of sex roles suggests that men are attracted to, stimulated by, and interested in other men. It is a process that is noticeable in early childhood and is channeled and encouraged by the entire range of social institutions within which males live. The stratification system, which ranks individuals and groups in terms of their value to society, systematically places males in more highly valued roles than females. Until very recently, the stratification system located men in such a way that they had virtually total and exclusive access to the entire range of resources available within the society.

The pragmatic recognition that males controlled economic, political, educational, occupational, legal, and social resources created a situation in which men identified with and sought help from other men. Women, recognizing the existential validity of the situation, also turned to men for help and protection. By now, it is practically a psychological truism that individuals identify with other individuals whom they perceive to be the controllers of resources in any given situation. This is true of children vis-à-vis parents as well as of workers in an occupational setting. It is no less true of the relations between the sexes.

Men can and commonly do seek satisfaction for most of their needs from other men. They can derive satisfaction for their intellectual, physical, political, economic, occupational, social, power, and status needs —and in some circumstances their sexual needs—from other men. The dominance order among men is based upon control of resources, including land, money, education, occupations, political connections, and family ties. Women, forced to seek resources from men, in turn become resources which men can use to further their own eminence in the homosocial world of men. The acquisition of a beautiful woman is a

1. Jean Lipman-Blumen, "Changing Sex Roles in American Culture: Future Directions for Research," *Archives of Sexual Behavior* 4 (July 1975): 433–46.
2. Robert K. Merton, *Social Theory and Social Structure* (Glencoe, Ill.: Free Press, 1949).

resource that heightens the status claims of a man vis-à-vis other men and provides him with a sexual resource as well.

The one basic need that men cannot meet for other men is paternity, in most societies the ultimate claim to masculinity. For that, men are forced to turn to women. Contrary to the claims of some theorists, men have not turned women into sex objects. Rather, from a structural viewpoint, women have been forced to fashion themselves as sex objects to attract men and distract them away from other men into the comforts of heterosexual relationships. Once involved in heterosexual relationships, most males are less likely to seek homosexual relationships. Nonetheless, as the existence of affluent men's clubs, working-class bowling leagues, unions, pool shooting, or corner groups attest,[3] the call of the homosocial world is still strong long after men become engaged in heterosexual relationships.

The origins of male control over resources are open to speculation. One possible explanation lies in the well-nigh universal historical male roles of warrior and hunter, roles inaccessible to women because of their childbearing and child-nursing functions. Warrior and hunter roles placed men in positions of protecting and acquiring territory and food—fundamental resources in any society. Men's positions in these resource-acquiring and resource-protecting roles also led to certain dominance hierarchies that persisted long after technology had obviated the need for such differentiation and stratification of roles.

Exchange between the Sexes

For some social scientists, a major portion of social interaction can be understood in terms of exchange systems.[4] In relationships between the sexes, males have had a disproportionate amount of resources under their control. They could bargain their power, status, money, land, political influence, legal power, and educational and occupational resources (all usually greater than women's) against women's more limited range of resources, consisting of sexuality, youth, beauty, and the promise of paternity. Men also could bargain their aggression, strength, competitiveness, and leadership capabilities against women's domestic and clerical services. In addition, men could offer women potential maternity, reciprocally the ultimate validation (in a sexist world) of a woman's

3. Mirra Komarovsky, *Blue-Collar Marriage* (New York: Vintage Press, 1962); Elliot Liebow, *Tally's Corner* (Boston: Little, Brown & Co., 1967).

4. Peter M. Blau, *Exchange and Power in Social Life* (New York: John Wiley & Sons, 1964); Sol Levine and Paul White, "Exchange as a Conceptual Framework for the Study of Interorganizational Relationships," *Administrative Science Quarterly* 5 (March 1961): 583–97; George C. Homans, "Social Behavior as Exchange," *American Journal of Sociology* 63 (May 1958): 597–606; and *Social Behavior* (New York: Harcourt, Brace & World, 1961).

femininity. But until recently, men did not need to offer competent sexuality.

As I have noted elsewhere, "this uneven array of resources systematically made men more interesting to women, women less interesting and useful to other women, and women fairly often unnecessary and/or burdensome to men."[5] This disparity of resources made it apparent that men were the most valued social beings.

With the recent advent of the feminist movement, we have begun to witness the redistribution of a small portion of these resources. We have begun to see the renaissance of female subcultures which have waxed and waned in earlier times.[6] Women are beginning to demand and receive legal power, which gives them access to educational, occupational, and financial resources. This, in turn, allows other women (and eventually men) to perceive them as the controllers of some resources. As a result, women are beginning to develop a new homosocial world of their own, turning to one another, rather than to men, for help in exchange relationships. There are indications of an emerging "new-girl network" analogous to the powerful "old-boy network" of the male world.

Examples of women turning to women for help are becoming more commonplace. Communication networks that pass along information about jobs, legislation, and women in trouble are developing. The myth that even women do not like female doctors is being put to rest by the advent of female-run obstetrical/gynecological clinics. When males dominated the obstetrics and gynecology departments of most universities and hospitals (as they usually still do), women had little choice but to go to male doctors. As female-run clinics have sprung up across the country, they have had more patients than they could handle easily.

Vicarious Patterns

But the development of a homosocial world for women that reaches beyond the domestic sphere is still in its infancy.[7] Traditionally, the homosocial world has existed for the benefit of men, who controlled all access to resources. As the Safilios-Rothschild paper suggests,[8] the Par-

5. Lipman-Blumen, p. 440.

6. Carroll Smith-Rosenberg, "The Female World of Love and Ritual: Relationships between Women in Nineteenth-Century America," *Signs: Journal of Women in Culture and Society* 1, no. 1 (Autumn 1975): 1–29; Jessie Bernard, *How to Think about Women in This Day and Age,* in progress.

7. Bernard's description of the thirteenth- and fourteenth-century German and French béguine collectives for women which performed economic, social, and political functions for a female homosocial world were a rare exception. She suggests that other comparable forms of female homosociality, as yet unknown to us because of the neglect of women's history, may indeed have existed.

8. Constantina Safilios-Rothschild, "Dual Linkages between the Occupational and Family System: A Macrosociological Analysis," in this volume.

sons formulation of the normative articulation between the family and the occupational world involved a single linkage—between the husband's work role and his familial role. Parsons concluded that comparable occupational roles for husband and wife would introduce a negative, competitive component in the marital relationship. Parsons, in effect, was providing an ex post facto explanation of a homosocial pattern in which only the husband had direct access to resources of income and occupation, and the wife and children gained their status through their relationship with the male figure.

In a male homosocial world, women derive their status and resources through relationships with fathers, brothers, husbands, sons, or lovers. Women's need to derive their status vicariously often has led to their adoption of a vicarious achievement pattern.[9] Safilios-Rothschild informs us that "working-class women . . . often have had a higher occupational status than their husbands when they worked as secretaries, teachers, or nurses, but clearly had a lower income than their husbands." Thus, even when women succeed in occupying work roles of higher status than their husbands, their access to the resource which offers the greatest potential for exchange—income—is limited. And the reported Havens and Tully data, which indicate that professional women's median earnings correspond to the median earnings of male laborers,[10] are another reflection of the multiple ways in which the homosocial world, created and protected by men, operates to limit women's access to significant resources.

Men have not singlehandedly created and perpetuated this world; women unwittingly have helped to preserve it by marrying men with higher status lines than themselves. This is a trap they could hardly avoid if they wished to have even indirect access to resources. Safilios-Rothschild correctly points out that this "marrying up" phenomenon was an "important mechanism that safeguarded a situation in which husbands would have higher-level occupational roles."

Influence of Law

In the Domestic Sphere

The division of labor in the family is another reflection of the homosocial world in which males control resources. Time budget studies

9. Jean Lipman-Blumen, "The Vicarious Achievement Ethic and Non-traditional Roles for Women" (paper presented at the annual meeting of the Eastern Sociological Society, April 1973); Jean Lipman-Blumen and Harold J. Leavitt, "Vicarious Achievement as a Factor in Adulthood," *Counseling Psychologist,* special issue, ed. Nancy Schlossberg and Alan Entine, forthcoming.

10. Elizabeth Havens and Judy Corder Tully, "Female Intergenerational Occupational Mobility: Comparisons of Patterns?" *American Sociological Review* 37 (December 1972): 774–77.

have indicated that, in many countries, husbands have more leisure time in the home than do their wives.[11] Often this time is spent in the company of males outside the family unit—in private men's clubs, male golf clubs, or working-class analogues to these more affluent patterns.

Safilios-Rothschild's paper, drawing from cross-national studies, suggests that the additional hours that women in the labor force must spend on home chores compared with men places them at a disadvantage in the marketplace. The additional work load at home presumably dampens their aspirations and limits the amount of extra time and energy they can devote to improving their occupational positions.

The Gates paper corroborates the link between the division of labor within the home and women's disadvantaged occupational position, a link buttressed by domestic law. Gates suggests that a marriage contract is more properly conceived as a contract between the couple and the state in which the individuals agree to "conform to the terms which government has agreed are appropriate for marriage. [These terms] include the man's obligation to support his wife and children [and] the woman's obligation to care for the home and children."[12] Such marriage contracts imply recognition of the male as head of the household. She argues that, "because men have a legal duty to support their families, they are considered [by employers] permanent members of the work force [and] women . . . are considered temporary workers who will leave their jobs to bear and rear families or to be homemakers, since that is their obligation as wives."[13] The law, promulgated and practiced by males, once again serves to create and protect a male homosocial world in which men are given preference in work situations where they are able to build resources.

The resource that women often use to establish a supposedly binding relationship with men—children—eventually becomes a very important means of further reducing women's access to other resources. Women's roles as childbearer and child rearer serve to eliminate them as serious competitors in the occupational world. As Gates and others have indicated, women and women's families often are reluctant to make the human capital investment in their own education in view of their projected roles as wife and mother.[14]

11. Claude Alzon, *La Femme potiche et la femme bonniche* (Paris: François Maspero, 1973); G. R. Barker, "La Femme en Union Sovietique," *Sociologie et sociétés* 4 (November 1972): 159–91; Magdelena Sokolowska, "Some Reflections on the Different Attitudes of Men and Women toward Work," *International Labor Review* 92 (July–December 1965): 35–50.

12. Margaret J. Gates, "Occupational Segregation and the Law," in this volume.

13. Ibid.

14. Jacob Mincer, "Labor Force Participation of Married Women: A Study of Labor Supply," in *Aspects of Labor Economics* (Princeton, N.J.: Princeton University Press, 1962), pp. 63–97; and "The Distribution of Labor Income: A Survey with Special Reference to the Human Capital Approach," *Journal of Economic Literature* 8 (March 1970): 1–26.

Employers similarly are resistant to hiring women or training them for jobs in which they are not readily replaceable or substitutable. As a result, women are kept in minimum-training, low–investment risk, substitutable positions from which there is no strong career ladder to jobs that offer meaningful resources of income, status, or power. The recent downtrend in fertility rates—if it continues—may have an effect upon this situation.[15] When more women choose to remain nonparents, their ability to develop human capital in terms of education and work experience and their access to more responsible, higher-status and higher-income jobs should increase.

In the Political Forum

A major resource is the political forum, from which women traditionally have been effectively barred. Access to the public forum is a potent means to political and legal power. It is the most important realm of power for determining the legal conditions of life. Legislation that creates or bars access to resources is developed within the political forum. It is only very recently that women's action groups in the United States have begun to develop meaningful, sustained, potent strategies for influencing the legislative process.[16]

Women are excluded from public decision-making domains —legislatures and departments of state where foreign-policy matters are determined. The exclusion of women from the political forum is evidenced by the underrepresentation of women in national legislatures around the world. In peacetime, women comprise approximately 1 percent of the national legislatures, a figure which has had remarkable cross-national stability.[17] It is only in times of war that the proportion of women rises to approximately 3 percent, again a figure with considerable cross-national consistency.Wars may be one form of the perturbations that Leavitt suggests disturb a system in equilibrium.[18]

In another context, we have argued that crisis is a condition which

15. Jean Lipman-Blumen and Ann R. Tickamyer, "Sex Roles in Transition: A Ten-Year Review," *Annual Review of Sociology* 1 (1975): 297–337; June Sklar and Beth Berkov, "Abortion, Illegitimacy, and the American Birthrate," *Science* 185 (September 1974): 909–15.

16. The very recent defeat of the Casey amendment in the U.S. Congress (that would have limited the power of Title IX of the Education Amendment of 1972 in prohibiting single-sex physical education classes and honorary societies) is an example of a developing homosocial world of women. In this instance women's action groups combined resources to lobby vigorously for the help of women legislators, who in turn could use their resources to influence the votes of their male legislative colleagues. We may be witnessing here the first cracks in the traditionally impervious political flank of the male homosocial world.

17. Jean Lipman-Blumen, "Role De-differentiation as a System Response to Crisis: Occupational and Political Roles of Women," *Sociological Inquiry* 43, no. 2 (1973): 105–29; Lionel Tiger, *Men in Groups* (New York: Random House, Vintage Books, 1970).

18. Harold Leavitt, "Comment," in this volume.

weakens the usually strong differentiation of roles in all social domains—the family, the occupational world, the political realm, etc.[19] This is so because of the fundamental need during crisis to reallocate resources in order to survive or to maintain the status quo. And social roles, indeed, are an important resource which may be reallocated (i.e., dedifferentiated) during crisis.

The stratification system, a mechanism for ordering individuals and groups in terms of ranked value to a society, undergoes serious deterioration during periods of crisis. This is so because its particularistic focus on who is occupying a role, rather than on the level of goal attainment, serves no crisis-resolving functions during these periods. As a result, the stratification system, which acts as a social grid keeping individuals in highly differentiated roles, begins to crumble in crisis periods. Individuals previously barred from certain roles are allowed access and even deliberately recruited into these roles.[20]

Holter has argued that the admission of women into national legislatures in increased numbers during periods of stability only occurs when these bodies have become obsolete as decision-making instruments.[21] Further support for this homosocial viewpoint is the fact that the greatest number of women in the Soviet political structure is within the Supreme Soviet, the political organ with largely ceremonial, rather than real, functions. The homosocial organization of society demands that, for ordinary purposes, women are excluded from the important realms of social life, except as adjuncts to men or until those realms lose their importance.

In Law Enforcement

In addition to limiting women's access to the political forum, the male homosocial world has seriously impeded women's equal entry into the military and police forces, the mechanisms for ensuring compliance with the legislative and political edicts of a society. Gates has documented the legal history of the police force in the United States, in which numerous "state and municipal laws establishing police departments provided for only male officers to carry out the general mission of the force, including patrol and investigations."

The police force offers an interesting example of job requirements that serve to circumvent the legal prohibition against discrimination on

19. Lipman-Blumen, "Role De-differentiation" and "A Crisis Framework Applied to Macrosociological Family Changes: Marriage, Divorce, and Occupational Trends Associated with World War II," *Journal of Marriage and the Family*, special issue, ed. Constantina Safilios-Rothschild (November 1975).

20. Lipman-Blumen, "Role De-differentiation."

21. Harriet Holter, "Sex Roles and Social Change," *Acta Sociologica* 14, nos. 1–2 (1971): 2–12.

the basis of sex. Height, physical strength, and agility requirements are used to eliminate women and males who do not meet the criteria of the male homosocial world, despite the fact that the "law requires that all selection criteria for employment be related to the tasks which the employee will actually perform." The exclusion of those individuals who cannot participate actively in the male homosocial world from the public forum, the legislative world and its processes, and the enforcement mechanisms of a society seriously reinforces the stranglehold that the male homosocial world has on the crucial resources of a society.

Through Protective Legislation

The law has worked in still other ways to keep women from gaining access to occupations and thereby financial resources. Protective laws, originally designed to protect women and children from exploitation by employers, have been used to prevent women from entering roles which could serve as stepping stones to managerial positions. The irony of this situation, as Gates notes, is that laws designed to protect women and children from sweatshop conditions have been used to protect men's jobs from infiltration by women.

Another example of so-called protective legislation that adversely affects the very group it is designed to protect is the legal prohibition against using women in combat. Women are prevented from entering high-risk-taking positions in the military which lead to high level, resource-wielding positions. Women are not similarly protected from caring for high-risk-takers close to the front lines in the nursing role characterized by lower pay, lower status, less resource availability, less decision-making power. This exclusion from high-risk-taking roles occurs in other domains—finance, industry, medicine, law, aerospace —domains which lead to high reward and, thus, access to resources.

Exclusion from Athletics

Another high-risk area, the world of sport, is predominantly reserved for males. This is symbolized by the higher economic stakes for male professional athletic contests. National honor is risked in athletic competitions at the Olympic level which pit one country against another in the form of an individual male or a team of males. Although women athletes compete in the Olympic games, the sports that command the greatest spectator attention and interest are those that feature male athletes. With few exceptions, in the Olympic games males are the guardians of their country's honor—a major resource not to be handed lightly to women. And the recent furor over the demand of Title IX of the Education Amendment of 1972 that equal amounts of money be expended on female and male athletic activities in educational institutions is still another reflection of the safeguarding of resources for males only.

Thus, we see that the different institutions of our society—the family, the labor market, athletics, the judiciary system, the political world—all act in an integrated and reinforcing way to maintain a male homosocial world in which only men are included and allowed access to the various resources of a society. In this way they perpetuate their control over the entire social system and maintain segregation of the marketplace as well as all other significant domains of social life. Women, children, and men who cannot meet the strict criteria of the male homosocial world are excluded and held in relatively servile positions in which it is virtually impossible to accumulate resources that would set them free. Males who refuse or are unable to meet the standards of the male homosocial world are "peripheralized" much as male monkeys who lose out in the male dominance order are peripheralized and allowed only the company of women and nonadult males.[22]

Psychoanalysis and Sexuality

The newest rationale for this male homosocial structure has been woven on a relatively recent and powerful loom—traditional Freudian psychoanalysis. Traditional psychoanalysis shapes women to feel it is "natural" and "feminine" to relinquish their autonomy and thereby to suppress any predilection for developing skills that lead to the accretion of power and other resources, including leadership. Greer has suggested that "women are contoured by their conditioning to abandon autonomy and seek guidance."[23] This only reinforces the male power structure and teaches women not even to attempt developing strategies for building reservoirs of power and other resources. Psychoanalysis suggests, instead, that women should look to men to meet such needs. Women, to be acceptable to men, must be "unmasculine" and resemble the male homosexual, the most undesirable form of male, according to the criteria of the male homosocial world.

Sexuality is a recognized form of power, and the "double standard" of sexual behavior for males and females systematically has taught women at an early age to repress this power, to repress even their awareness of their own desire to express their sexuality. The "double standard" of sexual behavior controls women's sexual power and trans-

22. Raphaela Best, *The Group, Sex and Learning in the Primary Grades*, in progress; and R. M. Rose, T. P. Gordon, and I. S. Bernstein, "Plasma Testosterone Levels in the Male Rhesus: Influences of Sexual and Social Stimuli," *Science* 178 (November 1972): 643–45.

23. Germaine Greer, *The Female Eunuch* (New York: McGraw-Hill Book Co., 1971), p. 91.

forms it into a resource for men, rather than for women. For women it serves only as a short-term power source—a means of attracting a male, hopefully to establish a permanent relationship. But, as most marriage counselors can attest, the power of female sexuality within the marriage structure soon begins to wane and becomes a resource which is very difficult for a woman to maintain over time vis-à-vis her husband.

Female sexuality is a resource which is negotiable legitimately only within limited spheres. Thus, under ordinary circumstances females cannot overtly and effectively use this power in other areas of social life—such as in interaction with the occupational world, the political arena, or the educational system. (This is not to say that female sexuality is never utilized in these areas but merely that, when it is, it usually is used in a covert and unsanctioned manner.) The crude aphorisms that a woman has "slept her way to the top" or "gotten her degree on her back" reflect the lack of legitimation for such uses of female sexual power.

The feminist movement has encouraged the development and expression of female sexuality as a form of power. This call for the growth of a significant form of female power is patently feared and serves as one of the major bases of objection to the feminist movement by the male world.

This homosocial view of sex roles does not rest on a biological predisposition to bonding, such as Tiger's work explicitly claims. Nor is it meant as a euphemistic way of insinuating that men are all repressed homosexuals. As noted elsewhere,[24] we have used Gagnon and Simon's term "homosocial" precisely to emphasize this distinction.[25]

Research Evidence

While we have spent considerable time drawing the outlines of this homosocial interpretation of sex roles, it is now important to ask the question "What research evidence supports such a view?" In the remaining space we shall try to marshall evidence from a broad range of sources, including research on early childhood development, adolescent and adult interaction patterns between the two sexes, as well as some suggestive material from animal studies (for those who find the leap from monkeys to men not too great to bear).

Males repeatedly find their behavior influenced by the presence of other males: "Summarizing from a broad range of sex differences research shows that boys more often attempt to dominate other boys, boys more often pick other boys as victims (despite equally nonreinforcing response patterns from both male and female victims), boys' activity

24. Lipman-Blumen, "Changing Sex Roles," p. 13.
25. John H. Gagnon and W. Simon, eds., *Sexual Deviance* (New York: Harper & Row, 1967).

levels increase when they are in the company of other boys, boys' competitiveness increases when in all-male groups, boys' aggression is stimulated by the presence of other boys, boys' reading problems are ameliorated when they are treated in male settings as opposed to female or individualized settings."[26]

Male competition, aggression, and dominance do not necessarily gainsay the more affectionate predilections Greer describes. They simply represent different aspects of the "stimulation and attraction" phenomenon. The more "negative" behavior of males toward one another is part of the jostling for rank and resources which makes the victorious male even more admirable and desirable to other males.

Dominance and Aggression

Influenced by the strong dominance hierarchies evident among lower primates, Omark and Edelman and Omark et al. attempted to study dominance behavior in the free play of children between the ages of four and ten.[27] They also developed a "hierarchy test" in which each child was asked to rate pairs of children in the classroom in terms of "which child in the pair they thought was 'tougher.' " Maccoby and Jacklin summarize the results in the following way: "Boys are rated as tougher than girls as early as nursery school age, though there is some overlap, with the toughest girls being tougher than the least tough boys. . . . There are dominance hierarchies for both sexes, but the boys' hierarchy tends to be more stable (that is, more agreed upon) than the girls' hierarchy."[28]

One of the most consistent findings in the highly inconsistent literature on sex differences is that boys tend to be more aggressive than girls.[29] This appears to be upheld in the seven-culture study reported by

26. Lipman-Blumen, "Changing Sex Roles," p. 441.

27. D. R. Omark and M. Edelman, "Peer Group Social Interactions from an Evolutionary Perspective" (paper presented at the Society for Research in Child Development Conference, Philadelphia, 1973); D. R. Omark, M. Omark, and M. Edelman, "Dominance Hierarchies in Young Children" (paper presented at the International Congress of Anthropological and Ethnological Sciences, Chicago, 1973).

28. Eleanor E. Maccoby and Carol N. Jacklin, *The Psychology of Sex Differences* (Stanford, Calif.: Stanford University Press, 1974), p. 236.

29. A. McIntyre, "Sex Differences in Children's Aggression," *Proceedings of the 80th Annual Convention of the American Psychological Association* 7 (1972): 93–94; R. M. Oetzel, "Annotated Bibliography," in *The Development of Sex Differences*, ed. Eleanor Maccoby (Stanford University Press, 1966), pp. 223–322; L. A. Serbin, K. D. O'Leary, R. N. Kent, and I. J. Tonick, "A Comparison of Teacher Response to the Pre-academic and Problem Behavior of Boys and Girls," *Child Development* 44 (December 1973): 796–804; P. K. Smith and K. Connolly, "Patterns of Play and Social Interaction in Pre-School Children," in *Ethological Studies of Child Behavior*, ed. N. B. Jones (London: Cambridge University Press, 1972), pp. 65–95; L. M. Terman and L. E. Tyler, "Psychological Sex Differences," in *Manual of Child Psychology*, ed. L. Carmichael, 2d ed. (New York: John Wiley & Sons, 1954), pp. 1064–1114.

Whiting and Pope,[30] who report that boys engaged in more mock fighting, more counterattacks, and more verbal insults than girls. But the important point here, as Maccoby and Jacklin note in the many studies they reviewed, is that boys are both more active and more aggressive "during play with other boys."[31] Male aggression appears to be directed more often toward other boys, and girls are significantly less often chosen as boys' victims despite the fact that they respond similarly to boys when attacked.[32] Maccoby and Jacklin conclude that "girls and women are less often the objects, as well as the agents of aggressive action. ... Males aggress primarily against each other, and seldom against females."[33]

While the activity level of boys often is observed to be higher than females, this is primarily true when they are involved in same sex groups. Halverson and Waldrop, in a study of two-and-one-half-year-old children in a nursery school setting, found no difference by sex in activity level of boys and girls when they were playing alone.[34] However, when boys played with same-sex peers, their activity level increased significantly, but this did not happen to girls when they played with other girls.

For those willing to extrapolate from monkeys to people, studies by Mitchell and Brandt suggest that infant monkeys of both sexes have comparable activity levels when they are caged individually or only with their mothers.[35] However, when these same infant monkeys are placed in cages where only a Plexiglas screen separates them from another infant-mother pair, the activity level of male infant pairs is higher than that of pairs of mixed-sex infants or female infants. The behavior of male infant pairs in this setting involves a greater number of threats toward one another and more play imitating.

Attraction

Boys appear to find each other more attractive as playmates at an early age. One study involving eighteen-month-old children revealed

30. Beatrice Whiting and C. Pope, "A Cross-cultural Analysis of Sex Difference in Behavior in Children Aged Three to Eleven," *Journal of Social Psychology*, forthcoming.

31. Maccoby and Jacklin, p. 229.

32. G. R. Patterson, R. A. Littman, and W. Bricker, *Assertive Behavior in Children: A Step toward a Theory of Aggression*, in *Monographs of the Society for Research in Child Development* 32, serial no. 114 (Chicago: University of Chicago Press, 1967); J. R. Shortell and H. B. Biller, "Aggression in Children as a Function of Sex of Subject and Sex of Opponent," *Developmental Psychology* 3 (July 1970): 143–44.

33. Maccoby and Jacklin, p. 239.

34. C. F. Halverson and M. R. Waldrop, "The Relations of Mechanically Recorded Activity Level to Varieties of Preschool Play Behavior," *Child Development* 44 (September 1973): 678–81.

35. G. D. Mitchell and E. M. Brandt, "Behavioral Differences Related to Experience of Mother and Sex of Infant in the Rhesus Monkey," *Developmental Psychology* 3 (July 1970): 149.

that boys hugged, stroked, and kissed each other, but girls did not. By age three years, when they were reobserved, the more affectionate male behavior took the form of rough-and-tumble play. Maccoby and Jacklin interpret the kissing-hugging-stroking behavior as "preaggressive play," that is, a prior developmental stage.

While we would argue that such affectionate behavior precedes aggressive behavior in a temporal sense only, we would argue, as we have elsewhere, that "it is preaggressive for somewhat different reasons" than ontological development:[36] "It is preaggressive behavior because the only way in which our present society can tolerate males touching one another is in an aggressive, competitive manner. Transforming natural affectionate behavior into aggressive rough-and-tumble behavior is one way of protecting valued males from falling into the (wasteful) trap of homosexuality. (The taboos against lesbianism are not nearly as stringent, partly because female roles are seen as potentially dispensable, or at least less valuable, in our society.)"[37]

Another study of one-year-old girls and boys offers additional suggestive evidence that males are more attracted by males. Ban and Lewis found that boys spent more time looking at their fathers than at their mothers, while no comparable difference was observed in girls.[38]

Further indication that adult males are more concerned with other males comes from research which reveals that in adulthood "normal" men report they dream twice as often about men as about women. Women, on the other hand, dream equally about both males and females.[39] An interesting side note on dream behavior and aggressive figures from this same study reveals that, in both male and female dreams about aggression, the aggressor is more often seen as a male.

Group and Team Play

Research on play patterns supports the suggestion that boys enjoy the company of male society more than girls enjoy an elaborated female social structure. There is ample evidence that, from an early age, boys tend to congregate in groups and girls tend to play in dyads.[40] There is cross-cultural evidence of this recurrent pattern. The group or gang behavior of little boys, which may be perceived as an early reflection of the male homosocial world, is a precursor of adolescent and later adult team sports, favored more by males than females.

36. Lipman-Blumen, "Changing Sex Roles," p. 14.
37. Ibid., pp. 14–15.
38. P. L. Ban and M. Lewis, "Mothers and Fathers, Girls and Boys: Attachment Behavior in the One-Year-Old" (paper presented at the meeting of the Eastern Psychological Association, New York, April 1971).
39. C. Hall and R. L. Van Der Castle, *The Content Analysis of Dreams* (New York: Appleton-Century-Crofts, 1966).
40. Best (see n. 22 above); Maccoby and Jacklin (n. 28 above), p. 257.

The effect of team membership is thought to be predominantly salutary. There is some research evidence that individuals involved in groups have higher self-esteem than individuals who are social isolates. Sociometric studies of "stars" and "isolates" gathered together in opposing teams reveal some interesting insights. As teammates, "stars" approve of themselves and one another more than the "isolates" do, even when joined together in a team. This has implications for our earlier discussion of the enjoyment, including camaraderie and loyalty, that comes from the male homosocial world. Until the emergence of "sisterhood," promulgated by the feminist movement, women had few analogous social structures beyond the confines of the domestic world which protected them from isolation with its myriad deprivations.[41]

Team sports offer two positive elements to males: first, the enjoyment of physical contact with other males and second, the power or strength that comes with numbers. Adolescent male athletic teams allow young males the enjoyment of physical contact with other males, under the "competitive/cooperative" rules sanctioned by society. Thus, one is allowed the camaraderie and loyalty of teammates, the hugging and backslapping that is part of team spirit, and the competitive physical jostling against members of the opposing team.

Blumfield and Remmers, in a study of 2,000 high school students aged fourteen to seventeen, found that, even in terms of spectator sports, from a possible eleven choices boys selected the contact sport of football as their favorite spectator sport more often than girls.[42] Girls, by contrast, chose basketball and baseball more often than boys did. This suggests that even when boys cannot partake actively in the competitive, physical contact sports of athletic teams, they prefer to watch the game that involves more body contact among males.

Interest in Power and Resources

Still other studies reveal the early onset of males' greater interest in power and resources than that evidenced by females. Ables studied the wishes of latency-age children by asking boys and girls aged seven to twelve what each would wish if (s)he had three wishes.[43] Males more often than females indicated their wish for money and material objects (i.e., resources), while females more often than males wished for another individual.

The interest in accumulating resources and the dependence upon

41. Bernard, forthcoming; Smith-Rosenberg (n. 6 above).

42. W. S. Blumenfield and H. H. Remmers, "Research Notes on High School Spectator Sports Preference of High School Students," *Perceptual and Motor Skills* 20 (February 1965): 166.

43. B. Ables, "The Three Wishes of Latency Age Children," *Developmental Psychology* 6 (January 1972): 186.

an all-male society to accomplish this purpose are apparent in the social structure of the Mafia. Territoriality, dominance, resource acquisition, and loyalty characterize this extreme example of a male homosocial world, from which women are excluded, not because they are seen as competitors but because they are irrelevant. It is a "family" without women. Presumably, a concept of male chivalry, in which women (i.e., wives) are to be protected from the gross realities of the male world or are used as media (i.e., prostitutes) for acquiring more resources, promotes the exclusion of women from this highly structured male homosocial world.

The upper-class male club bears structural similarities to the Mafia, albeit refined by generations of affluence and culture. It has its own emphasis upon territoriality, exclusivity, dominance, and resource accumulation, preservation, and enlargement. The affluent men's club excludes from its membership rolls women and unimportant or peripheralized men. Even as guests, women often must enter through a side door, if they are allowed entry at all.

Careers are advanced or potentially destroyed within the carpeted smoking rooms of these clubs which often are extensions of youthful male clubs in the Ivy League male colleges. In addition to explicit bargaining and support, advice on political, legal, economic, and social matters is traded within these enclaves. Women are excluded, partly because they would dilute the atmosphere and function of these bastions of male homosociality and, more importantly, because they usually do not have the economic, political, legal, or social resources to make it worth the men's while to negotiate with them.

Although women also form clubs, rarely have these groups pretended to have the same function or influence in the lives of women.[44] And, as Booth has told us, men belong to more voluntary groups than women.[45] Women's club activities are meant to keep women occupied while their men are away; they serve as a "divertissement" until the main act begins when men reenter the scene. This is in stark contrast to the activity that occurs in men's clubs, activity that takes place in "prime time," not as a diversion but as a primary function in the lives of affluent men.

In conclusion, we have tried to demonstrate that the absence of women from certain segments of the occupational world is part of a much larger pattern of a male homosocial world. Women are excluded from this world because their lack of resources makes them less useful

44. A partial exception is the Junior League, the closest female analogue to the upper-class men's club, which has functioned to maintain and allocate social resources *directly,* and economic and political resources only *indirectly* (Arlene Kaplan Daniels, *The Female Power Elite,* in progress.)

45. Alan Booth, "Sex and Social Participation," *American Sociological Review* 37 (April 1972): 183–93.

and interesting both to men and to other women. Men, recognizing the power their male peers have, find one another stimulating, exciting, productive, attractive, and important, since they can contribute to virtually all aspects of one another's lives.

The contributions that women can make to men's lives, under the constraints of our present segregated society, are decidedly less important—and offer less scope. Women, whose resources are limited to sexuality, beauty, charm, service, and parenthood, must focus upon this narrow range in order to distract men from the endless enticement of the male homosocial world. Women must emphasize what they feel men want most from them—sexuality, motherhood, service—in order to share their world at all.

The rationale of traditional Freudian theory serves as the mortar that holds the bricks of the male homosocial world in place. The emphasis upon the penis as power and the woman as a castrated male, passive and dependent, serves to reinforce women's condition. Women's attempt to amass resources, according to this theory, is an unfeminine act in itself. And the vicious circle is kept intact. The various institutions within society—the labor force, economic and legal institutions, the political forum, the military, and the family—all act in analogous and integrated ways to perpetuate the homosocial world of men. The result is a self-sufficient, male homosocial world which need not deliberately conspire to keep women segregated. Merely by ignoring the existence of women outside the domestic, sexual, and service realms the male homosocial world relegates women to the sidelines of life.

National Institute of Education

THE SOCIAL INSTITUTIONS OF OCCUPATIONAL SEGREGATION

Work Aspiration of Women: False Leads and New Starts

Judith Long Laws

The Motivational Context of Aspiration

"Aspiration" is a term psychologists use in a specific way. It is an integral part of a dynamic cycle involving goal-setting, effortful striving, events that provide feedback about success or failure, and the adjustment of aspiration. It has been shown to vary as a function of performance, and although less emphasized, as a function of other informational inputs as well.

Aspiration can scarcely be studied apart from the nexus of motivation that forms it. "Motivation," a particular state of affairs, is a function of two elements: Expectancy and Value. Expectancy can be as specific as the individual's subjective sense of probability that a certain event will occur, or it may include more definitive information in a broader sense. Value can be viewed cognitively, as the positive or negative incentive value a particular event has for an individual, or behaviorally, in terms of an organism's tendency to approach or avoid a given state of affairs. Aspiration as a psychological event is but one outcome of expectancy and value. Other outcomes include such molar behaviors as choice and effort.

The context of information and incentive should always be remembered when speaking of aspiration. In the laboratory, the informational component of motivation is frequently manipulated, creating systematic fluctuations in aspiration. So, too, in real-life situations. The information one has available is influenced by one's position in the social structure. Major transitions in the life cycle are occasions when new options and new information may reach any worker, changing the motivational equation. We should expect that changes in aspiration would be commonplace in all workers, as a function of changes in the work situation and life situation. In short, aspiration, formed by lawful but dynamic factors, is not a static entity.

While it has long been understood that women's labor-force participation is responsive to such major life-cycle events as education, marriage, divorce, bereavement, childbearing, and geographic mobility, the study of the motivational side has been neglected. Thus, when we turn to the theoretical work on work aspiration in women, and the empirical literature it has spawned, we find it both stagnant and unimaginative. Work aspiration (or occupational choice, or career commitment—rarely are these concepts distinguished) is usually treated as a discrete event, like the menarche, which occurs at some time in adolescence and never again. From this inadequate conceptualization derives a research methodology which further reifies what is in reality a complex and dynamic motivational entity. "Work aspiration" of women is then understood to mean that occupation or set of occupations in which some adolescent girls express interest—in response to widely differing inquiries phrased by different researchers.

In my opinion, the topic of women's occupational aspiration and the related vicissitudes of work motivation during the working history has gotten short shrift from the scholarly community. The gaps in our knowledge of these topics is not mere oversight but the result of systematic errors having their roots in specific sociological and psychological traditions. In dissecting the assumptions of existing work on women's work motivation, I have identified a body of interrelated myth and misconception that constitutes a present obstacle to scientific understanding of a complex set of phenomena.

Common Misconceptions about Women's Work Motivation

Most of the literature to be reviewed here has its roots in a sociology of occupations which is both class centric and sexist. Among its premises are:

1. *The myth of mom and pop.*—Men work; women do not.

2. *The sexualization of occupations.*—Working is a masculine activity and the "world of work" is a man's world. Woman's life is defined by exclusion from this world. The survival of the family unit requires, however:

3. *The myth of the male breadwinner.*—The assumption that every woman will marry *and* stay married *and* that her husband's income will

be sufficient to support the family and provide their consumption needs underlies much of the theorizing about women's relative indifference to preparing for and pursuing a career. In the real world, of course, a great many families find two incomes a necessity rather than an option. Many women who have lost their partner, through bereavement or divorce, find that they have no choice but to seek paid employment. Many are underemployed, and a third of households headed by women are living below the poverty level.

Facts aside, the myth of the male breadwinner is still prevalent. This being so, the public and the researcher are alerted to:

4. The myth of the career-woman freak.—The working woman is "masculine" and deviant, hence her working requires explanation. Furthermore, because the working woman is deviant, her working cannot be explained by the same factors as the work of men (for whom work is normal). The most popular explanation of the "differentness" of the woman worker is:

5. Myth of homemaking as a career.—Any paid employment is secondary and will be accommodated to or sacrificed for her true vocation. Related assumptions include the assertion that homemaking and paid employment are antithetical.[1] This gives rise to:

6. The shibboleth of role conflict.—Role conflict is inevitable for the woman who departs from her true vocation by seeking employment, especially the demanding sort of employment usually called a career.

Most of the foregoing are made explicit in the literature on women's orientation to paid employment. A powerful assumption which remains implicit is:

7. The fallacy of monism.—Men are assumed to give primacy to only one role obligation (employment). It is inconceivable that women could handle two sets of involvements. In point of fact, the majority of married women with husband and young children present in the home are now holding down two full-time jobs. Some variant of the dual role life-style is the dominant one among American women today. Family time-use studies show us, at the same time, that family responsibilities do not constitute a second job for American husbands. Walker's research shows that, on the average, the contribution of husbands to the household's domestic labor budget amounts to only 1.6 hours per day.[2] The contribution of children to the work of the household they share is even smaller.

These statistics are so impressive that one might well expect to find a large body of research on *how* women do it. However, the monistic

1. D. G. Zytowski, "Toward a Theory of Career Development for Women," *Personnel and Guidance Journal* 47 (1969): 660–64.
2. Kathryn Walker, "Time-Use Patterns for Household Work Related to Homemakers' Employment" (paper presented at the 1970 National Agricultural Outlook Conference, Washington, D.C.).

fallacy, the myth of homemaking as a career, and the image of the working woman as freak are so powerful that most research is still dead-ended at the question of *why* women work.

Related to the fallacy of monism, and often advanced as an "explanation" of why this must be true, is:

8. *The myth of the heroic male professional.*—This is a model of work motivation which is used as the standard for assessing all workers. The heroic male professional is characterized by zeal for his work—an internalized devotion to its tasks and demands independent of pay rates or the work week. Indeed, his work is the most important thing in his life. Self-motivated, he assumes complete responsibility for his work and routinely turns in a superior performance. He has high standards and ethics. Conversely, the male professional's career is so demanding as to preclude other major commitments; hence, the myth of monism. The heroic male professional sacrifices "selfish" concerns like personal and family life to the demands of his career. An invidious judgment concerning the worth of career and family is central to the implied comparison between the assumed motivation of the female worker—divided, uninspired, venial—and that of "the" male worker.

Research on working men has demonstrated that this myth does not describe either the motivation or the behavior of the great majority of employed men. The comparison among women and men is, however, rarely made. Rather, the myth of the heroic male professional is most often invoked as a context for comparison with (any) working woman. The more complex motivations and structural arrangements involved in women's employment are made to appear paltry and pedestrian in comparison with this mythical standard.

Sometimes, the characterization of "the" female's motivation for work is left implicit, with attention being focused on the male standard. Sometimes, however, the motivational syndrome postulated for the female is:

9. *The myth of female motivational deficit.*—This emphasizes women's "lack" of "career commitment," an undefined but honorific term usually associated with the myth of the heroic male professional.[3] It is not certain that we would need such a concept as "career commitment" if we were to specify fully conditions that facilitate and conditions that impede attachment to the labor force, to a particular job, or to a particular occupation. If there were a valid psychological entity operating independent of material constraints, we would expect it to manifest itself as perseverance in the face of obstacles. In that case we would scarcely attribute commitment to those for whom all the material conditions conduce to occupational attainment but rather to those who must overcome obstacles to attain the desired state.

3. L. Tyler, "Sex Differences in Vocational Interests and Motivation Related to Occupations" (testimony before the Federal Commerce Commission, Washington, D.C., August 1972).

Myths 8 and 9 operate in tandem to defeat empirical inquiry in two critical ways. First, as motivational myths, they locate the causes of different individuals' outcomes within the individual, diverting attention away from gross differences in the external instrumentalities that influence these outcomes. Second, they invite an inappropriate and misleading comparison between "all" working women and a privileged minority of working men. Such a comparison obscures the very differences that are the basis for predicting different motivational outcomes and assigns the latter to a spurious cause.

The myth of female motivational deficit has much in common with the deficit theories of black personality which, in the sixties, "accounted for" the "inferior" motivation and attainment of black Americans. Many psychologists have not yet applied this lesson to the study of women, another group subject to categorical discrimination affecting the expectancy term in the motivational equation.

Studies of Female Occupational "Choice"

Many times the misconceptions listed above are found in theoretical writings which float far above the level of fact. Where one finds appeals to evidence in this literature, however, they most often refer to prospective studies of occupational preference. The researcher almost never attempts to determine the antecedents of the preferences expressed. After more than thirty years of research the question of the formation of occupational aspiration remains virtually pristine. In studying the expressed preferences of young girls among various occupational options, we would like to know (1) how occupations come to be perceived as options, (2) how options are eliminated from consideration, (3) how occupations become imbued with attractiveness and unattractiveness, and (4) how these perceptions change. Clearly, this set of questions needs to be asked repeatedly at different points in the life cycle, when options and priorities change. Existing research suggests some "critical points" for life planning, but the educational policy implications of these have not yet been developed.[4]

The findings from existing prospective studies need to be taken with a large grain of salt. They are totally inadequate, conceptually, to tell us anything about such motivational phenomena as choice or aspiration. They afford the reader no basis for inferring whether the verbal behavior reported indexes Expectancy, Value, their product, or something else altogether (sex-role conventionalism, for example). Far from reflecting "occupational choice," they are at best studies of "occupational

4. I have suggested a series of critical decisions or transition points in the female life cycle in a chapter in a forthcoming book edited by Phyllis Wallace (*Some New Perspectives on Equal Employment Opportunity* [Cambridge, Mass.: M.I.T. Press, 1975]).

intention." Not surprisingly, they show poor predictive validity.[5] A more appropriate way to view such research is simply as a reading of the information and incentives perceived by young persons at a point in time. The respondents reproduce the maps they have learned; we know nothing of what it means. These maps reflect, and even exaggerate, the occupationally segregated dual labor market of the United States. Most occupations young women report considering fall within the female job ghetto. It would be interesting to know if, coupled with the "realism" reflected by their occupational intentions, prospective female jobholders are also informed about wage discrimination and prospects for advancement in the occupations they are considering. Researchers' failures to explore the context of occupational intention are perhaps responsible for two additional myths which are prominent in reports of this age group:

   10. *The teleological shibboleth.*—This holds that young women do not plan for their occupational future but rather, like the devout Navaho weaver, leave the design of their identity unfinished until knitted together by their future life partner. The faulty syllogism here is that since most women do intend to marry (true), and since marriage is the true and only, or at least major, vocation for women (questionable), their occupational intentions will be vague, undifferentiated, and indifferent. The germ of truth here is that the bulk of young women do show vocational interests that are undifferentiated and perhaps (though I have seen no empirical verification of this) show less than an all-consuming passion for them. This would seem part of the "realism" discussed above: if your options are lackluster, and none of them has irresistible incentives associated with it, why would you be excited about your occupational future? The true test of these competing interpretations would require comparisons between women and men where Expectancy, as well as Value, were equivalent. These instances are so rare in an unjust world that the test will probably require a laboratory experiment. The teleological shibboleth is, however, challenged by evidence showing that young women are in fact planning industriously and proactively for adult lives that will be more complex than those of their male peers,[6] and that in fact they have given more thought to their future occupation than have those male peers.[7]

      5. L. Tyler, "The Antecedents of Two Varieties of Vocational Interests," *Genetic Psychology Monographs* 70 (1964): 177–227; L. W. Harmon, "Women's Working Patterns Related to Their SVIB Housewife and 'Own' Occupational Scores," *Journal of Counseling Psychology* 14, no. 4 (1967): 299–301; and "Anatomy of Career Commitment in Women," *Journal of Counseling Psychology* 17, no. 1 (1970): 77–80.
      6. L. M. Rand and A. L. Miller, "A Developmental Cross-Sectioning of Women's Careers and Marriage Attitudes and Life Plans," *Journal of Vocational Behavior* 2 (1972): 317–31.
      7. E. Davis, "Careers as Concerns of Blue Collar Girls," in *Blue Collar World: Studies of the American Worker,* ed. A. Shostak and W. Gomberg (New York: Prentice-Hall, Inc., 1964), pp. 154–64.

A related fallacy results from researchers' inadequate attention to the constraints on women's work histories that are largely outside their individual control:

11. The fallacy of voluntarism.—This assumes that outcomes which befall women in the labor force reflect their personal choice. This assumption is found frequently in the retrospective literature, as well as in the prospective literature. This assumption is highly untenable, in view of the poor predictive validity of women's preferences, but it is to be expected where the Expectancy term is neglected in predicting aspiration and the modification of preference through experience is not investigated. At its worst, this fallacy conduces to "blaming the victim"; at its best, to the continued neglect of obstacles to women's occupational actualization.

Two more misconceptions appear prominently in the design and interpretation of research on women's work motivation rather than in the conceptualization:

12. The fallacy of stasis.—This is based on what I believe to be a mistaken model of social causality. As a problem in measurement, the fallacy of stasis assumes that, having once measured a construct in a psychometrically reputable way, we are prepared to use it as a predictor. It assumes that the phenotypic manifestations of any genotypic regularities are similar enough that a measure validated at time 1 will afford prediction at time 2 . . . *n*. This assumption has proved embarrassing to the whole realm of personality research and is even less justifiable in the realm of occupational behavior. Women's lives, even more than men's, are characterized by major discontinuities, and this is especially true of women's work histories.

If predictive research of the traditional sort is a risky enterprise at the empirical level, it is even more precarious at the conceptual level. The fundamental validity of linear-prediction models based on current orthodox statistical methodology is questionable. Research on work motivation suggests that it involves a complex constellation of factors, which shifts over time. This suggests the need not for more research, but for different research.[8] Typical research design and interpretation fall into:

13. The labeling trap.—This is an error that affects both the researcher and the object of study. It implies a retrospective strategy,

---

8. Leona Tyler was aware of this problem and stated it decisively: "If these dynamic structures for selecting from among life's possibilities are essentially *programs rather than traits,* and if such programs are constructed, modified or given up during successive developmental stages, the psychometric methods used in this research will never really tell us what they are like. *Instead of trying to trace continuous variables, we must analyze successive states of organization*" (1964, p. 221; italics mine). This recommendation implies such a radical change in thought and research procedures that not even Tyler has responded to the challenge in the intervening years.

though it can be found in concurrent and prospective studies as well. The researcher selects some marked outcome of interest (commonly, unusual occupational attainment or even aspiration) and seeks to find the "causes" of the exceptional or deviant event. The effects on the subject become apparent when the researcher enlists the subject's help in answering the question, Why are you different? Deviance, rather than the phenomenon of interest, becomes the focus of the inquiry. One of the many regrettable effects of this mistaken focus is that control groups or comparison groups are not included, or are not comparable. The literature on "achieving women" is rife with examples of this error.

Research on Women's Occupational Histories

The shortcomings of prospective research lead us to seek more information on women's work motivation from research differently located on the time dimension: cross-sectional comparisons of women presently in the work force and retrospective and longitudinal studies. These strike a decisive blow against some of the prevailing myths and illuminate many remaining research needs.

Both cross-sectional and retrospective studies demonstrate that employment of the wife and mother is a majority phenomenon, not a minority phenomenon, and there is evidence that once the employment of the adult woman living in a family ceases to be statistically "deviant," it gradually becomes less normatively "deviant." This would lead us to expect that in the future we will see less research on the why and more on the how, when, and under what conditions, of female employment. Among women, employment will be a normal part of future expectations.

Indeed, current prospective studies indicate that the great majority of young women intend to work while married; only 8 percent prefer the life-style of marriage-only,[9] and it is possible that marriage-only has always been a minority preference. Furthermore, in Mulvey's retrospective study 39 percent of the women interviewed had not been employed since marriage, although some would have preferred to hold a job.[10]

These studies suggest that preferences (the value term of the motivational equation) and outcomes may be quite different. Thus, among young black women the proportion of adult life they anticipate spending in paid employment exceeds their preference.[11] Among samples of

9. Rand and Miller.

10. M. C. Mulvey, "Psychological and Sociological Factors in Prediction of Career Patterns of Women," *Genetic Psychology Monographs* 68 (1963): 309–86.

11. B. F. Turner, "Socialization and Career Orientation among Black and White College Women" (paper presented at the meeting of the American Psychological Association, Honolulu, 1972).

older, white women (particularly college educated) there is indication of a reverse pattern. Many women, it appears, made their life-style choices at a time when options were restricted and express strong interest in careers only at mid-life.[12] Opportunities for entering paid employment may not keep pace with interest. This question deserves further research. Indeed, the issue of preparing for the second thirty-five years of life is one that cries out for serious study and planning.

The more research we review, the clearer it becomes that we are lacking certain kinds of vital information on how women move through the labor force and through the life cycle. We need more micro studies, at critical transition points, of the options and incentives women perceive, and we need to coordinate research with these critical choice points. Additionally, we need to develop programs to rationalize and expand the options and upgrade the incentives.

Contemporaneous Determinants of Work Motivation

The comparison of facts with theoretical explanations about women's motivations leads to new questions. We observe that not all women have the same preferences and priorities; that these preferences and priorities appear to be changing over time, both for individuals and in the aggregate. We observe that preferences do not seem to determine what women actually experience, and we are led to examine the other determinants of women's outcomes. This leads to the Expectancy term in the motivational equation and the realization that very little is known about how these cognitions are formed. We thus examine the cognitive map of occupational intentions and then the real matrix of employment options. This leads us out of the world of contrived theories restricted to women and into the domain of research on workers and managers. I will not attempt to summarize the substantial findings of this literature, based almost entirely on male workers and managers, but rather to point out the research questions they indicate with reference to women workers and managers.

A good deal of research on the worker has focused on job satisfaction, largely because this is correlated with job performance, productivity and profits. Research in this tradition has uncovered a number of factors that operate as incentives; that is, which contribute to "work motivation," both positive and negative. Other things being equal, a worker who enjoys high pay, autonomy, prestige, opportunity for advancement, opportunities for skill utilization and skill development, and who has high interest in the task itself, will have high job satisfaction and

12. Mulvey; R. Baruch, "The Achievement Motive in Women: Implications for Career Development," *JPSP* (May 1967), pp. 260–67.

productivity. Another way of saying this is that jobs which are characterized by offering these positive incentives will motivate the workers who hold them to be highly satisfied and productive.

Existing studies on the distribution of women and men over the occupational structure would lead us to predict substantial differences in job satisfaction, if not productivity. A description of the characteristics of "women's occupations" reads like an inventory of *dis*incentives.[13] The least motivating jobs are reserved for women. Even where women and men occupy jobs in the same occupational category, however, we find that women receive lower levels of reward (pay and rank being the outcomes most commonly studied). Very few studies have looked at the motivational effects of discrepancies in incentives provided for women and men workers. Research in progress indicates, however, that satisfaction of women professionals is lower than that of their male colleagues. This, indeed, is what our theory of motivation would predict. More research is needed in comparing work performance and job satisfaction of women and men as a function of the level of incentives associated with the job.

Social Factors in Work Motivation

For the most part, research on job satisfaction and productivity has concentrated on variables that take the individual worker as the unit of analysis. There are, in addition, predictors at the group or social level. A general process of social comparison seems to be part of basic learning early in the socialization process. The individual learns to satisfy certain kinds of information needs by making comparisons between himself and others.[14] There are two research traditions which have explored this phenomenon in organizational contexts: Stouffer et al. studied satisfaction outcomes among servicemen in the Second World War.[15] They discovered that relative deprivation (or relative gratification) resulted when individuals compared their outcomes with others who were better off (or worse off). Relative deprivation thus results, not from a situation of objective deprivation, but from the subjective deprivation occasioned by comparing with someone more fortunate. These ideas have not been

13. Valerie K. Oppenheimer, *The Female Labor Force in the United States: Demographic and Economic Factors Governing Its Growth and Changing Composition,* in *Population Monograph,* ser. 5 (Berkeley, 1970).

14. Leon Festinger, "A Theory of Social Comparison Process," *Human Relations* 7 (1954): 117–39.

15. S. A. Stouffer, E. A. Suchman, L. C. Vinney, S. A. Star, and R. M. Williams, *The American Soldier: Adjustment during Army Life* (Princeton, N.J.: Princeton University Press, 1949).

extended to women workers, but the implications for women —underpaid relative to men—are evident.

Social comparison processes also seem to underlie the phenomenon of equity, a newer tradition of research in industrial psychology. Experimenters have found that workers will increase or decrease their production—either qualitatively or quantitatively—in order to bring about an "equitable" rate of reward. The judgment of equity is arrived at by the worker's comparing his own qualifications and rate of pay with those of other workers. The "information" about other workers can be provided indirectly, by the experimenter, and the motivational mechanism of equity can be activated.

The worker need not have firsthand information for this to occur. This has interesting implications for the effects of comparisons between men and women workers. Many researchers have pointed out the extraordinary degree of sex segregation in the occupational structure of the United States. These statistics may be an underestimate if, as some suggest, sex segregation is even more pronounced at the level of the employing establishment. If women's only source of information about inequitable qualifications-to-pay ratios is direct observation, this state of affairs will muffle working-women's discontent and the likelihood of activism based on discontent. If, however, information can enter the motivational calculus vicariously, as equity research suggests—through the media, for example—the prediction will be quite different.

It appears from the foregoing that a number of viable research problems can be discovered simply by extending the work that has been done with men in the work situation. Additional questions have not yet been broached.

The literature on leadership, for example, shows a progression from "great-man" (*sic*) formulations restricted to psychological variables to the inclusion of situational variables.[16] The current understanding is that different combinations of structural and personnel factors represent different kinds of leadership problems, requiring dissimilar leadership styles for optimal outcomes. The question of whether women and men have contrasting leadership styles has not been systematically investigated.

Even more basic research questions are suggested by including gender as a variable in the leadership equation. Does the sex of the leader (independent of leadership style) have an effect on the willingness of workers to follow her/him? What is the effect of the sex composition of the work group on the effectiveness of the individual worker? Informal and attitudinal data are rich in hypotheses regarding these phenomena, but systematic research has yet to begin.

16. F. E. Fiedler, "Leadership and Leadership Effectiveness Traits: A Reconceptualization of the Leadership Trait Problem," in *Interpersonal Behavior*, ed. L. Petrullo and B. M. Bass (New York: Holt, Rinehart & Winston, 1961).

Careers, Intermittent Work Patterns, and Reentry

Another interesting set of questions is suggested by the work on career patterns. It would be fruitful to ascertain whether women's work histories follow the patterns proposed for men[17]—but perhaps an even more fundamental query is whether these theoretical formulations have validity for men. The study of careers brings into focus two related issues that have received inadequate study. The first is intermittency of labor-force participation and its relationship to such outcomes as earnings and advancement. Though intermittency has been assumed to be strictly a "female problem" and to account for the lower rates of returns to women, the former assumption has not been documented, and the latter has been decisively challenged.[18] The issues underlying intermittency (employer's return on his training investment; worker's increased value as a function of work experience) also have relevance to job turnover. A second issue is the prevalence and concomitance of a heterogeneous work history. The theoretical models posit a single, lifelong career, but we are not now in a position to conclude that such a pattern is either modal or optimal. Empirical investigation of multiple-career, interrupted-career, and noncareer work histories would enlarge our understanding of all workers, including women.

The relationship of heterogeneity to outcomes may be more critical for women; I suspect that we will find that earnings and advancement underestimate time in the work force more drastically for women than for men. Heterogeneity thus becomes the new shibboleth of the intellectuals, replacing intermittency as the dominant rationale for sex differentials in returns for labor-force participation.

Intellectual footwork avoids the serious issues of social justice and social policy. The problem of the heterogeneous work history is one of many which have not yet come to concern the typical worker. However, all of the organizational theory reviewed points to the same predictions: as women workers' information level concerning the material conditions of their employment rises, so will their discontent. Trends in labor-force participation predict that a greater proportion of women will be spending a higher proportion of their adult years in paid employment. Oppenheimer has suggested that women will become more invested in their job outcomes as the job becomes more central in their lives.[19] More experience with sex discrimination can only have a depressing effect on work motivation and aspiration. The motivational consequences of the

17. D. Miller and W. Form, *Industrial Sociology* (New York: Harper & Row, 1964).
18. Isabel V. Sawhill, "The Economics of Discrimination against Women: Some New Findings," *Journal of Human Resources* 8 (Summer 1973): 383–96.
19. V. K. Oppenheimer (paper delivered at Radcliffe Institute Conference, Cambridge, Mass., May 1972).

labor market into which women are moving have not yet received serious consideration.

In general, much interesting and vital research remains to be done along lines laid out by previous publications on work organizations. Additional research questions have been generated in a context where women are uniquely the focus. These involve the socialization, elicitation, and inhibition of achievement motivation in women. Of particular interest here is the operation of the achievement motive in the occupational sphere.

Sex-Role Issues in Women's Motivation for Paid Employment

Achievement motivation is thought to be a relatively enduring propensity to strive for success in any situation where standards of excellence are applicable. Most research and theoretical development have focused on academic achievement and occupational aspiration. However, the same behavioral tendencies to strive for success can be attached to goals other than academic or occupational achievement. McClelland et al. did not deal with the possibility[20] raised by more recent work,[21] that females are socialized toward different achievement *goals* but exhibit all the components of the achievement syndrome—effortful striving, persistence, overcoming obstacles, etc. By this argument, females' achievement motive would not be aroused by the cues most often employed in research on men; hence they would test low in the motive. Moreover, as we have seen, achievement situations arouse other, competing motives in women, besides the achievement motive. Consequently we commit the error of oversimplification if we infer the strength of the achievement motive from the level of occupational aspiration. The achievement motive is only one among several determinants of aspiration.

Stein and Bailey's critique raises an important issue of general interest in the study of motivation: the channeling of motivation, or how valence becomes attached to some outcomes and not others. Our major interest here, however, is the motivational import to women of the situations culturally defined as achievement, especially in occupations. The public elementary school is commonly thought of as an institution oriented toward the development of individual talent, irrespective of gender. "Success" presumably means the same thing to girls and boys. Yet there is considerable evidence that girl children orient differently to achievement situations even during elementary school. Girls perform

20. D. C. McClelland, J. W. Atkinson, R. A. Clark, and E. L. Lowell, *The Achievement Motive* (New York: Appleton-Century-Crofts, 1953).

21. A. Stein and M. Bailey, "The Socialization of Achievement Orientation in Females," *Psychological Bulletin* 80, no. 5 (November 1973): 345–66.

better on tasks defined as "feminine," or sex appropriate.[22] This tendency seems to accelerate through puberty, and related effects become clear. Girls are unwilling to compete with boys, though the converse is not true. When college women receive feedback that their performance has exceeded a male peer's, they immediately cut back their effort.[23] As females and males move closer to adulthood, they seem more strongly affected by a sex role ideology that says work is the destination of (only) males and marriage (only) the destination of females. The world of work (and by extension the world of achievement) is declared off limits for women, "or else." The "or else" is failure as a female and rejection by men. In motivational terms, achievement of success in male terms comes to be perceived as *negatively* instrumental for the female goal of marriage. This approach-avoidance conflict is what Horner documented in her research on the Motive to Avoid Success in women. Research shows us that only a small minority of women reject marriage as a goal; all others are vulnerable to this conflict.

The fear of a threat to femininity through successful achievement is the result of cultural learning so prevalent as to affect most women. The workplace is a situation likely to elicit this conflict and the arena most likely to show its day-to-day effects.

In the laboratory, the effect of arousal of the Motive to Avoid Success is to inhibit the task performance of women. Future research should seek ways to eliminate the counterproductive effects of this conflict. For example, what do we know at present about ways of coping with the fear of invalidation of femininity?

A number of responses seem to "solve" the problem by lessening the conflict, but at the expense of women's full achievement. In their fantasy stories, women solved the sex-role dilemma by denying their success, lowering their aspirations, or subordinating their achievements to those of a male partner. The real-life analogue of these events seems apparent in the occupational realm. Research repeatedly shows that women lower their occupational aspirations as they move into adolescence,[24] even when achievement remains high.[25]

Other individual solutions to the femininity/achievement conflict seek to assert femininity in an incontrovertible way. One way, which has

22. G. A. Milton, "Sex Differences in Problem Solving as a Function of Role Appropriateness of the Problem Content," *Psychological Reports* 5 (1959): 705–8; A. H. Stein, "The Effects of Sex-Role Standards for Achievement Motivation," *Developmental Psychology* 4 (1971): 219–31; E. S. Battle, "Motivational Determinants of Academic Task Persistence," *Journal of Personality and Social Psychology* 4 (1966): 634–42.

23. P. Weiss, "Some Aspects of Femininity," *Dissertation Abstracts* 23 (1962): 1083.

24. E. Matthews and D. V. Tiedeman, "Attitudes toward Career and Marriage and the Development of Life Style in Young Women," *Journal of Counseling Psychology* 11, no. 4 (1964): 375–83.

25. M. Schwenn, "Arousal of the Motive to Avoid Success" (Junior honors paper, Harvard University, 1970).

several variations, is to solve the challenge to femininity by marrying and then get on with the achievement interests. Another is to choose a partner so overwhelming in ability or ambition that one's own aspirations can be overlooked; or, in the absence of such a superman, to perceive one's partner as a superman.

Other strategies lessen the conflict by reducing the "masculinity" of the chosen achievement activity. Pilot research conducted under my direction indicates that young women aspiring to sex-atypical occupations engage in "cognitive feminization" of the occupation, perceiving it in terms of attributes sex-typed as feminine. It would be of great interest to see whether recruits to other archetypically "masculine" occupations exhibit a similar trend.

The traditionally feminine occupations deserve another look, in this connection. Past research, adopting the dominant male set of values (e.g., with respect to the prestige of occupations), has tended to dismiss women making "traditional" career choices. To the extent that we are interested in continuous labor-force attachment, advancement, and lifetime earnings, however, the work histories of women in traditional occupations may make a more interesting study than those of women in "masculine" occupations. These occupations offer advantages heretofore overlooked: the debilitating sex-role conflict is minimized, and the achievement motive is given full rein. A second advantage is afforded, to the extent that the work group is composed of women: the *situational* arousal of the Motive to Avoid Success will be minimized.

Means of Neutralizing Sex-Role Conflict in the Work Place

The discussion so far has emphasized individual and accidental "solutions" to the motivational conflict evoked by fear of male disapproval of female achievement. Let us speculate about intentional and collective means of neutralizing these conflicts.

Horner has conceived of the Motive to Avoid Success much as McClelland conceived of the need for achievement[26]—as a stable disposition, early learned and not particularly malleable. I conceive of it, rather, as a form of role conflict, and as such subject to situational evocation or neutralization. The experimental research tells us that the conflict is situationally aroused. My reading of the literature suggests at least two kinds of factors that may maximize the fear of "loss" of femininity and consequent disruption of task effectiveness. One is the presence of an eligible male (a potential partner). By implication, this stimulus will be more disruptive for the single than for the married

26. M. S. Horner, "Sex Differences in Achievement Motivation and Performance" (Ph.D. diss., Harvard University, 1968).

woman. The other factor is a direct evaluation concerning femininity. This can be effectively manipulated by any co-worker, female or male. These points of special vulnerability are also points of intervention for training and change. Employers and co-workers sometimes treat female workers in ways which neutralize task orientation and elicit sex-role orientation. Women workers, employers, and co-workers can be trained to be aware of and to avoid styles of interaction that disrupt task effectiveness.

In general, research has neglected the immediate interactions of working women and the ways in which role partners—most notably co-workers, employers, and husbands—reward and discourage aspiration and effort. Existing research suggests that many of these role partners may be more punishing than rewarding, if their measured attitudes are any indication of their behavior.

The worker's own awareness of the role pressures producing this conflict can do much to disarm its effectiveness. Most women workers have a greater stake in doing the job well than in gaining male approval for their femininity. Many women have discovered that other women are a major source of support in rethinking the cultural patterns and reasserting personal priorities.

The existing research on women's aspiration, at all ages, also reaffirms the importance of the support of a male partner. Women who believe that men approve female competence permit themselves higher aspirations; those who believe men disapprove radically restrict their goals. Bringing about changes in these perceptions needs to go back to adolescence, and probably before. However, much can be accomplished by monitoring and modifying the behavior of male co-workers, and especially male employers, in the contemporaneous work situation of the woman worker.

Summary

In this paper, an approach to work motivation is developed which emphasizes information and incentive. Motivation is seen as dynamic and responsive to events in the work life. Hence attention is directed toward the contemporaneous environment rather than static attributes of the individual. Dubious motivational inferences (e.g., "career commitment") are avoided, and the attempt is made to identify the determinants of options and incentives perceived by women at varying stages of experience in the life cycle and the work cycle.

The focus on the work environment as a source of information and incentives leads to an evaluation of the opportunities and incentives available to working women. These predict systematic negative effects on working-women's motivation, a problem which has been virtually

ignored in the current concern over alienation among American workers. The focus on the work environment also directs attention to the
working-woman's role partners: those with whom employment brings
her into direct and regular contact. These are a major source of positive
and negative experiences which modify perceived possibilities and incentives.

Finally, a balanced emphasis on information and incentive directs
our attention to vocational education. Our review of women's occupational aspiration leads to the conclusion that women need better occupational maps *and* better occupational options.

Cornell University

THE SOCIAL INSTITUTIONS OF OCCUPATIONAL SEGREGATION

Dual Linkages between the Occupational and Family Systems: A Macrosociological Analysis

Constantina Safilios-Rothschild

Talcott Parsons formalized in sociological theory the widespread assumption that a dual linkage with the occupational system on the part of both spouses is detrimental to the marital relationship due to the introduction of competition in an "expressive" relationship. This competition is introduced because the spouses' status lines with respect to income, prestige, and power would most probably be unequal. Disruptive effects would result from comparing each other's status lines. Therefore, the ideal model became one in which the family was linked with the occupational system only through the husband's work. In this way, both spouses had the same status lines in terms of income and prestige,[1] since the husband conferred his on his wife and children. In cases of financial need the model allowed the wife also to link with the occupational system, as long as her link was clearly secondary and supplementary and her achieved status lines significantly lower than those of her husband. Partly due to the prevailing sex-role socialization patterns and partly due to sex discrimination practices, married women who worked did so in low-prestige, low-pay "feminine" occupations and in positions auxiliary to those held by men. They might also work part time or seasonally, so

---

1. It is not accurate to say that the husband's power-status line is conferred on the wife to the extent that this is true for income and prestige. It is, in fact, rare that the wife can exercise any power in the name of her husband, except within the context of rigid social stratification systems. Otherwise, the husband's power line may only increase the wife's prestige but not give her any power.

that their occupational link remained safely marginal and secondary and all their status lines consistently lower than those of their husbands.

Occasionally, however, the safeguards keeping wives' occupational link weak, secondary, or marginal did not work satisfactorily, due either to structural unemployment of unskilled and semiskilled husbands or the wives' relatively higher degree of formal education that entitled them to occupations with higher status than those of their husbands. Because, in the past, black males experienced relatively more racial discrimination than black females in educational and occupational contexts, this frequently held true in the case of black couples. Thus, the black wife often had a higher education than her husband and held a job of higher status. In this way, low-income, and particularly black low-income, wives were occasionally forced to become the main breadwinners, their case considered to be "deviant" and to constitute a "social problem."

In March 1957 over half (53.9 percent) of the working wives of craftsmen, foremen, and kindred workers and nearly two-fifths (38.8 percent) of the working wives of operatives and kindred workers had jobs classified as white collar or professional.[2] In other words, working-class women (particularly black women) often have had a higher occupational status than their husbands when they worked as secretaries, teachers, or nurses, but clearly had a lower income than their husbands. The 1960 census data show that when the criterion of median earnings is used important discrepancies between males' and females' median earnings in the same occupational category are revealed. For example, professional women's median earnings correspond to the median earnings of male laborers, that is, of males at the lowest occupational category.[3]

It seems, therefore, that working women's higher occupational prestige in working-class couples was not disruptive to the relationship or threatening to the husbands, despite the prevalence of negative sex-role stereotypes against the wife's superiority on any status line. The reason for this tolerance on the part of the wife may be due to the fact that the income line is the most salient one in American society, permitting the husband to continue to enjoy overall occupational status superior to his wife.[4]

2. Lincoln Day, "Status Implications of the Employment of Married Women in the U.S.," *American Journal of Economic Sociology* 20 (December 1961): 390–98.

3. Elizabeth Havens and Judy Corder Tully, "Female Intergenerational Occupational Mobility: Comparisons of Patterns," *American Sociological Review* 37 (December 1972): 774–77.

4. It is interesting to note here that in a society like Greece the most stable type of status inequality between husband and wife has been the one in which the wife earns a higher income than her husband, but the husband has a higher degree of education and of occupational prestige. This is so because education and prestige are the most salient status lines within the context of the Greek society (see Constantina Safilios-Rothschild, "La Mobilité sociale des femmes en Grèce," *Sociologie et sociétés* 6 [February 1974]: 105–26).

Thus, wives' occupational roles have been acceptable as long as the wives' achieved status lines were lower (or could be perceived or interpreted as lower) than those of the husbands. The extent to which the wives' achieved status lines being higher than those of the husbands represented deviance is clearly demonstrated by the anxious efforts of successful professional women to stay below their husbands' achievements and the husbands' great dissatisfaction when these efforts were not successful.[5]

Increasingly, however, dual linkages between the occupational and family system are occurring, and their nature is changing. The diffusion of the Women's Liberation ideology has freed wives of the compulsion to keep their status lines lower than those of their husbands, and a number of structural changes are responsible for married women's greater interest in work, their higher achievement aspirations, and their increasing entry into previously masculine, high-prestige, high-pay occupations such as medicine and law. Therefore, some married women's occupational roles have already changed. They are expected increasingly to resemble the range of occupational roles of married men as sex discrimination with respect to pay and promotions decreases. In addition, since more women will increasingly have access to individually achieved income, prestige, and power-status lines, they will more often marry men to whom they are attracted because of appearance, personality, or other status-irrelevant skills and characteristics (such as being good lovers) than those with satisfactory or promising status lines. The probability will increase that wives will have the same or similar occupational roles as their husbands, and that in some cases their achieved status lines will be higher than those of their husbands. For it must not be forgotten that another important mechanism that safeguarded a situation in which husbands would have higher-level occupational roles has been the women's selection of mates primarily in terms of high actual or projected status lines.[6]

As long as the linkage between the familial and the occupational system was made only through the husband or as long as the second linkage through the wife remained marginal and secondary, no changes had to be made in either system. For even when women worked they often worked only part time, thus being able to carry out all their familial responsibilities with some minor adjustments. Or they withdrew from the labor force during periods in which the familial responsibilities were too demanding as, for example, when the children were young. Or they only had jobs from 8:00 to 5:00 and refused additional responsibilities in

5. Margaret M. Poloma, "Role Conflict and the Married Professional Woman," in *Toward a Sociology of Women*, ed. C. Safilios-Rothschild (Lexington, Mass.: Xerox Publishing Co., 1972).

6. Constantina Safilios-Rothschild, "Sex Role Theories as Explanatory Theories of Ongoing Changes in the Dynamics of the Husband-Wife Relationship" (paper presented at the International Sociological Association Meetings, Toronto, Ontario, August 1974).

terms of time or psychological commitment that interfered with their lives and familial responsibilities, even when these refusals were made at the expense of promotions and advancement. This type of limited work commitment on the part of married women was possible because of their socialization to limited achievement aspirations and occupational ambitions and a lack of confidence that created doubts that they could aspire higher or have a chance to reach their aspirations.

The USSR and the Eastern European societies present a model in which, even though a sizable number of husbands and wives have the same or similar occupations, no structural changes are brought about in the familial or the occupational systems. As a consequence many strains are apparent, and women are doubly oppressed. Time-budget studies, for example, have shown that Russian women work at home from two and one-half to four hours on weekdays after they return from work and five hours on Sunday, while many husbands help with housework one hour a day or not at all. As a result, Russian husbands have one and one-half times more leisure than their wives to read, study, listen to the radio or to music, to nap, or to go out.[7] The lack of structural changes in the familial or the occupational system is possible partly because men and women are still socialized according to sex-role stereotypes and partly because husbands and wives do not, in fact, play the same type of occupational roles even when they are engaged in the same occupations and occupy the same positions. Due to sex discrimination, women are paid significantly less than their husbands and are not promoted (and are too tired to aspire) to responsible, top positions.[8] Women's linkage with work is still secondary to men's, despite the fact that they are expected to work as hard and to perform as well as men.

In many developing nations, on the other hand, wives often (especially in the middle and upper classes) may occupy the same or a similar position as their husbands. They may enjoy similar upward occupational mobility, again without any changes being brought about in either system. Such changes are not necessary in this case, primarily because of the existence of an extended or a "modified" extended family and the availability of a helpful grandmother or hired help that facilitiates married women's linkage with the occupational system without heavy penalties in terms of the entire package of household and child-care responsibilities.

In developed societies, however, in which the "modified" extended family does not entail a maternal grandmother willing to function as an unpaid housekeeper and babysitter, hired help is too expensive and

7. G. R. Barker, "La Femme en Union Soviétique," *Sociologie et sociétés* 4 (June 1972): 159–91.

8. Magdalena Sokolowsha, "Some Reflections on the Different Attitudes of Men and Women toward Work," *International Labor Review* 92 (July–December 1965): 35–50; Claude Alzon, *La Femme potiche et la femme bonniche* (Paris: François Maspero, 1973); Barker.

scarce, and child care and "service" house facilities are limited, dual linkages of a similar nature between the familial and the occupational system bring about tensions and strains that can be resolved only by means of a series of structural changes in both systems. The appearance of equal status dual linkages between the familial and occupational systems is an important structural change with far-reaching consequences for both systems. As a matter of fact, it is doubtful that such equal status dual linkages can become institutionalized unless a number of structural changes take place in both systems.

Turning first to the family, a macro and micro redefinition of familial roles is necessary so that the division of labor equally taxes the time, energy, and resources of spouses with similar occupational roles. At the macro level the redefinition of family roles can be made in family law, and at the micro level the redefinition can be made through private negotiations between spouses (especially before and at the onset of marriage). It must be remembered, however, that even with a redefinition of family roles dual linkages with occupational systems of equal salience and work commitment leave little time to either spouse for leisure (although it is more equalized between them), and often require elaborate and precise time schedules so that all responsibilities and tasks can be taken care of.[9] Such careful scheduling and rational utilization of all the available time implies a rushed and hectic life-style.

Furthermore, conditions are such that in most occupations, whether semiskilled or skilled, clerical, or professional, and even when overtime is optional or not part of the work contract, overtime is occasionally or regularly expected if one aspires to salary raises, promotions, or just to holding the job. Hence, husbands and wives with occupational roles often find themselves totally drained of energy and ability to meet all the job and family tasks and responsibilities. Their performance in one or both systems is seriously hampered. In some cases the solution is found by compromising. Depending upon one's hierarchy of values and satisfactions, the compromises may take place with respect to obligations vis-a-vis the family or the occupational system or both. Up to now, in terms of sex-role stereotypes, wives were always expected to, and consistently did, compromise their occupational obligations, but they are becoming increasingly reluctant to do so.

At present, therefore, two sets of solutions are theoretically feasible: one entailing structural changes in the occupational system; the other structural changes in the family system. Both sets require deep-rooted sociopsychological changes and are expected to run into strong resistances on the part of both men and women. But a combination of both is most probably necessary in order for equal status dual linkages between

9. Rhona Rapoport and Robert Rapoport, *Dual Career Families* (London: Pelican Books, 1971); Margaret Poloma, "Role Conflict and the Married Professional Woman," in *Toward a Sociology of Women.*

the family and the occupation to become institutionalized in a society in which sex-role stereotypes are no longer dominant.

Structural changes in the occupational system have already begun in Sweden. Part-time work is now available to all men and women during the child-rearing years without incurring any type of economic or occupational penalty. In addition, a parental (instead of a maternity) six-month paid leave can be shared equally by the mother and the father, as can a paid leave (up to twenty-one days per year) for fathers or mothers to stay home and take care of sick children. These leaves provide both working spouses equally with a certain degree of institutionalized flexibility.[10] But these changes represent only a beginning in the structural changes needed within the occupational system. The concept of work continuity needs to be rethought. Is it really necessary and desirable that people have uninterrupted work records if they are to be considered serious, reliable, and committed? Are the "blind spots" in work records not accounted for in terms of related work necessarily stigmata? Is taking time out to travel, to paint, to think and write, to have fun and enjoy life necessarily an indication of unreliability and lack of commitment?

The increasing strain in the efforts to provide everyone with employment, and the increasing desire of people for a high "quality of life" that includes some adequate leisure time, may represent facilitating factors in bringing about some profound structural changes in the world of work. It has to be recognized that a flexible occupational structure would not only benefit the workers and their families but most probably would also raise the level of productivity, the quality of and enthusiasm for work. The prevailing high unemployment rates and the increasing tendency to retire people at an earlier age suggest that the option for people in all types of occupations to take time off from their work at different intervals, and with varying pay arrangements, may be not only a feasible and acceptable but also a necessary solution. Under such a flexible occupational structure people could take off a month, six months, or a year or more for a variety of personal reasons at a fraction of their pay (or at no pay) *without losing their job or being otherwise penalized.* Depending on the type of occupation and the manpower picture, people could have the option to continue working after the retirement age for as many years as they took out from work, thus providing more options to retired people. Such flexibility would tend to "normalize" work discontinuity and to lessen the strains on men and women with equal commitment to family and occupational roles. Thus, compromises in the performance of one's job could be avoided by temporarily withdrawing from the work force to attend to demanding family responsibilities, or to care for and enjoy a

10. Constantina Safilios-Rothschild, *Women and Social Policy* (Englewood Cliffs, N.J.: Prentice-Hall, Inc., 1974).

growing baby, or to concentrate on a pet project, or to live some desirable life experiences. The normalization of breaks in one's work record would render such temporary withdrawals from work only minor occupational setbacks rather than indications of failure and long-term handicaps. Besides, the availability of a fraction of the salary during the time off may be an extremely important feature that has to be thought out carefully by economists. Perhaps it is possible to find some formula by which one could trade off some percentage of the after-retirement income for some income during "flexible, free" preretirement periods, especially if the option to make up for this time after "retirement" exists.

Undoubtedly, such an alteration will be slow to come. It will meet a great variety of resistances, partly rational and partly emotional, since it taps a very fundamental work ethic. Yet this is a change for which scientists and policymakers must prepare since its attraction lies in the fact that it combines many different sets of emerging work-related values as well as aspirations for leisure and a good life and the availability of options.

Within the family system, on the other hand, the emergence of equal status dual linkages with the occupational system is affecting the very basis of exchanges between men and women. As noted before, women who plan and aspire to full-fledged occupational roles may increasingly feel free to choose a mate on the basis of his attractiveness, tenderness, understanding, or sexual ability rather than on the basis of aspirations and access to high status lines. The probability therefore increases that at least some women may be attracted to a low-achievement-oriented man with desirable affective and interpersonal skills and characteristics. Furthermore, it is also possible that at least some men may become attracted to successful, high-income women.

A 1971 study of college students showed that 77 percent of the men, instead of 8 percent of the men in Horner's original 1965 study, gave responses that can be coded as "motive to avoid success" and seriously questioned the value of success, at least academic and professional success.[11] While we do not know the extent to which such trends may be found in the noncollege population or the long-range implications of these findings, it is possible that some young men may enter into marital exchanges similar to those undertaken up to now predominantly by women. That is, some young men may like to work only occasionally or part time. If they work full time it may be without the necessary efforts and sacrifices needed for high achievement and success. They may exchange their youth, attractiveness, sexual prowess, cooking skills, and zest for living for the higher status lines of a woman. While such changes in the family system would diminish considerably the strains

11. Lois Wladis Hoffman, "Fear of Success in Males and Females, 1965–1971," *Journal of Consulting and Clinical Psychology* 42 (June 1974): 353–58.

produced by linkages by reducing the husband's occupational role to a secondary one, they can be expected to be quite slow and only sporadic since they go against powerful sex-role stereotypes. So far, the internalization of sex-role stereotypes makes men resistant and unable to fall in love with and marry a woman with higher status lines. Women are equally resistant and unable to admire, love, and marry a man with status lines lower than their own.[12]

Marriages of older women to younger men may represent a different type of structural change that allows equal status dual linkages even when both are highly achievement oriented. It represents an accommodation to equal status dual occupational linkages because the younger husband is usually at an earlier occupational stage that renders his occupational linkage different and often secondary to that of the wife.

Still another type of structural change in the family system has occurred and does occur relatively more easily because it tends to be subtler and does not necessarily involve striking (or predictable) discrepancies between husbands' and wives' status lines. This change involves the matching of men and women who, despite aspirations to equal status occupational roles, have different degrees of family-and-work orientation. While the extent of incompatibility existing between husbands' occupational and familial roles has seldom been investigated, in one study in which men were asked whether they thought that family and occupational responsibilities interfere with each other, 40 percent of them responded affirmatively. In addition, 70 percent of the men in the same study (and 85 percent of the women) designated the family as the primary source of satisfaction, and 22 percent of them (and 6 percent of the women) chose the occupation as the primary source of satisfaction.[13] Since this study was carried out in 1966 and the women were in "feminine" fields such as home economics and education, it is possible that in the middle 1970s many more women will choose the occupation as the primary or as an equal source of satisfaction with the family. Thus, a possible matching could involve women for whom the primary source of satisfaction is their occupation with men for whom the family is the primary source of satisfaction, assuming that this value orientation implies a hierarchization that influences behavior and the relative allocation of time, energy, interest, and concern.

Actually, there is some evidence that in dual-career families the greater degree of marital satisfaction is found when husbands give relatively greater importance to their family than to their work while the wives give equal importance to family and occupation.[14] It is, therefore, this type of mix that seems to be the best for equal status dual linkages in

12. *Women and Social Policy.*

13. Raymond J. Adamek and Willis J. Goudy, "Identification, Sex and Change in College Major," *Sociology of Education* 39 (Spring 1966): 183–99.

14. Lotte Bailyn, "Career and Family Orientations of Husbands and Wives in Relation to Marital Happiness," *Human Relations* 23 (April 1970): 97–113.

the absence of structural changes in the occupational system. But how well can men and women plan for such a mix at the time that they are looking for a partner? Such a matching becomes especially problematic since it represents a delicate balance that can be easily upset by developmental changes in either spouse. And how much more importance must the husband give to the family over his work when the wife gives more importance to her work in order for an equilibrium to be established?

Finally, one can question what happens to marital satisfaction and the established balance when the husband's granting a lower degree of importance to his work results in a low degree of achievement and low status lines. What takes place if meanwhile the wife, due to a higher degree of importance given to her work rather than to the family, achieves higher status lines than her husband? Here again we face the necessity for sociopsychological changes that would allow men and women to love and enjoy each other regardless of the relative position of their status lines. Such sociopsychological changes probably cannot occur until women can feel confident enough in their own ability to achieve and choose men, not in terms of higher status lines, but in terms of affective and interpersonal criteria.

It must be noted, however, that it is possible that status inequalities between spouses in terms of the stratification criteria of income, prestige, and power may become of less crucial importance, to the extent that it becomes recognized that other factors can be of equal relevance and value. They may include love, sex, companionship. Thus, status inequalities between spouses that go against sex-role stereotypes may be more easily accepted because they are balanced out by differential value attached to love, sex, and/or understanding provided by the other spouse.

Some of the structural changes that are or will be occurring in the family system may be universal, while others may be more relevant to specific occupational groups or families. Childlessness, for example, may be one type of structural change that may be adopted by some couples who desire equal status dual linkages with the occupational system and who aspire to high occupational achievements. Though childlessness alleviates, it does not solve the problems created by such linkages. There is demographic evidence that this type of change has been increasingly occurring in the United States during the last decade; but it cannot be universal, and it may deprive some highly achievement-oriented individuals who would like to have children of the option to have them. Other types of structural family changes that may be adopted by at least some individuals may involve (a) serial polygamy involving two or three marriages at different occupational and life stages, each marriage representing the best adaptation for that particular stage; (b) nonmarital, semipermanent "living together" arrangements or different types of communal arrangements that may provide considerable flexibility to facilitate equal status dual occupational linkages.

The structural changes that allow both spouses to have equal em-

ployment and occupational options should not, however, drastically cut
down their options in marital and familial alternatives. There is little
doubt that the lagging structural changes in the occupational system
briefly outlined in this paper are necessary and must be universal if
equal status dual linkages of *all* types of couples are to be accommodated. To the degree that it will be possible, through legislation and
social policies, to bring about the changes in the occupational system
discussed earlier there will be less need for specific universal structural
changes to occur in families with equal status dual linkages with the
occupational system. Families, therefore, will be freer to choose those
arrangements most appealing to their members. Such options as different types of marital partners and of marriages, or childlessness will not
have to be limited by the structural strains resulting from equal status
occupational dual linkages.

Wayne State University

THE SOCIAL INSTITUTIONS OF OCCUPATIONAL SEGREGATION

Occupational Segregation and the Law

Margaret J. Gates

> The humane movements of modern society, which have for their objective the multiplication of avenues for woman's advancement, and of occupations adapted to her condition and sex, have my heartiest concurrence. But I am not prepared to say that it is one of her fundamental rights and privileges to be admitted into every office and position, including those which require highly special qualifications and demanding special responsibilities.[1]

These are the words which Mr. Justice Miller, writing for the Supreme Court of the United States in 1873, used to uphold an Illinois statute which denied women admission to the practice of law. They eloquently illustrate both the role which our laws and judicial perspectives have played in reinforcing occupational segregation and the fact that our legal institutions themselves are bastions of sex-segregated occupations, most of which are reserved for men. In the century which has transpired since this opinion was written, the law has changed dramatically, but the problem of occupational segregation remains.

Because all the relevant law reforms and legal remedies have been enacted in the past decade, and most within the last five years, it is not yet possible to assess their effectiveness. Neither is it possible to ignore

1. Bradwell v. Illinois, 83 U.S. (16 Wall.) 130, 31 L. Ed. 442 (1873).

the shadow which now invalidated discriminatory laws still cast across the staffing patterns of major industries, institutions, and governmental agencies. The oblique effects on occupational choice of apparently unrelated statutes such as domestic relations laws must also be considered.

This paper will therefore be divided into several sections. Two will consider past and present laws and judicial attitudes that cause (or at least reinforce) occupational segregation directly and indirectly. A third explores the remedies which the law provides. Woven throughout and in the final section is a discussion of sex segregation within legal institutions.

Legal Prohibitions against Employment of Women in Certain Occupations

Although many private and public employers have traditionally limited hiring for certain job categories to one sex or the other, only twenty-six states have ever statutorily required them to do so. Those statutory limitations which have existed have generally been with respect to work which is considered dangerous, such as mining, bartending, and policing. In each of these fields, the laws and ordinances reinforced previously existing cultural patterns, and in some cases a sincere legislative intent to protect women from dangerous conditions can be inferred. In other instances it is less clear whose interests the law was designed to serve.

An important occupation and a legal institution from which in the past women have been legally barred from full participation is policing. Not uncommonly the state and municipal laws establishing police departments provided for only male officers to carry out the general mission of the force, including patrol and investigations. Typically another, much smaller corps of policewomen was provided to do clerical work, guard and search female offenders, and deal with juveniles. In 1971 there were only seven policewomen on patrol in the United States. The others were outside the structure of the department through which male officers are promoted to positions of power and so had little upward mobility.[2] However, despite several federal laws requiring equal employment opportunity for women in policing,[3] cities and states which have integrated women into their police forces are still the exception rather than the rule.

Evaluation reports on programs which have employed women on

2. Catherine Milton, *Women in Policing* (Washington, D.C.: Police Foundation, 1972).
3. Title VII of the Civil Rights Act of 1964, 42 U.S.C. 2000e et seq., as amended; Crime Control Act of 1973, Act of August 6, 1973, Pub. L. 93–83, 87 Stat. 197. Sec. 518(c) (1); State and Local Fiscal Assistance Act of 1972, Pub. L. 92–512, 86 Stat. 919.

patrol show that on the average they perform as well as men.[4] If one considers that it is better to defuse a violent situation than to make an arrest, one might consider women officers superior to their male counterparts. Yet most police chiefs are reluctant to assign women to do the same work as men, even though the penalty for not doing so may be a law suit or the loss of valuable federal grants or revenue-sharing funds.

Since women can no longer be excluded simply because of their gender, their representation on police forces is kept low by certain entrance requirements which have an adverse impact on women as a class. For example, many departments have minimum height requirements which discriminate against not only women but Spanish-speaking and Oriental men as well. Physical strength and agility tests utilized in the selection process of some departments require a candidate to perform exercises in which women are characteristically untrained or which are difficult for women because of differences between male and female musculature. Although the law requires that all selection criteria for employment be related to the tasks which the employee will actually perform,[5] few departments are prepared to prove that relationship. A few have been required to do so in courtrooms as a result of suits brought against them by women who did not qualify for jobs.[6]

Another kind of law which has indirectly made policing a male enclave is veterans' preference statutes. In Massachusetts, for example, where competition for law-enforcement jobs is keen, the absolute nature of the veterans' preference law has made it all but impossible for women applicants, few of whom are veterans, to reach a position on civil service lists which enables them to qualify for police positions—or for that matter any position for which veterans are competing. The constitutionality of veterans' preference laws has been unsuccessfully challenged by women in Pennsylvania (*Feinerman* v. *Jones*)[7] and in Minnesota (*Koelfgen* v. *Jackson*).[8] The latter opinion was summarily affirmed by the Supreme Court.

This problem suggests another occupation in which women and men have been segregated—military service. Although all the major services have a women's branch, the female component was traditionally limited by law and is now limited by policy to a tiny percentage of the total strength of the service. The number of jobs for which women are

4. Peter Bloch, Deborah Anderson, and Pamela Gervais, *Policewomen on Patrol* (Washington, D.C.: Police Foundation, February 1973).

5. Griggs v. Duke Power Co., 401 U.S. 424 (1971).

6. See, e.g., Smith v. City of East Cleveland, 363 F. Supp. 1131 (N.D. Ohio, 1973) rev'd. in part; aff'd. in part 520 F.2d 492 (6th Cir. July 3, 1975); and The Officers for Justice et al. v. The Civil Service Commission of the City and County of San Francisco, Civil no. C-73-0657RFP (N.D. Cal.), memorandum and order dated May 2, 1975.

7. Feinerman v. Jones, 356 F.Supp. 252 (M.D. Pa. 1973).

8. Koelfgen v. Jackson, 355 F. Supp. 243 (Minn. 1972) *aff'd without opinion*, 410 U.S. 976 (1973).

eligible to train has recently been dramatically increased, particularly in the air force. Nevertheless few women are in fact being trained for or serving in job categories which are related to combat. This is so because there are specific laws which prohibit the service of women on combat ships (whether or not in combat)[9] and on planes in combat.[10] The army has interpreted the intent of Congress in passing these statutes to have been to preclude female participation in any form of combat—in other words, a codification of what was an already firmly established tradition of male-only combat. These laws have survived because the military services are not covered by any of the laws prohibiting sex discrimination in employment. Of course they are not compatible with equal rights amendment (ERA) principles and often become a focal point of debate over the amendment.

Like other laws apparently written to protect women as a class, these statutes have had a profound adverse impact on opportunities for women in the military services. They prevent women being trained in combat arms—the fields which have traditionally been the path to high rank—and were also the chief argument made against the admission of women to the military academies, which have historically produced most of our military leaders.[11] Nevertheless, a bill to admit women to the academies has been passed by Congress and approved by the President.[12]

Although military careers have not usually been particularly appealing to women, enormous efforts have been made to make them so during wartimes when women were needed. Even a year ago, before the recession increased the manpower supply, the services seemed to have perceived that without the draft they had a choice between second-rate men or first-rate women to meet their recruitment goals—hence the opening up of more jobs to women. For many young women who cannot afford education after high school and who would be channeled into dead-end jobs, the military offers training, travel, and a chance to become self-sufficient.

Another notoriously sex-segregated occupation which may not be every woman's cup of tea is serving liquor. Bartending under the laws of many states and cities was restricted to men. Challenges to these rules have coincidentally occasioned two decisions decades apart which have been extremely important to the women's legal movement. In 1948 the Supreme Court in *Goesaert* v. *Cleary*[13] upheld a Michigan statute which limited employment of women as bartenders to establishments owned by

9. 10 U.S.C. Sec. 6015.

10. 10 U.S.C. Sec. 8549.

11. Edwards v. Schlesinger and Waldie v. Schlesinger, consolidated as 377 F. Supp. 1091 (1974).

12. Pub. L. No. 94–106, Sec. 8 (October 7, 1975).

13. Goesaert v. Cleary, 335 U.S. 464 (1948).

the father or husband of the female employee. In doing so it said: "The fact that women may now have achieved the virtues that men have long claimed as their prerogatives and now indulge in vices that men have long practiced, does not preclude the States from drawing a sharp line between the sexes, certainly in such matters as the regulation of the liquor traffic. The Constitution does not require legislatures to reflect sociological insight, or shifting social standards, any more than it requires them to keep abreast of the latest scientific standards."

This infamous case is often cited to support the proposition that legislatures are not restrained by the federal Constitution from limiting the social and economic opportunities of certain classes of people so long as legislation enacted does not interfere with specific freedoms guaranteed under the Bill of Rights. The fact that federal courts have been constrained in their treatment of employment cases for many years by this case and its progeny played a large role in the renewed demand for ERA.

Fortunately, two state supreme courts have managed to distinguish *Goesaert* from cases arising from similar statutes or ordinances. The Supreme Court of New Jersey in *Patterson Tavern and Grill Owners Ass'n.* v. *Borough of Hawthorne*[14] struck down a no-women-in-bartending law and specifically repudiated the language of the Supreme Court quoted above by saying: "While the law may look to the past for the lessons it teaches, it must be geared to the present and towards the future if it is to serve the people in just and proper fashion. In the current climate the law may not tolerate blanket municipal bartending exclusions grounded solely on sex."

More important, the California Supreme Court in *Sail'er Inn* v. *Kirby*[15] held that its statute prohibiting women from tending bar violated the equal protection clause of the Fourteenth Amendment, and in so doing a state supreme court declared for the first time that sex is a "suspect classification," like race and national origin, and requires a court to scrutinize the classification carefully.

Other Laws Which Contribute Indirectly to Occupational Segregation

"Protective Legislation"

The U.S. Department of Labor Women's Bureau reported in 1969 that forty-six states, the District of Columbia, and Puerto Rico had laws or regulations governing in some way the hours which women were permit-

14. Patterson Tavern and Grill Owners Ass'n. v. Borough of Hawthorne, 57 N.J. 180, 270 A.2d 628 (1970).
15. Sail'er Inn v. Kirby, 5 Cal. 3d 1, 485 P.2d 529 (1971).

ted to work. Some set a maximum number of hours to be worked daily or weekly; some prohibited night work; others required a day off or certain rest periods. Other "protective" legislation for women barred them categorically from certain jobs in twenty-six states. In forty-five states employers were required to provide seats for women workers, and in ten there were statutory maximum weights which women could be required to lift.[16]

These laws were the culmination of years of effort on the part of feminists, labor unions, and social reformers to protect women from sweatshop conditions. Despite its noble origins, however, the legislation became an excuse which employers were able to use to refuse women jobs when they chose to do so. For example, when investigating the employment practices of American Telephone and Telegraph (AT & T) in 1970, the Equal Employment Opportunity Commission (EEOC) found an almost total sex segregation of jobs. In its prehearing analysis and summary of evidence, the EEOC outlined the defenses of the operating companies of the Bell system. One of the major bases of the companies' defense was reliance on state protective laws. This legislation, the companies asserted, prevented them from employing women in the craft jobs which typically lead to management positions.

Long before the EEOC and Title VII of the Civil Rights Act of 1964 existed, it was widely recognized that protective legislation created obstacles for women seeking work in certain trades. However, there did not seem to be a way of correcting the situation through existing law, since the Supreme Court had upheld the constitutionality of maximum-hours laws for women in 1908.

Three years earlier the Court had said in *Lochner* v. *New York*[17] that the states could not regulate the hours of all workers, because to do so would interfere with the constitutionally protected right of the employer to contract with labor on whatever terms could be bargained. However, in 1908 in *Muller* v. *Oregon*,[18] it was confronted with the original "Brandeis Brief" giving social science data concerning the impact of the working conditions of women on their health and reproductive capacity. In the face of this evidence, the court relented and upheld the state laws for women, distinguishing its opinion in *Lochner* by saying of woman: ". . . She is properly placed in a class by herself, and legislation designed for her protection may be sustained, even when like legislation is not necessary for men and could not be sustained. It is impossible to close one's eyes to the fact that she still looks to her brother and depends upon him."

16. U.S. Department of Labor, Women's Bureau, *Summary of State Labor Laws for Women* (Washington, D.C.: Government Printing Office, 1969).
17. Lochner v. New York, 198 U.S. 45 (1905).
18. Muller v. Oregon, 208 U.S. 412 (1908).

Following the *Muller* decision, protective labor legislation for women was always upheld until 1971, when the Ninth Circuit Court in *Mengelkoch* v. *Industrial Welfare Commission*[19] struck down a state hours law on equal protection grounds. The circuit court explained that its holding was inconsistent with the sixty-three-year old Supreme Court ruling, because the *Muller* case was brought by an employer eager to preserve its inexpensive female labor source while Mengelkoch was an employee who had been denied a job because of the state law. Specifically it said, "In *Muller,* the statute was upheld in part because it was thought to be a necessary way of safeguarding women's competitive position. Here the statute is attacked on the ground that it gives male employees an unfair economic advantage over females."

During the period between *Muller* and *Mengelkoch,* women's rights advocates looked to the proposed equal rights amendment for a solution to the problem created by the protective laws. They argued that under ERA the legislation would be extended to men, thereby protecting both sexes from oppressive working conditions and at the same time removing the incentive for employers to hire men rather than women. To a large measure the Congress was discouraged from acting on ERA because of the controversy over protective legislation between the amendment's proponents and its opponents, many of whom were labor unions. The latter's ardent defense of the protective laws led their opposition to speculate that what was actually being "protected" was, not women, but men's jobs.

Ultimately it has been litigation under Title VII rather than the prospects of ERA which has begun the demise of state protective legislation. The impact of Title VII on these laws and other factors contributing to occupational segregation will be discussed in Part III below.

Domestic Relations Law

Even more subtly than the protective legislation, the domestic relations laws of the states have contributed to sex segregation in employment. The states have dictated the reciprocal rights and responsibilities which all couples agree to when they are joined in wedlock in that particular jurisdiction. Marriage is less a contract between a husband and wife than it is an agreement which the couple makes with the state to conform to the terms which government has agreed are appropriate for marriage. They include the man's obligation to support his wife and children, the woman's obligation to care for the home and children, and the husband's position as head of the household. It is true that not all marriages follow this pattern, but in most states the total breach of any of

19. Mengelkoch v. Industrial Welfare Commission, 442 F.2d 1119 (9th Cir. 1971).

these terms is still grounds for divorce. It is also true that none of these terms is really enforceable during the life of the marriage.[20]

Nevertheless, because the law defines marital roles as it does, employers are comfortable with presumptions concerning the labor-force participation of married men and women. Because men have a legal duty to support their families, they are considered permanent members of the work force. Women, on the other hand, are considered temporary workers who will leave their jobs to bear and rear families or to be homemakers, since that is their obligation as wives. On this assumption, employers are reluctant to invest in the training of women to do skilled work. They also do not encourage women to take on job responsibility, because they believe that working wives give priority to their occupation as homemakers. Women are believed to be good at, and therefore are assigned to, supportive and service jobs such as secretarial and nursing, because these roles are so similar to the stereotype of wife and mother.

Because a man is the legally appointed breadwinner, he is considered to be serious about his work, ambitious, and responsible. Jobs with a future must be reserved for him so that he can meet the financial needs of his growing family. Since he has been crowned head of the household, he can dictate where the family lives and so is available for transfer and travel, which is usually not the case with his wife. In addition, his place as head of the family grooms him for a position of authority in his job. A woman, on the other hand, makes a poor foreman or sergeant if she is not even boss in her own home.

If marriage were legally a partnership, a real contractual relationship, employers might be less inclined to channel young men and women into jobs believed to be appropriate for them as stereotypical husbands and wives. Quite likely increasingly fewer marriages correspond to traditional patterns, but so long as the law remains the same, employer behavior in this regard is not apt to change.

The Law as a Remedy for Occupational Segregation

The most important legal prohibition against occupational segregation is Title VII of the Civil Rights Act of 1964. It proscribes discrimination on the basis of sex as well as race, color, national origin, and religion in any term or condition of employment. It specifically forbids an employer "to limit, segregate, or classify his employees in any way which would deprive or tend to deprive any individual of employment oppor-

20. Barbara Allen Babcock, Ann E. Freedman, Eleanor Holmes Norton, and Susan C. Ross, *Sex Discrimination and the Law: Causes and Remedies* (Boston: Little, Brown & Co., 1975), pp. 561–66.

tunities . . . because of such individual's sex."[21] The EEOC was established under the act to enforce these provisions.

Title VII was broadened and strengthened by amendments in 1972 so that it now applies to most employers in the private and public spheres with the already mentioned exception of the military services. Although the effectiveness of the EEOC has been jeopardized by an enormous backlog of complaints, it has had some notable successes, such as the previously described AT & T case. In addition, private individual and class actions may be brought under the act. Within the appreciable body of law which has been developed under Title VII, there are several important principles which should be outlined in connection with this discussion.

The Bona Fide Occupational Qualification (BFOQ)

Employers are forbidden to refuse to hire persons because of their race, color, sex, national origin, and religion, except that any of the last three of these characteristics may be considered if it is a "bona fide occupational qualification reasonably necessary to the normal operation of that particular business or enterprise."[22] When the telephone company told Claudine Cheatwood she could not be their commercial representative because this position was inappropriate for women, she sued. The court said the company failed to show that "all or substantially all women would be unable to perform safely and efficiently the duties of the job involved" and that they therefore could not limit the job to men.[23] When Celio Diaz wanted to be a flight attendant, and Pan American said he could not meet the psychological needs of the passengers as well as a woman could, he sued.[24] The court applied a business-necessity test and decided that transportation, not meeting the psychological needs of travelers, was the essence of Pan American's services. Therefore there was no necessity to hire women only. The case which drastically limited the use of the BFOQ defense was *Rosenfeld* v. *Southern Pacific Company*,[25] a suit by Lea Rosenfeld, who wanted to become an agent-telegrapher. The court said: "In the case before us there is no contention that the sexual characteristics of the employee are crucial to the successful performance of the job, as they would be for the position of wet-nurse, nor is there need for authenticity or genuineness as in the

21. Sec. 703a, 42 U.S.C. 2000e 2(a) (1972).

22. Sec. 703e, 42 U.S.C. 2000e 2 (1972).

23. Cheatwood v. South Central Bell Telephone & Telegraph Co., 303 F.Supp. 754 (M.D. Ala. 1969).

24. Diaz v. Pan American World Airways, Inc., 442 F. 2d 385 (5th Cir. 1971), *cert. denied*, 404 U.S. 950 (1971).

25. Rosenfield v. Southern Pacific Company, 444 F.2d 1219 (9th Cir. 1971).

case of an actor or actress. Rather, on the basis of a general assumption regarding the physical capabilities of female employees, the company attempts to raise a commonly accepted characterization of women as the 'weaker sex' to the level of a BFOQ."

Protective Labor Legislation

The protective legislation discussed earlier was claimed to be a BFOQ in many cases of male-only employment. This was true in the *Rosenfeld* case noted above. However, the Ninth Circuit concurred with the determination of the EEOC that the BFOQ exception is so narrow that it encompasses only sexual characteristics and does not extend to assessments of physical capabilities and endurance, which are presumed to be sex linked and which form the rationale for state protective laws.

The "Sex-Plus" Theory

A variation on the theme of excluding one sex or another from certain jobs is disqualifying persons of one sex because of some characteristic other than gender. For example, in *Phillips* v. *Martin Marietta Corporation*,[26] the company did not hire women with pre-school-age children but did hire men in the same circumstances. The Supreme Court said the corporation had failed to show that for persons with pre-school-age children being male was a BFOQ, leaving open the possibility of doing so on remand. Martin Marietta did not accept the challenge, and the sex-plus theory has fallen in disuse. A number of cases decided in lower courts after *Phillips* dealt with no-marriage and under-thirty-two rules for female flight personnel but not male. The airlines lost all of them.[27]

Sex-neutral Policies with a Discriminatory Impact

As we observed above in the discussion of women in policing, where women are not overtly denied certain jobs they may nevertheless be effectively excluded by the use of apparently sex-neutral policies which have a disproportionate impact on them as a class. The Supreme Court in *Griggs* v. *Duke Power Company*[28] dealt with a similar situation, in which the employer's requirement of a high school diploma or passing of a standardized intelligence test eliminated a disproportionate number of black applicants. Once this was proved by the plaintiff, the burden shifted to the employer to justify this effect as a "business necessity" and to show that the business purpose could not be accomplished as well by

26. Phillips v. Martin Marietta Corporation, 400 U.S. 542 (1971).
27. See, e.g., Sprogis v. United Air Lines, Inc., 444 F.2d 1194 (7th Cir. 1971).
28. Griggs v. Duke Power Company, 401 U.S. 424 (1971).

some alternative, nondiscriminatory means. The rule of the *Griggs* case was recently applied to strike down the minimum height requirement and a physical agility test which had made it all but impossible for women to qualify for positions as police officers in San Francisco. In *The Officers for Justice et al.* v. *The Civil Service Commission of the City and County of San Francisco,*[29] a district court judge said that studies made by the police department failed to show any correlation between the height requirement and an officer's ability to perform police duties. He also discounted an attempt by the government to validate the physical agility test, saying that even if it could be shown to accurately test an applicant's ability to perform the tasks of a police officer, the defendant would still have to prove that there was no alternative way of assuring that all officers are physically able to carry out their jobs. In light of the experience of other major city police departments which give no preselection test at all but rely on the police academy training to develop the necessary abilities, the court did not believe that San Francisco's test could be justified. It is noteworthy that the *The Officers for Justice* case had been in litigation for several years and predated the extension of Title VII to government employment. Even though the case was brought on equal protection grounds under the Civil Rights Act of 1871,[30] the court did not hesitate to apply Title VII principles.

Numerical Quotas for Hiring and Firing

When a court has found that an employer has engaged in illegally discriminatory hiring practices against a class of people, it can institute a hiring quota. This kind of affirmative relief has been used in various forms to compel police departments to hire women. The Philadelphia Police Department was ordered to hire 50 per cent women for one police academy class only, so that the performance of the men and women could be compared.[31] Similarly, San Francisco was required to hire fifteen women for every class of forty until sixty women had been hired whose performance could be studied.[32] A court in Detroit simply ordered a 50 percent hiring quota for the purpose of redressing past discrimination.[33]

Because the economic recession has caused some departments to lay off officers, the jobs of women who were recently hired under these quotas have been jeopardized. They were scheduled to be fired or de-

29. See n. 6 above.

30. 42 U.S.C. Sec. 1983.

31. Brace v. O'Neill, et al., Civil no. 74-399 (E.D. Pa.); and United States v. City of Philadelphia, Civil no. 74-400 (E.D. Pa.), order of the court dated January 29, 1975.

32. The Officers for Justice et al. v. The Civil Service Commission of the City and County of San Francisco (n. 6 above).

33. Schaefer v. Tannian, 394 F.Supp. 1128 (6th Cir. 1974).

moted first because of a "last-hired, first-fired" seniority system which is often part of a collective bargaining agreement. Most departments that accomplished a reduction in force in this manner would lose a disproportionate number of women and minority men, most of whom were also recently hired.

Courts which have been called upon to deal with the dilemma are divided in their decisions. It would seem directly contrary to Title VII principles to allow classes of people who were previously victims of discrimination to lose their jobs because of a lack of seniority which resulted from the discrimination.[34] However, some courts have decided this way because of their interpretation of the validity of language in the legislative history of Title VII which guarantees that the act will not interfere with the operation of seniority systems.[35]

This is but a cursory review of developments in Title VII law as it affects job segregation. It should be mentioned that other laws of more recent vintage are expected to aid women and men entering nontraditional careers. Title IX of the Education Amendments of 1972, because it prohibits sex discrimination in education, including vocational and professional programs, should eventually contribute substantially to opening new careers to both men and women.

The Crime Control Act of 1973 is beginning to be used more vigorously to open law-enforcement jobs to women. For example, payments to the Chicago Police Department of funds administered under the act were deferred in the fall of 1974 because of failure to hire women officers. Another $38 million due to be paid to Chicago under the General Revenue-Sharing Act was also withheld under court order. Tough federal enforcement of these laws against Chicago has reportedly had a "ripple effect" around the country. The usefulness of all this legislation obviously depends on the effectiveness of the agencies charged with enforcing it, which may in turn be determined by the amount of public pressure placed on those agencies.

This proved to be true with respect to the enforcement of Executive Order 11246, as amended by 11375, which prohibits federal government contractors from discriminating in employment practices. The Women's Equity Action League and the National Organization for Women have used the order to press for equal opportunity for women, especially those seeking to teach in colleges and universities, which until 1972 were not covered by Title VII. Although this has proved a useful device for educating institutions of higher learning with respect to their equal employment opportunity obligations, it has not yet resulted in

34. See Schaefer v. Tannian, 394 F.Supp. 1136 (6th Cir. May 13, 1975); Loy v. City of Cleveland F.Supp. , 8 F.E.P. Cases 614 (N.D. Ohio, 3/29/74); Watkins v. Steelworkers Local 2369, 369 F.Supp. 1221 (E.D. La. 1974).
35. See Waters v. Wisconsin Steel, 502 F.2d 1306 (7th Cir. 1974).

increased numbers of jobs or promotions for women. Another effect of the feminist effort to enforce the executive order has been an increase in concern about the concept of affirmative action which the order embodies. It requires a contracting organization to determine whether it has failed to hire and promote women and minorities commensurate with their availability, and if so to set goals and timetables for correcting this failure.

Although the burden on the employer for affirmative action is not so great as when a hiring quota has been set by a court, it is more onerous than a simple promise of nondiscrimination. A good-faith effort to hire more women into some lines of work may require convincing them that they want the job in the first place. For example, the telephone company might encourage a female applicant for an operator's job to be a lineman instead.

It is clear that in many industries, affirmative action plans, if carried out in good faith, could have substantial impact on the problem of occupational segregation. Whether or not this will happen may be again a question of the government's dedication to enforcement.

The Law as a Sex-segregated Profession

The legal profession remains a stronghold of male chauvinism despite the recent influx of young women into law schools. Few women lawyers have yet found their way into legislatures, onto judicial benches, or into the upper echelons of law firms. Women students lack role models because of the dearth of female law professors. Recent graduates still have trouble obtaining clerkships with judges and positions with prestigious firms. Those who do secure jobs are often restricted in the kinds of cases they are assigned—typically they are denied courtroom experience and contact with important clients who are believed to prefer a male attorney. Women lawyers tend to know their rights better than do other women workers, however, so they have been able to practice their skills against employers who disdain them. More than one prominent firm has had to defend itself against an attorney alleging sex discrimination in hiring or other conditions of employment.[36]

Unfortunately, asserting one's legal rights in this way can be expensive, time consuming, and difficult. Plaintiffs in suits against employers are sometimes ostracized, harassed, and branded as troublemakers. Financial, legal, and moral support for workers who are willing to challenge employers in court on behalf of a class is woefully inadequate. Feminist and public-interest litigators attempting to provide these services often lack the resources to do so. They are nevertheless responsible

36. Kohn v. Royall, Koegal and Wells, 59 F.R.D. 515 (S.D.N.Y. 1973.)

for much of the test-case and precedent-setting litigation in the area of
sex discrimination and are perhaps the only bright spot in this otherwise
gloomy catalog of male-dominated legal institutions.

Conclusions

Occupational segregation has often been reinforced by, but seldom
created by, the law. In the past five years, legislators and jurists have
created powerful legal remedies for workers who attempt to break down
gender-related barriers in the work force. It is too early to judge
whether these laws will have a substantial remedial effect on the problems of sex segregation in the work force. However, at least one dramatic breakthrough of women into a field previously reserved exclusively
for men—police patrol—is noteworthy. There has been a clear numerical increase of women on patrol, and a significant proportion of those
positions are known to have been filled by women because of court
orders or under financial duress by federal enforcement agencies.

Center for Women Policy Studies
Washington, D.C.

The Social Institutions of Occupational Segregation

Comment I

Kenneth Boulding

We are, perhaps, today assisting at the birth of a new science, or at least a new interdiscipline. I am not quite sure what to call it. We can't call it sexology because that is something else. I thought of calling it dimorphics, because it is the study of sexual dimorphism in the total social system and the study of the fact that the human race is dimorphic. It is, particularly, divided into two sexes of approximately equal numbers.

The present state of dimorphics can be considered primitive in the extreme. Cross-cultural studies very much need to be done. Then we must get into sociology and law, and the study of institutions, economics, and all of the social sciences. We have a 100-year job ahead.

This set me to thinking how we can do this: what is the strategy of a new science? It starts out, I think, with descriptive science. This is very important, something the social sciences have badly neglected, outside of anthropology. We are highly deficient in simple description. Still, there is a good deal of it here, and a good many of the materials for this conference are, quite rightly, concerned with it.

This leads to a positive science. Descriptive science is not enough. Essentially positive science is a science of constraints. That is, it is the study of what the constraints on the system are. As we know, positive science is difficult, especially in complex systems.

But positive science is something very real. If you jump off a high building with the belief you can fly, positive science will settle the issue. Now positive social science is the study of social constraints, but you must be careful not to fall into equilibrium science, as equilibrium is a figment of the human imagination. Equilibrium is unknown in the real world, although it is useful for passing examinations or for certain other uses in economics and other sciences. Equilibrium is important because the world has what I call equilibrating constraints. Dynamic systems do not explode indefinitely but are pressed into loose molds.

Laws, correlations, and the like are equilibrating constraints. If one is a true scientist, believing in such things as correlations, one should see these only as preludes to dynamics. Correlation, and indeed most of the prime statistical techniques, are only a prologue to science. As I have said, real positive science is to find the real boundaries. Boundaries are hard to find, especially when we have to think of them in dynamic terms, and all constraints are really dynamic. Equilibrium is a special case of dynamic constraints which are equally difficult to study.

Positive science is the study of boundaries that divide the possible from the impossible. And beyond this we have normative science, a legitimate part of science. Normative science studies what should be instead of what can be. The fundamental principle here is what should be cannot be what cannot be. The positive constraints must limit the proposals of normative principle.

Obviously it is important to keep positive and normative science both separate and related, and it is very dangerous to confuse the two. It is very dangerous to say that because something should be, it is. And it is also dangerous to be too positive about positive science since one can be wrong. The limits may be wider than we think. Normative science can force us to widen the boundaries of the possible, for if something which is not now possible should be, we have an incentive to find out how to make it possible. A very important pattern we still have to discover is why things so often end up between the positive and the normative. The image of the normative is not stable either, as the norms change all the time. We have to be careful not to get into the fallacy of assuming unchangeable norms.

But norms also change under positive constraints, and it is tragically easy to fail to reach normative ends because of a failure to understand the positive constraints. But the positive constraints on normative change are hard to discover; the inquiry is a very large order.

I think, then, that we are at the beginnings of a discipline. Its fruits should be a better understanding of what the positive constraints are on social systems, especially in regard to change of norms. Certainly error in regard to this has been appallingly costly to the human race. When one thinks of the constant failure of liberations, revolutions, reforms, and prohibitions to improve the human condition, and when one thinks of the catastrophic effects of normative principles applied in positive misunderstanding, one is tempted to formulate a law of political irony—that everything one does to help people hurts them, and everything one does to hurt people helps them. While this is not true, there is enough truth in it to hurt. Values are no substitute for positive knowledge. They have to operate under known constraints. Otherwise they are not fulfilled.

The thing I like in all these papers is that one sees the nice mix of the positive and the normative, which I think we have to strive for. I have not discussed these papers in detail, but I think someone may look back on this occasion 100 years from now and say it was here that something began.

University of Colorado

THE SOCIAL INSTITUTIONS OF OCCUPATIONAL SEGREGATION

Comment II

Harold J. Leavitt

It seems to me that we have to begin our analysis at a point in time, perhaps a decade or so ago, with a system that is in equilibrium but which is also unjust: the stereotyped system in which the man is the breadwinner and the woman is the housewife. Then we perturb that system. I am not sure of the source of the social forces that cause the perturbation, but essentially we raise the consciousnesses of women and, to some extent, of men. So the system must now deal with a new element, the increased level of aspiration of many women. The papers express a great deal of concern about the extent to which that perturbation has been effective in modifying the system. For example, Safilios-Rothschild's paper is concerned with the effects of that perturbation on the traditional man-woman relationship. The legal issues Gates considers raise questions about modification of the larger structure in which the male-female unit operates and whether or not one can loosen up the system at the macro level to give the new aspirations of women someplace to exert themselves.

What I have been worrying about is how to draw the causal arrows in the whole complex picture. One thing that struck me is that *time* is one of the critical issues; that the many changes involved in the rising female levels of aspiration are occurring at different rates. For example, although the legal problems are large and complex, I thought I heard an optimistic note in what was being said, a note that implied that the macro structure was already changing in a direction that enables women to move into new kinds of occupations. The progress may be slow, but there is legal progress.

The next thing I heard was that as larger systems loosen to permit newly aspiring women an opportunity, at least a partial one, to fulfill those aspirations, we should expect a secondary backup effect on the man-woman relationship. We generate problems of disequilibrium in a relationship whose structure has been in some kind of equilibrium. The woman now works; the man continues to work, but the housework still has to be done. So we search for compensatory modifications of the household which lead to notions about getting rid of specialization between husband and wife, or alternation between outside work and housework by both members, or a variety of other ways of handling this new problem. But my personal feeling about those ideas is that many of the things that Safilios-Rothschild was projecting are likely to be a lot slower in coming than some of the more macro structural changes.

When we back up to the effects on the individual, I suspect that what we have done is to take a generation of people, both men and women during their adult years, and we have somehow succeeded in changing their attitudes and raising their levels of aspriation without making contemporaneous modifications of other related attitudes. I have the feeling that a lot of women are caught up in this dilemma. They have *not* given up those notions and role pursuits because they learned them very early and very deeply. In this realm as elsewhere the imposition of the new does not necessarily automatically and immediately wash out the old. It might well wash out the old over a generation, but in the middle run the new and the old coexist and cause conflicts.

The more I look at this complex change process, the more it seems that most of the pressure is bound to fall on the woman herself and on the man-woman relationship. That is what a lot of this discussion has been about. How do you modify and deal with old attitudes about the man-woman relationship in the presence of a presumably increasingly benign world in which women can go out and make it where they want to? Maybe what we are doing is offering up a sacrificial generation—a generation of people who will have to absorb the conflicts until a new equilibrium swings itself ponderously into place.

I should like to conclude with a comment of a different sort. I vacillate between being optimistic and pessimistic about the structural side of these issues: whether or not, for example, business organizations are going to change very rapidly. A few things look reasonably positive. One of them is that there has been a rather strong trend toward participative management in business organizations. The modern, good manager's ideal is to be a much more humanistic and a much more group-oriented manager than his father was. The old model of the command-post executive has been giving way rather rapidly, I think, to a softer model, partially as a consequence of the education that young managers are getting. That kind of more group-oriented viewpoint does seem more open to the idea that we not only can use women in our organization, but we ought to. This is so because the values that go along with that participative style tend to be more democratic and less autocratic, more contemporary and less traditional.

Stanford University

The Social Institutions of Occupational Segregation

Comment III

Karen Oppenheim Mason

Occupational segregation appears to be caused by the operation of *most* social institutions, not just the labor market itself. Such segregation is, in other words, just one reflection of a society-wide system of sex differentiation which promotes different roles, temperaments, opportunities, and rewards for women and men.

If this is true, then an important question is the extent to which we can end occupational segregation without changing these basic institutions. How far can we go, trying to change *only* the labor market and its behavior? To answer this we must learn the extent to which differing expectations and opportunities for women and men in the family, the educational system, the community, and the political system will continue to present barriers to occupational equality, even in the face of all possible efforts to end the discriminatory behavior of employers, trade unions, and the professions.

We already have research that speaks to this question, but not enough. Thus, it would be helpful to think about the *immediate* causes of workers' occupational placements so we can disaggregate the question of why women work in positions so different from men's. At least five such causes of individual occupational placement come readily to mind:

1. Human capital formation prior to labor-market entry (i.e., how much education people obtain and what they train themselves for).

2. Their ability or willingness to forego short-run rewards in favor of long-run occupational advantages at the time of labor-market entry.

3. Their ability or willingness to meet workplace demands for temporary or permanent geographic movement, or for change in their pattern or amount of work effort.

4. Their ability or willingness to accumulate continuous experience in the labor market, in a particular field or trade, or in a particular firm, bureaucracy, or union.

5. Employers', co-workers', and clients' stereotypes and "tastes" regarding women versus men workers.

We suspect that women's position on all five of these factors tends to differ from men's. Because of their traditional roles as wives and mothers, perhaps their acquiescence to a general principle of male privilege, or their recognition of market discrimination, women tend to prepare themselves for different fields than do men. Probably for similar reasons they are also less likely than men to forego early market rewards for long-term payoffs; are less able or willing than men to meet employers' labor-supply demands; and are less likely than men to work continuously. They are also probably more likely than men to suffer from negative stereotypes and distastes.

We need to know in more detail why each of these differences exists and also the extent to which each contributes to the overall segregation of the work force. Such information would, at least, help us understand where our personal and political efforts to end occupational segregation might most effectively be applied.

We do not yet know the relative importance of different institutions for maintaining sex segregation in the work force, but I guess that one institution presents an especially serious barrier to occupational equality in our society and is likely to do so for some time. This is parenthood. What we know about the determinants of female labor-force participation, about women's household time budgets, and about people's reasons for having children, all suggest that caring for children (and enjoying them) is a far more serious barrier to continuous and intensive market work than are other domestic responsibilities. And caring for children is, of course, usually women's responsibility.

Safilios-Rothschild's paper talks about the increasing proportion of women who are choosing to not have children and the salutary effects this might have on women's careers. I agree these effects may exist but think the emphasis on women is misplaced. Even today, it is only a small minority of women who anticipate never having children. And it is hard to imagine conditions under which this minority would grow much beyond one-quarter or one-third of all women. Thus, unless future patterns of child rearing are very different from today's, most American women, relative to most American men, are likely to remain at a disadvantage on the factors that determine occupational placement. A sex-role revolution in which men's domestic roles and employment patterns change as much as do women's may thus be necessary for ending occupational segregation.

Population Studies Center
University of Michigan

The Social Institutions of Occupational Segregation

Comment IV

Sandra S. Tangri

I noted that none of the papers proposed a definition of occupational segregation, so I am going to propose one and see where it takes us. I would like to propose that occupational segregation exists in an occupation when the work force in that occupation does not contain a representative distribution of persons on the major demographic variables according to their proportion in the adult population. This definition includes, for example, those occupations in which sex is a BFOQ (bona fide occupational qualification), like wet nurse, but there are very few of those kinds of occupations, and they are not full time. It also includes occupations in which the sex ratio may be fifty-fifty but minorities of either sex or persons from either end of the age continuum are over- or underrepresented. That is something that I think has been very much neglected, at least in the papers I have read so far. When we talk about occupational segregation, we seem to be focusing almost exclusively on sex segregation of occupations. Yet segregation of occupations on these other dimensions, by race and age, is at least equally important. It might broaden our view on how we treat the subject of occupational segregation to consider the similarities and differences among those. As Representative Griffiths said, it is true that the vast majority of the female labor force is in teaching, health, and service occupations. But if we break those categories down further, the female labor force is further segregated by race (black and other minority women are highly overrepresented among private household workers and seasonal farm workers) and by age (airline stewardesses are seldom over thirty and they are seldom nonwhite). So we do have other dimensions of occupational segregation to take into account. I think we would be very remiss if we ignored that fact.

I think that ignoring that fact produces certain limitations in treatments of the subject. For instance, Safilios-Rothschild's paper, while speaking of equal status dual linkages, addresses more specifically the problem of equally *high*-status occupational linkages much more than the question of equally *low*-status occupational linkages. Because of the general association between status and race, her discussion fails to note that there has been in this country for some time both equal status and reverse status dual linkages for black wives and husbands and that this experience offers us valuable lessons on equal status marriages. Some very good examples of this were given by Patricia Harris in a talk she gave to the American Council on Education at their annual meeting in 1972. It would be particularly instructive to study such marriages because they endure under very hostile conditions, and the hostility is derived not just from the conflict between status assumptions based on occupational reversals but also from the conditions of race.

There is, of course, a further assumption in the definition of the problem as presented in Safilios-Rothschild's paper: once marital choice is exercised, it *ought* to be a permanent one, a problem already raised when we talked about the issue of divorce. It is my feeling that this may be an unnecessarily limiting assumption and that marital or consort choices, like occupational choices may increasingly be singular and permanent (our standard model), singular and serial, or multiple and simultaneous. Furthermore, they may not be heterosexual or exclusively heterosexual. We ought to be wondering how these options affect occupational choice over time and, in particular, how they affect women's occupational mobility.

Whereas Safilios-Rothschild looks at the relationship between family institutions and occupational segregation, Gates examines the laws and legal institutions that perpetuate and enforce our occupational segregation and the ways in which these can be turned around to reverse the phenomenon. It is clear from her paper that both aspects of the legal impact on occupational segregation apply to the entire range of occupations and not just high-status occupations.

Nancy Gordon told me recently about a lawsuit brought by a woman machinist in which she testified as an expert witness and which, technically, was won by the woman. However, the amount to be awarded had been in the hands of a municipal judge—I hate to say she was a woman—for two years. Representative Griffiths said that only half of the awards to women by the courts on sex discrimination have actually been paid.

It would be extremely useful in counteracting the premature backlash to women's "gains" to gather data on the duration of court cases, the costs, the legal outcome, the amounts awarded, and ultimate amounts actually paid. My feeling has been that the track record is similar to that in alimony and child-support cases: dismal. When I called a meeting at the Commission on Civil Rights for persons interested in research on affirmative action, the major theme that emerged was that we do not even know what the track record is in any detail. This is the first major research task for any studies on affirmative action. Until we know how many such actions have occurred and what the outcomes have been, we cannot really assess the effectiveness of this strategy or evaluate what progress we have made.

Although the family and the law are important social institutions supporting occupational segregation, two others are the educational system and the social structure of work itself. We are probably all aware of how the educational system tracks individuals into particular segments of the occupational structure through sex- and class-segregated courses, curriculum content, biased textbooks, counseling, etc. We also have to look at problems such as the distribution of men and women at various levels and curriculum areas of the educational system.

In terms of the social structure of work, its most compelling fact is its rigidity, and any workers who fail to conform pay a stiff price in wages and prestige. In terms of professional careers, I think there is a terrible rigidity in defining a professional career as requiring fifty to sixty hours a week, and that makes the system of dual professional career linkages an unbearable strain. The restructuring of these interlocking systems must become a high priority social program.

I think there are other factors that coincide with and reinforce the rigidity of the social structure of work, such as transportation, the system for delivery of services that presume in many cases a permanent housewife at home all day, and the absolute lack of any institutionalized childcare system. Collecting follow-up data on women's postgraduate experiences, I found that many of them said that they were not going to need any outside help in caring for children because the family could take care of its own needs in this area. It turns out that what they see as the self-sufficiency of the family is really the self-sufficiency of the wife.[1]

U.S. Commission on Civil Rights

1. Sandra Tangri, "Effects of Background, Personality, College and Post-College Experiences on Women's Post-Graduate Employment" (Final Report to U.S. Department of Labor, grant 91-34-71-02, 1974).

The Historical Roots of Occupational Segregation

Historical and Structural Barriers to Occupational Desegregation

Jessie Bernard

The following three papers document in convincing detail the fact that occupational segregation has an ancient, if not necessarily always an honorable, history, both predating and postdating traditional capitalism. A thread running through them is emphasis on the dysfunctional consequences for women of such occupational segregation as evidenced by the disproportionate amount of the work load they carry in societies and by the relatively low rewards they receive for their work.

Four introductory comments seem to me to warrant some attention: (1) that there have been times and places when occupational segregation was highly valued rather than resented by women, (2) that occupational segregation may have more than a simply economic foundation, (3) that occupational desegregation may have productivity-enhancing consequences, and (4) that occupational desegregation need not result in across-the-board sex equality in occupational distribution.

1. The present point of view has not always obtained among women. Nor does it even today, either in this country or in some others. In America, for example, there was a time when "the sphere of women" was highly exalted. Occupational segregation was, in fact, a desideratum devoutly longed for. The concept of women's sphere, the cult of true womanhood, arose when the labor of middle- and upper-class women began to decline. Catharine Beecher, one of the greatest proponents of the cult of domesticity, apotheosized it.

Her ideas on class and sex were derived in large part from

deTocqueville. She referred to his belief that "in no country has such constant care been taken, as in America, to trace two clearly distinct lines of action for the two sexes" and saw societal divisions on the basis of sex as a safeguard against societal divisions on the basis of class. In the words of Kathryn Kish Sklar, her biographer, Beecher "decried the abandonment of the sexual division of labor and its replacement with a class system. . . . The increasing division of labor along class lines had disrupted this natural order. . . . The effect of class was debilitating women [as well as men]. Catharine Beecher's conscience and her social fears were aroused by the increasing signs of class divisions in American life, but there was very little she was able to do to assuage her fears beyond insisting on the maintenance of gender boundaries rather than class boundaries to mark the basic divisions in American society."[1]

When increasing urbanization and industrialization began to erode women's sphere, Beecher sought new ways to continue occupational segregation. She felt a strong need to "discover new ways to maintain the boundaries between men and women in an urban environment where both sexes might be performing similar functions. . . . The inclusion of women alongside men in the class of industrial workers was but one example of the ways in which an increasingly complex urban society blurred the lines that separated men from women. Victorianism was an effort to retain the old ideological goal of domesticity by continuing the belief that society's fundamental social divisions were the 'natural' ones of sex, rather than the pernicious ones of class."[2] As a sop to women who might not appreciate the beauties of the women's sphere, Beecher reassured them of the value of their contribution to building the nation: "The woman who is rearing a family of children; the woman who labors in the schoolroom; the woman who, in her retired chamber, earns, with her needle, the mite, which contributes to the intellectual and moral elevation of her Country; even the humble domestic, whose example and influence may be moulding and forming young minds, while her faithful services sustain a prosperous domestic state:—each and all may be animated by the consciousness, that they are agents in accomplishing the greatest work that ever was committed to human responsibility."[3]

In an extraordinarily stimulating paper, Johnny Faragher and Christine Stansell have shown how hard women on the covered-wagon trail tried to maintain their feminine sphere and how, when the going got really rough, they had to join with the men in the hard labor:

> The vicissitudes of the trail opened new possibilities for expanded work roles for women, and in the cooperative work of the family

1. Kathryn Kish Sklar, *Catharine Beecher: A Study in American Domesticity* (New Haven, Conn.: Yale University Press, 1973), pp. 212–13.
2. Ibid., p. 211.
3. Ibid., p. 160.

there existed a basis for a vigorous struggle for female-male equality. But most women did not see the experience in this way. They viewed it as a male enterprise from its very inception. Women experienced the breakdown of the sexual division of labor as a dissolution of their own autonomous "sphere." Bereft of the footing which this independent base gave them, they lacked a cultural rationale for the work they did, and remained estranged from the possibilities of the enlarged scope and power of family life on the trail. Instead, women fought *against* the forces of necessity to hold together the few fragments of female subculture left to them.[4]

The occupational segregation of women was something they wanted. It was, however, a luxury the pioneers could not afford. Life on the trail began with the customary division of labor, but "the relegation of women to purely domestic duties . . . soon broke down under the vicissitudes of the Trail. . . . By mid-journey, most women worked at male tasks."[5]

Still the women tried valiantly to salvage what they could of their female culture: "Woman's sphere provided them with companionship, a sense of self-worth, and most important, independence from men in a patriarchal world. The Trail, in breaking down sexual segregation, offered women the opportunities of socially essential work. Yet this work was performed in a male arena, and many women saw themselves as draftees rather than partners. . . . On the Overland Trail, cultural roles and self-definitions conflicted with the immediate necessities of the socioeconomic situation. Women themselves fought to preserve a circumscribed role [even] when material circumstances rendered it dysfunctional."[6] The authors see this clinging to a dysfunctional paradigm as retarding for women: "They refused to appropriate their new work to their own ends and advantage. In their deepest sense of themselves they remained estranged from their function as 'able bodies.' "[7]

At trail's end the opportunity to reconceptualize occupational roles was over: "The ideal wife in the West resembled a hired hand more than a nurturant Christian housekeeper."[8] The women continued to try to recapture the culture of domesticity, but the basis for such a world was missing: "Their work as virtual hired hands rendered obsolete the material base of separate arenas for women and men."[9]

4. Johnny Faragher and Christine Stansell, "Women and Their Families on the Overland Trail, 1842–1867," *Feminist Studies* 2 (November 1975): 151.
5. Ibid., pp. 155, 157.
6. Ibid., p. 161.
7. Ibid.
8. Ibid., p. 154.
9. Ibid., p. 162.

Hanna Papanek has given us an analysis of occupational segregation at its greatest extreme in the form of purdah.[10] She notes that it makes possible a whole occupational structure for serving women at high professional levels. There is room for women doctors and professors. I have even heard women argue that it is to the advantage of women to have large blocks of occupations "reserved" for them, both protected from competition and more sheltered against recessions.

2. My second introductory comment has to do with some noneconomic, nontechnological aspects of occupational segregation. All three of the papers focus on economic and technological factors, as is appropriate in a conference organized by economists. But at the end of her paper, Hartmann widens the scope of her perspective and invokes a new explanatory variable, the rules of behavior that constitute the microunderpinnings or complements of the discriminatory institutions she has so meticulously analyzed.

The "rules" to which she refers have now been expanded to include a wide variety of behaviors that have discriminatory consequences for women in the work force. Mary P. Rowe's classic paper, "The Saturn's Rings Phenomenon," lists some of them.[11] Elsewhere I have also begun to look into the subtle forms of behavior that have discriminatory consequences for women.[12] The Committee on the Status of Women in the Economics Profession of the American Economic Association has also explored behaviors at the professional level that result in discrimination against women.[13]

Caplow gives as explanations for these exclusionary rules the rebellion of men against the female figures which dominate the socializing

10. Hanna Papanek, "Purdah in Pakistan: Seclusion and Modern Occupations for Women," *Journal of Marriage and the Family* 33 (August 1971): 517–30; "Purdah: Separate Worlds and Symbolic Shelter," *Comparative Studies in Society and History* 15, no. 3 (June 1973): 289–325.

11. Rowe has a typology with four overlapping categories, including harassment and invisibility. Under harassment she gives illustrations of this nature: ". . . if she is given tenure, I will see that she is so miserable that she goes." Or there is systematic humiliation in the form of comments about appearance, or extra work. Under invisibility, she notes that a woman's name is mysteriously missing from a list, that she does not receive the announcement, invitation, reservations, planned vacation (see Mary P. Rowe, "The Saturn's Rings Phenomenon" [unpublished, 1973; available from author at Massachusetts Institute of Technology, $2.00]).

12. I have been looking at what I call the "stag effect," i.e., the complex of habits, customs, and practices which have the effect of excluding women from male meetings, contacts, communication networks. This would fall into Rowe's category of invisibility. I am also looking at putdowns, verbal and nonverbal in expression. These fall into Rowe's category of harassment. See Jessie Bernard. "What Will Equality Mean?" (paper presented to Educational Staff Seminar, George Washington University and Institute for Educational Leadership, April 17, 1975), and "Women of the World Unite! An *International* Year" (address at the opening session of National Commission on Observance of International Women's Year, April 15, 1975).

13. Kenneth E. Boulding and Barbara B. Reagan, "Combatting Role Prejudice and Sex Discrimination," *American Economic Review* 63, no. 5 (December 1973): 1049–61.

process in childhood, the scorn heaped upon boys who associate with girls, and the desire to protect the "male culture":

> Especially in the male group, which tends to reject overtly, if superficially, the official morality sponsored by women in the family, there is a culturally recognized atmosphere which symbolizes the exclusion of women. The use of tabooed words, the fostering of sports and other interests which women do not share, and participation in activities which women are intended to disapprove of —hard drinking, gambling, practical jokes, and sexual essays of varying kinds—all suggest that the adult male group is to a large extent engaged in a reaction *against* feminine influence, and therefore cannot tolerate the presence of women without changing its character entirely.[14]

Lionel Tiger makes an analogous point. On admittedly impressionistic evidence, he argues: "(1) that, when they can, males choose their workmates in processes analogous to sexual selection; (2) that the bond established generates considerable emotion; (3) that males derive important satisfactions from male bonds and male interactions which they cannot derive from male-female bonds and interactions; and (4) that the sexual division of labor is a *consequence* of males' wishes to preserve their unisexual bonds and not simply a result of physical and temperamental differences with females in any culture."[15] Tiger goes further than other observers in attributing a biological basis to this male bonding: "Males dominate females in occupational and political spheres. . . . They consciously and emotionally *exclude* females from these bonds. The significant notion here is that these broad patterns are biologically based."[16] They are part of the human "biogram."

Accepting a great deal of the data on the existence of male bonding but, unlike Tiger, attributing a sociological rather than a genetic basis to it, Jean Lipman-Blumen is exploring the concept of homosociality. The term, borrowed from John Gagnon, refers to a preference men have for the company of men. She adduces evidence from early childhood development studies, patterns of adolescent and adult interaction, as well as animal studies ("for those who are willing to extrapolate from monkeys to men").[17] But even more cogent is her own sociological analysis in terms of control of resources. She notes that since men have control of most of the sources of power they can more readily than women satisfy most of the intellectual, physical, emotional, social, and sexual needs of men. Even women have realistically identified with males. The only re-

14. Theodore Caplow, *The Sociology of Work* (New York: McGraw-Hill Book Co., 1964), p. 239.

15. Lionel Tiger, *Men in Groups* (New York: Random House, 1969), p. 128.

16. Ibid., pp. 143–44.

17. Jean Lipman-Blumen, "Changing Sex Roles in American Culture: Future Directions for Research," *Archives of Sexual Behavior* 4, no. 4 (1975): 433–92, esp. p. 441.

source on which women have a monopoly is that of conferring paternity
on men. Lipman-Blumen concludes from this array of evidence that it is
not difficult to see women's absence from the world of power *not* as a
deliberate or hostile conspiracy against women, but rather as evidence of
a self-sufficient homosocial male society. If we are, indeed, up against
this kind of barrier to occupational desegregation, our strategies will
have to take a radical turn.

3. My third comment, though it has no relevance for historical
research on occupational segregation, may be justified as a precursor of
future history. It follows logically from the comments on the work
group, and it has to do with the results that may be expected when or if
we finally overcome the male bias against the presence of women in the
work group. Hartmann lays great stress on the schooling many more
men than women have received in hierarchical organization techniques.
Their ability to use it gave them an advantage over women, who were
more isolated and less schooled in organization. It is now dawning on
students of industrial organization that horizontal, as contrasted with
hierarchical, organization has a lot to be said for it and may, in fact, be
the wave of the future. At this point, I would like to suggest that the way
women operate organizationally may be superior even on the basis of
male criteria of success. Harold Leavitt has shown me the results of the
most interesting experimental study I know of "male" and "female" styles
of working together in which the effect of the sex ratio on group decision
making was explored.[18] Individuals were asked to rank fifteen items according to their importance for survival in a contrived desert situation,[19]
first individually without discussion as a team and then together as a
five-member team after discussion.[20] The individual scores for each
team were averaged so that there were two scores for each team, one the
average of five individual prediscussion scores and one postdiscussion
consensual team score.[21] The averaged prediscussion individual scores
were about the same for both men (69.9) and women (69.1), but the
consensual team scores for all-female groups were spectacularly better
than the consensual team scores of all-male groups—53.8 and 62.8, re-

18. E. L. M. Publications, *The Survival Problem*, developed by Human Synergistics,
1973. The individuals who worked on this project were J. Clayton Lafferty, Patrick M.
Eady, and Jon M. Elmers, in consultation with Alonzo W. Pond.
19. The items were a flashlight, a jackknife, a sectional air map of the area, a plastic
raincoat, a magnetic compass, a compress kit with gauze, a .45 caliber loaded pistol, a
parachute, a bottle of salt tablets, a quart of water per person, a book on edible animals of
the desert, a pair of sunglasses per person, two quarts of 180-proof vodka, a topcoat per
person, and a cosmetic mirror.
20. Rankings were validated on the basis of the ranking of a survival expert. High
scores showed low conformity with the expert's ranking; low scores showed high conformity with it.
21. Forty-eight five-member teams varying in sex composition from all female to all
male were studied. There were five all-female teams; seven with four females, four with
three females; five with two females; eight with one female; and nineteen with no females.

spectively, a difference in favor of the women of 9.0 score points. It was especially striking to me that although team discussion improved the performance of both sexes it improved the scores of female teams more than twice as much (15.3 score points) as it did male team scores (7.1 score points). The inference seems to be legitimate that the women could work together, learn from one another, accept suggestions, modify their own position more easily than the men could. The competitiveness of the men probably interfered with their acceptance of the logic of others; they had to protect their macho. In terms of a male-bond theory the findings are rather anomalous. The male bond did not seem to work as well among the men as the female-bond did among women. If men could overcome their homosocial bias enough to work comfortably with women, their own performance might well be improved. In the survival experiment, the best-performing teams were those composed of three women and two men. The dynamics are not altogether clear. Perhaps the civilizing effect of three women was enough to tone down the macho competitiveness of the two men.

4. A final comment is also related to future, rather than past, history. What would constitute occupational nonsegregation? What would be a sex-fair distribution of work? A fair distribution would, it seems to me, have to take into account both the distribution of talent in the work force and the distribution of individual preferences or aspirations. I am not one who insists that there are no sex differences in the distributions of talents. I am not prepared to state just how these talents are distributed in the two sexes, but I am convinced—as much from Lapidus's data as from any—that more women than men have certain skills and motivations and more men than women other skills and motivations. Although disparities in female participation as wide as those shown in table 4 of the Lapidus paper—ranging from 24 percent in transport to 85 percent in public health, physical culture, and social welfare—undoubtedly do reflect socialization and power relationships, they seem to me to reflect more. Any sex-free concept of occupational nonsegregation must allow options to women based on talents. It seems to me contrary to the interests of women to pressure them to enter professional occupations for which they do not have talents or at least qualifications. The increase in the number of women engineers in the USSR between 1941 and 1970—from 44,000 to 1 million—suggests to me that there are a great many women with talents for engineering formerly untapped, and perhaps still untapped, waiting for the encouragement that education and employment patterns could release. On the other hand, I note also that "Soviet emphasis on scientific and technical skills" has not greatly increased the proportion of female scientific workers since 1947. There may be an asymptote here. Of course we will never know what sex differences there are in the distribution of all kinds of talents until opportunities and rewards are totally equalized.

A second factor, in addition to talent, that will have to be taken into account in occupational nonsegregation will have to be aspirations. Here we are on a most sensitive spot. As Lapidus reminds us, "women's lower aspirations may reflect not only the effects of socialization but also a realistic assessment of the likely returns on investments of additional time and energy." How to raise them is still by no means clear. If, despite high aspirations, a woman finds herself always at the lower levels of her profession, why try?

If we may anticipate a solution to the problem of measuring both talent and aspiration[22] and a way of eliminating the effects of past socialization and present power relations on women, we could then devise an occupational nonsegregated scheme. It would not necessarily take the form of across-the-board numerical equality.[23] If sex differences persist when opportunities and rewards are equalized, I would not fight them. Any attempt to deny or explain away all sex differences seems to me to reflect too low an opinion of women. It indicates that they are viewed as valuable or worthy only as they conform to male patterns. I am personally less concerned about occupational segregation per se than I am with its almost universal concomitant, namely, the custom of according less recognition and less value to the work women do, almost regardless, than to the work men do. I believe that organizing women in the labor force to achieve power and to demand greater recognition and reward for what they do is a first step in upgrading the status of the work they do. What I covet for women is the realization not only among men but even, more important, among themselves, of their own value and the feeling of self-worth that will gain for them the recognition their contribution deserves.

United States Civil Rights Commission

22. Although it is difficult to measure talent and aspirations, one proxy in the academic labor market is the proportion of women obtaining M.A.'s and the proportion receiving Ph.D.'s in a given field. Universities have used such percentages to estimate the availability of qualified women in setting affirmative-action goals, even though at present the figures represent a combination of aspirations, socialization, talent, and power relations.

23. In the United States in 1973, there were, roughly, 55 million men in the civilian labor force and, again roughly, 35 million women. If, let us say, 10 percent of the men and 50 percent of the women have both talent and high aspirations for occupation A, there would be 3.5 million men suitable for occupation A and 17.5 million women, a ratio of one man to five women. If 25 percent of the men and 10 percent of the women have talent and high aspirations for occupation B, there would be 11 million men and 3.5 million women in that occupation, a ration of three-plus men to one woman. If the talent and aspiration levels were equal—say 10 percent of both men and women had talent and high aspirations for occupation C—the ratio in occupation C would be the same as in the labor force, namely, eleven men to seven women.

THE HISTORICAL ROOTS OF OCCUPATIONAL SEGREGATION

Familial Constraints on Women's Work Roles

Elise Boulding

The nature of the familial constraints on woman's role as worker in every type of human society is perhaps best captured by the triple role concept of "breeder-feeder-producer." From the earliest and simplest hunting and gathering folk to the most industrialized society of the twentieth century, the breeding of babies[1] and the feeding of humans of all ages is almost exclusively the work of the woman,[2] above and beyond other productive processes she is engaged in. In addition, the woman participates in certain producer roles, usually but not always differentiated from male producer roles.

It should be clear that all three categories in the breeder-feeder-producer triad are in fact producer roles, but I am distinguishing between the first two categories, which are assigned to women only, and the third, which is divided between women and men. In a subsistence society, the producer role exists primarily to create material for domestic consumption. It is only when trading begins that sticky questions about

Some of the material in this article is taken from *The Underside of History: A View of Women through Time* (Boulder, Colo.: Westview Press, 1976, in press). I wish to thank my associate, Dorothy Carson, for assistance in preparing this manuscript.

1. I include in the concept of breeding both the bearing of children and caring for them until they are self-sufficient. The biological aspect of childbearing is only one component of breeding thus defined.

2. Men may prepare special feast foods, but in no society is the preparation of food for consumption in the home the regular daily work of men.

the agents and measurements of production arise. Woman's production is normally noticed by statisticians only when it leaves the home. Man's production is more apt to be noticed whether it leaves the home or not.

At the simplest level the producer roles for women outside the breeder-feeder complex have to do with the gathering or growing of food, carrying water and fuel to the hearth, erection of shelters, making domestic utensils and clothing, and the creation of ceremonial objects. The triple role tends to give women more hours of work in a day than men, although this is not universally true. We will begin by examining the working day of women in different kinds of societies.

Different Work Settings for Women through History

Hunting and Gathering Societies

In hunting and gathering societies the producer role of the male is encompassed by hunting and the making of tools associated with hunting. These activities consume all of his working hours and generally provide about 20 percent of the food of the band.[3] Hunting has been described as a high-risk, low-yield activity, in contrast to food gathering as a low-risk, high-yield activity.[4] Women seem to be able to provide the other 80 percent of the band's food through gathering activities and still carry out the breeder-feeder roles, the procuring of water and fuel, building of shelters, making of utensils, etc. They also catch small game close to the campsite with their bare hands, but do not run great distances after game—an impractical proposition with small children to care for. It is sometimes said that the hunting and gathering way of life is the only leisure society we know of. Reports from many of the 250 hunting and gathering bands extant today indicate that women and men work shorter hours than in any other type of society and have more time for ceremonies and celebrations.[5]

Due to the constraints of the nomadic life, there is a strict limitation on family size. Hunting and gathering bands manage zero population growth through a combination of abortion, infanticide, and infant mortality. In this leisure society there are few sex-differentiated reward systems. Women and men have different ceremonial roles but participate equally in ceremonials and band decision making, including decisions about marriages. There is no accumulation of resources to serve as a power base for individuals of either sex, and monogamy is the rule. Although it is said that twenty hours of work per person per week may meet all maintenance needs, it is not clear whether the anthropologist

3. Richard B. Lee and Irven DeVore, eds., *Man the Hunter* (Chicago: Aldine Publishing Co., 1968).
4. Ibid.
5. Ibid.

observers have actually clocked the full working time of women around the campfire after the food has been brought there. There is probably a component of "invisible" work which needs to be more accurately recorded before this way of life disappears. It is also difficult to clock time spent in care of small children. When are they being "cared for," and when is interaction with them pure recreation and enjoyment? When all these considerations are taken into account, the chances are that even in this most egalitarian of all types of human societies the women are "working" longer hours than men.

The Early Agrovillages

Agriculture probably emerged out of discoveries of stands of wild grain at revisited campsites—stands that represented accidental harvests of the previous year's gathering activities. This was clearly women's work and still is wherever simple digging-stick type of planting in the slash-and-burn cultivation pattern is found, notably in Africa. In the agrovillage existence that developed when people began settling down near good supplies of wild grain, and planting their own crops besides, the work load began to shift more heavily toward women. Men in these agrovillages were still contributing their share of the food through hunting. Because of game scarcity by 12,000 B.C., the contributions of the now sedentary hunters, even with improved tools, were probably kept to 20 percent of the total food supply. Men would be gone for days at a time in pursuit of game, and women's producer roles in the agrovillage multiplied. The herding pattern for men, which was an offshoot of hunting, involved similar movement patterns, although it may have increased the economic contribution of men to family sustenance. With settlement came buildings, courtyards, the making and accumulation of domestic objects and ceremonial materials. The following outline summarizes women's daily activities in the agrovillage based on my interpretation of archeological evidence in the Near East from 10,000 to 6000 B.C., plus more contemporary anthropological evidence.

1. The hearth
   a) Cooking
   b) Feeding family
   c) Care of small infants (carried out concurrently with all other activities during day and night)
   d) Childbearing (one of primary productive processes of women, carried out concurrently with all other activities during day and night)
   e) Cleaning and maintenance of hearth
2. The courtyard
   a) Production processes
      (1) Food: processing of foods to be cooked (sometimes cooking and baking also done in courtyard, combining 1 and 2a)

    (2) Crafts: sewing, weaving, basket and pottery making, stone-
ware and implement making, jewelry, production of
cosmetics
    (3) Building activities: houses, cult centers, etc.
  b) Social organization
    (1) Council meetings
    (2) Ritual and ceremony preparations
    (3) Teaching of children
    (4) Other village affairs
3. The fields
  a) Gathering fruit and nuts
  b) Clearing fields (with help from men)
  c) Planting, cultivating, and harvesting food
  d) Caring for sheep and goats
  e) Collecting fuel for hearth fires
  f) Collecting material for building
  g) Carrying water to the courtyard and hearth

These first agrovillages had populations of from 100 to 200 people. If
the work load assigned to women seems improbably heavy, compare it
with the summary of workloads for women (table 1) based on surveys of
women engaged in subsistence agriculture in Africa today.[6]

I suggest that the point of transition from these early agrovillages
(such as Eynan, Jarmo, Hacilar) to the larger trading towns (like Jericho,
Beidha, Catal Huyuk) was the point at which the woman's economic
contribution started to "weigh" less than the man's, even though the sheer
quantity of productive labor was greater. Initially, the egalitarianism of
the hunting and gathering society must have carried over into the earliest
agrovillages. The sheer fact of the continuing presence of women and
long absences of men may have given rise to occasional examples of a
"rule of women" during this first village life. Aberle suggests that matriliny arises in situations where there are all-women work groups, where
women control the residence bases, and where there is "a certain range of
productivity and a certain range of centralization—ranges narrower than
those of either patrilineal or bilateral systems."[7]

6. The data base for discussion on the interrelations between the integration of
women in development, their situation, and population factors in Africa is the Regional
Seminar on the Integration of Women in Development, with Special Reference to Population Factors, held by the Economic Commission for Africa of the United Nations Economic
and Social Council in Addis Ababa, May 1947, mimeographed report (New York: United
Nations, 1974).
7. David F. Aberle, "Matrilineal Descent in Cross-cultural Perspective," in *Matrilineal
Kinship,* ed. David M. Schneider and Kathleen Gough (Berkeley: University of California
Press, 1974), pp. 655–730. I agree with him that matriliny is not a general evolutionary
stage but only arises under certain conditions. Not all agrovillage development would
follow the pattern I am suggesting.

Table 1

Participation by Women in the Traditional Rural
and Modernizing Economy in Africa

Responsibility	Unit of Participation*
A. Production/supply/distribution:	
1. Food production	0.70
2. Domestic food storage	0.50
3. Food processing	1.00
4. Animal husbandry	0.50
5. Marketing	0.60
6. Brewing	0.90
7. Water supply	0.90
8. Fuel supply	0.80
B. Household/community:	
1. Household:	
a) Bearing, rearing, initial education of children	1.00
b) Cooking for husband, children, elders	1.00
c) Cleaning, washing, etc.	1.00
d) Housebuilding	0.30
e) House repair	0.50
2. Community:	
Self-help projects	0.70

Source.—Mimeographed report of the Regional Seminar on the Integration of Women in Development (n. 6 above). Data base from "The Changing and Contemporary Role of Women in African Development (1974); "Country Reports on Vocational and Technical Training for Girls and Women" (1972–74); studies, mission reports, discussions, all available from the United Nations. As noted in the text, units of participation should be determined first for areas within countries, then on the national level, then for Africa.

*Estimates are given in terms of the unit of participation for women's labor, i.e., women as a percentage of the total population in a given activity.

The Trading Towns

Women's range of productivity increasingly narrowed as men, during their hunting journeys, began locating sources of flint and other materials valued for tools and for ceremonials. This immediately gave them a competitive advantage over stay-at-home women. The first specialization between villages, according to the archaeological evidence, appears when hunters (some from agrovillages, some of them probably still nomadic) begin supplying other villages with flint and receiving craft and food products in return. Women are not able to work the trading networks to the extent the men are, because they are too busy with production for family consumption. Some of the craft products of women enter the trading networks, but by and large the diversity of women's tasks prevents specialization. Thus, when their products do enter the market they are marginal, and probably do not command "prices" comparable with those of the male specialists in the new stone and bone shops of the later trading towns.

The Rise of Urban Civilization

By the time major urban centers in Sumer and Egypt arose, a system of social stratification had developed that complicates the picture. In Sumerian Erech, 4000 B.C., there were few distinctions between rich and poor. There were "street scribes" available to any woman or man for business purposes, and there were no great differences in housing style and size. By 2500 B.C., however, nomadic incursions, wars, and gifts of land and booty from kings to their supporters had created an aristocracy based in the palace, the temple, and the landed estates. On the new urban scene there were large palace-temple complexes, rich landholders, and elaborate tables of law. From there a certain class of women—the aristocracy—became visible and would remain visible until the industrial revolution. Women in the scribal and small-merchant class, on the contrary, became invisible, working-class women somewhat less so. Thus, while the emergence of early trading towns tipped the scales against recognition of the productive role of the mass of women, the first urban civilizations finished the process.

The Role of Law in Redefinition of Women's Work

The emergence of law contains the emergence of the concept of the male-headed household and of the administration of property by the male. The earlier, more fluid, clan rights to land and property that left resources available to the women and men who were prepared to work with them were transformed into rigidly spelled out male rights. This was no simple process; as late as 1751 B.C. the Code of Hammurabi contained sixty-eight sections on family and women, fifty on land and territory (dealing with clan rights), and seven on priestesses. While descent of the elites was usually recorded in government records through the male, a woman was sometimes named and descent traced through her. Women sometimes also appear in land deeds as heads of households and as donors and recipients of ritualized food offerings. They are recorded as doing long-distance trading under their own names. Ancient legal records show that the women of the elite often fought successfully to keep their rights to land under the new system that in principle recorded land in the name of males only. No study has been made of the percentage of women holding land in their own name throughout history, but in Europe from A.D. 900 to 1200 it was sometimes as high as 18 percent. When land administered by women on behalf of children is included, the figures was as high as 25 percent.[8] The amount of attention given to women's rights, both in Egyptian and Sumerian law,[9] and the numerous

8. David Herlihy, "Land, Family, and Women in Continental Europe, 701–1200," *Traditio* 18 (1962): 89–120.
9. Steffen Wenig, *Women in Egyptian Art* (New York: McGraw-Hill Book Co., 1970); Samuel Noah Kramer, *The Sumerians: Their History, Culture, and Character* (Chicago: University of Chicago Press, 1963).

references in contemporary documents to court battles fought by women in Greece and Rome, indicates that declaring the male the legal head of the household and building legal and administrative practices around him never fully covered the real-life economic and social exigencies with which women and men had to deal. What the male head of household device did do, however, was to make second-class citizens of the great mass of middle- and working-class women, who had no independent power base as the women of the elite did. By defining them as subsidiary household members, it became possible to avoid the issue of equal work for equal pay. This mainly affected working-class women, since the scribal and small-merchant class—the urban bourgeoisie of the ancient civilizations—were as apt to promote women as display objects as their brothers centuries later. Middle-class urbanites in the Mediterranean civilizations enclosed their women from the beginning. Europe, ancient and modern, followed suit.

There were two classes of "working women," then, from about 2000 B.C. on: the wealthy overseas merchants and the estate and temple administrators on the one hand, and, on the other, the poor women who worked in textile workshops, ran the corner bakery and brewery, and provided the upper classes with much the same range of domestic, health, and beauty services that working women do today. The occupational roles for women in the Age of Pericles can be classified in the following way.[10]

1. Occupations for women slaves (there were an estimated 90,000 women slaves in Athens in the fourth century according to Wallon's *Histoire d'esclavage*)
   a) Food processing: threshing grain, grinding flour
   b) Agricultural work in the fields
   c) Mining: gold and silver mining; separating metal from slag, washing metal; transporting ore from underground corridors of mines to the surface
   d) Textile workers: all operations connected with carding, spinning, and weaving carried on by women in workshops—no indication whether these were state owned or privately owned. Weaving also carried on as cottage industry in private homes
   e) Variety of craft production carried on as cottage industry in private homes
   f) Domestic service
2. Occupations open to free women
   a) Agriculture, unspecified except for "fieldwork"
   b) Textile work as above
   c) Trade: selling of vegetables, processed foods, baked goods,

---

10. This listing represents a synthesis of information about Greek women from a great variety of sources, including material summarized in Evelyne Sullerot, *Histoire et sociologie du travail féminin* (Paris: Société Nouvelle des Editions Gonthier, 1968).

other home-manufactured products, unspecified. Selling of cloth, garments, headdresses
d) Innkeeping
e) Being a courtesan (combination intellectual, artist, and entertainer)
f) Running schools for courtesans
g) Midwifery, nursing
h) Music
i) Dancing
j) Vase painting
3. Occupations specifically forbidden to women
a) Medicine (there are records of illegal practice and punishment of women practitioners)
4. Occupations possible but not encouraged
a) Scribe; schools for women are rare (ex. Sappho) but if a woman could write she was not forbidden to exercise her skill.

Poor working women had several disadvantages compared with men from the beginning. They had to compete with slave labor for one thing.[11] Most of the textile workshops in Egypt and Greece were operated by female slave labor, and many services were rendered by slave women in the Mediterranean cities. Since slaves were only given subsistence, a double force operated to give free women pittance wages: (1) the availability of slave labor and (2) the fiction of male head of household. The woman supposedly had someone to support her, and so her wages needed only be supplemental.

Characteristic Constraints on the Woman Worker

In the foregoing analysis, I have traced the work settings for women in hunting and gathering societies, the early agrovillages, the trading towns, and in the first urban civilizations. From the first urbanism until the industrial revolution, it is my view that there were no substantial differences in the work situation for women. The following discussion of the social, legal, and familial constraints on women will apply primarily but not exclusively to the Western world from Greek and Roman times onward.

The Male Head of Household Fiction

One of the most enduring constraints is the male head of household concept. I have labeled the term a fiction, for, while a careful study still needs to be done, it appears that in any setting—urban or rural—in any period of history for which data is available, one fifth to one-half of the

11. Free men had so many other advantages in ancient societies that the existence of male slaves did not affect their situation to the extent that female slaves affected the situation of free women (see William L. Westermann, *The Slave Systems of Greek and Roman Antiquity* [Philadelphia: American Philosophical Society, 1955]).

heads of households were women. Many of these women were rearing children without male partners because of widowhood, desertion, divorce, or because they were plural wives infrequently visited by the husband and with full responsibility for the care and feeding of their children.[12] Some were never-married women who had been driven by poverty to sell sexual services and who raised children with minimal resources. Or they were never-married women who had chosen an independent way of life as entertainers, intellectuals, or merchants (variously labeled hetaira, courtesans, and prostitutes); they might or might not have chosen to raise children of their own. Most of these women, except for the wealthy and the independent entrepreneurs, had to struggle to make ends meet. They had to accept the low wages established through the fiction of male support and the reality of the competition of slave labor.

What family arrangements did women heads of household make for the care of their children while they were at work? Women in great poverty had to leave children without care to run the streets or locked them in airless rooms. Probably the institution of the neighbor who takes in children for a few pennies is as ancient as the urban working woman. For the most part, however, what care such children received throughout the Christian Era came from women who chose celibacy rather than motherhood, the women of the religious orders. They ran the soup kitchens, the orphanages, and the schools for the very poor. When many of the earlier religious orders declined and before the nineteenth-century growth in religious service orders began, the plight of children of the poor became desperate. In 1770 thousands of children of Parisian working mothers were rounded up from the streets by the "authorities" to be deported as labor for overseas settlements.[13] Only the mass exodus of their mothers from their places of work stopped this roundup. Indeed, it was around the problems of these "ragged children," as the British called them, that the nineteenth-century philanthropic and social service movements developed. For the women heads of household who were the mothers of these children, however, there was never much more than pious exhortation to "stop sinning." They were fallen women in the eyes of the middle and upper class, not working women with family responsibilities. That notion continues even today.

Familial Division of Labor

Rural areas. —The division of labor between women and men in rural areas throughout the world has varied depending on the scale of agricul-

---

12. A common situation in parts of Africa today (see Ester Boserup, *Woman's Role in Economic Development* [London: George Allen & Unwin, 1970]; out of print, but reissued as a paperback [New York: St. Martin's Press, 1974]).

13. George Rude, *The Crowd in History, 1730–1848* (New York: John Wiley & Sons, 1964).

ture. With cash cropping and plantation agriculture comes the development of labor-saving machinery and the dominance of the male.[14] In developing countries, the development of large-scale agriculture usually puts heavier work loads on women in terms of working hours because they are required to weed and carry water to the cash-crop fields while still growing food in their own plots to feed the family. Since the breeding-feeding activities are not counted as productive labor, the wages of Third World women agriculturalists are often of some indeterminate minus quantity. That is, they subsidize, even more than other working women, the men of their households and of their community. In a society with large-scale urban migration, the women are usually left behind to do the farming. Rarely do they share the urban wages of male family members, although these wages may be invested in buying more land for the woman to farm.

In Europe during the Middle Ages the situation of farm women varied. There was the prosperous but hardworking peasant household where length of working hours was perhaps fairly equally divided. On the other hand, there were the widows who had an incredible work load because they were compelled to render, unaided, feudal services that were shared in husband-wife households.[15] There was also the desperate situation of laboring women without partners who sometimes died, with their babies, of exhaustion and starvation in the very fields that were yielding unprecedented harvests.[16]

Wave and labor differentials in rural areas.—With the decline of the feudal estates in the later Middle Ages, the new phenomenon of detached wage labor began in rural areas. Here the outlines of women's subservient economic situation as wage laborer became clear. The state tried to establish control over manpower movements but in effect controlled the movement of women. The 1563 Elizabethan Statute of Artifices, for example stated: "By this Act [the Statute of Laborers] every woman free or bound, under 60, and not carrying on a trade or calling, provided she had no land, and was not in domestic or other service, was liable to be called upon to enter service either in the fields or otherwise, and if she refused, she was imprisoned until she complied; whilst all girls who for twelve years had been brought up to follow the plough, were not allowed to enter any other calling, but were forced to continue working in the fields."[17]

14. See Boserup.
15. For an incredible account of the work load under feudalism, see G. Duby, *Rural Economy and Country Life in the Medieval West,* trans. C. Pasten (London: E. Arnold, 1968).
16. Julia O'Faolian and Laura Marines, eds., *Not in God's Image: A History of Women in Europe from the Greeks to the Nineteenth Century* (New York: Harper & Row, 1973).
17. Arthur Rackham Cleveland, *Woman under the English Law* (London: Hurst, 1896), p. 76.

Men continued to move to get jobs, but women with family responsibilities felt the full force of the compulsion to work in the fields and took
home piecework which they could do while still caring for children. With
the unity of capital and labor gone, the only limit set on the exploitation of
the poorest class of laboring women was death by starvation. That grim
scenario became more fully developed in the next century.

It is with the appearance of wage labor that the manifestations of
wage differentials (which may in fact have existed all the time) became
visible. Because of their immobility women have no bargaining power and
so suffer wage discrimination everywhere. In 1422 the scholars of
Toulouse paid women grape pickers half what they paid the men, who
only had to carry the full baskets back to the college cellar. (The monks of
Paris did the same.)[18] Women construction workers who worked side by
side with men in building the College of Toulouse were paid far less than
the men for the same labor.[19] Not even the labor shortage resulting from
the Black Death improved women's wages; they remained substantially
the same on the Continent for nearly 100 years.[20] The supposed labor
shortages from the Black Death did not help the laboring poor in England, either.[21] While this could be interpreted as reflecting widespread
underemployment in the previous century, one could also say that laborers in that century had "shorter hours, better working conditions."
Fourteenth-century workers had to work longer and harder for the same
pay, especially women.

The opportunities for the woman of the rural upper classes were
limited only by her abilities; entrepreneurship was rewarded. With plenty
of hands to help, the breeding-feeding role posed no problem to her.
During the Middle Ages and as a result of the absence of men in crusades,
there may have been an increase in the number of women in landholding
and public roles, but the basic pre-Crusade participation level was already
high, as the Herlihy study shows.[22]

Urban areas.—It is difficult to construct a clear picture of the situations of urban middle-class women. The enclosure concept that I have
emphasized is only part of the picture. In addition to the unknown
number of women who had no significant activities beyond supervision of
children and servants, there were women who acted as partners in their
husbands' enterprises, including trading. It is hard to determine how
many of the women who became known as successful traders in their own

18. Sylvia L. Thrupp, *Changes in Medieval Society Europe North of the Alps, 1050–1500*
(New York: Appleton-Century-Crofts, 1964), pp. 240–41.

19. Ibid., p. 244.

20. E. Perroy, as quoted in Thrupp, p. 241.

21. Philip Ziegler, *The Black Death* (New York: John Day Co., 1969; reprint ed., Baltimore: Penguin Books, Pelican Books, 1970), pp. 240–59.

22. See n. 8 above.

right began as partners with their husbands and expanded the business after widowhood. The well-to-do middle-class woman trader was a familiar figure in all the port cities of the Mediterranean from Phoenician times on. Many of the first converts to Christianity were well-to-do women merchants who put their homes and their wealth at the disposal of the early Christian communities. The wealthiest Greek trader in Byzantium in the Middle Ages was a woman,[23] and women traders were major figures in Bristol in the 1400s.[24] These were all middle-class women whose enterprise and ability enabled them to "earn" the help they needed to free themselves from the burdens of the breeder-feeder role.

Somewhere on this continuum of producer roles for the urban middle-class woman, which runs the gamut from the almost totally nonproductive display wife through the independent trader, there exists the craft partner, the woman who was jointly engaged with her spouse in home-workshop production as a member of a craft guild. Where this kind of economic partnership existed, there may have been considerable sharing of the child-care part of the breeder role with the spouse. The craft-guild tradition, which began in the Mediterranean before the Christian Era, was one of husband-wife partnership which involved both more equality in the producer roles and more joint involvement with the children. The dividing line between teaching and nurturance faded away when both spouses were engaged in the craft role. In addition, every craft-guild household had outside children of the age of seven and up in an apprentice relationship. Even in non-craft-guild families it was common to send one's own children out to other households in the community and take others' children into one's home to rear. This practice seems to have been a combination of mutual boarding out, a way of getting extra household help, and a device for involving others in the education of one's children.[25] Because people were raising each others' children, men became more involved in the process than they might have been had children stayed in their own home.

The whole history of the craft-guild movement in England and on the Continent (though more so in the former than the latter) is a history of the involvement of women in the productive process in partnership roles with men. (There is less information about the relative roles of father and mother in relation to children and production in rural settings.) It may well be that the small-scale craft-guild enterprise that predated the industrial revolution provided the setting of a more egalitarian, less exploitative work and parenting partnership than any other kind of work setting.

23. Philip Sherrard, *Byzantium* (New York: Time, Inc., 1966).
24. Eileen Power and M. M. Postan, *Studies in English Trade in the Fifteenth Century* (London: George Routledge & Sons, 1933).
25. Peter Laslett, ed., *Household and Family in Past Time* (Cambridge: Cambridge University Press, 1972).

Household Size and Familial Constraints

In the sixteenth century, the process of pushing women back inside their families, denying then economic and other extradomestic involvements, gained momentum. Household size became an important constraint and should be considered. Recent studies of local records in various parts of Europe reveal the surprising fact that household size has changed very little from the Middle Ages to the present.[26] Apart from the great manor houses of the nobility and the homes of rich merchants, most people lived in families with an average size of 4.75 persons per family, plus a servant.[27] Not only were families small, but the marriage age for women and men was beginning to rise. For European women in the 1500s the average age at marriage was about twenty-one, rising in succeeding centuries to twenty-five and twenty-eight. Furthermore, because multigenerational families were very much the exception, most women were confined to very small domestic spaces in small families before and after marriage. While women certainly had larger households during their childbearing years, high infant death rates and the practice of older couples and widows maintaining their own separate quarters left women in increasing domestic isolation as they lost freedom of movement in other spheres.

The tension level between mothers and daughters was apparently very high in this period. There are many mentions of brutal child rearing, and particularly of mothers beating daughters who resisted parental marriage plans. Even the gentle peace queen, Margaret of Navarre, beat her daughter daily for weeks on end to make her agree to a politically designed marriage choice. Agnes Paston of the lively Paston family, known for its voluminous intrafamily correspondence and numerous lawsuits, beat her daughter so badly that "her head was broke in 2 or 3 places." Lady Jane Gray's mother beat her. Since the records all refer to mothers, not fathers, beating their daughters, and this in the context of an otherwise "good" family life, it would seem that women of this period were subject to severe emotional pressure which they relieved by child beating. Sending daughters out to other families as servants was one of the few available means of relieving the strain, but this required reciprocity and acceptance of someone else's daughter into the home. The disappearance of convents in England and in many places in Europe,[28] and the closing down of other occupational options for women, made

26. Ibid.
27. These "servants," it turns out, are not servants in the contemporary sense of the word but rather children of neighboring families in the same parish.
28. The pressure on mothers to get rid of daughters also existed in the Middle Ages at the height of convent life, and many daughters were beaten half to death by mothers who were trying to force them into convents against their wills. There are interesting records of lawsuits of nuns who claimed that they had been forced to take vows by their parents (see O'Faolian and Martines, pp. 270–75).

marriage arrangements increasingly important and also made marriages harder to achieve. Mothers bore the brunt of these problems in terms of pressure to get their daughters out of their small households.

The effect of a lowering status of women on mother-daughter relations is a subject that needs much more attention. Obviously not all mothers beat their daughters, and when there were beatings they do not seem to have led to ruptured relations. There was, rather, some continued expression of affection between mothers and daughters in later life. Women seem to have fled from confining extended family situations whenever possible. This is supported by the fact that in the 1500s, even with housing shortages, 16 percent of all English households in the 100 communities Laslett examined were headed by women.[29] Of these, 12.9 percent were widows, 1.1 percent single females, and 2.3 percent "unspecified females" in humble households, as well as estates. There are many references to the joy with which women set up their own households after widowhood and the vigor with which they resisted courting by amourous widowers. The extended family togetherness we nostalgically refer to as part of our golden past simply did not exist in the European heritage, and there is some evidence that it never really existed on a large scale anywhere.

More important, perhaps, the picture of women that emerges from this material is a useful corrective to the popular misconception that women have throughout history submissively endured everything. They endured a great deal, but they were not necessarily submissive.

Alternatives to Familial Roles

During the entire historical period from 500 B.C. to the industrial revolution, there were important alternatives for women to being the wife/mother in a male headed household or the family-burdened female head of a household. One alternative was celibacy. The nun role has existed from early times in Hinduism, in Buddhism, and finally in Christianity and Islam. Although religious orders for women took different forms in Asia, the Middle East, and Europe, the basic pattern of an alternative role that did not involve the breeder-feeder function was present in all these societies. Between A.D. 500 and 1400 there was an extraordinary flowering of convent culture in Europe. This culture produced science, art, and literature, and a social service infrastructure in the fields of health, education, and welfare unparalleled until the nineteenth century. While nuns were in one sense isolated within the male-dominant structure of the Catholic church, in another sense they lived in protected niches within which they could be free. And if the

29. Laslett, p. 147.

price they paid for that freedom was celibacy, there is real evidence of the creativity and joy of convent life in those centuries (as well as before and since). The nineteenth and twentieth centuries have seen a second explosion of creativity through celibacy, partly within religious orders and partly outside of them. Today, there are approximately 2 million nuns in the world from all the major religious traditions.

In addition to the celibacy in the convent, there was the beguinage[30]—an urban secular commune for rural women migrants to the city during the major urban migrations of the 1200s and 1300s. Invented by women, the beguinages were so successful that they were seen as serious threats to some of the existing craft guilds and were persecuted by them. Besides the beguines there were also hermitesses—women solitaries who lived in huts by bridges, on the edges of towns, and in forest solitudes all over England and, to a lesser extent, in Europe. These were a special class of independents in the Middle Ages—able to support themselves through their knowledge of human nature and folk medicine. With no institutional protection of any kind, most of them were burned as witches during the height of the medieval witch mania. Last, there were the vagabonds, the hardworking fun-loving women who moved partnerless through the Middle Ages, always able to pick up the pennies they needed at a fair or celebration of some kind. When they were willing to settle in a town, they were not infrequently supported by town councils, glad to have resident entertainers for their community. Besides being entertainers, they ran the soup kitchens and the first-aid stations in wars, including the Crusades. They were good soldiers when they were needed as fighters. Altogether, they were a social category for which we would have no labels today. Marriage was not on their agenda, and at times up to one-fourth of the women of Europe belonged in their company.

The End of an Era

During the late 1500s and the 1600s many of the phenomena described above began to disappear. The craftwomen, the celibates, and the vagabonds all declined in numbers and status. In the guilds in particular there was a rapid loss of rights and statuses for women. Men were feeling the pressure of women as competitors in the labor market and successfully pressed for their expulsion from guild after guild. This transition era intiated the prolonged suffering of both rural and urban female laborers as they were squeezed out of secure medieval work statuses. The hermitess or vagabond of the fourteenth century became

30. This was a religiously based social movement, but the women were *not* in religious orders (see Ernest W. McDonnell, *The Beguines and Beghards in Medieval Culture* [New York: Octagon Books, 1969]).

the work-deadened automaton of the seventeenth and eighteenth centuries. Rural laboring women went hungry, and the children of women in the factories were rounded up like cattle. Married and single women alike were trapped by the formula of "supplemental" pittance wages for women.

This was also the period when the gentlewoman in straitened circumstances appeared—the middle-class woman without training and resources who could not enter domestic service because of her social status. She became a governess or a companion in homes of slightly better off middle-class people, working for little more than bread and board, often in a position close to that of the household slave of Greek and Roman times. Just below her in station was the domestic, even more of a household slave. By the 1700s, these women began to emigrate overseas to new hardships, but also to new opportunities.

It is this period that witnessed the emergence of the Marxist analysis of the situation of women. Women and men alike, whether Saint-Simonians or anarchist socialists or Marxian socialists, all saw the necessity for society to deal with the burden of the breeder-feeder role that entrapped women by providing child care and domestic maintenance for everyone. However, no one looked back to the time when men had shared part of the breeder-feeder role. Everything (except biological childbearing) was to be taken over by the state. If this proposal asked nothing of men, it had the virtue of helping married and single women heads of household equally.

Since no socialist state could afford to duplicate the individualized breeder-feeder role of women as a public service, and no capitalist state wanted to, it was easy to turn this task back to women in the end. The famous Ellen Key "return to matriarchy movement" to restore full legal head of household rights to women independently of marital status has to be seen in that context. Indeed, all the nineteenth-century utopian movements from Brook Farm to New Harmony left women's roles unchanged. Only the Shakers and the Mormons offered something different; the former the freedom of celibacy, the latter the freedom of co-wives with whom to share farm labor. Both attracted women in droves.

It was a hard century for working women, and it was an unsettling one for middle-class women who had been led to expect something different—some kind of equality. All the women-triggered social reform movements of the nineteenth century and all their concrete achievements—protective legislative enactments and new types of social service institutions—could not take the edge off the bitterness of unacknowledged colleagueship. Women were invited, welcomed, urged into the labor force—but at bargain prices; working was to be an avocation. The breeder-feeder role was here to stay as the unremitting background rhythm to all other activities of women. Even in the socialist countries, where women were the most needed and most welcomed into the labor

Table 2

Workday Time Budgets of Employed Women and Employed Men
(Percentage of Each Sex Participating in Primary Activities)

Work (Job)	Six Cities of France		Torun, Poland		Jackson, Miss., USA		Pakov, USSR	
	Women	Men	Women	Men	Women	Men	Women	Men
Housework*	95.2	58.4	98.2	58.2	93.8	50.3	98.7	73.4
Other household obligations†	52.9	63.5	45.3	53.9	56.6	48.4	65.6	53.8
Child care‡	31.0	24.8	41.6	30.8	35.8	18.7	48.2	40.1
Personal needs§ (includes sleep)	100.0	100.0	100.0	100.0	100.0	100.0	100.0	100.0
Study and participation‖	8.8	9.7	18.0	19.2	13.6	18.9	19.8	34.3
Mass media#	69.0	82.7	75.1	88.0	76.1	83.1	75.6	92.2
Leisure**	79.2	83.4	64.1	74.8	74.7	61.3	65.8	81.7
Travel††	88.8	95.0	99.1	98.5	100.0	100.0	99.8	99.5

SOURCE.—From Alexander Szalai, *The Use of Time* (The Hague: Mouton & Co., 1972), pp. 584, 588.
NOTE.—Data are weighted to ensure equality of days of the week and number of eligible respondents per household.
*Includes cooking, home chores, laundry, marketing.
†Includes garden, animal care, errands, shopping, other household activities.
‡Includes child care, other child-related activities.
§Includes personal care, eating, sleep.
‖Includes study, religion, organization.
#Includes radio, TV (home), TV (away), read paper, read magazine, read books, movies.
**Includes social (home), social (away), conversation, active sports, outdoors, entertainment, cultural events, resting, other leisure.
††Includes travel to work, personal travel, leisure travel.

force, they were expected to carry on the same breeder-feeder role at home after hours.

The Present and Possible Futures

The UNESCO Time Budget Series shows with startling clarity that every married woman who works today still bears the triple burden of breeder-feeder-producers. The Szalai study,[31] from which tables 2 and 3 are taken, included twelve countries and show remarkable consistence. I have selected four countries that represent four distinct types of "work culture." Because time budgets would differ for different groups within the same city, as well as between cities in the same country, and between countries, all figures must be treated as giving general indications only.

Table 2 gives the percentage of women and men participating in primary activities and table 3 the number of minutes spent per day on these activities. Not surprisingly, more employed women than men do housework and child care; the differences range from 25 to 45 percent. Fewer women engage in study and participation, or in use of the mass-media than men. Everyone sleeps, has some free time, and travels (whether on foot or otherwise) to work and to do errands, so here any figures under 100 percent are artifacts of the enumeration procedures.

It is in table 3 that we begin to get the concrete picture of daily life. In no country do employed men spend more than half an hour on housework, and employed women less than an hour and a half, even though women's working hours outside the home are sometimes longer than men's. In some areas men spend a few more minutes on "other household obligations" than women, in some not. Time spent in child care alone as a primary activity is, according to this data, never more than half an hour, even for women. But this is somewhat misleading, since most child care runs concurrently with other activities —housework, use of media, and free time. In fact, child care is continuous for women during all hours they are not at work. Only in Pakov, USSR, do employed fathers give as much "primary care" to children as employed mothers. Only in the United States do women spend more time on personal needs and sleep than men.

The most consistent differences between women's and men's use of time, apart from housework, show up in the figures for study and participation, for mass media, and for leisure. Women have substantially fewer minutes to spend on each activity within these categories. Given the wide variations in the cultures represented, there is a remarkable overall consistency in the use of time by employed females as compared with employed males. Women's time is far more constrained than men's, as it has probably always been since hunting and gathering days. Household appliances and ready-to-use products or services for domestic

31. Alexander Szalai, *The Use of Time* (The Hague: Mouton & Co., 1972).

Table 3

Workday Time Budgets of Employed Women and Employed Men
(Time Spent in Primary Activities, in Average Minutes per Day)

Work (Job)	Six Cities of France		Torun, Poland		Jackson, Miss., USA		Pakov, USSR	
	Women	Men	Women	Men	Women	Men	Women	Men
Housework*	156	26	180	31	133	21	170	28
Other household obligations†	17	32	20	29	31	29	27	39
Child care‡	24	8	27	20	16	8	30	30
Personal need (includes sleep)§	621	621	543	560	590	572	546	573
Study and participation‖	7	9	23	25	17	27	27	52
Mass media#	47	76	70	117	65	114	73	125
Leisure**	60	70	56	71	63	59	48	55
Travel††	57	75	86	91	73	85	81	20
Total minutes	1,440	1,440	1,440	1,400	1,440	1,436	1,440	1,440

SOURCE.—Szalai, pp. 583, 587. Data are weighted to ensure equality of days of the week and number of eligible respondents per household.
NOTE.—See notes to table 2.

maintenance or child care help somewhat, but the stubborn fact remains that the private spaces of the home and the private shapes of individual lives cannot be fully mass serviced. Something remains that individuals must do. Must these individuals always be women?

If the private spaces of the home were closed down and everyone adopted communal living, home maintenance could be simplified. And if one simply stopped having children. . . . But there is no evidence that these are happening. In the United States, for example, there has been a steady decrease in the number of married couples without their own households (fig. 1). First marriages, and remarriages for the divorced,

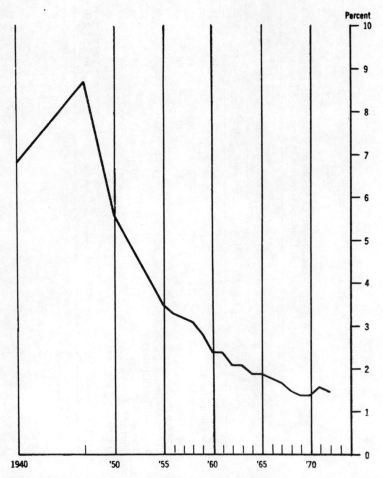

Fig. 1.—Married couples without their own households: United States, 1940–72. Source.—From *Social Indicators, 1973,* written and compiled by the Statistical Policy Division, Office of Management and Budget, and prepared for publication by the Social and Economic Statistics Administration, U.S. Department of Commerce (Washington, D.C.: Government Printing Office, 1973), p. 199.

continue at a rate that makes American society much more "married" than the European society of the Middle Ages. And although families are decreasing in size in the West, there are no signs of children being given up as a project of the human race. Commune formation may be continuing at about the same rate as in the previous decade, but so does commune dissolution. Most young people in the United States who are attracted to communes evidently go through a commune initiation and then "go private." Private quarters, in socialist countries, in kibbutz-proud Israel, and commune-proud China, are valued as much as anywhere.

In the Middle Ages there were beguinages, hermitages, and small family households. In the twentieth century there are communes, single-person households, and nuclear families. However we label them, these various types of social organization to meet human maintenance needs are probably all enduring features of the human landscape. The mix simply differs in different periods of history, depending on the ratio of single to attached women and on reproductive rates. Children are also enduring features of the human landscape. When women have too heavy a work burden with the triple breeder-feeder-producer role, the whole society suffers. Women suffer role overstrain, men suffer role deprivation, and children suffer from inadequate experiences of relating to the human community.

Marxist analysis failed to put its finger on one aspect of the oppression of women: the confining of breeder-feeder roles to women. It thought that by turning the state into the breeder-feeder all would be well. But human liberation depends on sharing breeder-feeder roles between women and men, as well as on having state-administered support services. The problems of scale in human nurturance are such that relatively small living units will always be required, no matter how closely integrated into larger communal sharing units. There is no way out for men but to confront parenthood, and no way out for women but to confront sharing their centuries-old monopoly on the breeder-feeder role. The biological aspect of breeding is a minute part of the total care that goes into the production of an autonomous human being; there is really very little that men need to be excluded from if one looks at the totality of the child-breeding process.

Another element missing in Marxist analysis is love. By failing to deal in theoretical terms with the special role of love and tenderness that enhances all other social interactions when present, and diminishes them when absent, Marx left love as women's work by default. It simply could not be taken over by the state.

One of the properties of love is that it acts to modify dominance relations. For this reason love has been rejected by some women's liberationists as one more element in a constellation of role expectations that has led to women's oppression. It has taken the twentieth century to produce the insight that the particular kind of reciprocity represented by love as *agape,* or caring, is a trait that is equally desirable in men and women. The men's liberation movement, in setting out to destroy both the image and the reality of sex-linked dominance behavior, may in the end be the most significant social movement of the twentieth century. By liberating the potential for tenderness in men, it undercuts much of the rationale for sex-based dominance and sets the stage for a new kind of involvement of men with children.

Equal involvement of women and men with children does not imply that every woman, or every man, must have a partner for parenting. Part of the new understanding of parenting is reflected in court decisions that allow sometimes men, sometimes women, sole custody of a child when single-parenting becomes necessary. Single parenting involves extra burdens, but when it is not sex linked it becomes clearer that society should provide generalized "drawing rights" for persons of either sex who undertake the care of small children alone. A concept developed by Gösta Rehn, such a generalized set of rights "would make available to women in monetary form the help no longer available to them in the form of unpaid mutual aid" and would include income maintenance during time out for motherhood.[32] (The generalized drawing rights idea was developed in connection with the needs of women, but in a dual parenting society they should be available to any parent who needs them.)

The alternative to a new role sharing, supplemented with a variety of support services for single parents, is to concentrate on producing a race of superwomen who can excel in the breeder-feeder roles and also in the producer roles. The research on role transcendence, and the type of woman who excels in all three of her human roles,[33] suggests that what some women acquire by chance, through a biologically inherited metabolic pattern that ensures abundant physical energy, could be deliberately provided to all women by chemical intervention and genetic engineering. Is that the way we want to do it? Would men enjoy living in the shadow of a race of superwomen? Would women enjoy being superwomen? A reversal of dominance patterns might be enjoyable for some in the short run, but in the long it runs leaves us with all the limitation of the old male-dominance pattern.

The occupational roles of woman as producer and the constraints of familial breeder-feeder roles on that occupational role are the problems this paper set out to consider. Through historical analysis I have shown that the triple role has always been present. This is no new phenomenon of the industrial revolution, or of the twentieth century; nor is the wage differential related to the triple-role handicap new. What is new is a

32. Gösta Rehn, as quoted in Jessie Bernard, *Women, Wives, Mothers: Values and Options* (Chicago: Aldine Publishing Co., 1975), p. 273.

33. Ibid., pp. 51–54.

vision of human potential which is being applied to women as well as to men and which inevitably leads to the affirmation of equal rewards and equal opportunities for both sexes. The kind of creativity that we now see as possible for all human beings, and that needs to be fostered from earliest childhood, depends in a very direct sense on the exposure of men to breeder-feeder roles. This is where the male areas of freedom lie. This is where the male constraints, ones that were not discussed in this paper,[34] but which are as punitive in their way as the female constraints, must be broken. What is involved here is not the old battle of the sexes, which was a battle for dominance, but a process of mutual liberation on behalf of that gentler and more creative generation to come—our children's children.

University of Colorado

34. The reader interested in the phenomenon of male liberation, highly relevant to this closing discussion, is referred to Warren Farrell, *The Liberated Man: Beyond Masculinity, Freeing Men and Their Relationships with Women* (New York: Random House, 1974).

The Historical Roots of Occupational Segregation

Occupational Segregation and Public Policy: A Comparative Analysis of American and Soviet Patterns

Gail Warshofsky Lapidus

The revolutionary leadership which proclaimed the establishment of the new Soviet state in October 1917 promised a radical social transformation to bring about the full equality of women in economic, political, and family life. Soviet efforts to draw women into new economic and political roles, to redefine the relationship between the family and the larger society, and above all to alter deeply ingrained cultural values, attitudes, and behavior represent the first and perhaps the most far-reaching effort ever undertaken to transform the status and role of women.

The full participation of women in economic life was viewed as the key to this effort. Rejecting the path of legal political reform, and with it the tactics and goals of bourgeois feminism, the revolutionary socialist movement had insisted that the full liberation of women was dependent upon a larger economic and social transformation. The nationalization of the means of production on the one hand, and the shift of women's traditional domestic responsibilities to the socialized economy on the other, were considered the necessary conditions for their full participation in productive labor. The entry of women into social production was viewed in turn as the key to personal independence and sexual equality.

Early Soviet policies insisted upon the full equality of women in political, economic, and social life and challenged the network of traditional values, expectations, opportunities, and sanctions which had defined their roles in prerevolutionary Russia. In subsequent decades pressing economic needs buttressed ideological commitments, drawing women into the nonagricultural labor force in massive numbers and

transforming in dramatic ways the possibilities open to them. The values
and priorities which guided Soviet efforts and the patterns of economic
and political organization which shaped them had important consequences for the redefinition of women's roles. They created new opportunities for the participation of women in economic life even as they
imposed new constraints, resulting in patterns of occupational segregation which share many features in common with those of other industrial
societies but which have certain distinctive characteristics which this
paper will attempt to explore.

Occupational Segregation: The American Pattern

A brief review of the nature of occupational segregation in the
United States, and of the forces which sustain it, provides a useful starting point for an analysis of Soviet policy and its outcomes. Occupational
segregation is defined in the economic and sociological literature in
terms of three distinct, if somewhat overlapping, features. First, it involves what might be called horizontal segregation, a distribution of
workers which results in the domination of certain sectors or occupations by women, and others by men, out of all proportion to their overall
participation in the labor force. The indices developed to measure this
concentration demonstrate that, while the sexual structure of individual
occupations has changed over time, the overall degree of segregation
appears to be strikingly unaffected by fundamental changes in the structure and composition of the labor market over the past few decades.[1]

A second dimension of occupational segregation involves the vertical stratification of individual occupations. The tendency for the proportion of women to decline at successively higher levels of skill, responsibility, status, and income is almost universal, even in professions in which
women predominate. A third dimension of occupational segregation is
income inequality, a differential between average male and female
wages which is in part a reflection of the horizontal and vertical distribution of women in the occupational structure, in part a consequence of
differences in education, skills, and experience, and also a result of some
degree of direct discrimination.[2]

1. Edward Gross, "Plus ça change . . . ? The Sexual Structure of Occupations over
Time," *Social Problems* 26 (Fall 1968): 198–208 (see also Valerie Oppenheimer, "The Sex-
Labelling of Jobs," *Industrial Relations* 7 [May 1968]: 219–34). According to a recent study by
Barbara R. Bergmann and Irma Adelman, some 72.6 percent of all employed women in
the United States in 1970 were found in occupations which were 45–100 percent female
("The 1973 Report of the President's Council of Economic Advisors: The Economic Role
of Women," *American Economic Review* 68 [September 1973]: 510).
2. *The Economic Report of the President, January 1973* (Washington, D.C.: Government
Printing Office, 1973) calculates that the ratio of female to male earnings, adjusted for age

The forces which have contributed to this situation, and which presently sustain it, are the subject of what is by now a vast literature. For our purposes, three features deserve emphasis. A political culture which treats freedom, equality, and achievement as supreme and universal norms collides with pervasive cultural assumptions about the need for a sexual division of labor, for differentiation and complementarity between male and female roles.[3] Instrumental roles in political and economic life are regarded as appropriately the domain of men, while expressive roles are treated as preeminently the sphere of women. The primacy assigned to the homemaking and maternal roles of women encourages the treatment of their participation in the labor force as secondary and residual.

These cultural norms are reinforced by patterns of socialization which receive formal expression in educational institutions. Differential expectations for boys and girls are embedded in educational curricula: boys are channeled into mathematical and scientific disciplines, girls into humanistic programs which affect their later opportunities for advanced training and employment. And, of course, differential expectations elicit differences in behavior; boys are encouraged to be assertive and achievement-oriented while girls are rewarded for nurturing and compliance.[4]

Finally, these values are mirrored and reinforced by public policy. Across the broad spectrum of governmental programs, ranging from taxation measures to the provision of social services, public policy in the

---

and education, ranges from 72 percent for professional and technical workers to 47.8 percent for sales personnel (p. 91). Other studies calculate the differential to be between 35 and 57 percent, depending on the data base used. The authors of the presidential report, after adjusting for every possible factor, including experience, found a residual differential of about 20 percent but stopped just short of attributing it to direct discrimination (pp. 103–6). Six recent econometric studies, reviewed in Bergmann and Adelman, variously calculated the differential due to discrimination to be between 29 and 43 percent. See, e.g., Larry Suter and Herman Miller, "Income Differences between Men and Career Women," in *Changing Women in a Changing Society*, ed. Joan Huber (Chicago: University of Chicago Press, 1973), pp. 210–12, for a demonstration that women receive smaller increments of income for equal increases in educational level and occupational status. A study of university faculty salaries by the Carnegie Commission on Higher Education, *Opportunities for Women in Higher Education* (New York: Carnegie Commission, 1973), reveals a similar pattern and concludes that women faculty members earn an average of $1,500–$2,000 less a year than men in comparable positions for comparable qualifications (see also Myra Strober, "Lower Pay for Women: A Case of Economic Discrimination," *Industrial Relations* 11 [May 1972]: 279–84).

3. A classic theoretical statement of this view is found in Talcott Parsons and Robert Bales, *Family, Socialization and the Interaction Process* (Glencoe, Ill.: Free Press, 1955).

4. For two studies among many on this question, see Naomi Weisstein, "Psychology Constructs the Female," in *Woman in Sexist Society*, ed. Vivian Gornick and Barbara Moran (New York: Basic Books, 1971); Lenore J. Weitzman, "Sex-Role Socialization," in *Women: A Feminist Perspective*, ed. Jo Freeman (Palo Alto, Calif.: Mayfield Publishing Co., 1975).

United States reflects the premise that marriage is an institution for the economic support of women. The inadequacy of measures designed to guarantee equal educational and employment opportunities to women and the failure to develop social services which would support the dual roles of women workers intensify the conflict between the traditional cultural norms that define family roles and the social realities of rising female employment.

Women and Work in Soviet Policy

The cultural values, educational orientations, and public policies which have sustained occupational segregation in the United States are explicitly repudiated in the Soviet Union. From the earliest days of the new regime, Soviet ideology has insisted upon the link between sexual equality and female employment.[5] The right as well as the obligation to work represented a central feature of Soviet conceptions of citizenship, and women shared with men what one sociologist has called an "equal liability to mobilization."[6] Productive employment for women, official sources insist, is a condition of individual independence, a source of personal satisfaction, and a way of contributing to the larger community.

The labor shortage which accompanied rapid Soviet industrialization made the increased employment of women not merely a politically desirable objective but a pressing economic need. At the same time, a combination of economic, demographic, and social forces increased the supply of female labor. War and civil war, political deportations, and military service transformed wives and widows into heads of households, while the scarcity of men deprived a whole generation of women of the opportunity to marry. Almost 30 percent of all Soviet households in 1959 were headed by women, and as one Soviet economist noted, "Women could not but work, because their earnings are the basic source of income for the family."[7] Under these circumstances, the congruence

5. For a more extensive treatment of the evolution of Soviet policy and its consequences, see Gail Warshofsky Lapidus, *Women in Soviet Society: Equality, Development and Social Change 1917–1975* (Berkeley: University of California Press, forthcoming).
6. I am indebted to Reinhard Bendix for suggesting this formulation.
7. Cited in Murray Feshbach, "Manpower Trends in the U.S.S.R.: 1950 to 1980," mimeographed (Foreign Demographic Analysis Division, Bureau of the Census, U.S. Department of Commerce, May 1971), p. 9. The massive impact of losses of males is further indicated by the fact that in 1959 only 62.3 percent of women aged forty to forty-five and only 54.9 percent of women aged forty-five to forty-nine were married (Frederick Leedy, "Demographic Trends in the USSR," in *Soviet Economic Prospects for the Seventies*, U.S. Congress, Joint Economic Committee [Washington, D.C.: Government Printing Office, 1973], p. 441). The structure of Soviet wages and incomes also actively encourages female employment. According to official Soviet sources, the minimum per capita income necessary for "material well-being" is 620 rubles per year, or 2,480 rubles for a family of four.

of ideological norms and social realities sustained high rates of female labor-force participation.

The dependence of new female social and economic roles upon new educational opportunities was explicitly recognized in Soviet policy. Early measures established a network of coeducational schools that offered a uniform educational experience to boys and girls alike and a curriculum that stressed scientific and technical training. Deliberate efforts were made to draw women into technical and scientific fields where they were not previously represented, and for a time official decrees obliged higher-education institutions to use preferential admissions and quotas to increase the proportion of women in such programs. Vocational training, part-time and correspondence programs, and a network of Party schools were designed to raise the qualifications of men and women already in the labor force and to prepare them for more skilled and responsible positions. As a consequence, the gap between male and female educational attainment has been progressively narrowed at all levels of the educational system. Women presently constitute half the student body in higher-education institutions, and among the younger age cohorts the proportion of women with higher or secondary education actually exceeds that of men.[8]

By contrast with the American pattern, public policy in the Soviet Union assumes from the start the dual role of women as workers and mothers and makes substantial provision for the support of both roles. Early legislative measures amounted to an equal rights amendment, Soviet style, and guaranteed women full and equal civil, political, and economic rights, including the right to equal pay for equal work. At the same time Soviet codes insist that equal rights for women are not incompatible with special protective measures governing female employment; indeed, genuine equality requires such differentiated treatment in order to make it possible for women to combine employment with motherhood. An elaborate network of regulations governs the nature and terms of female employment and makes special provision for the needs of pregnant women and mothers of infants. Maternal legislation entitles women to 112 days of paid maternity leave and up to a full year of

---

The average monthly wage in 1972 was 130.3 rubles, or less than two-thirds of what would be required to support such a family.

8. By 1973 for every 1,000 persons aged ten or over, 504 men and 448 women had at least an incomplete secondary education, while 56 men and 43 women had completed higher education. In the age cohort presently attending secondary specialized or higher educational institutions, women outnumber men (see Tsentral'noe statisticheskoe upravlenie, *Narodnoe khoziaistvo SSSR v 1972 g.* [Moscow: Statistika, 1973], p. 39; Tsentral'noe statisticheskoe upravlenie, *Itogi vsesoiuznoi perepisi naseleniia 1970 goda,* vol. 3 [Moscow: Statistika, 1972], pp. 6–7). At the same time women are underrepresented in vocational-technical schools, where they form roughly one-fourth of enrollments, primarily in the less skilled specialties.

unpaid leave without loss of job or seniority. The care of young children during working hours is also assumed by a network of public institutions embracing some 11 million preschool children, while a growing number of regular schools with extended day programs, supplemented by the efforts of the Pioneer movement and the Komsomol, offer extracurricular activities for school-age children during the hours when parents are at work.

Patterns of Female Employment in the Soviet Union

The effects of Soviet values, educational efforts, and public policy have resulted in patterns of female labor-force participation which differ in important ways from those found in the United States. The sharpest difference is in overall participation rates. In 1974 more than 51 million women were employed in the socialized sector of the Soviet economy, where they formed 51 percent of the labor force. These participation rates are close to the demographic maximum; some 85 percent of all women aged twenty to fifty-five are employed, almost exclusively full time (table 1). The very scale of female employment in the USSR itself affects the distribution of women within the labor force.

A second major difference between Soviet and American patterns of female employment is the high proportion of Soviet women in scientific, technical, and industrial occupations. Women constitute 44 percent of all engineers and technicians in the Soviet labor force, three-fourths of all physicians, and half of all personnel employed in science and scientific services.[9] The 1970 census, for example, lists roughly

Table 1

Female Labor-Force Participation Rates, Soviet Union,
by Age Cohort, 1959–80

Age Cohort (Years)	1959	1965	1970	1975 (Est.)	1980 (Est.)
14–15	17.1	11.6*	7.0*	6.0	6.0
16–19	66.5	41.7	21.0	20.0	20.0
20–29	80.4	86.1	88.4	88.4	88.4
30–39	77.7	83.2	85.6	85.6	85.6
40–49	75.4	80.8	83.2	83.2	83.2
50–54	67.7	72.5	74.7	74.7	74.7
55–59	48.5	51.9	53.0	53.0	53.0
60+	33.8	36.2	37.0	37.0	37.0

SOURCE.—Murray Feshbach, "Manpower Trends in the U.S.S.R.: 1950 to 1980," mimeographed (Foreign Demographic Analysis Division, Bureau of the Census, U.S. Department of Commerce, May 1971).
*The falling rate reflects increased school attendance.

9. It should be noted that teachers and physicians, two occupations in which women predominate, have a shorter workday than the average and that a certain flexibility of scheduling at scientific institutions as well benefits women technical and professional personnel.

400,000 women chemists, over 1 million engineers, and 25 million medical workers.

The extensive role of women in industrial jobs further distinguishes Soviet employment patterns. Soviet women are heavily concentrated in such traditionally female industries as textiles, clothing, and food, but they are also employed in heavy industrial sectors such as machine building, metallurgy, and construction, which in the United States are almost exclusively male. The penetration of women into such occupations, combined with their substantial training in engineering, gives them some access to positions of managerial responsibility. According to Soviet census data, women constitute 15 percent of foremen and shop heads in Soviet enterprises, 24 percent of heads of production-technical departments, and 13 percent of enterprise heads.[10] While the complexities of gathering comparable data make direct comparisons extremely difficult, it would appear that the role of women in positions of authority in industry is somewhat higher in the Soviet Union than it is in the United States.

In other respects, however, the distribution of women within the Soviet economy suggests the existence of a dual labor market similar to that found in the United States and Western Europe. Although industrialization has expanded the range of opportunities for women, occupations which were female at an earlier time tend to remain female. By and large, women predominate in economic sectors and occupations which are low in status and pay, while they are underrepresented in more prestigious and highly rewarding occupations.

The distribution of women within the Soviet labor force by economic sector reveals interesting patterns (table 2). First, there is a high degree of continuity in the patterns of employment from 1940 to 1972; the changes in the proportion of women in different economic sectors increase in proportions which follow closely their overall ratio within the labor force. In some respects the gap between those sectors in which women are overrepresented and those in which they are underrepresented has actually widened in the intervening years. The proportion of women in industry, transport, and construction has actually declined in relation to the proportion of women in the labor force overall, while in several fields with a high proportion of women in 1940 it has risen still further.

The rapid growth of the service sector in recent years, from 30 percent of the nonagricultural labor force in 1960 to 38 percent by 1970, has tended to increase the degree of occupational segregation in Soviet economic life. The proportion of women engaged in trade, procurement, supplies, and public dining, for example, has risen to 76 percent. Credit and state insurance, a sector which employs large numbers of

10. *Itogi vsesoiuznoi perepisi 1970 . . .* , vol. 6, p. 167.

Table 2

Distribution of Women within the Soviet Labor Force
by Economic Sector, 1940–74

Economic Sector	Percentage of Women Workers by Economic Sector			Ratio of Women in Given Sector to Proportion of Total Labor Force	
	1940	1960	1974	1940	1974
Women in total labor force (%)	39	47	51	...	...
Industry.........................	38	45	49	0.97	0.96
Agriculture (socialized sector)	30	41	44	0.77	0.86
Transportation	21	24	24	0.54	0.47
Communications	48	64	68	1.23	1.33
Construction	24	30	29	0.62	0.57
Trade, public catering, material-technical supplies and marketing, and procurement...............	44	66	76	1.12	1.49
Municipal housing and consumer services.......................	43	53	53	1.10	1.04
Public health, physical culture, and social culture..................	76	85	85	1.94	1.66
Education and culture	59	70	73.	1.51	1.43
Art	39	36	45	1.00	0.88
Science and scientific services	42	42	49	1.07	0.96
Banking and state insurance.......	41	68	81	1.05	1.59
Apparatus of organs of state and economic administration, of co-operatives and of social organizations	34	51	63	0.87	1.23

Source.—Calculated from figures given in "Zhenshchiny v SSSR," *Vestnik statistiki* 1 (January 1975): 86.

secretaries and bookkeepers, is 81 percent female, while the mass of clerical workers drawn into government and economic administration is 63 percent female. In comparison to manufacturing, however, the service sector has relatively low status in the Soviet Union, a status reinforced by the distinction in Marxist economic theory between "productive" and "nonproductive" activities.

The sex stereotyping of individual occupations further contributes to horizontal segregation. A number of occupations listed in the all-union tabulations of the 1970 census have no counterpart in the tables summarizing female employment. Mechanical engineering and metallurgy represent two fields that are overwhelmingly or exclusively male. The garment and textile industries, on the other hand, are largely female. Women are also heavily concentrated in trade and public catering (91 percent of all employees) and nursing (98 percent); they also comprise three-fourths of all teachers, 98 percent of nursery school personnel, 95 percent of librarians, 96 percent of telephone operators, and 99 percent of typists and stenographers.[11] Despite the extensive

11. Ibid., pp. 165–69.

penetration of women into previously male fields, there has been no reciprocal flow of men into these "female" occupations.

The Soviet census data further suggest that in recent years occupational segregation has tended to increase with development. In 1959 just under 16 million women were employed in occupations in which they formed 70 percent or more of the labor force; in 1970, more than 30 million women, or 55 percent of the female labor force, fell into this category. Whereas one-fifth of the female labor force was concentrated in occupations which are 85 percent or more female in 1959, by 1970 the proportion rose to almost one-third.

If it is true that Soviet women first entering the labor force chose fields in which they felt most at ease,[12] or which were most closely associated with their traditional roles, then we see that this pattern has not been altogether reversed. Indeed, the polarization of certain sectors into male-dominated or female-dominated ones has intensified with development.

The Vertical Structure of Occupations

The patterns of employment of women by industrial sector, however, tell us little about the actual structure of occupations within each sector and provide no indication of the extent to which women have moved from unskilled jobs to those involving professional skills and executive responsibility. A more complete picture would require comparing the employment pyramid for women with that for men. Although such a broad comparison is beyond this study's scope, the detailed analysis of particular fields may illuminate the larger picture. For this purpose we shall focus on four occupations involving four different levels and types of skills: agriculture, industrial engineering, education and medicine, and advanced scientific work.

The most striking feature of Soviet agriculture is the high proportion of women involved—roughly 20 million. The bulk of these are members of collective or state farms, and the rest are in private subsidiary agriculture, producing for home consumption or the local market.[13] This female labor force is aging, unskilled, and engaged in physically demanding labor, particularly on the collective farms. In a pattern common to other less developed societies, Soviet men are moving into more skilled and better-paid positions, often involving

12. For this point of view, see William Mandel, "Soviet Women in the Work Force and Professions," *American Behavioral Scientist* 14 (November-December 1971): 255–80.

13. The figures for 1970 were derived from Tsentral'noe statisticheskoe upravlenie, *Narodnoe khoziaistvo SSSR: 1922–1972* (Moscow: Statistika, 1972), p. 283. Using the figure 26.6 million for the total agricultural labor force in 1971 (16.5 million for the collective farm sector and 10 million for the state farms), the number of women in the total was

mechanized operations, while women are left to perform heavy manual labor.[14] Soviet commentators themselves have drawn attention to this situation: "In many instances, work demanding manual labor falls to women, while the men work as accountants, section leaders, and farm managers."[15]

While official encouragement is given to enlisting women in skilled agricultural labor, and while women have been trained for such specialties as agronomy, tractor driving, and veterinary medicine in some numbers, the traditional and sharply defined sexual division of labor prevails in many areas as it did in prerevolutionary peasant communities.[16] Collective-farm women constitute more than 90 percent of milking personnel, swineherds, and poultry workers, and 80 percent of vegetable growers; they form under 10 percent of the workers in traditionally male agricultural activities and in the more mechanized modern sectors. As Khrushchev once remarked at an agricultural conference, ". . . it is the men who do the administrating and the women who do the work."[17]

Industrial occupations appear to offer women opportunities for more satisfying and responsible work than do those in agriculture. The first women to enter industry in the early thirties were unskilled with little education. In subsequent decades extensive governmental encouragement and expanding educational attainment produced growing numbers of women with specialized skills, although within blue-collar categories women are concentrated at lower levels.

In technical and professional categories such as engineering, women are found in larger proportions. The number of women engineers with higher education increased between 1941 and 1964 from

computed by using the 1959 ratios. The figure arrived at is almost identical with the 12,632,741 reported in the 1970 census data (see n. 10 above). The figure of 7–8 million additional women engaged in private subsidiary agriculture is based on estimates of the Foreign Demographic Analysis Division of the U.S. Department of Commerce. For a discussion of the female agricultural labor force, based on 1959 census data, see Norton Dodge and Murray Feshbach, "The Role of Women in Soviet Agriculture," in *Soviet and East European Agriculture*, ed. Jerry Karcz (Berkeley: University of California Press, 1967), pp. 265–305; Norton Dodge, "Recruitment and the Quality of the Soviet Agricultural Labor Force," in *The Soviet Rural Community*, ed. James Millar (Urbana: University of Illinois Press, 1971), pp. 180–213.

14. For a discussion of the impact of development on the agricultural division of labor see Ester Boserup, *Woman's Role in Economic Development* (New York: St. Martin's Press, 1970).

15. *Komsomolskaia pravda* (February 16, 1969).

16. See, e.g., the description of patterns of labor in prerevolutionary and post-revolutionary rural Russia in the famous ethnographic study of Viriatino: Sule Benet, ed. and trans., *The Village of Viriatino* (New York: Doubleday & Co., Anchor Books, 1970), pp. 95–96, 255–56, and compare them with the occupational distributions of Soviet farm workers presented in Dodge, p. 183.

17. *Izvestiia* (December 26, 1961).

44,000 to 460,000 and then doubled to 1 million in 1970. Engineering remains a profession in which women are slightly underrepresented, but the total number of women engineers is far greater than the total number of women physicians, a field in which women predominate. This is one important illustration of how Soviet emphasis on the training of large numbers of industrial technicians and specialists, male and female, has resulted in female employment patterns substantially at variance with those found in other industrial societies.

A background in engineering is almost a prerequisite for advancement to responsible positions in Soviet industry, and it is possible that the concentration of women at lower levels of authority may be partly explained by their late entrance into this field. The proportion of women in high-level managerial positions did rise from 13 percent to 16 percent between 1959 and 1970, but the figure remains lower than one might expect given the extensive training and work experience of women, as well as the existence of large industries, such as textiles, which are largely female in composition. Women tend to hold responsible positions in technical and clerical categories that do not involve executive leadership and authority.

Medicine and education, two professions dominated by women, clearly indicate the extent to which the proportion of women declines as the level of responsibility rises. While women are 71 percent of the total number of teachers, 80 percent of the teachers of grades 1–10, and 80 percent of the directors of primary schools, they constitute 31 percent of the directors of eight-year schools and 27 percent of the directors of secondary schools.[18] The proportions of women in teaching and administration at higher levels of the educational system are lower still.

A similar situation prevails in medicine. While seven out of ten physicians are women, chief physicians and supervisory personnel are frequently male.[19] This situation has been noted even in Soviet commentaries: "Even given an equal level of professional preparation, representatives of the stronger sex as a rule hold the managerial posts. How does one explain that while men comprise 15 percent of all medical personnel, they are 50 percent of all chief physicians and executives of medical

18. "Zhenshchiny v SSSR," *Vestnik statistiki* 1 (January 1975): 89. For purposes of comparison, women constitute about 50 percent of elementary teachers in Denmark, Norway, and the Federal Republic of Germany, 66 percent in France, 75 percent in Sweden and Great Britain, and 85 percent in the United States (see Marjorie Galenson, *Women and Work* [Ithaca: New York School of Industrial Relations, 1973], p. 27).

19. Medicine has traditionally been regarded as a suitable occupation for women in Europe, along with dentistry and pharmacy. While the proportion of women physicians is particularly high in the Soviet Union, the low proportion of women in the American medical profession is also exceptional. Women constitute 6.7 per cent of physicians in the United States, 12.8 percent in France, 17.4 percent in Sweden, 18 percent in Great Britain and Italy, 20 percent in the Federal Republic of Germany, and 23.4 percent in Finland (see Galenson, p. 24).

institutions . . . ? In the overwhelming majority of cases, it is men who
head departments, enterprises, and administrative agencies."[20]

This pattern appears to be the outcome of deliberate policy choices
in the training and assignment of specialists. Preferential treatment of
males in admissions to medical schools appears to reflect lower expectations for women's professional productivity. For example, in response to
a letter of complaint from a young woman who had spent ten years
unsuccessfully seeking admission to a medical institute, a Soviet news-
paper elicited this explanation from a professor of surgery: "Medical
institutes' entrance requirements are lower for boys than for girls. Problems with women doctors arise because of marriage, relocation
difficulties, and temporary or permanent retirement when family considerations are placed above professional ones, especially when the
family's material situation makes this possible. This is the rationale for
higher requirements for girls."[21]

Upon completion of their training, a high proportion of women
teachers and physicians are assigned to relatively undesirable positions
in rural regions, where they have little opportunity to improve their
skills and to qualify for more responsible positions. The argument that
the low proportion of women in the top positions of their professions is
caused by the time lag necessary to overcome earlier educational disadvantages would not seem valid for these two professions where the
proportion of women with specialized secondary or higher-education
credentials was already high in the thirties and forties.

Soviet emphasis on scientific and technical skills in economic and
educational planning has encouraged women's entry into these fields in
large numbers. Table 3 indicates the rapid growth in the total number of
women scientific workers in the past two decades: from 59,000 in 1950
to 439,500 in 1973. However, their proportion of the total has remained
fairly stable: 35 percent in 1947, 36 percent in 1959, 38 percent in 1967,
and 40 percent in 1973.

The number of women receiving higher degrees has also grown
dramatically in recent years. Between 1950 and 1972 the number of
women Candidates of Science, a degree corresponding roughly to an
American Ph.D., increased from 11,400 to 79,600, while the number of
women Doctors of Science, a degree requiring great scholarly accom-
plishment, grew from 600 to 4,000. Despite the rise in absolute numbers,
the increase of men has been so great that the proportion of women in
the total has grown only slightly.

In academic and scientific life, as in other areas, women have advanced to positions of some responsibility but are largely absent at the
apex of authority and power. Women constitute one-fourth of junior

20. M. Sonin, *Literaturnaia gazeta* (April 16, 1969).

21. J. Doletsky, "Two Points Higher than a Dream," *Komsomolskaia pravda* (December
22, 1970); trans. in *Current Digest of the Soviet Press* 22, no. 52 (1971): 27.

Table 3

Distribution of Higher Degrees among Soviet Scientific Workers, 1950–70

	1950	1960	1965	1970	1972	1973
Number of scientific workers	162,500	354,200	664,600	927,700	1,056,000	1,100,000
Number of women	59,000	128,000	254,000	359,900	414,000	439,500
Percentage of women	36.3	36.1	38.2	38.8	39.2	40.0
Total of scientific workers with scholarly degree Candidate of Science	45,000	98,300	134,400	224,500	269,500	285,000
Number of women	11,400	28,800	34,800	60,700	73,700	79,600
Percentage of women	25.0	29.3	25.9	27.0	27.3	28.0
Total of scientific workers with scholarly degree Doctor of Science	8,300	10,900	14,800	23,600	28,100	28,570
Number of women	600	1,100	1,400	3,100	3,700	4,000
Percentage of women	7.2	10.0	9.4	13.0	13.2	14.0

Source.—Calculated from figures given in Tsentral'noe statisticheskoe upravlenie SSSR, *Narodnoe obrazovanie nauka i kultura v SSSR* (Moscow, 1971), pp. 246, 271; *Narodnoe khoziaistvo v SSSR 1972 g*, p. 129; "Zhenshchiny v SSSR," *Vestnik Statistiki* 1 (January 1975): 91. General totals for 1973 are approximations, inferred from numbers and percentages of women.

scientific workers and assistants, 10 percent of senior scientific workers, and only 2 percent of academicians and professors.[22] As of 1973 there were twelve women among the 705 members of the powerful and prestigious USSR Academy of Sciences, of whom four were full members and eight corresponding members.[23]

Finally, the proportion of women also declines at higher levels of the political system. While Soviet sources point with pride to the large proportion of women deputies elected to the soviets, women play a rather small role in the Party and government apparatus at the regional and national level. Women form 23 percent of the total membership of the Communist party, under 5 percent of the membership of the Central Committee, and only one woman—Ekaterina Furtseva—has ever been a member of the powerful Politburo.[24]

The Male-Female Income Gap

No Soviet data are available which would permit a detailed and comprehensive comparison of the average annual earnings of women with those of men at comparable levels of education. Nonetheless, substantial disparities might be anticipated for several reasons. First, Soviet branches of industry are divided into groups depending upon their political and economic importance, with established wage levels for each. The preferred economic sectors have an underrepresentation of women, while those with lower wage levels show an overrepresentation of women (table 4).[25] Moreover, the virtual absence of women in the highly skilled categories of the labor force, combined with their lower seniority and mobility,[26] exerts added downward pressure on wage levels. The paucity of women in managerial positions further prevents them from earning substantial bonuses to supplement basic salaries. Finally, although Soviet law requires equal pay for equal work, women are not necessarily assured of positions commensurate with their training and skills. Because the place of residence of married women is usu-

22. Tsentral'noe statisticheskoe upravlenie, *Narodnoe obrazovanie, nauka, i kul'tura v SSSR* (Moscow: Statistika, 1971), p. 271.

23. *Membership, USSR Academy of Sciences,* Reference Aid, Central Intelligence Agency (Washington, D.C.: Government Printing Office, May 1973).

24. For a more detailed analysis of the role of women in the political system, see Gail W. Lapidus, "Political Mobilization, Participation and Leadership: Women in Soviet Politics," *Comparative Politics* 8, no. 1 (October 1975): 90–118.

25. The monthly wages of a chief engineer in the coal industry, e.g., are 380 rubles, in ferrous metallurgy 270–320, in machine building 260–300, in light industry 200–210, and in the food industry 180–200 (see Andreas Tenson, "Wage and Salary Rates in the Production Sphere of the Soviet Economy," *Radio Liberty Dispatch* [June 15, 1973], pp. 11–12).

26. Valentina Borisovna Mikhailyuk, *Ispol'zovanie zhenskogo truda v narodnom khoziaistve* (Moscow: Ekonomika, 1970), pp. 73–81. The low proportion of women in technical-vocational schools probably accounts for their low proportion among skilled workers.

Table 4

Female Participation and Average Earnings
by Economic Sector

Economic Sector	Women as Percentage of Labor Force	Average Monthly Earnings (Rubles)
Construction	29	159.4
Transport	24	150.8
Science and scientific services	49	143.6
Industry (production personnel)	48	142.1
Apparatus of government and economic administration, and of cooperative and voluntary organizations	63	124.4
Credit and insurance	68	118.0
Education and culture	73	112.7
Agriculture	44	111.8
Communications	68	102.9
Housing and municipal economy	53	99.6
Trade, public catering, materials and equipment, supply and sales, agricultural procurement	76	99.3
Arts	45	97.5
Public health, physical culture, and social welfare	85	95.5
Nationwide average	51	130.2

SOURCES.—Tsentral'noe statisticheskoe upravlenie, *Narodnoe khoziaistvo SSSR v 1972 g.* (Moscow, 1973), p. 516; "Zhenshchiny v SSSR," *Vestnik statistiki* 1 (January 1975): 86.

ally determined by the husband's job, they experience greater difficulty in finding suitable employment, and they often fill jobs which could have been filled by less qualified persons. The absence of Soviet data makes it impossible to explore the weight of these different factors or to calculate with any precision the differential between average male and female earnings. Some of the factors which contribute to the male-female income gap in the United States may exert less influence in the Soviet Union because of the high rates and continuity of female labor-force participation, the relative equality of younger women's educational attainment with that of younger men, and the high proportion of women among technical and engineering personnel and in professional occupations.

A crude calculation of the magnitude of the male-female income differential can nevertheless be made by utilizing occupational census data in conjunction with an official Soviet breakdown of wages published in 1968.[27] Such a calculation yields a per capita female income roughly 87 percent that of males, but this excludes collective farming, ignores the way in which the occupational and hierarchical distribution of women within sectors affects average wages, and omits the weight of some bonuses in actual income. It is clear that this figure understates the

27. Tsentral'noe statisticheskoe upravlenie, *Trud v SSSR* (Moscow: Statistika, 1968), pp. 140–45.

real differential. Calculations for other socialist countries where more detailed data are available yield a larger differential: in a recent study the median full-time earnings of women were estimated to be 67.1 percent those of men in Czechoslovakia, 66.5 percent in Poland, and 73 percent in Hungary (state sector only).[28]

The Social Bases of Occupational Segregation in the Soviet Union

Despite cultural norms, educational efforts, and public policy designed to support high levels of female employment, some degree of occupational segregation nevertheless persists in the USSR, and indeed appears to be increasing with economic development. Differences in the occupational aspirations of men and women are one major factor underlying these employment patterns. Soviet studies show that from a relatively early age female schoolchildren express a preference for occupations in teaching, medicine, and, more generally, the humanities, while boys are more strongly oriented toward scientific and technical fields.[29] As one sociologist commented: ". . . the selective attitudes of boys and girls toward different kinds of activities emerge at an early school age, and continue during the period of intensive formation of interests and inclinations. All this testifies to the existence in society of certain stereotypes of occupational preference according to sex, which is confirmed by differences in the ratings of occupations by secondary school graduates and teachers, and by the actual feminization of a number of occupations in whole branches of the economy."[30] Aside from orientation, it is the intensity of occupational commitment that appears to distinguish men and women. Fewer Soviet women than men express an interest in a career rather than a job; only one-third of the women in a recent opinion survey expressed a desire to upgrade their skills, compared with more than half of the male respondents.[31]

28. For the Soviet Union, see William Moskoff, "An Estimate of the Soviet Male-Female Income Gap," *ACES Bulletin* 16 (Fall 1974): 24. For Eastern Europe, see Jan Michal, "An Alternate Approach to Measuring Income Inequality" (paper presented at the International Slavic Association Conference, Banff, August 1974).

29. P. Petrov, "The Formation of Career Plans in School" (based upon data for Nizhnii Tagil), in *The Career Plans of Youth,* ed. M. V. Rutkevich (White Plains, N.Y.: International Arts and Sciences Press, 1969), p. 42; L. F. Liss, "The Social Conditioning of Occupational Choice," in *Social Stratification and Mobility in the USSR,* by Murray Yanowitch and Wesley Fisher (White Plains, N.Y.: International Arts and Sciences Press, 1973), pp. 281–82; V. V. Vodzinskaia, "Orientations toward Occupations," ibid., pp. 168–73.

30. Liss, p. 282.

31. G. V. Osipov and S. F. Frolov, "Vnerabochee vremia i ego ispol'zovanie," cited in David Lane, *Politics and Society in the USSR* (New York: Random House, 1971), p. 355.

Differential aspirations, preferences, and valuations, however, are not unrelated to the real structure of opportunities. Women's lower aspirations may reflect not only the effects of socialization but also a realistic assessment of the likely returns on investments of additional time and energy. In addition, the claims on women's time and energy of household chores and child rearing, which are still viewed as "women's work," severely limit professional mobility. Recent time-budget studies demonstrate that working wives have significantly less leisure time for enhancing professional skills than do their male counterparts.[32] Similarly, the pervasive sex labeling of jobs, in the absence of strong economic or political incentives to alter prevailing patterns, shapes the pattern of women's occupational choices.

Both the expansion of opportunities available to women and the continuing constraints upon full sexual equality have been shaped in significant ways by the political and developmental priorities of the Soviet system. The concern to maximize labor-force participation rates while simultaneously maintaining a high rate of reproduction has inspired a wide range of measures to make it possible for women to combine employment with motherhood. Moreover, the centralization of political and economic authority has facilitated efforts to alter attitudes and behavior in desired directions and to shift part of the costs of social engineering from the individual economic and family unit to the larger social community.

If the structure and priorities of the Soviet system have expanded the opportunities available to women in some important respects, they have also done so at a very high cost. The organization of the Soviet economy permits a high degree of control over the *terms* of women's entry into the labor force. Even in the absence of adequate child-care facilities and other supporting institutions, the maintenance of low wage levels forced women into full-time employment with little freedom not to work or to reshape the terms of their employment to meet individual needs. Indeed a declining birth rate in the more urbanized regions of European Russia may reflect in part the strain of women's "double shift."

Moreover, this strain was accentuated by a pattern of industrialization which placed extremely heavy burdens upon the individual household. In an effort to economize on urbanization and to limit investment in consumer goods and services, Soviet industrialization required the household to perform functions which in other countries at comparable levels of development are performed by the market. This additional burden fell heavily upon the shoulders of women. It is in this sense that "consumerism" is a genuinely feminist issue in the USSR and a reorien-

32. Ibid.

tation of economic priorities the condition of a durable improvement in the welfare of women.

Finally, the whole Soviet approach to sexual equality has been imbued with an authoritarian paternalism characteristic of the system more generally. The Soviet approach to the liberation of women was ultimately shaped less by the individualistic and liberatarian concerns of nineteenth-century feminism or Marxism than by an instrumental concern to utilize the mobilization of women to enhance the economic and political capacity of the Soviet system. It was concerned with increasing participation but not with equal power. Indeed, the very emphasis on women's participation in production as the guarantee of full equality neglected the political and cultural dimensions of sex roles, and these dimensions have proved less responsive to economic arrangements than was anticipated. Moreover, the commitment to rapid industrialization, and with it the mobilization of manpower, created a climate hostile to changes in social relationships and values which might threaten the overriding objectives of efficiency and productivity.

The Soviet experience seems to suggest that, contrary to earlier expectations shaped by Marxian theory, economic participation does not, in and of itself, guarantee equality of status and authority for women. In no less than an avowedly socialist society, the structure of authority remains hierarchical and stratified, and the proportion of women at successively higher levels of that hierarchy, even in the occupations they dominate, declines. Arrangements to sustain high rates of female employment, and to enable women to penetrate previously male occupations, may diminish to some degree the scope of occupational segregation. But a more comprehensive attack on the cultural values and institutional arrangements which sustain occupational segregation requires not merely the partial assimilation of women to male roles but the reciprocal redefinition of both.

University of California, Berkeley

The Historical Roots of Occupational Segregation

Capitalism, Patriarchy, and Job Segregation by Sex

Heidi Hartmann

The division of labor by sex appears to have been universal throughout human history. In our society the sexual division of labor is hierarchical, with men on top and women on the bottom. Anthropology and history suggest, however, that this division was not always a hierarchical one. The development and importance of a sex-ordered division of labor is the subject of this paper. It is my contention that the roots of women's present social status lie in this sex-ordered division of labor. It is my belief that not only must the hierarchical nature of the division of labor between the sexes be eliminated, but the very division of labor between the sexes itself must be eliminated if women are to attain equal social status with men and if women and men are to attain the full development of their human potentials.

The primary questions for investigation would seem to be, then, first, how a more sexually egalitarian division became a less egalitarian one, and second, how this hierarchical divison of labor became extended to wage labor in the modern period. Many anthropological studies suggest that the first process, sexual stratification, occurred together with the increasing productiveness, specialization, and complexity of society;

I would like to thank many women at the New School for sharing their knowledge with me and offering encouragement and debate, in particular, Amy Hirsch, Christine Gailey, Nadine Felton, Penny Ciancanelli, Rayna Reiter, and Viana Muller. I would also like to thank Amy Bridges, Carl Degler, David Gordon, Fran Blau, Grace Horowitz, Linda Gordon, Suad Joseph, Susan Strasser, and Tom Vietorisz for helpful comments.

for example, through the establishment of settled agriculture, private property, or the state. It occurred as human society emerged from the primitive and became "civilized." In this perspective capitalism is a relative latecomer, whereas patriarchy,[1] the hierarchical relation between men and women in which men are dominant and women are subordinate, was an early arrival.

I want to argue that, before capitalism, a patriarchal system was established in which men controlled the labor of women and children in the family, and that in so doing men learned the techniques of hierarchical organization and control. With the advent of public-private separations such as those created by the emergence of state apparatus and economic systems based on wider exchange and larger production units, the problem for men became one of maintaining their control over the labor power of women. In other words, a direct personal system of control was translated into an indirect, impersonal system of control, mediated by society-wide institutions. The mechanisms available to men were (1) the traditional division of labor between the sexes, and (2) techniques of hierarchical organization and control. These mechanisms were crucial in the second process, the extension of a sex-ordered division of labor to the wage-labor system, during the period of the emergence of capitalism in Western Europe and the United States.

The emergence of capitalism in the fifteenth to eighteenth centuries threatened patriarchal control based on institutional authority as it destroyed many old institutions and created new ones, such as a "free" market in labor. It threatened to bring all women and children into the

1. I define patriarchy as a set of social relations which has a material base and in which there are hierarchical relations between men, and solidarity among them, which enable them to control women. Patriarchy is thus the system of male oppression of women. Rubin argues that we should use the term "sex-gender system" to refer to that realm outside the economic system (and not always coordinate with it) where gender stratification based on sex differences is produced and reproduced. Patriarchy is thus only one form, a male dominant one, of a sex-gender system. Rubin argues further that patriarchy should be reserved for pastoral nomadic societies as described in the Old Testament where male power was synonomous with fatherhood. While I agree with Rubin's first point, I think her second point makes the usage of patriarchy too restrictive. It is a good label for most male-dominant societies (see Gayle Rubin, "The Traffic in Women," in *Toward an Anthropology of Women*, ed. Rayna Reiter [New York: Monthly Review Press, 1975]). Muller offers a broader definition of patriarchy "as a social system in which the status of women is defined primarily as wards of their husbands, fathers, and brothers," where wardship has economic and political dimensions (see Viana Muller, "The Formation of the State and the Oppression of Women: A Case Study in England and Wales," mimeographed [New York: New School for Social Research, 1975], p. 4, n. 2). Muller relies on Karen Sacks, "Engels Revisited: Women, the Organization of Production, and Private Property," in *Woman, Culture and Society,* ed. Michelle Z. Rosaldo and Louise Lamphere (Stanford, Calif.: Stanford University Press, 1974). Patriarchy as a system between and among men as well as between men and women is further explained in a draft paper, "The Unhappy Marriage of Marxism and Feminism: Towards a New Union," by Amy Bridges and Heidi Hartmann.

labor force and hence to destroy the family and the basis of the power of men over women (i.e., the control over their labor power in the family).[2] If the theoretical tendency of pure capitalism would have been to eradicate all arbitrary differences of status among laborers, to make all laborers equal in the marketplace, why are women still in an inferior position to men in the labor market? The possible answers are legion; they range from neoclassical views that the process is not complete or is hampered by market imperfections to the radical view that production requires hierarchy even if the market nominally requires "equality."[3] All of these explanations, it seems to me, ignore the role of men—ordinary men, men as men, men as workers—in maintaining women's inferiority in the labor market. The radical view, in particular, emphasizes the role of men as capitalists in creating hierarchies in the production process in order to maintain their power. Capitalists do this by segmenting the labor market (along race, sex, and ethnic lines among others) and playing workers off against each other. In this paper I argue that male workers have played and continue to play a crucial role in maintaining sexual divisions in the labor process.

Job segregation by sex, I will argue, is the primary mechanism in capitalist society that maintains the superiority of men over women, because it enforces lower wages for women in the labor market. Low wages keep women dependent on men because they encourage women to marry. Married women must perform domestic chores for their husbands. Men benefit, then, from both higher wages and the domestic division of labor. This domestic division of labor, in turn, acts to weaken women's position in the labor market. Thus, the hierarchical domestic division of labor is perpetuated by the labor market, and vice versa. This process is the present outcome of the continuing interaction of two interlocking systems, capitalism and patriarchy. Patriarchy, far from being vanquished by capitalism, is still very virile; it shapes the form modern capitalism takes, just as the development of capitalism has transformed patriarchal institutions. The resulting mutual accommodation between patriarchy and capitalism has created a vicious circle for women.

My argument contrasts with the traditional views of both neoclas-

2. Marx and Engels perceived the progress of capitalism in this way, that it would bring women and children into the labor market and thus erode the family. Yet despite Engels's acknowledgment in *The Origin of the Family, Private Property, and the State* (New York: International Publishers, 1972), that men oppress women in the family, he did not see that oppression as based on the control of women's labor, and, if anything, he seems to lament the passing of the male-controlled family (see his *The Condition of the Working Class in England* [Stanford, Calif.: Stanford University Press, 1968], esp. pp. 161–64).

3. See Richard C. Edwards, David M. Gordon, and Michael Reich, "Labor Market Segmentation in American Capitalism," draft essay, and the book they edited, *Labor Market Segmentation* (Lexington, Ky.: Lexington Books, forthcoming) for an explication of this view.

sical and Marxist economists. Both ignore patriarchy, a social system with a material base. The neoclassical economists tend to exonerate the capitalist system, attributing job segregation to exogenous *ideological* factors, like sexist attitudes. Marxist economists tend to attribute job segregation to capitalists, ignoring the part played by male workers and the effect of centuries of patriarchal social relations. In this paper I hope to redress the balance. The line of argument I have outlined here and will develop further below is perhaps incapable of proof. This paper, I hope, will establish its plausibility rather than its incontrovertibility.

The first part of this paper briefly reviews evidence and explanations offered in the anthropological literature for the creation of dominance-dependence relations between men and women. The second part reviews the historical literature on the division of labor by sex during the emergence of capitalism and the Industrial Revolution in England and the United States. This part focuses on the extension of male-female dominance-dependence relations to the wage-labor market and the key role played by men in maintaining job segregation by sex and hence male superiority.

Anthropological Perspectives on the Division of Labor by Sex

Some anthropologists explain male dominance by arguing that it existed from the very beginning of human society. Sherry Ortner suggests that indeed "female is to male as nature is to culture."[4] According to Ortner, culture devalues nature; females are associated with nature, are considered closer to nature in all cultures,[5] and are thus devalued. Her view is compatible with that of Rosaldo,[6] who emphasizes the public-private split, and that of Lévi-Strauss, who assumes the subordination of women during the process of the creation of society.

4. Sherry B. Ortner, "Is Female to Male as Nature Is to Culture?" *Feminist Studies* 1, no. 2 (Fall 1972): 5–31. "The universality of female subordination, the fact that it exists within every type of social and economic arrangement, and in societies of every degree of complexity, indicates to me that we are up against something very profound, very stubborn, something that cannot be remedied merely by rearranging a few tasks and roles in the social system, nor even by rearranging the whole economic structure" (pp. 5–6).

5. Ortner specifically rejects a biological basis for this association of women with nature and the concomitant devaluation of both. Biological differences "only take on significance of superior/inferior within the framework of culturally defined value systems" (ibid., p. 9). The biological explanation is, of course, the other major explanation for the universality of female subordination. I, too, deny the validity of this explanation and will not discuss it in this paper. Female physiology does, however, play a role in supporting a cultural view of women as closer to nature, as Ortner argues persuasively, following DeBeauvoir (ibid., pp. 12–14). Ortner's article was reprinted in *Woman, Culture, and Society* in slightly revised form.

6. Michelle Z. Rosaldo, "Woman, Culture, and Society: A Theoretical Overview," in *Woman, Culture, and Society*.

According to Lévi-Strauss, culture began with the exchange of women by men to cement bonds between families—thereby creating *society*.[7] In fact, Lévi-Strauss sees a fundamental tension between the family (i.e., the domestic realm in which women reside closer to nature) and society, which requires that families break down their autonomy to exchange with one another. The exchange of women is a mechanism that enforces the interdependence of families and that creates society. By analogy, Lévi-Strauss suggests that the division of labor between the sexes is the mechanism which enforces "a reciprocal state of dependency between the sexes."[8] It also assures heterosexual marriage. "When it is stated that one sex must perform certain tasks, this also means that the other sex is forbidden to do them."[9] Thus the existence of a sexual division of labor is a universal of human society, though the exact division of the tasks by sex varies enormously.[10] Moreover, following Lévi-Strauss, because it is men who exchange women and women who are exchanged in creating social bonds, men benefit more than women from these social bonds, and the division of labor between the sexes is a hierarchical one.[11]

While this first school of anthropological thought, the "universalists," is based primarily on Lévi-Strauss and the exchange of women, Chodorow, following Rosaldo and Ortner, emphasizes women's confinement to the domestic sphere. Chodorow locates this confinement in the mothering role. She constructs the universality of patriarchy on the universal fact that women mother. Female mothering reproduces itself via the creation of gender-specific personality structures.[12]

Two other major schools of thought on the origins of the sexual divison of labor merit attention. Both reject the universality, at least in

7. Claude Lévi-Strauss, "The Family," in *Man, Culture and Society,* ed. by Harry L. Shapiro (New York: Oxford University Press, 1971).

8. Ibid., p. 348.

9. Ibid., pp. 347–48. "One of the strongest field recollections of this writer was his meeting, among the Bororo of central Brazil, of a man about thirty years old: unclean, ill-fed, sad, and lonesome. When asked if the man was seriously ill, the natives' answer came as a shock: what was wrong with him?–nothing at all, he was just a bachelor. And true enough, in a society where labor is systematically shared between men and women and where only the married status permits the man to benefit from the fruits of woman's work, including delousing, body painting, and hair-plucking as well as vegetable food and cooked food (since the Bororo woman tills the soil and makes pots), a bachelor is really only half a human being" (p. 341).

10. For further discussion of both the universality and variety of the division of labor by sex, see Melville J. Herskovits, *Economic Anthropology* (New York: W. W. Norton & Co., 1965), esp. chap. 7; Theodore Caplow, *The Sociology of Work* (New York: McGraw-Hill Book Co., 1964), esp. chap. 1.

11. For more on the exchange of women and its significance for women, see Rubin.

12. Nancy Chodorow, *Family Structure and Feminine Personality: The Reproduction of Mothering* (Berkeley: University of California Press, forthcoming). Chodorow offers an important alternative interpretation of the Oedipus complex (see her "Family Structure and Feminine Personality" in *Woman, Culture, and Society*).

theory if not in practice, of the sex-ordered division of labor. One is the "feminist-revisionist" school which argues that we cannot be certain that the division of labor is male supremacist; it may be separate but equal (as Lévi-Strauss occasionally seems to indicate), but we will never know because of the bias of the observers which makes comparisons impossible. This school is culturally relativist in the extreme, but it nevertheless contributes to our knowledge of women's work and status by stressing the accomplishments of females in their part of the division of labor.[13]

The second school also rejects the universality of sex-ordered division of labor but, unlike relativists, seeks to compare societies to isolate the variables which coincide with greater or lesser autonomy of women. This school, the "variationist," is subdivided according to the characteristics members emphasize: the contribution of women to subsistence and their control over their contribution, the organization of tribal versus state societies, the requirements of the mode of production, the emergence of wealth and private property, the boundaries of the private and public spheres.[14] A complete review of these approaches is impossible here, but I will cite a few examples from this literature to illustrate the relevance of these variables for the creation of a sex-ordered division of labor.

Among the !Kung, a hunting and gathering people in South West Africa, the women have a great deal of autonomy and influence.[15] Draper argues that this is the result of (1) the contribution of 60–80 percent of the community's food by the women and their retention of control over its distribution; (2) equal absence from the camp and equal range and mobility of the male hunters and the female gatherers (the women are not dependent on the men for protection in their gathering range); (3) the flexibility of sex roles and the willingness of adults to do the work of the opposite sex (with the exception that women did not hunt and men did not remove nasal mucous or feces from children!); (4) the absence of physical expression of aggression; (5) the small size (seventeen to sixty-five) of and flexible membership in living groups; (6)

13. Several of the articles in the Rosaldo and Lamphere collection are of this variety (see particularly Collier and Stack). Also, see Ernestine Friedl, "The Position of Women: Appearance and Reality," *Anthropological Quarterly* 40, no. 3 (July 1967): 97–108.

14. For an example of one particular emphasis, Leavitt states: "The most important clue to woman's status anywhere is her degree of participation in economic life and her control over property and the products she produces, both of which factors appear to be related to the kinship system of a society" (Ruby B. Leavitt, "Women in Other Cultures," in *Woman and Sexist Society*, ed. Vivian Gornick and Barbara K. Moran [New York: New American Library, 1972], p. 396). In a historical study which also seeks to address the questions of women's status, Joanne McNamara and Suzanne Wemple ("The Power of Woman through the Family in Medieval Europe: 500–1100," *Feminist Studies* 1, nos 3–4 [Winter–Spring 1973]: 126–41) emphasize the private-public split in their discussion of women's loss of status during this period.

15. Patricia Draper, "!Kung Women: Contrasts in Sexual Egalitarianism in Foraging and Sedentary Contexts," in *Toward an Anthropology of Women*.

a close, public settlement arrangement, in which the huts were situated in a circle around the campfire.

In the late 1960s when Draper did her fieldwork, some of the !Kung were beginning to settle in small villages where the men took up herding and the women agriculture, like other groups (e.g., the Bantu) who were already settled. The agriculture and the food preparation were more time consuming for the women than gathering had been and, while they continued to gather from time to time, the new agricultural pursuits kept the women closer to home. The men, in contrast, through herding, remained mobile and had greater contact with the world outside the !Kung: the Bantus, politics, wage work, and advanced knowledge (e.g., about domesticated animals). These sex roles were maintained with more rigidity. Boys and girls came to be socialized differently, and men began to feel their work superior to the women's. Men began to consider property theirs (rather than jointly owned with the women), and "[r]anking of individuals in terms of prestige and differential worth ha[d] begun. . . ."[16] Houses, made more permanent and private, were no longer arranged in a circle. The women in particular felt that the group as a whole had less ability to observe, and perhaps to sanction, the behavior of people in married couples. Doubtless these changes occurred partly because of the influence of the male-dominated Western culture on the !Kung. The overall result, according to Draper, was a decrease in the status and influence of women, the denigration of their work, and an increase, for women, in the importance of the family unit at the expense of the influence of the group as a whole. The delineation of public and private spheres placed men in the public and women in the private sphere, and the public sphere came to be valued more.

Boserup, in *Woman's Role in Economic Development,* writes extensively of the particular problems caused for women when Third World tribal groups came into contact with Western colonial administrations.[17] The usual result was the creation or strengthening of male dominance as, for example, where administrations taught men advanced agricultural techniques where women were farmers, or schooled men in trading where women were traders. The Europeans encouraged men to head and support their families, superseding women's traditional responsibilities. Previous to colonization, according to Leavitt: "In regions like Africa and Southeast Asia, where shifting agriculture and the female farmer predominate, the women work very hard and receive limited support from their husbands, but they also have some economic independence, considerable freedom of movement, and an important place in the community. . . . In traditional African marriages the woman is expected to support herself and her children and to feed the family,

16. Ibid., p. 108.
17. Ester Boserup, *Woman's Role in Economic Development* (London: George Allen & Unwin, 1970).

including her husband, with the food she grows."[18] Boserup supports this view of the economic role of women before the influence of Europeans began to be felt.

Europeans also entrusted local governance to male leaders and ignored women's traditional participation in tribal society. That the women had highly organized and yet nonhierarchical governmental structures, which were unknown and ignored by the colonists, is illustrated by the case of the Igbo in Nigeria. Allen reports that Igbo women held *mikiri,* or meetings, which were democratic discussions with no official leaders and "which articulated women's interests *as opposed to* those of men."[19] The women needed these meetings because they lived in patrilocal villages and had few kinship ties with each other, and because they had their own separate economic activities, their own crops, and their own trading, which they needed to protect from men. When a man offended the women, by violating the women's market rules or letting his cows into the women's yam fields, the women often retaliated as a group by "sitting on a man"—carrying on loudly at his home late at night and "perhaps demolishing his hut or plastering it with mud and roughing him up a bit."[20] Women also sometimes executed collective strikes and boycotts. With the advent of the British administrators, and their inevitably unfavorable policies toward women, the Igbo women adapted their tactics and used them against the British. For example, in response to an attempt to tax the women farmers, tens of thousands of women were involved in riots at administrative centers over an area of 6,000 square miles containing a population of 2 million people. The "Women's War," as it was called, was coordinated through the market *mikiri* network.[21] Allen continues to detail the distintegration of the *mikiri* in the face of British colonial and missionary policies.

In a study of a somewhat different process of state formation, Muller looks at the decline of Anglo-Saxon and Welsh tribal society and the formation of the English nation-state, a process which occurred from the eighth to the fifteenth century. Muller writes:

> The transition from tribe to state is historically probably the greatest watershed in the decline in the status of women. . . . This is not to deny that in what we call "tribal," that is, pre-state, society there is not a wide variation in the status of women and even that in certain pre-state societies, women may be in what we would consider an abject position *vis à vis* the men in that society. . . . We

18. Leavitt, pp. 412, 413.
19. Judith Van Allen, " 'Sitting on a Man': Colonialism and the Lost Political Institutions of Igbo Women," *Canadian Journal of African Studies* 6, no. 2 (1972): 169.
20. Ibid., p. 170.
21. Ibid., pp. 174–75. The British naturally thought the women were directed in their struggle by the men, though very few men participated in the riots.

believe that the causes for these variations in status can be found, as in the case of State Societies, in the material conditions which give rise to the social and economic positions therein.[22]

Muller stresses that, in the Welsh and Anglo-Saxon tribes, "the right of individual maintenance was so well entrenched that these rights were not entrusted to a patriarchal head of a nuclear family, but were, rather, vested in the larger social group of the *gwely* [four-generation kinship group]."[23] Both men and women upon adulthood received a share of cattle from the *gwely*. The cattle provided their personal maintenance and prevented an individual from becoming dependent upon another. Thus, although in the tribal system land inheritance was patrilineal and residence patrilocal, a married woman had her own means of economic subsistence. Women were political participants both in their husbands' and in their natal lineages. Like a man, a woman was responsible for her children's crimes, and she and her natal lineages (*not* her spouse's) were responsible for her crimes. Tribal customs were, however, undermined by the emergence of the state. ". . . we can observe the development of public—as opposed to social—male authority, through the political structure imposed by the emerging state. Since the state is interested in the alienation of the tribal resource base—its land and its labor power —it finds it convenient to use the traditional gender division of labor and resources in tribal society and places them in a hierarchical relationship both internally (husband over wife and children) and externally (lords over peasants and serfs)."[24] The king established regional administrative units without regard to tribal jurisdictions, appointed his own administrators, bypassed the authority of the tribal chiefs, and levied obligations on the males as "heads" of individual households. Tribal groups lost collective responsibility for their members, and women and children lost their group rights and came under the authority of their husbands. Woman's work became private for the benefit of her husband, rather than public for the benefit of the kin group. As Muller points out, there must have been tendencies evident in tribal society that created the preconditions for a hierarchical, male-dominated state, for it was not equally likely that the emerging state would be female. Among these tendencies, for example, were male ownership of land and greater male participation in military expeditions, probably especially those farther away.[25]

22. Muller, p. 1. I am very grateful to Viana Muller for allowing me to summarize parts of her unpublished paper.

23. Ibid., p. 14.

24. Ibid., p. 25.

25. The examples of the !Kung, the Igbo, the Anglo-Saxons, and the groups discussed by Boserup all suggest that the process of expansion of state or emerging-state societies and the conquest of other peoples was an extremely important mechanism for

This summary of several studies from the third school of anthropology, the variationist school, points to a number of variables that help to explain a decrease in woman's social status. They suggest that increased sexual stratification occurs along with a general process of social stratification (which at least in some versions seems to depend on and foster an increase in social surplus—to support the higher groups in the hierarchy). As a result, a decrease in the social status of woman occurs when (1) she loses control of subsistence through a change in production methods and devaluation of her share of the division of labor; (2) her work becomes private and family centered rather than social and kin focused; and/or (3) some men assert their power over other men through the state mechanism by elevating these subordinate men in their families, using the nuclear family against the kin group.[26] In this way the division of labor between men and women becomes a more hierarchical one. Control over women is maintained directly in the family by the man, but it is sustained by social institutions, such as the state and religion.

The work in this school of anthropology suggests that patriarchy did not always exist, but rather that it emerged as social conditions changed. Moreover, men participated in this transformation. Because it benefited men relative to women, men have had a stake in reproducing patriarchy. Although there is a great deal of controversy among anthropologists about the origins of patriarchy, and more work needs to be done to establish the validity of this interpretation, I believe the weight of the evidence supports it. In any case, most anthropologists agree that patriarchy emerged long before capitalism, even if they disagree about its origins.

In England, as we have seen, the formation of the state marks the end of Anglo-Saxon tribal society and the beginning of feudal society. Throughout feudal society the tendencies toward the privatization of family life and the increase of male power within the family appear to strengthen, as does their institutional support from church and state. By the time of the emergence of capitalism in the fifteenth through eigh-

---

spreading hierarchy and male domination. In fact, the role of warfare and imperialism raises the question of whether the state, to establish itself, creates the patriarchal family, or the patriarchal family creates the state (Thomas Vietorisz, personal communication). Surely emerging patriarchal social relations in prestate societies paved the way for both male public power (i.e., male control of the state apparatus) and the privatization of patriarchal power in the family. Surely also this privatization—and the concomitant decline of tribal power—strengthened, and was strengthened by, the state.

26. This point is stressed especially by Muller but is also illustrated by the !Kung. Muller states: "The men, although lowered from clansmen to peasants, were elevated to heads of nuclear families, with a modicum of both public power [through the state and religion] and a measure of private power through the decree of the Church-State that they were to be lords over their wives" (p. 35).

teenth centuries, the nuclear, patriarchal peasant family had become the basic production unit in society.[27]

The Emergence of Capitalism and the Industrial Revolution in England and the United States

The key process in the emergence of capitalism was primitive accumulation, the prior accumulation that was necessary for capitalism to establish itself.[28] Primitive accumulation was a twofold process which set the preconditons for the expansion of the scale of production: first, free laborers had to be accumulated; second, large amounts of capital had to be accumulated. The first was achieved through enclosures and the removal of people from the land, their subsistence base, so that they were forced to work for wages. The second was achieved through both the growth of smaller capitals in farms and shops amassed through banking facilities, and vast increases in merchant capital, the profits from the slave trade, and colonial exploitation.

The creation of a wage-labor force and the increase in the scale of production that occurred with the emergence of capitalism had in some ways a more severe impact on women than on men. To understand this impact let us look at the work of women before this transition occurred and the changes which took place as it occurred.[29] In the 1500s and 1600s, agriculture, woolen textiles (carried on as a by-industry of ag-

27. Both Hill and Stone describe England during this period as a patriarchal society in which the institutions of the nuclear family, the state, and religion, were being strengthened (see Christopher Hill, *Society and Puritanism* [New York: Schocken Books, 1964], esp. chap. 13; Lawrence Stone, *The Crisis of the Aristocracy, 1558–1641,* abridged ed. [New York: Oxford University Press, 1967], esp. chap. 11). Recent demographic research verifies the establishment of the nuclear family prior to the industrial revolution (see Peter Laslett, ed., *Household and Family in Past Time* [Cambridge: Cambridge University Press, 1972]). Because of limitations of my knowledge and space, and because I sought to discuss, first, the concept and establishment of patriarchy and second, its transformation in a wage-labor society, I am skipping over the rise and fall of feudal society and the emergence of family-centered petty commodity production and focusing in the next section on the disintegration of this family-centered production, creation of the wage-labor force, and the maintenance of job segregation in a capitalist context.

28. See Karl Marx, "The So-called Primitive Accumulation," in *Capital,* 3 vols. (New York: International Publishers, 1967), vol. 1, pt. 8; Stephen Hymer, "Robinson Crusoe and the Secret of Primitive Accumulation," *Monthly Review* 23, no. 4 (September 1971): 11–36.

29. This account relies primarily on that of Alice Clark, *The Working Life of Women in the Seventeenth Century* (New York: Harcourt, Brace & Howe, 1920). Her account is supported by many others, such as B. L. Hutchins, *Women in Modern Industry* (London: G. Bell & Sons, 1915); Georgiana Hill, *Women in English Life from Medieval to Modern Times,* 2 vols. (London: Richard Bentley & Son, 1896); F. W. Tickner, *Women in English Economic History* (New York: E. P. Dutton & Co., 1923); Ivy Pinchbeck, *Women Workers and the Industrial Revolution, 1750–1850* (London: Frank Cass & Co., 1930; reprinted 1969).

riculture), and the various crafts and trades in the towns were the major sources of livelihood for the English population. In the rural areas men worked in the fields on small farms they owned or rented and women tended the household plots, small gardens and orchards, animals, and dairies. The women also spun and wove. A portion of these products were sold in small markets to supply the villages, towns, and cities, and in this way women supplied a considerable proportion of their families' cash income, as well as their subsistence in kind. In addition to the tenants and farmers, there was a small wage-earning class of men and women who worked on the larger farms. Occasionally tenants and their wives worked for wages as well, the men more often than the women.[30] As small farmers and cottagers were displaced by larger farmers in the seventeenth and eighteenth centuries, their wives lost their main sources of support, while the men were able to continue as wage laborers to some extent. Thus women, deprived of these essential household plots, suffered relatively greater unemployment, and the families as a whole were deprived of a large part of their subsistence.[31]

In the 1700s, the demand for cotton textiles grew, and English merchants found they could utilize the labor of the English agricultural population, who were already familiar with the arts of spinning and weaving. The merchants distributed materials to be spun and woven, creating a domestic industrial system which occupied many displaced farm families. This putting-out system, however, proved inadequate. The complexities of distribution and collection and, perhaps more important, the control the workers had over the production process (they could take time off, work intermittently, steal materials) prevented an increase in the supply of textiles sufficient to meet the merchants' needs. To solve these problems first spinning, in the late 1700s, and then weaving, in the early 1800s, were organized into factories. The textile factories were located in the rural areas, at first, in order both to take advantage of the labor of children and women, by escaping the restric-

30. Women and men in England had been employed as agricultural laborers for several centuries. Clark found that by the seventeenth century the wages of men were higher than women's and the tasks done were different, though similar in skill and strength requirements (Clark 1920, p. 60). Wages for agricultural (and other work) were often set by local authorities. These wage differentials reflected the relative social status of men and women and the social norms of the time. Women were considered to require lower wages because they ate less, for example, and were expected to have fewer luxuries, such as tobacco (see Clark and Pinchbeck throughout for substantiation of women's lower standard of living). Laura Oren has substantiated this for English women during the period 1860–1950 (see n. 60 below).

31. The problem of female unemployment in the countryside was a generally recognized one which figured prominently in the debate about poor-law reform, for example. As a remedy, it was suggested that rural families be allowed to retain small household plots, that women be used more in agricultural wage labor and also in the putting-out system, and that men's wages be adjusted upward (see Ivy Pinchbeck, *Women Workers and the Industrial Revolution, 1750–1850*, pp. 69–84).

tions of the guilds in the cities, and to utilize waterpower. When spinning was industrialized, women spinners at home suffered greater unemployment, while the demand for male handloom weavers increased. When weaving was mechanized, the need for handloom weavers fell off as well.[32]

In this way, domestic industry, created by emerging capitalism, was later superseded and destroyed by the progress of capitalist industrialization. In the process, women, children, and men in the rural areas all suffered dislocation and disruption, but they experienced this in different ways. Women, forced into unemployment by the capitalization of agriculture more frequently than men, were more available to labor, both in the domestic putting-out system and in the early factories. It is often argued both that men resisted going into the factories because they did not want to lose their independence and that women and children were more docile and malleable. If this was in fact the case, it would appear that these "character traits" of women and men were already established before the advent of the capitalistic organization of industry, and that they would have grown out of the authority structure prevailing in the previous period of small-scale, family agriculture. Many historians suggest that within the family men were the heads of households, and women, even though they contributed a large part of their families' subsistence, were subordinate.[33]

We may never know the facts of the authority structure within the preindustrial family, since much of what we know is from prescriptive literature or otherwise class biased, and little is known about the point of view of the people themselves. Nevertheless, the evidence on family life and on relative wages and levels of living suggests that women were subordinate within the family. This conclusion is consonant with the anthropological literature, reviewed in Part I above, which describes the emergence of patriarchial social relations along with early societal

32. See Stephen Marglin, "What Do Bosses Do? The Origins and Functions of Hierarchy in Capitalist Production," *Review of Radical Political Economics* 6, no. 2 (Summer 1974): 60–112, for a discussion of the transition from putting out to factories. The sexual division of labor changed several times in the textile industry. Hutchins writes that the further back one goes in history, the more was the industry controlled by women. By the seventeenth century, though, men had become professional handloom weavers, and it was often claimed that men had superior strength or skill—which was required for certain types of weaves or fabrics. Thus, the increase in demand for handloom weavers in the late 1700s brought increased employment for men. When weaving was mechanized in the factories women operated the power looms, and male handloom weavers became unemployed. When jenny and waterframe spinning were replaced by mule spinning, supposedly requiring more strength, men took that over and displaced women spinners. A similar transition occurred in the United States. It is important to keep in mind that as a by-industry, both men and women engaged in various processes of textile manufacture, and this was intensified under putting out (see Pinchbeck 1969, chaps. 6–9).

33. See Clark; Pinchbeck; E. P. Thompson, *The Making of the English Working Class* (New York: Vintage Books, 1963).

stratification. Moreover, the history of the early factories suggests that capitalists took advantage of this authority structure, finding women and children more vulnerable, both because of familial relations and because they were simply more desperate economically due to the changes in agriculture which left them unemployed.[34]

The transition to capitalism in the cities and towns was experienced somewhat differently than in the rural areas, but it tends to substantiate the line of argument just set out: men and women had different places in the familial authority structure, and capitalism proceeded in a way that built on that authority structure. In the towns and cities before the transition to capitalism a system of family industry prevailed: a family of artisans worked together at home to produce goods for exchange. Adults were organized in guilds, which had social and religious functions as well as industrial ones. Within trades carried on as family industries women and men generally performed different tasks: in general, the men worked at what were considered more skilled tasks, the women at processing the raw materials or finishing the end product. Men, usually the heads of the production units, had the status of master artisans. For though women usually belonged to their husbands' guilds, they did so as appendages; girls were rarely apprenticed to a trade and thus rarely become journeymen or masters. Married women participated in the production process and probably acquired important skills, but they usually controlled the production process only if they were widowed, when guilds often gave them the right to hire apprentices and journeymen. Young men may have married within their guilds (i.e., the daughters of artisans in the same trade). In fact, young women and girls had a unique and very important role as extra or casual laborers in a system where the guilds prohibited hiring additional workers from outside the family, and undoubtedly they learned skills which were useful when they married.[35] Nevertheless, girls appear not to have been trained as carefully as boys were and, as adults, not to have attained the same status in the guilds.

Although in most trades men were the central workers and women the assistants, other trades were so identified by sex that family industry did not prevail.[36] Carpentry and millinery were two such trades. Male carpenters and female milliners both hired apprentices and assistants

34. In fact, the earliest factories utilized the labor of poor children, already separated from their families, who were apprenticed to factory owners by parish authorities. They were perhaps the most desperate and vulnerable of all.

35. Hutchins, p. 16 (see also Olive J. Jocelyn, *English Apprenticeship and Child Labor* [London: T. Fisher Unwin, 1912], pp. 149–50, on the labor of girls, and Clark, chap. 5, on the organization of family industry in towns).

36. The seventeenth century already found the crafts and trades sex divided. Much work needs to be done on the development of guilds from the point of view of shedding light on the sexual division of labor and on the question of the nature of women's organizations. Such work would enable us to trace more accurately the decline in women's status from the tribal period, through feudalism, to the emergence of capitalism.

and attained the status of master craftspersons. According to Clark, although some women's trades, such as millinery, were highly skilled and organized in guilds, many women's trades were apparently difficult to organize in strong guilds, because most women's skills could not be easily monopolized. All women, as part of their home duties, knew the arts of textile manufacturing, sewing, food processing, and to some extent, trading.

In the seventeenth and eighteenth centuries the family industry system and the guilds began to break down in the face of the demand for larger output. Capitalists began to organize production on a larger scale, and production became separated from the home as the size of establishments grew. Women were excluded from participation in the industries in which they had assisted men as they no longer took place at home, where married women apparently tended to remain to carry on their domestic work. Yet many women out of necessity sought work in capitalistically organized industry as wage laborers. When women entered wage labor they appear to have been at a disadvantage relative to men. First, as in agriculture, there was already a tradition of lower wages for women (in the previously limited area of wage work). Second, women appear to have been less well trained than men and obtained less desirable jobs. And third, they appear to have been less well organized than men.

Because I think the ability of men to organize themselves played a crucial role in limiting women's participation in the wage-labor market, I want to offer, first, some evidence to support the assertion that men were better organized and, second, some plausible reasons for their superiority in this area. I am not arguing that men had greater organizational abilities at all times and all places, or in all areas or types of organization, but am arguing here that it is plausible that they did in England during this period, particularly in the area of economic production. As evidence of their superiority, we have the guilds themselves, which were better organized among men's trades than women's, and in which, in joint trades, men had superior positions—women were seldom admitted to the hierarchical ladder of progression. Second, we have the evidence of the rise of male professions and the elimination of female ones during the sixteenth and seventeenth centuries. The medical profession, male from its inception, established itself through hierarchical organization, the monopolization of new, "scientific" skills, and the assistance of the state. Midwifery was virtually wiped out by the men. Brewing provides another example. Male brewers organized a fellowship, petitioned the king for monopoly rights (in exchange for a tax on every quart they brewed), and succeeded in forcing the numerous small-scale brewsters to buy from them.[37] Third, throughout the formative period

37. See Clark, pp. 221–31, for the brewers, and pp. 242–84, for the medical profession.

of industrial capitalism, men appear to have been better able to organize themselves as wage workers. And as we shall see below, as factory production became established men used their labor organizations to limit women's place in the labor market.

As to why men might have had superior organizational ability during this transitional period, I think we must consider the development of patriarchal social relations in the nuclear family, as reinforced by the state and religion, a process briefly described above for Anglo-Saxon England. Since men's superior position was reinforced by the state, and men acted in the political arena as heads of households and in the households as heads of production units, it seems likely that men would develop more organizational structures beyond their households. Women, in an inferior position at home and without the support of the state, would be less likely to be able to do this. Men's organizational knowledge, then, grew out of their position in the family and in the division of labor. Clearly, further investigation of organizations before and during the transition period is necessary to establish the mechanisms by which men came to control this public sphere.

Thus, the capitalistic organization of industry, in removing work from the home, served to increase the subordination of women, since it served to increase the relative importance of the area of men's domination. But it is important to remember that men's domination was already established and that it clearly influenced the direction and shape that capitalist development took. As Clark has argued, with the separation of work from the home men became less dependent on women for industrial production, while women became more dependent on men economically. From a position much like that of the African women discussed in Part I above, English married women, who had supported themselves and their children, became the domestic servants of their husbands. Men increased their control over technology, production, and marketing, as they excluded women from industry, education, and political organization.[38]

When women participated in the wage-labor market, they did so in a position as clearly limited by patriarchy as it was by capitalism. Men's control over women's labor was altered by the wage-labor system, but it was not eliminated. In the labor market the dominant position of men was maintained by sex-ordered job segregation. Women's jobs were lower paid, considered less skilled, and often involved less exercise of

38. Ibid., chap. 7. Eli Zaretsky ("Capitalism, the Family, and Personal Life," *Socialist Revolution*, nos. 13, 14 [1973]), follows a similar interpretation of history and offers different conclusions. Capitalism exacerbated the sexual division of labor and created the *appearance* that women work for their husbands; in reality, women who did domestic work at home were working for capital. Thus according to Zaretsky the present situation has its roots more in capitalism than in patriarchy. Although capitalism may have increased the consequence for women of the domestic division of labor, surely patriarchy tells us more about why men didn't stay home. That women worked for men in the home, as well as for capital, is also a reality.

authority or control.[39] Men acted to enforce job segregation in the labor market; they utilized trade-union associations and strengthened the domestic division of labor, which required women to do housework, child care, and related chores. Women's subordinate position in the labor market reinforced their subordinate position in the family, and that in turn reinforced their labor-market position.

The process of industrialization and the establishment of the factory system, particularly in the textile industry, illustrate the role played by men's trade-union associations. Textile factories employed children at first, but as they expanded they began to utilize the labor of adult women and of whole families. While the number of married women working has been greatly exaggerated,[40] apparently enough married women had followed their work into the factories to cause both their husbands and the upper classes concern about home life and the care of children. Smelser has argued that in the early factories the family industry system and male control could often be maintained. For example, adult male spinners often hired their own or related children as helpers, and whole families were often employed by the same factory for the same length of working day.[41] Technological change, however, increasingly made this difficult, and factory legislation which limited the hours of children, but not of adults, further exacerbated the difficulties of the "family factory system."

The demands of the factory laborers in the 1820s and 1830s had

39. William Lazonick argues in his dissertation, "Marxian Theory and the Development of the Labor Force in England" (Ph.D. diss., Harvard University, 1975), that the degree of authority required of the worker was often decisive in determining the sex of the worker. Thus handloom weavers in cottage industry were men because this allowed them to control the production process and the labor of the female spinners. In the spinning factories, mule spinners were men because mule spinners were required to supervise the labor of piecers, usually young boys. Men's position as head of the family established their position as heads of production units, and vice versa. While this is certainly plausible, I think it requires further investigation. Lazonick's work in this area (see chap. 4, "Segments of the Labour Force: Women, Children, and Irish") is very valuable.

40. Perhaps 25 percent of female textile factory workers were married women (see Pinchbeck, p. 198; Margaret Hewitt, *Wives and Mothers in Victorian Industry* [London: Rockliff, 1958], pp. 14 ff.). It is important to remember also that factory employment was far from the dominant employment of women. Most women worked as domestic servants.

41. Neil Smelser, *Social Change and the Industrial Revolution* (Chicago: University of Chicago Press, 1959), chaps. 9–11. Other researchers have also established that in some cases there was a considerable degree of familial control over some aspects of the work process. See Tamara Hareven's research on mills in New Hampshire; e.g., "Family Time and Industrial Time: The Interaction between Family and Work in a Planned Corporation Town, 1900–1924," *Journal of Urban History* 1, no. 3 (May 1975): 365–89. Michael Anderson, *Family Structure in Nineteenth Century Lancashire* (Cambridge: Cambridge University Press, 1971), argues, based on demographic data, that the "practice of allowing operatives to employ assistants, though widespread, can at no period have resulted in a predominantly parent-child pattern of employment" (p. 116). Also see Amy Hirsch's treatment of this question in her "Capitalism and the Working Class Family in British Textile Industries during the Industrial Revolution," mimeographed (New York: New School for Social Research, 1975).

been designed to maintain the family factory system,[42] but by 1840 male factory operatives were calling for limitations on the hours of work of children between nine and thirteen to eight a day, and forbidding the employment of younger children. According to Smelser this caused parents difficulty in training and supervising their children, and to remedy it male workers and the middle and upper classes began to recommend that women, too, be removed from the factories.[43]

The upper classes of the Victorian Age, the age that elevated women to their pedestals, seem to have been motivated by moral outrage and concern for the future of the English race (and for the reproduction of the working class): "In the male," said Lord Shaftesbury, "the moral effects of the system are very sad, but in the female they are infinitely worse, not alone upon themselves, but upon their families, upon society, and, I may add, upon the country itself. It is bad enough if you corrupt the man, but if you corrupt the woman, you poison the waters of life at the very fountain."[44] Engels, too, appears to have been outraged for similar reasons: ". . . we find here precisely the same features reappearing which the Factories' Report presented,—the work of women up to the hour of confinement, incapacity as housekeepers, neglect of home and children, indifference, actual dislike to family life, and demoralization; further the crowding out of men from employment, the constant improvement of machinery, early emancipation of children, husbands supported by their wives and children, etc., etc."[45] Here, Engels has

42. "[The factory operatives'] agitation in the 1820's and 1830's was one avenue taken to protect the traditional relationship between adult and child, to perpetuate the structure of wages, to limit the recruitment of labourers into industry, and to maintain the father's economic authority" (Smelser, p. 265). Lazonick argues that the workers' main interest were not in maintaining their familial dominance in industry but in maintaining their family life outside industry. According to Smelser, agitation before 1840 sought to establish equal length days for all workers, which would tend to maintain the family in the factory, whereas after 1840 male workers came to accept the notion that married women and children should stay at home.

43. The question of the motives of the various groups involved in passing the factory acts is indeed a thorny one. Women workers themselves may have favored the legislation as an improvement in their working conditions, but some undoubtedly needed the incomes longer hours enabled. Most women working in the mills were young, single women who perhaps benefited from the protection. Single women, though "liberated" by the mills from direct domination in their families (about which there was much discussion in the 1800s), were nevertheless kept in their place by the conditions facing them in the labor market. Because of their age and sex, job segregation and lower wages assured their inability to be completely self-sufficient. Ruling-class men, especially those associated with the larger firms, may have had an interest in factory legislation in order to eliminate unfair competition. Working-class and ruling-class men may have cooperated to maintain men's dominant position in the labor market and in the family.

44. From Mary Merryweather, *Factory Life,* cited in *Women in English Life from Medieval to Modern Times,* 2: 200. The original is recorded in *Hansard Parliamentary Debates,* 3d ser., House of Commons, June 7, 1842.

45. Frederick Engels, *The Condition of the Working Class in England in 1844* (London: Geo. Allen & Unwin, 1892), p. 199.

touched upon the reasons for the opposition of the male workers to the situation. Engels was apparently ambivalent about whose side he was on, for, while he often seems to share the attitudes of the men and of the upper classes, he also referred to the trade unions as elite organizations of grown-up men who achieved benefits for themselves but not for the unskilled, women, or children.[46]

That male workers viewed the employment of women as a threat to their jobs is not surprising, given an economic system where competition among workers was characteristic. That women were paid lower wages exacerbated the threat. But why their response was to attempt to exclude women rather than to organize them is explained, not by capitalism, but by patriarchal relations between men and women: men wanted to assure that women would continue to perform the appropriate tasks at home.

Engels reports an incident which probably occurred in the 1830s. Male Glasgow spinners had formed a secret union: "The Committee put a price on the heads of all blacklegs [strikebreakers] . . . and deliberately organized arson in factories. One factory to be set on fire had women blacklegs on the premises who had taken the places of men at the spinning machines. A certain Mrs. MacPherson, the mother of one of these girls, was murdered and those responsible were shipped off to America at the expense of the union."[47] Hostility to the competition of young females, almost certainly less well trained and lower paid, was common enough. But if anything, the wage work of married women was thought even less excusable.

In 1846 the *Ten Hours' Advocate* stated clearly that they hoped for the day when such threats would be removed altogether: ". . . It is needless for us to say, that all attempts to improve the morals and physical condition of female factory workers will be abortive, unless their hours are materially reduced. Indeed we may go so far as to say, that married females would be much better occupied in performing the domestic duties of the household, than following the never-tiring motion of machinery. We therefore hope the day is not distant, when the husband will be able to provide for his wife and family, without sending the former to endure the drudgery of a cotton mill."[48] Eventually, male trade unionists realized that women could not be removed altogether, but their attitude was still ambivalent. One local wrote to the Women's Trade Union League, organized in 1889 to encourage unionization among women workers: "Please send an organizer to this town as we

---

46. Ibid., p. xv.

47. Engels, *The Condition of the Working Class in England in 1844* (Stanford, Calif.: Stanford University Press, 1968), p. 251.

48. Smelser, p. 301. Similarly, Pinchbeck quotes from a deputation of the West Riding Short-Time Committee which demands "the gradual withdrawal of all females from the factories" because "home, its cares, its employments, is woman's true sphere." Gladstone thought this a good suggestion, easily implemented by appropriate laws, e.g., "forbidding a female to work in a factory after her marriage and during the life-time of her husband" (Pinchbeck, p. 200, n. 3, from the *Manchester and Salford Advertiser* [January 8, 15, 1842]).

have decided that if the women here cannot be organized they must be exterminated."[49]

The deplorable situation of women in the labor market was explained in a variety of ways by British historians and economists writing in the early twentieth century. Some accepted the logic of the male unions that women belonged at home if possible and men's wages should be increased. Ivy Pinchbeck, for example, stated: ". . . the industrial revolution marked a real advance, since it led to the assumption that men's wages should be paid on a family basis, and prepared the way for the more modern conception that in the rearing of children and in homemaking, the married woman makes an adequate economic contribution."[50] Others argued that this system would only perpetuate women's low economic status. Examining the literature from this period, especially the Webb-Rathbone-Fawcett-Edgeworth series in the *Economic Journal,* is important because it sets the framework for nearly all the explanations of women's position in the labor market that have been used since. In addition, this literature tends to support the argument, delineated in this paper, that job segregation was detrimental to women and that male unions tended to enforce it.

Several writers who focused on job segregation and noncompeting groups as the central mechanism discussed the actions of male unionists as well. Webb offered as a justification for the lower wages women received the explanation that they rarely did the same grade of work, even when engaged in the same occupation or industry. He cited cigar making, where men made fancy cigars and women made cheap ones requiring less skill.[51] Yet he also acknowledged the role male unions played in preventing women from gaining skills and admitted the possibility that, even for equal work, women received lower wages.[52]

49. Quoted in G. D. H. Cole and Raymond Postgate, *The Common People, 1746–1946,* 4th ed. (London: Methuen, 1949), p. 432.

50. Pinchbeck, pp. 312–13. The history of the emergence of capitalism and the Industrial Revolution clearly shows that the "family wage" is a recent phenomenon. Before the late 1800s, it was expected that working-class (and earlier, middle- and upper-class) married women would support themselves. Andrew Ure, a manufacturer, wrote in 1835: "Factory females have also in general much lower wages than males, and they have been pitied on this account with perhaps an injudicious sympathy, since the low price of their labour here tends to make household duties their most profitable as well as agreeable occupation, and prevents them from being tempted by the mill to abandon the care of their offspring at home. Thus Providence effects its purposes with a wisdom and efficacy which should repress the short-sighted presumption of human devices" (*The Philosophy of Manufacturers* [London: C. Knight, 1835], p. 475). The development of the family wage is discussed in somewhat greater detail in Heidi Hartmann, "Capitalism and Women's Work in the Home, 1900–1930" (Ph.D. diss., Yale University, 1974). More work needs to be done on this concept.

51. Sidney Webb, "The Alleged Differences in the Wages Paid to Men and Women for Similar Work," *Economic Journal* 1, no. 4 (December 1891): 639.

52. The competition between men and women in industry is, indeed, not so much a direct underselling in wages as a struggle to secure the better paid kinds of work (ibid., p. 658).

Millicent Fawcett argued that equal pay for equal work was a fraud for women, since having been kept from obtaining equal skills their work (at the same jobs) was, in fact, not equal.[53] The essence of trade-union policy, she felt, was to exclude women if they were less efficient and, furthermore, to keep them less efficient.[54] As Eleanor Rathbone put it in 1917, male union leaders will support equal pay as "an effective way of maintaining the exclusion of women while appearing as the champions of equality between the sexes." Many of the followers, she thought, "are obviously rather shocked in their hearts at the idea of a woman earning a man's pay."[55]

Rathbone also considered seriously the different family responsibilities of women. They are a reality, she insisted; men do support their families more often than women do, and men want sufficient money to do this. But she did not necessarily agree with this arrangement; she simply acknowledged that most people considered it "a fundamental part of the social structure":

> The line of argument I have been following usually either irritates or depresses all women who have the interests of their own sex at heart, because it seems to point to an impasse. If the wages of men and women are really based upon fundamentally different conditions, and if these conditions cannot be changed, then it would seem . . . that women are the eternal blacklegs, doomed despite themselves to injure the prospects of men whenever they are brought into competition with them. . . . If that were really so, then it would seem as if men were justified in treating women, as in practice they have treated them—as a kind of industrial lepers, segregated in trades which men have agreed to abandon to them, permitted to occupy themselves in making clothes or in doing domestic services for each other, and in performing those subsidiary processes in the big staple trades, which are so monotonous or unskilled that men do not care to claim them.[56]

World War I, however, had raised women's expectations, and women were not likely to go back to their place willingly—even though the male

53. Millicent G. Fawcett, "Mr. Sidney Webb's Article on Women's Wages," *Economic Journal* 2, no. 1 (March 1892): 173–76.

54. In her review of *Women in the Printing Trades*, ed. J. Ramsay Mac Donald, Fawcett wrote that a trade union in Scotland "decided that women must either be paid the same rates as men or got rid of altogether" (p. 296). She cites "the constant and vigilant opposition of Trades Unions to the employment and the technical training of women in the better paid and more skilled branches of trade" (p. 297). As one example, she cites the London Society of Journeymen Bookbinders who tried to get the highly skilled job of laying gold leaf—a women's job—assigned to the male union members (*Economic Journal* 14, no. 2 [June 1904]: 295–99).

55. Eleanor F. Rathbone, "The Remuneration of Women's Services," *Economic Journal* 27, no. 1 (March 1917): 58.

56. Ibid., pp. 62, 63.

unions had been promised that the women's jobs were only temporary—especially since in addition to their wages, married women whose husbands were at war received government allowances according to family size. Rathbone wrote: ". . . the future solution of the problem is doubtful and difficult, and . . . it opens up unpleasant possibilities of class antagonism and sex antagonism; . . . for women especially it seems to offer a choice between being exploited by capitalists or dragooned and oppressed by trade unionists. It is a dismal alternative."[57] She recommended the continuation of allowances after the war because they would insure that families would not have to rely on men's wages, that women who stayed at home would be paid for their work, and that women in the labor market could complete equally with men since their "required" wages would not be different. By 1918, Fawcett also thought equal pay for equal work a realizable goal. Advancement in the labor market required equal pay in order not to undercut the men's wages. The main obstacles, she argued, were the male unions and social customs. Both led to overcrowding in the women's jobs.[58]

In 1922, Edgeworth formalized Fawcett's job segregation and overcrowding model; job segregation by sex causes overcrowding in female sectors, which allows men's wages to be higher and forces women's wages to be lower, than they would be otherwise. Edgeworth agreed that male unions were the main cause of overcrowding.[59] He argued that men *should* have an advantage because of their family responsibilities, and the corollary, that since women do not have the same family responsibilities as men, and may even be subsidized by men, their participation will tend to pull wages down. And he seemed to suggest that equal competition in the job market would result in lower wages even for single women vis-à-vis single men, because women required 20 percent less food for top efficiency. In this last, Edgeworth was simply taking seriously what many had remarked upon—that women have a lower standard of living than men and are willing to work for less.[60] Edgeworth concluded that restrictions on women's work should be removed but that, since unfet-

57. Ibid., p. 64.
58. Millicent G. Fawcett, "Equal Pay for Equal Work," *Economic Journal* 28, no. 1 (March 1918): 1–6.
59. "The pressure of male trade unions appears to be largely responsible for that crowding of women into comparatively few occupations, which is universally recognized as a main factor in the depression of their wages" (F. Y. Edgeworth, "Equal Pay to Men and Women for Equal Work," *Economic Journal* 32, no. 4 [December 1922]: 439).
60. While this reasoning may sound circular, I believe it is quite valid. As Marx said, wages are determined by the value of the socially necessary commodities required to maintain the worker, and what is necessary is the product of historical development, of customs of comfort, of trade union activity, etc. (*Capital*, 1: 171). Laura Oren has examined the literature on the level of living of work-class families and found that, indeed, within the family, women have less food, less leisure, and less pocket money ("The Welfare of Women in Laboring Families: England, 1860–1950," *Feminist Studies* 1, nos. 3–4 [Winter-Spring 1973]: 107–25). That women, like immigrant groups, can reproduce themselves on less, and have for centuries, is a contributing factor in their lower wages.

tered competition would probably drag down the wages of men for the reasons noted above, men and families should be compensated for their losses due to the increased participation of women.[61]

The main explanation the English literature offers for lower wages is job segregation by sex, and for both lower wages and the existence of job segregation it offers several interdependent explanations: (1) the exclusionary policies of male unions, (2) the financial responsibility of men for their families, (3) the willingness of women to work for less (and their inability to get more) because of subsidies or a lower standard of living, and (4) women's lack of training and skills. The English historical literature strongly suggests that job segregation by sex is patriarchal in origin, rather longstanding, and difficult to eradicate. Men's ability to organize in labor unions—stemming perhaps from a greater knowledge of the technique of hierarchical organization—appears to be key in their ability to maintain job segregation and the domestic division of labor.

Turning to the United States experience provides an opportunity, first, to explore shifts in the sex composition of jobs, and, second, to consider further the role of unions, particularly in establishing protective legislation. The American literature, especially the works of Abbott and Baker,[62] emphasizes sex shifts in jobs and, in contrast to the English literature, relies more heavily on technology as an explanatory phenomenon.

Conditions in the United States differed from those in England. First, the division of labor within colonial farm families was probably more rigid, with men in the fields and women producing manufactured articles at home. Second, the early textile factories employed young single women from the farms of New England; a conscious effort was made, probably out of necessity, to avoid the creation of a family labor system and to preserve the labor of men for agriculture.[63] This changed, however, with the eventual dominance of manufacture over agriculture as the leading sector in the economy and with immigration. Third, the shortage of labor and dire necessity in colonial and frontier America perhaps created more opportunities for women in nontraditional pursuits outside the family; colonial women were engaged in a wide variety

61. Edgeworth's conclusions are typical of those of neoclassical economists. In furthering Fawcett's analysis he further abstracted from reality. Whereas Fawcett had realized that women were not less efficient than men, and Rathbone had argued similarly, Edgeworth clung to the notion that men deserved more and sought to justify it theoretically. He opposed family allowances, also with neoclassical reasoning because they would raise taxes, discourage investment, encourage the reproduction of the poorer classes, and remove the incentive for men to work. Edgeworth reports the comment of a lady-inspector: "I almost agree with the social worker who said that if the husband got out of work the only thing that the wife should do is to sit down and cry, because if she did anything else he would remain out of work" (p. 453).

62. Edith Abbott, *Women in Industry* (New York: Arno Press, 1969); Elizabeth F. Baker, *Technology and Woman's Work* (New York: Columbia University Press, 1964).

63. See Abbott, esp. chap. 4.

of occupations.[64] Fourth, shortages of labor continued to operate in women's favor at various points throughout the nineteenth and twentieth centuries. Fifth, the constant arrival of new groups of immigrants created an extremely heterogeneous labor force, with varying skill levels and organizational development and rampant antagonisms.[65]

Major shifts in the sex composition of employment occurred in boot and shoe manufacture, textile manufacture, teaching, cigar making, and clerical work.[66] In all of these, except textiles, the shift was toward more women. New occupations opened up for both men and women, but men seemed to dominate in most of them, even though there were exceptions. Telephone operating and typing for example, became women's jobs.

In all of the cases of increase in female employment, the women were partially stimulated by a sharp rise in the demand for the service or product. During the late 1700s and early 1800s, domestic demand for ready-made boots went up because of the war, a greater number of slaves, general population expansion, and the settling of the frontier. Demand for teachers increased rapidly before, during, and after the Civil War as public education spread. The demand for cheap, machine-made cigars grew rapidly at the end of the nineteenth century. The upward shift in the numbers of clerical workers came between 1890 and 1930, when businesses grew larger and became more centralized, requiring more administration, distribution, transportation, marketing, and communication.

In several cases the shift to women was accompanied by technical innovations, which allowed increased output and sometimes reduced the skill required of the worker. By 1800, boot- and shoemakers had devised a division of labor which allowed women to work on sewing the uppers at home. In the 1850s, sewing machines were applied to boots and shoes in factories. In the 1870s, the use of wooden molds, rather than hand bunching, simplified cigar making, and in the 1880s, machinery was brought in. And in clerical work, the typewriter, of course, greatly increased the productivity of clerical labor. The machinery introduced in textiles, mule spinners, was traditionally operated by males. In printing, where male unions were successful in excluding women, the unions insisted on staffing the new linotypes.[67]

64. Ibid., chap. 2.

65. These antagonisms were often increased by employers. During a cigar-makers strike in New York City in 1877 employers brought in unskilled native American girls. By printing on the boxes, "These cigars were made by American girls," they sold many more boxes of the imperfect cigars than they had expected to (Abbott, p. 207).

66. This summary is based on Abbott and is substantiated by both Baker and Helen L. Sumner, *History of Women in Industry in the United States, 1910,* United States Bureau of Labor, *Report on Condition of Women and Child Wage-Earners in the United States* (Washington, D.C.: Government Printing Office, 1911), vol. 9.

67. Baker and Abbott rely heavily on technological factors coupled with biological sex differences as explanations of shifts in the sex composition of jobs. Increased speed of

The central purposes of subdividing the labor process, simplifying tasks, and introducing machines were to raise production, to cheapen it, and to increase management's control over the labor process. Subdivision of the labor process ordinarily allowed the use of less skilled labor in one or more subportions of the task. Cheapening of labor power and more control over labor were the motive forces behind scientific management and earlier efforts to reorganize labor.[68] Machinery was an aid in the process, not a motive force. Machinery, unskilled labor, and women workers often went together.

In addition to greater demand and technical change, often a shortage of the usual supply of labor contributed to a change in the labor force. In textiles, for example, in the 1840s the young New England farm women were attracted to new job opportunities for middle-class women, such as teaching. Their places in the mills were taken by immigrants. In boots and shoes the increased demand could not be met by the available trained shoemakers. And in clerical work the supply of high school educated males was not equal to the increase in demand. Moreover, in clerical work in particular the changes that occurred in the job structure reduced its attractiveness to men—with expansion, the jobs became dead-end ones—while for women the opportunities compared favorably with their opportunities elsewhere.[69]

Cigar making offers ample opportunity to illustrate both the opposition of male unionists to impending sex changes in labor-force composition in their industries and the form that opposition took: protective

---

machines and sometimes increased heaviness are cited as favoring men, who are stronger and have longer endurance, etc. Yet often each cites statistics which indicate that the same types of machines are used by both sexes; e.g., mule spinning machines. I would argue that these perceived differences are merely rationalizations used to justify the current sex assignment of tasks. Social pressures were powerful mechanisms of enforcement. Abbott gives several examples of this. A woman had apparently learned the mule in Lawrence and went to Waltham when mules were introduced there. She had to leave, however, because according to a male operative: "The men made unpleasant remarks and it was too hard for her, being the only woman" (p. 92). And: "Some of the oldest employees in the New England mills to-day [1910] say they can remember when weaving was so universally considered women's work that a 'man weaver' was held up to public ridicule for holding a 'woman's job' " (p. 95).

68. See Harry Braverman, *Labor and Monopoly Capital* (New York: Monthly Review Press, 1974), esp. chaps. 3–5.

69. Elyce J. Rotella, "Occupational Segregation and the Supply of Women to the American Clerical Labor Force, 1870–1930" (paper presented at the Berkshire Conference on the History of Women, Radcliffe College, October 25–27, 1974). Despite the long-standing recognition of job segregation and shifts in sex composition, there are surprisingly few studies of the process of shifting. In addition to Rotella for clerical workers there is Margery Davies, "Woman's Place Is at the Typewriter," *Radical America* 8, no. 4 (July-August 1974): 1–28. Valerie K. Oppenheimer discusses the shift in elementary teaching in *The Female Labor Force in the United States* (Berkeley: Institute of International Studies, University of California, 1970). And Abbott and Baker discuss several shifts.

legislation.[70] Cigar making was a home industry before 1800, when women on farms in Connecticut and elsewhere made rather rough cigars and traded them at village stores. Early factories employed women, but they were soon replaced by skilled male immigrants whose products could compete with fancy European cigars. By 1860, women were only 9 percent of the employed in cigar making. This switch to men was followed by one to women, but not without opposition from the men. In 1869, the wooden mold was introduced, and so were Bohemian immigrant women (who had been skilled workers in cigar factories in Austria-Hungary).[71] The Bohemian women, established by tobacco companies in tenements, perfected a division of labor in which young girls (and later their husbands)[72] could use the molds. Beginning in 1873 the Cigarmakers International Union agitated vociferously against home work, which was eventually restricted (for example, in New York in 1894). In the late 1880s machinery was introduced into the factories, and women were used as strikebreakers. The union turned to protective legislation.

The attitude of the Cigarmakers International Union toward women was ambivalent at best. The union excluded women in 1864, but admitted them in 1867. In 1875 it prohibited locals from excluding women, but apparently never imposed sanctions on offending locals.[73] In 1878 a Baltimore local wrote Adolph Strasser, the union president: "We have combatted from its incipiency the movement of the introduction of female labor in any capacity whatever, be it bunch maker, roller, or what not."[74] Lest these ambiguities be interpreted as national-local conflicts, let Strasser speak for himself (1879): "We cannot drive the females out of the trade, but we can restrict their daily quota of labor through factory laws. No girl under 18 should be employed more than eight hours per day; all overwork should be prohibited. . . ."[75]

70. This account is based primarily on Abbott, chap. 9, and Baker, pp. 31–36.

71. According to Abbott, Samuel Gompers claimed the Bohemian women were brought in for the express purpose of strikebreaking (p. 197, n.).

72. Bohemian women came to America first, leaving their husbands behind to work on the fields. Their husbands, who were unskilled at the cigar trade, came over later (ibid., p. 199).

73. In 1877 a Cincinnati local struck to exclude women and was apparently successful. The *Cincinnati Inquirer* said: "The men say the women are killing the industry. It would seem that they hope to retaliate by killing the women" (ibid., p. 207).

74. Baker, p. 34.

75. John B. Andrews and W. D. P. Bliss, *History of Women in Trade Unions* in *Report on Condition of Woman and Child Wage-Earners in the United States*, vol. 10. Although the proportion of women in cigar making did increase eventually, in many other manufacturing industries the proportion of women decreased over time. Textiles and clothing are the outstanding examples (see Abbott, p. 320, and her "The History of Industrial Employment of Women in the United States," *Journal of Political Economy* 14 [October 1906]: 461–501). Sumner, cited in U.S. Bureau of Labor Statistics, Bulletin 175, concluded that men had taken over the skilled jobs in

Because women are unskilled workers, it may be erroneous to interpret this as animosity to *women* per se. Rather it is the fear of the skilled for the unskilled. Yet male unions denied women skills, while they offered them to young boys. This is quite clear in the case of printing.[76]

Women had been engaged as typesetters in printing from colonial times. It was a skilled trade, but required no heavy work. Abbott attributed the jealousy of the men in the trade to the fact that it was a trade "suited" to women. In any case, male unions seem to have been hostile to the employment of women from the beginning. In 1854 the National Typographical Union resolved not to "encourage by its act the employment of female compositors."[77] Baker suggests that the unions discouraged girls from learning the trade, and so women learned what they could in nonunion shops or as strikebreakers.[78] In 1869, at the annual convention of the National Labor Union, of which the National Typographical Union was a member, a struggle occurred over the seating of Susan B. Anthony, because she had allegedly used women compositors as strikebreakers. She had, she admitted, because they could learn the trade no other way.[79] in 1870 the Typographical Union charted a women's local in New York City. Its president, Augusta Lewis, who was also corresponding secretary of the National Typographical Union did not think the women's union could hold out for very long, because, although the union women supported the union men, the union men did not support the union women: "It is the general opinion of female compositors that they are more justly treated by what is termed 'rat' foremen, printers, and employers than they are by union men."[80] The women's local eventually folded in 1878.

Apparently, the general lack of support was successful from the men's point of view, for, in 1910, Abbott claimed that: "Officers of other trade unions frequently refer to the policy of the printers as an example of the way in which trade union control may be successful in checking or preventing the employment of women."[81] The Typographical Union

---

women's traditional fields, and women had to take unskilled work wherever they could find it (p. 28).

76. This account is based primarily on Abbott and Baker. The hostility to training women seems generalizable. The International Molders Union resolved: "Any member, honorary or active, who devotes his time in whole or in part to the instruction of female help in the foundry, or in any branch of the trade shall be expelled from the Union" (Gail Falk, "Women and Unions: A Historical View," mimeographed [New Haven, Conn.: Yale Law School, 1970]. Published in somewhat shortened form in *Women's Rights Law Reporter* 1 [Spring 1973]: 54–65).

77. Abbott, pp. 252 3.

78. Baker, pp. 39–40.

79. See Falk.

80. Eleanor Flexner, *Century of Struggle* (New York: Atheneum Publishers, 1970), p. 136.

81. Abbott, p. 260.

strongly backed equal pay for equal work as a way to protect the men's wage scale, not to encourage women. Women who had fewer skills could not demand, and expect to receive, equal wages.[82]

Unions excluded women in many ways,[83] not the least among them protective legislation. In this the unions were aided by the prevailing social sentiment about work for women, especially married women, which was seen as a social evil which ideally should be wiped out,[84] and by a strong concern on the part of "social feminists"[85] and others that women workers were severely exploited because they were unorganized. The social feminists did not intend to exclude women from desirable occupations but their strategy paved the way for this exclusion, because, to get protection for working women—which they felt was so desperately needed—they argued that women, as a sex, were weaker than men and more in need of protection.[86] Their strategy was successful in 1908 in *Muller* v. *Oregon*, when the Supreme Court upheld maximum hours laws

82. Baker observed that the testimony on the Equal Pay Act in 1963 was about evenly divided between those emphasizing women's needs and those emphasizing the protection of men (p. 419).

83. Falk noted that unions used constitutional exclusion, exclusion from apprenticeship, limitation of women to helper categories or nonladder apprenticeships, limitation of proportion of union members who could be women, i.e., quotas, and excessively high fees. Moreover, the craft unions of this period, pre-1930, had a general hostility toward organizing the unskilled, even those attached to their crafts.

84. Such a diverse group as Caroll Wright, first U.S. Labor Commissioner (Baker, p. 84), Samuel Gompers and Mother Mary Jones, traditional and radical labor organizers, respectively (Falk), James L. Davis, U.S. Secretary of Labor, 1922 (Baker, p. 400), Florence Kelley, head of the National Consumers League (Hill), all held views which were variations of this theme. (Hill is Ann C. Hill, "Protective Labor Legislation for Women: Its Origin and Effect," mimeographed [New Haven, Conn: Yale Law School, 1970], parts of which have been published in Barbara A. Babcock, Ann E. Freedman, Eleanor H. Norton, and Susan C. Ross, *Sex Discrimination and the Law: Causes and Remedies* [Boston: Little, Brown & Co., 1975], a law text which provides an excellent analysis of protective legislation, discrimination against women, etc.)

85. William O'Neill characterized those women who participated in various reform movements in the late nineteenth and early twentieth centuries "social feminists" to distinguish them from earlier feminists like Stanton and Anthony. The social feminists came to support women's rights because they thought it would help advance the cause of their reforms; they were not primarily interested in advancing the cause of women's rights (*Everyone Was Brave* [Chicago: Quadrangle Books, 1969], esp. chap. 3). William H. Chafe, *The American Woman* (New York: Oxford University Press, 1972), also provides an excellent discussion of the debate around protective laws.

86. What was achievable, from the legislatures and the courts, was what the social feminists aimed for. Because in Ritchie v. People (155 Ill 98 [1895]), the court had held that sex alone was not a valid basis for a legislature to abridge the right of an adult to contract for work and, thus, struck down a maximum-hours law for women, and because a maximum-hours law for baking employees had been struck down by the U.S. Supreme Court (Lockner), advocates of protective labor legislation believed their task would be difficult. The famous "Brandeis Brief" compiled hundreds of pages on the harmful effects of long hours of work and argued that women needed "especial protection" (see Babcock et al.).

for women, saying: "The two sexes differ in structure of body, in the
capacity for long-continued labor particularly when done standing, the
influence of vigorous health upon the future well-being of the race, the
self-reliance which enables one to assert full rights, and in the capacity to
maintain the struggle for subsistence. This difference justifies a difference in legislation and upholds that which is designed to compensate for
some of the burdens which rest upon her."[87]

In 1916 in *Bunting* v. *Oregon* Brandeis used virtually the same data
on the ill effects of long hours of work to argue successfully for
maximum-hours laws for men as well as women. *Bunting* was not, however, followed by a spate of maximum-hours law for men, the way *Muller*
had been followed by laws for women. In general, unions did not support protective legislation for men, although they continued to do so for
women. Protective legislation, rather than organization, was the preferred strategy only for women.[88]

The effect of the laws was limited by their narrow coverage and
inadequate enforcement, but despite their limitations, in those few occupations where night work or long hours were essential, such as printing, women were effectively excluded.[89] While the laws may have protected women in the "sweated" trades, women who were beginning to
get established in "men's jobs" were turned back.[90] Some of these women
fought back successfully, but the struggle is still being waged today along
many of the same battle lines. As Ann C. Hill argued, the effect of these
laws, psychically and socially, has been devastating. They confirmed
woman's "alien" status as a worker.[91]

Throughout the above discussion of the development of the wage-
labor force in England and the United States, I have emphasized the role
of male workers in restricting women's sphere in the labor market. Although I have emphasized the role of men, I do not think that of employers was unimportant. Recent work on labor-market segmentation
theory provides a framework for looking at the role of employers.[92]
According to this model, one mechanism which creates segmentation is

87. Ibid., p. 32.
88. In 1914 the AFL voted to abandon the legislative road to reform (see Ann C. Hill).
89. Some states excluded women entirely from certain occupations: mining, meter
reading, taxicab driving, core making, streetcar conducting, elevator operating, etc. (ibid.).
90. These conclusions are based on Ann C. Hill and are also supported by Baker.
91. At the same time that women were being excluded from certain skilled jobs in the
labor force and otherwise protected, the home duties of women were emphasized in
popular literature, through the home economics movement, in colleges and high schools,
etc. A movement toward the stabilization of the nuclear family with one breadwinner, the
male, is discernible (see Hartmann).
92. Edwards, Gordon, and Reich use labor-market segmentation to refer to a process
in which the labor market becomes divided into different submarkets, each with its own
characteristic behaviors; these segments can be different layers of a hierarchy or different
groups within one layer.

the conscious, though not necessarily conspiratorial, action of capitalists; they act to exacerbate existing divisions among workers in order to further divide them, thus weakening their class unity and reducing their bargaining power.[93] The creation of complex internal job structures is itself part of this attempt. In fact, the whole range of different levels of jobs serves to obfuscate the basic two-class nature of capitalist society.[94] This model suggests, first, that sex segregation is one aspect of the labor-market segmentation inherent in advanced capitalism, and, second, capitalists have consciously attempted to exacerbate sex divisions. Thus, if the foregoing analysis has emphasized the continuous nature of job segregation by sex—present in all stages of capitalism and before [95]—and the conscious actions of male workers, it is important to note that the actions of capitalists may have been crucial in calling forth those responses from male workers.

Historically, male workers have been instrumental in limiting the participation of women in the labor market. Male unions have carried out the policies and attitudes of the earlier guilds, and they have continued to reap benefits for male workers. Capitalists inherited job segregation by sex, but they have quite often been able to use it to their own advantage. If they can supersede experienced men with cheaper women, so much the better; if they can weaken labor by threatening to do so, that's good, too; or, if failing that, they can use those status differences to reward men, and buy their allegiance to capitalism with patriarchal benefits, that's okay too.[96]

But even though capitalists' actions are important in explaining the current virility of sex segregation, labor-market-segmentation theory overemphasizes the role of capitalists and ignores the actions of workers themselves in perpetuating segmentation. Those workers in the more desirable jobs act to hang onto them, their material rewards, and their

93. Michael Reich's thesis, "Racial Discrimination and the White Income Distribution" (Ph.D. diss., Harvard University, 1973), sets forth this divide-and-rule model more thoroughly. In the labor-market-segmentation model there is another tendency toward segmentation in addition to the divide-and-rule mechanism. It arises out of the uneven development of advanced capitalism, i.e., the process of creation of a core and a peripheral economy. In fact, in the Edwards, Gordon, and Reich view, labor-market segmentation only comes to the fore under monopoly capitalism, as large corporations seek to extend control over their labor markets.

94. Thomas Vietorisz, "From Class to Hierarchy: Some Non-Price Aspects on the Transformation Problem" (paper presented at the Conference on Urban Political Economy, New School for Social Research, New York, February 15–16, 1975).

95. The strong divisions of the labor market by sex and race that existed even in the competitive phase of capitalism call into question the dominance of labor homogenization during that phase—as presented by Gordon, Edwards, and Reich.

96. Capitalists are not always able to use patriarchy to their advantage. Men's ability to retain as much of women's labor in the home as they have may hamper capitalist development during expansive phases. Men's resistance to female workers whom capitalists want to utilize also undoubtedly slows down capitalist advance.

subjective benefits.[97] Workers, through unions, have been parties to the creation and maintenance of hierarchical and parallel (i.e., separate but unequal) job structures. Perhaps the relative importance of capitalists and male workers in instituting and maintaining job segregation by sex has varied in different periods. Capitalists during the transition to capitalism, for example, seemed quite able to change the sex composition of jobs—when weaving was shifted to factories equipped with power looms women wove, even though most handloom weavers had been men, and mule spinning was introduced with male operators even though women had used the earlier spinning jennies and water frames. As industrialization progressed and conditions stabilized somewhat, male unions gained in strength and were often able to preserve or extend male arenas. Nevertheless, in times of overwhelming social or economic necessity, occasioned by vast increases in the demand for labor, such as in teaching or clerical work, male capitalists were capable of overpowering male workers. Thus, in periods of economic change, capitalists' actions may be more instrumental in instituting or changing a sex-segregated labor force—while workers fight a defensive battle. In other periods male workers may be more important in maintaining sex-segregated jobs; they may be able to prevent the encroachment of, or even to drive out, cheaper female labor, thus increasing the benefits to their sex.[98]

Conclusion

The present status of women in the labor market and the current arrangement of sex-segregated jobs is the result of a long process of interaction between patriarchy and capitalism. I have emphasized the actions of male workers throughout this process because I believe that emphasis to be correct. Men will have to be forced to give up their favored positions in the division of labor—in the labor market and at home—both if women's subordination is to end and if men are to begin to escape class oppression and exploitation.[99] Capitalists have indeed

97. Engels, Marx, and Lenin all recognized the *material* rewards the labor aristocracy reaps. It is important not to reduce these to *subjective* benefits, for then the problems arising out of intraclass divisions will be minimized. Castles and Kosack appear to make this error (see their "The Function of Labour Immigration in Western European Capitalism," *New Left Review*, no. 73 [May–June 1972], pp. 3–12, where references to Marx et al. can be found).

98. David Gordon suggested to me this "cyclical model" of the relative strengths of employer and workers.

99. Most Marxist-feminist attempts to deal with the problems in Marxist analysis raised by the social position of women seem to ignore these basic conflicts between the sexes, apparently in the interest of stressing the underlying class solidarity that should obtain among women and men workers. Bridges and Hartmann's draft paper (n. 1 above)

used women as unskilled, underpaid labor to undercut male workers, yet this is only a case of the chickens coming home to roost—a case of men's co-optation by and support for patriarchal society, with its hierarchy among men, being turned back on themselves with a vengeance. Capitalism grew on top of patriarchy; patriarchal capitalism is stratified society par excellence. If non-ruling-class men are to be free they will have to recognize their co-optation by patriarchal capitalism and relinquish their patriarchal benefits. If women are to be free, they must fight against both patriarchal power and capitalist organization of society.

Because both the sexual division of labor and male domination are so long standing, it will be very difficult to eradicate them and impossible to eradicate the latter without the former. The two are now so inextricably intertwined that it is necessary to eradicate the sexual division of labor itself in order to end male domination.[100] Very basic changes at all levels of society and culture are required to liberate women. In this paper, I have argued that the maintenance of job segregation by sex is a key root of women's status, and I have relied on the operation of society-wide institutions to explain the maintenance of job segregation by sex. But the consequences of that division of labor go very deep, down to the level of the subconscious. The subconscious influences behavior patterns, which form the micro underpinnings (or complements) of social institutions and are in turn reinforced by those social institutions.

I believe we need to investigate these micro phenomena as well as the macro ones I have discussed in this paper. For example, it appears to be a very deeply ingrained behavioral rule that men cannot be subordinate to women of a similar social class. Manifestations of this rule have been noted in restaurants, where waitresses experience difficulty in giving orders to bartenders, unless the bartender can reorganize the situation to allow himself autonomy; among executives, where women executives are seen to be most successful if they have little contact with others at their level and manage small staffs; and among industrial workers, where female factory inspectors cannot successfully correct the work of male production workers.[101] There is also a deeply ingrained fear of

---

reviews this literature. A few months ago a friend (female) said, "We are much more likely to be able to get Thieu out of Vietnam than we are to get men to do the dishes." She was right.

100. In our society, women's jobs are synonymous with low-status, low-paying jobs: ". . . we may replace the familiar statement that women earn less because they are in low paying occupations with the statement that women earn less because they are in *women's jobs*. . . . As long as the labor market is divided on the basis of sex, it is likely that the tasks allocated to women will be ranked as less prestigious or important, reflecting women's lower social status in the society at large" (Francine Blau [Weisskoff], "Women's Place in the Labor Market," *American Economic Review* 62, no. 4 [May 1972]: 161).

101. Theodore Caplow, *The Sociology of Work* (New York: McGraw-Hill Book Co.,

being identified with the other sex. As a general rule, men and women must never do anything which is not masculine or feminine (respectively).[102] Male executives, for example, often exchange handshakes with male secretaries, a show of respect which probably works to help preserve their masculinity.

At the next deeper level, we must study the subconscious—both how these behavioral rules are internalized and how they grow out of personality structure.[103] At this level, the formation of personality, there have been several attempts to study the production of gender, the *socially* imposed differentiation of humans based on biological sex differences.[104] A materialist interpretation of reality, of course, suggests that gender production grows out of the extant division of labor between the sexes,[105] and, in a dialectical process, reinforces that very division of labor itself. In my view, because of these deep ramifications of the sexual division of labor we will not eradicate sex-ordered task division until we eradicate the socially imposed gender differences between us and, therefore, the very sexual division of labor itself.

In attacking both patriarchy and capitalism we will have to find ways to change both society-wide institutions and our most deeply ingrained habits. It will be a long, hard struggle.

New School for Social Research

1964), pp. 237 ff., discusses several behavioral rules and their impact. Harold Willensky, "Women's Work: Economic Growth, Ideology, Structure," *Industrial Relations* 7, no. 3 (May 1968): 235–48, also discusses the implication for labor-market phenomena of several behavioral rules.

102. "The use of tabooed words, the fostering of sports and other interests which women do not share, and participation in activities which women are intended to disapprove of—hard drinking, gambling, practical jokes, and sexual essays of various kinds—all suggest that the adult male group is to a large extent engaged in a reaction *against* feminine influence, and therefore cannot tolerate the presence of women without changing its character entirely" (Caplow, p. 239). Of course, the lines of division between masculine and feminine are constantly shifting. At various times in the nineteenth century, teaching, selling in retail stores, and office work were each thought to be totally unsuitable for women. This variability of the boundaries between men's jobs and women's jobs is one reason why an effort to locate basic behavioral principles would seem to make sense —though, ultimately, of course, these rules are shaped by the division of labor itself.

103. Caplow based his rules on the Freudian view that men identify freedom from female dominance with maturity, i.e., they seek to escape their mothers.

104. See Rubin (n. 1 above), and Juliet Mitchell, *Feminism and Psychoanalysis* (New York: Pantheon Books, 1974), who seek to re-create Freud from a feminist perspective. So does Shulamith Firestone, *The Dialectic of Sex* (New York: Bantam Books, 1971).

105. For example, the current domestic division of labor in which women nurture children profoundly affects (differentially) the personality structures of girls and boys. For a non-Freudian interpretation of this phenomenon, see Chodorow (n. 12 above).

The Historical Roots of Occupational Segregation

Comment I

Carl N. Degler

Hartmann's paper is really two papers. The first is an abbreviated anthropological examination of the origins of women's suppression. The second, somewhat longer, is more properly historical in that it uses documentary evidence and deals with modern times, that is, the history of women in industry in England and the United States. The problem Hartmann sets for herself is, How is it that we find women in subordinate positions economically throughout the cultures of the world, that throughout time and space they have been disadvantageously segregated in occupations? What interests me hugely in her paper is her observation that we have too often or too easily ignored the role of men, ordinary men, men as workers, not as capitalists or rulers, as the prime source of occupational subordination. With this point I have long been in agreement. I have some specific reservations, to be sure, and I cannot go into them here, but they are not as important as the large point, which is the principal one from Hartmann's point of view, I believe, and which constitutes a major revision of traditional Marxian analysis of the suppression of women. I can only welcome a Marxist scholar's recognition of what has always seemed to me to be very important for women to acknowledge, namely, that the male sex—as a gender acting in society in its own interest—has been at the root of the disadvantages which women suffer in occupations and work.

On the other hand, I am not persuaded by her argument that there are some anthropological exceptions to the general pattern of women's subordination to men throughout the known human societies. I think we can find exceptions to the general pattern, but what we must address ourselves to is that general pattern, not those contrary examples that exist here and there in which women seem to be on an equal basis occupationally with men. More important, I missed in Hartmann any explanation of how this widespread subordination from equality came about, leaving aside the question of whether there ever was an egalitarian situation. As I say, I still have doubts as to whether there ever was.

Notwithstanding these doubts, there does seem to be a need to ascertain how women were subordinated by men. I missed in Hartmann's paper any reference to what seem to me obvious differences between men and women that might account for women's subordination. One of these differences is the greater strength of men on the average, both in weight and in musculature, a difference that must have played some role in all of this. Another is the disability that women periodically underwent, and in the days before contraception bearing and nursing children was not a part-time or seasonal occupation. In most societies children simply could not survive without nursing, for artificial means of feeding young children were not adequate. I am raising this more as a question for Heidi Hartmann than as a settled matter in my own mind. Is not this, too, a part of the explanation for women's subordination? That is, is not there a physical difference between the sexes that explains the ability of men to put women into this inferior position?

As to the situation that prevails when one moves into historical times, the industrial revolution, and so forth, I wonder if it is proper to talk, as Hartmann does, about capitalist society? It is true that England and America are capitalist societies, but I question if this same kind of disadvantageous job segregation has not been well documented for socialist societies like the Soviet Union or Yugoslavia. In fact, if one is going to talk about men as the originators and perpetuators of segregation of women on jobs, as Hartmann has done, one ought to generalize across societies and not confine the observation to capitalist societies or even only, as she says in one place, to advanced societies.

I have the feeling at times that Hartmann cannot decide whether she wants to indict capitalism or men; I would suggest that she recognize that both played their parts. Certainly capitalism reinforces the interests of men in using their superior power, whatever it might be, whether, as in ancient times their physical strength, or in modern times their control of the state or of social institutions, to impose occupational subordination on women. One of the social institutions that men controlled is labor unions. I will make one observation about them that might be useful to those interested in the history of women. It also provides a good example of what I think of as the way in which history affected women differently from the way in which it affected men. Often in discussing the history of unionization one talks about it as a great social gain, but when one does so for general American or European history one is really thinking about the gains for men. One ought to recognize that in many times and in many places in the past the experience of women has been quite different from that of men and might even be exactly the opposite in impact. There is a way, for example, in which one might describe unionization as a loss for women, at least at a certain time and under certain circumstances, for male unions in the nineteenth century often discriminated against women. When this difference in impact is recognized, one begins to write history in a different way. No longer can one say that unionization was an unalloyed gain for all workers.

Another example of the different interests of women and men in the past that affect how one writes history is a movement like temperance. Women had a disproportionate interest in Prohibition; more women were in the protemperance movement than in the suffrage movement throughout the nineteenth century and into a good part of the twentieth. The reason was because of the role that women occupied in the home (not because of their innate nature); as wives and mothers they were aware of what alcohol could do to men and therefore to them in their dependent roles. The Women's Christian Temperance Union, for example, was the largest women's organization in the whole nineteenth century. To recognize this interest of women in temperance and later Prohibition causes one to see the history of the Prohibition movement in a quite different light than when only men are included in the explanations for Prohibition.

In general I disagree with Elise Boulding's emphasis upon the prevalence of the female headed household in the past. No one has thought there were *no* female headed households, but on the other hand I do not think she is convincing that the existence of such households were important. Most women, like most men, lived in families. Certainly the women who headed households are a part of women's past, but beyond that I do not think we can go. If I interpret her paper properly, she is suggesting that female headed households succeeded and that therefore we ought to see this as a viable alternative to the traditional family. If this is indeed her point, I think her evidence is not convincing. In one of her statistics she points out that the vast majority of female headed households were those of widows. These are not women who chose the role of heading a household. And their failure to remarry cannot be assumed to be voluntary in a society in which men traditionally initiate the unions. I still think that a household headed by only one progenitor is a burden on that one, regardless of the sex. Rather than celebrating, as I think Boulding is, the female headed household, one ought to emphasize the burden it must always be. In short, I still contend that what history tells us is that women would like to have the help of men, just as men would like to have the help of women, in rearing children and maintaining a household. They have, admittedly, been unable to do this in certain circumstances, but that fact does not give us much on which to generalize about women.

Stanford University

THE HISTORICAL ROOTS OF OCCUPATIONAL SEGREGATION

Comment II

Hanna Papanek

The most interesting thing about all three papers is that they give us a broader perspective for looking at occupational segregation. The perspective of the white, affluent middle class in the United States is not the most fruitful basis for generating good social science theory or methods about anything. I am particularly aware of that because I have done most of my work on societies outside the United States—I recently figured out that I have spent ten of the last twenty years in Asia.

Second, it seems to me that we need to ask ourselves what the purpose is of our looking at the history of women, above and beyond the intellectual satisfaction of doing so. In one sense, it enables us to understand our own situation better in order to develop better means of coping with it. It also enables us to fulfill one of our civic responsibilities, which I personally consider extremely important. Let me explain what I mean here.

All of these three papers deal in part with the beginnings of industrialization. Most of the women alive in the world today are living in societies where industrialization is only beginning to be introduced. Most of these women are going to be part of the new "female proletariat." As researchers in affluent countries, we have a responsibility toward them, because it is from our countries that industrialization and "modernization" are being exported. As citizens of these countries, we must pay a great deal of attention to the possible consequences of the ways in which our countries' economies (and not only the political actions) affect others. More specifically, we need to find ways to understand what is happening to women in these countries as a result of economic changes. Elise Boulding has done this in another recent paper, "Women, Bread and Babies,"[1] which I find very exciting. In that paper she points out how the burdens of women in subsistence agriculture are being doubled and tripled as a result of changes in the economy, such as an increase in cash cropping. Not surprisingly, in most of these countries most of the new technology and advice on crops is going to the men in the cash-crop sector and not to the women.

I will not comment specifically on the Boulding paper, since this is part of Carl Degler's job, except to say that it adds important material to our understanding of women's economic roles as seen from Elise Boulding's new perspective. The most crucial point—and one which needs constant reiteration—is her point that a substantial number of unpartnered women at any given time may be heads of households and that therefore it is legitimate to call the "male head of household concept . . . a fiction." I wholeheartedly agree, especially because this concept very conveniently enables most societies and most employers to perpetuate working arrangements and pay scales which are very damaging to women and their families. Moreover, it needs to be made very clear that the existence of a "female proletariat," especially in the "developing" countries, also injures the bargaining position of men by providing an available labor force which will work for less than the male labor force. This is an important factor in countries with high unemployment and poorly organized trade unions. In these countries it turns out to be surprisingly easy to transform "traditional men's jobs" into "women's occupations" when that serves to keep labor costs down.

In the Lapidus paper, I was particularly interested in her demonstration of the interplay between ideology and values on the one hand and the constraints of resource base, class differences, and poverty on the other. It is particularly interesting to see how Soviet economic planning has worked to shape the life and work of both men and women explicitly as well as implicitly. For example, I think one of the most interesting points in the whole paper is hidden in a footnote (n. 7) which tells us that "the average monthly wage in 1972 was 130.3 rubles, or less than two-thirds of what would be required to support" a family of four. The consequences of this important aspect of wage policy are, of course, that women are under greater pressure to seek employment and also to restrict fertility.

In this connection, one needs to ask several questions on the basis of

1. Elise Boulding, "Women, Bread, and Babies: Directing Aid to Fifth World Farmers" (paper prepared for conference on World Food and Population Crisis: A Role for the Private Sector, Dallas [April 1975]), mimeographed (available from Program of Research on General Social and Economic Dynamics, Institute of Behavioral Science, University of Colorado).

her material. Most women are employed outside the home in the Soviet Union. Is this a deliberate policy in the Soviet economic plan? Which women are *not* employed? Is nonemployment of wives a privilege of high-status couples where the man receives much more than the average wage? What are some of the arguments presented by nonemployed women for their choice? What kinds of reciprocal redefinitions of female and male roles would it take to bring into play an institutional arrangement for equal participation? To what extent have these roles already been redefined by sixty years of female labor-force participation when this is compared with the earlier situation of female employment?

In looking further at the interplay between ideology and implementation of values concerning equal economic participation of women, I think that Lapidus is telling us very clearly that the cultural values and institutional arrangements in the USSR are not supportive of full and equal participation, even though it is "more equal" there than in most other industrial nations. The most important point here seems to be the provision of consumer services. If these are inadequate and there is no social commitment to sharing household management between husbands and wives, then the burden of coping with household work falls more heavily on the Soviet woman than on women in societies with better consumer services and equally uncooperative husbands. Another example of social values not supportive of fully equal participation is given in Lapidus's point that where there is a question of moving elsewhere in connection with a job, the wife moves along with the husband.

I was also impressed with a very imaginative use of available statistics, particularly in table 2, indicating the distribution of employed women by economic sector which suggests the existence of a dual labor market. Lapidus's materials also suggest the functioning of segregative mechanisms in the labor force of industrial countries which seem to be influenced relatively little by whether the system is capitalist or not. These are points with which an internationally oriented study of occupational segregation needs to concern itself.

In that connection, let me mention a few other examples of changes in occupational segregation in other countries to round out the picture a little. In Pakistan, where women are often secluded by the purdah system and where nonsecluded women are also affected by the general values on which the system is based, there exist two major high-status professions for educated women. These women can become "lady doctors" and teachers (often in all-female schools) in order to meet the needs of women for education and medical care. This is an example of constituency needs creating career opportunities for women in a segregated system. However, in the very recent past new opportunities for women which support the notion of a new "female proletariat" have been opening up in Pakistan. For example, I am told that jobs in spinning mills, which were previously held largely by Bengali men, have been opened up to women factory workers. This is a radical departure in Pakistani practice. It resulted from the departure of the Bengali workers since the creation of Bangladesh in 1971, and the presumption that women workers are less likely to be integrated into active trade-union activities, at least for the time being. Another occupation which has recently opened up to women, possibly for similar reasons, is in the processing of fish and shellfish for marketing and export. This is an unpleasant and low-paid occupation which men are perhaps eager to leave as soon as other opportunities are open.

Another example of rapid shifts in apparently well-established norms governing women's occupations is provided by the recent decision to take women into an occupation in which men have predominated in the past: public primary-school teaching. This is the result of several factors. There has recently been a great expansion of educational facilities, including education for girls. In the past, teachers —particularly in village primary schools—have been paid extremely low wages. Few girls attended primary schools in the village. Educated women were usually unwilling to move from urban areas to villages in order to work as teachers. These women did, however, teach in secondary schools for girls in the cities. Now the provision of more primary schools has led to a large increase of demand for teachers. Young women who complete ten years of schooling are being trained as primary-school teachers in special programs. At the same time, wages in occupations that are open to men with this level of education have often increased, while there are still comparatively few alternative employment opportunities for women. The opening up of these jobs is, therefore, a definite advantage for individual women and their families, even though it is likely that the future development of primary-school teaching as a specialized "women's occupation"—as has happened in many other countries along with the rationalization that it is a "natural" job for women—will limit the opportunities and wages for men who may still want to enter the occupation.

These instances from Pakistan illustrate how shifts can occur in the system of occupational segregation as the result of economic pressures coupled with changes in government policy. Another example in which the work of women has been seriously affected by changes in government policy can be found in the displacement of women from an occupation as a result of the introduction of technology. In Indonesia, small inexpensive rice mills for hulling have been introduced into rural areas relatively recently.[2] Previously, rice had been hand pounded by

2. William A. Collier, Jusef Colter, Sinarhadi, Robert d'A. Shaw, "Choice of Technique in Rice Milling in Java," *Bulletin of Indonesian Economic Studies* 10, no. 1 (March 1974): 106–20; Peter C. Timmer, "Choice of Technique in Rice Milling in Java," *Bulletin of Indonesian Economic Studies* 9, no. 2 (July 1973): 57–76; Peter C. Timmer, "Choice of Technique in Rice Milling in Java: A Reply," *Bulletin of Indonesian Economic Studies* 10, no. 1 (March 1974): 121–26.

women both for home consumption and for marketing. Since the introduction of the rice-hulling machinery, many farm women are still pounding rice for home consumption because of taste preferences and possibly because pounding small daily quantities for the family is considered part of women's household duties. However, the work is arduous, and some of the women to whom I talked about this informally said they would be glad to be relieved of it. For the women who pounded rice commercially, however, the introduction of the rice mills has meant a serious loss of income. What substitutes now for their earnings? Here again, there is a complicated process involved in which overall gains in terms of rice production and market quality must be balanced against the loss in income suffered by a section of the labor force which is now displaced.

There are many other examples, all of which have led me to the conviction that occupational segregation must be studied on a comparative basis. This is particularly important if we are to understand the role of international economic relationships in the process, as well as the decisions made by individual women in search of employment. For example, the women who work in the electronics factories of Singapore and Taiwan need the supplementary earning opportunities to help support their families and cannot consider the possible long-range effect of their work on the earning opportunities of the men in their families. Nor can they possibly consider its effects on women workers in the United States, who may be priced out of their "women's occupation" jobs because of the lower-cost alternative now available to internationally organized companies. The women who till the subsistence fields of Africa do not necessarily do this by choice—they work because they and their children need to eat.

What we as researchers share is the responsibility for understanding these processes in the first place and communicating our findings to others so that some of the damaging effects of segregating women in the labor force are also eliminated in the countries to which we export products, aid, and influence.

Boston University

ECONOMIC DIMENSIONS OF OCCUPATIONAL SEGREGATION

Economists' Approaches to Sex Segregation in the Labor Market: An Appraisal

Francine D. Blau and Carol L. Jusenius

The purpose of this paper is to appraise the contribution of economic theory to an understanding of the causes of sex segregation and pay differentiation between men and women in the labor market. We do not attempt to review the large and growing body of empirical literature in this area,[1] although our assessment of alternative theoretical approaches does rely upon a broad knowledge of the empirical findings. In particular, three points are taken as given:

1. Sex segregation in the labor market exists, and it is of considerable magnitude.

2. Women are segregated by occupational categories and within occupations by industry and firm.[2] (While we concentrate primarily on

This article was prepared while the authors were research associates at the Center for Human Resource Research, Ohio State University. We would like to thank our colleagues at the center, A. Kohen, S. Sandell, and R. Shortlidge for their helpful comments on an earlier draft of this paper, and P. Brito for her research assistance. We would also like to express our gratitude to M. Wachter and to the participants in the workshop conference on occupational segregation for their valuable input. The authors alone are responsible for the views expressed here, as well as for any errors which may remain.

1. See the extensive bibliography provided by Andrew I. Kohen, *Women and the Economy: A Bibliography and a Review of the Literature on Sex Differentiation in the Labor Market* (Columbus, Ohio: Center for Human Resource Research, Ohio State University, 1975).

2. For empirical documentation of the existence, depth, and dimensions of sex segregation, see, e.g., Barbara Bergmann and Irma Adelman, "The 1973 Report of the President's Council of Economic Advisers: The Economic Role of Women," *American Economic Review* 63 (September 1973): 509–14; Francine D. Blau, "Pay Differentials and

occupational segregation, much of the discussion is relevant to an analysis of these other dimensions.)

3. Aggregate pay differentials between men and women in the labor market exist.

Contemporary economic analysis may be divided into several schools of thought. Considerations of time and space have compelled some degree of selectivity, and this paper provides an evaluation of only two main approaches: the neoclassical and institutional schools. An additional school—radical economics—has also contributed important insights into an understanding of labor market segmentation. For the most part, however, we feel that the radicals' major contribution in this area has been to raise and analyze a number of important questions which are often ignored in traditional economic analyses. Thus, given the disparity in the questions posed by radical and other approaches, it was simply not possible to deal adequately with the radical perspective as well in this paper.[3]

In both their theoretical and empirical work, neoclassical economists have concentrated their attention primarily on the male-female pay differential and only secondarily on sex segregation per se. Their examination of segregation has largely been a by-product of investigations of wage-related issues. Such an emphasis is indeed understandable, since, to the neoclassical economist, the monetary manifestation of possible labor market inequities is an obvious focal point for the analysis. However, the coexistence in the labor market of both pay differentiation by sex and sex segregation along occupational and other dimensions

Differences in the Distribution of Employment of Male and Female Office Workers" (Ph.D. diss., Harvard University, 1975); Francine Blau Weisskoff, " 'Women's Place' in the Labor Market," *American Economic Review* 62 (May 1972): 161–66; John E. Buckley, "Pay Differences between Men and Women in the Same Job," *Monthly Labor Review* 94 (November 1971): 36–39; Edward Gross, "Plus ça Change . . . ? The Sexual Structure of Occupations over Time," *Social Problems* 16 (Fall 1968): 198–208; Carol L. Jusenius and Richard L. Shortlidge, Jr., *Dual Careers: A Longitudinal Study of Labor Market Experience of Women*, Manpower Research Monograph no. 21, vol. 3 (Washington, D.C.: Department of Labor, 1975); Donald J. McNulty, "Differences in Pay between Men and Women Workers," *Monthly Labor Review* 90 (December 1967): 40–43; Valerie Kincade Oppenheimer, *The Female Labor Force in the United States: Demographic Factors Governing its Growth and Changing Composition* (Berkeley: Institute of International Studies, University of California, 1970); Elizabeth Waldman and Beverly J. McEaddy, "Where Women Work—an Analysis by Industry and Occupation," *Monthly Labor Review* 97 (May 1974): 3–14.

3. For expositions of the radical approach, see, e.g., David M. Gordon, ed., *Problems in Political Economy: An Urban Perspective* (Lexington, Mass.: D. C. Heath Company, 1971) and Gordon, *Theories of Poverty and Underemployment: Orthodox, Radical and Dual Labor Market Perspectives* (Lexington, MASS.: D. C. Heath Co., 1972); Michael Reich, Richard C. Edwards, and David M. Gordon, "A Theory of Labor Market Segmentation," *Proceedings of the Twenty-fifth Anniversary Meeting, Industrial Relations Association Series*, ed. Gerard G. Somers (Madison, Wis.: Industrial Relations Research Association, 1973), pp. 269–76; and Michael Reich, David M. Gordon, and Richard C. Edwards, eds., *Labor Market Segmentation* (Lexington, Mass.: Lexington Books, 1975).

strongly suggests (although it certainly does not prove) a link between the two. This posited linkage may be considered an underlying assumption of this paper and thus a major criterion in our evaluation of the merits of alternative approaches.

The paper is divided into three main sections. The first section examines the neoclassical approach and variations within this school. The second section develops the application of an institutional model —the internal labor market analysis—to the questions under consideration. The final section provides a brief summary.

Neoclassical Approaches

In their attempts to explain the wage differential between men and women, some neoclassical economists employ models of perfect competition in which wages equal the value of workers' marginal products. Within this school are two particular approaches which are at variance with one another. One approach advocates the "overcrowding" hypothesis in which the low productivity of women workers is explained by the exclusionary behavior of employers. The other approach is based on human capital theory which argues that women's productivity is low because women have relatively low stocks of accumulated human capital. Other neoclassical economists reject the assumption of a perfectly competitive labor market. Instead, they focus on the wage implications of monopsony, that is, monopoly power on the buyer's side—in this case, the firm's power in the labor market.

The Competitive Model: The Overcrowding Approach

To begin the analysis we must first define "overcrowding." Put simply, overcrowding is the interplay of a relatively low demand for a particular type of worker with a relatively large supply of that same type of worker. Thus, overcrowding can result from an excessive number of individuals trained (in a broad sense) for a given occupation or set of occupations and/or it can result from an excessive number of limitations being placed on the total set of occupations open to an identifiable group of workers.

The first mention of what has come to be termed overcrowding is found in Fawcett[4] and Edgeworth.[5] "It is quite true to say that, although the doctrine of demand and supply has fallen of late years into unpopularity, it is nevertheless a fact that if demand for a particular class of

4. Millicent G. Fawcett, "Equal Pay for Equal Work," *Economic Journal* 28 (March 1918): 1–6.

5. F. Y. Edgeworth, "Equal Pay to Men and Women for Equal Work," *Economic Journal* 32 (September 1922): 431–57.

labor is either destroyed or very much restricted, 'a downward pull' on wages is called into existence for the whole class."[6] It was not until the early 1970s, however, that Bergmann[7] formalized the overcrowding hypotheses in her analyses of occupational segregation. Bergmann argued that women are restricted by demand factors to a limited set of occupations. This restriction results first in women receiving lower wages, and second in the nonrestricted group (men) receiving higher wages than if the constraints to mobility between the male and female sectors did not exist. In other words, Bergmann contrasts two equilibrium positions. In both these positions workers earn the value of their marginal products. Women, however, because they are forced into a relatively small number of occupations and the capital-labor ratio associated with these occupations are thus relatively low, have a lower productivity than men.

Two key elements comprise the Bergmann formulation. The first is that workers are identical with respect to potential productivity; that is, they are perfectly substitutable for one another but they have clearly differentiable ascriptive characteristics. The second important element, already noted, is that demand-side conditions are responsible for the overcrowding. Tastes of employers prevent integration.

It is important to note here that through her inclusion of employer tastes, Bergmann unites Becker's theory of discrimination[8] with Fawcett's and Edgeworth's. In Becker, employers who have a taste for discrimination against women workers will hire them only when the wage difference between male and female labor is large enough to compensate for the disutility they incur by hiring women.[9] Thus, the Bergmann approach is an extreme case of Becker; only if employer tastes for discrimination against women in male occupations are "very large" will total exclusion, as posited by Bergmann, exist.

This reliance on employer tastes as the causal factor of occupational segregation does not appear to be sufficient. It is not clear why so many employers would have such tastes against women in certain occupations, nor is it clear why employers' aversion should be so "strong" that they

6. Fawcett, p. 2.

7. Barbara R. Bergmann, "The Effect on White Incomes of Discrimination in Employment," *Journal of Political Economy* 79 (March/April 1971): 294–313, and "Occupational Segregation, Wages and Profits When Employers Discriminate by Race or Sex," *Eastern Economic Journal* 1 (April–July 1974): 103–10.

8. Gary S. Becker, *The Economics of Discrimination* (Chicago: University of Chicago Press, 1957).

9. Becker identifies three sources of discrimination: employer, employee, and customer. Tastes for discrimination on the part of either employees or customers may provide the motivating force for discriminatory action on the part of employers (see also Kenneth Arrow, "The Theory of Discrimination," in *Discrimination in Labor Markets,* ed. Orley Ashenfelter and Albert Rees [Princeton, N.J.: Princeton University Press, 1973], pp. 3–33).

are not compensated for their disutility by the prevailing male-female pay differential. However, in the Bergmann model, complete occupational segregation depends upon a highly skewed distribution of employer tastes.[10] Furthermore, it is not obvious that the case of perfect substitutability between men and women in the production process is general enough to shed light on the whole pattern of occupational segregation. In sum, we are forced to conclude that Bergmann's contribution lies more in her analysis of the *consequences* of occupational segregation than in her approach to explanations of its *causes*.

The Competitive Model: The Human Capital Approach

At first glance, human capital theory would seem to contribute more to an understanding of the causes of segregation than the overcrowding hypothesis. Yet in the final analysis, human capital theorists also rely heavily on a factor termed "tastes." While human capital models have not explicitly considered women's concentration in selected occupations, it is possible to draw seemingly reasonable inferences about this problem from their models. The basic argument of human capital theory is outlined below.

The major point of the human capital approach is that men and women are not perfectly substitutable for one another. Although they may be similarly distributed across IQ categories and levels of education, women accumulate less human capital through work experience because they spend proportionately fewer years in the labor force than men.[11] Thus, productivity differentials between men and women will appear.[12] In other words, the quality of labor supplied by the two groups varies because of their different patterns of labor force participation, of which the presumedly higher turnover rates among women are a short-run manifestation. Pay differentials merely reflect the quality differentials between men and women.[13]

Closing the circle of this argument is the human capital school's

10. One difficulty which troubles economists about the existence of discrimination in the labor market is why, in the long run, competitive forces do not tend to weaken and indeed eliminate it (see Arrow).

11. Work experience in this context may be broken down into general labor force experience and firm-specific experience.

12. The most rigorous formulation of this argument is found in Jacob Mincer and Solomon Polacheck, "Family Investments in Human Capital: Earnings of Women," *Journal of Political Economy* 82 (March/April 1974): 76–111 (see also Larry E. Suter, "Occupation, Employment, and Lifetime Work Experience of Women" [paper presented at the meetings of the American Sociological Association, New York, August 27, 1973]).

13. While the (actual or potential) market wage does figure in their models of the determinants of female labor force participation, in their discussions of pay differentials proponents of the human capital approach tend not to consider that labor market discrimination may, by lowering female wages, reduce women's incentive for engaging in market work.

model of the family and women's role within it. By revising the traditional work-leisure dichotomy in economic theory, they have been able to conceptualize the effects of the family on a woman's supply curve of labor.[14] Arguments in their household utility functions include not only leisure and goods derived from market work, but also goods derived from nonmarket work—work traditionally performed by women. Thus, from the perspective of a utility-maximizing household, a woman's decision not to work continuously, that is, not to accumulate a relatively large stock of human capital, is a rational one.[15]

It should be noted that this theory is one of pay differentials and that occupational segregation is *not* a necessary adjunct. Wage rates sufficiently flexible to allow for quality differences among workers in the same occupation are theoretically possible. Yet the human capital approach can be used to explain the phenomenon of occupational segregation. The theory would predict that women would tend to enter those occupations which provide few opportunities for increases in productivity through labor market experience.[16] Anticipating or reacting to the needs of the family, women would enter occupations which, while they may not reward work experience, also do not penalize their incumbents for discontinuities in employment (such as waitressing). This same line of reasoning suggests that women would tend to exclude themselves from a second type of occupation, that is, those which embody a lengthy process of general training (such as lawyers)—the costs of which the women themselves must bear—unless they planned to work throughout the greater part of their life span. Also implied is that employers would tend to exclude women from a third type of occupation—that which

14. Gary S. Becker, "A Theory of the Allocation of Time," *Economic Journal* 75 (September 1965): 493–517; Becker, "A Theory of Marriage: Part I," *Journal of Political Economy* 81 (July/August 1973): 813–46; and Jacob Mincer, "Labor Force Participation of Married Women: A Study of Labor Supply," in *Aspects of Labor Economics,* National Bureau of Economic Research (Princeton, N.J.: Princeton University Press, 1962), pp. 63–105.

15. While it might appear from their analysis that the source of women's inequality in the labor market is derived from women's role in the family, this does not appear to perturb the human capital theorists. According to Becker, "A Theory of Marriage," the institution of marriage in its current form produces an "optimal" division of labor within the family.

16. This interpretation is based on Sawhill's attempt to incorporate Becker's human capital theory with the overcrowding hypothesis of Bergmann. It should be mentioned that Sawhill concludes by arguing that women may be overcrowded in low-skill occupations and that this "oversupply" would tend to depress wages in a fashion similar to that posited by Bergmann. While wages reflect marginal productivity, productivity is low. Our major criticism of Sawhill's paper is provided in the text below. See Isabell V. Sawhill, "The Economics of Discrimination against Women: Some New Findings," *Journal of Human Resources* 8 (Summer 1973): 383–95; and Gary S. Becker, *Human Capital: A Theoretical and Empirical Analysis, with Special Reference to Education* (New York: Columbia University Press, 1964).

embodies a lengthy firm-specific training process (such as executive-trainee programs or, more broadly conceived, any "learning by doing" process)—because of actual or perceived high turnover rates (labor quality differences).

However, a major problem exists with this logic; *both* male and female occupations require varying amounts and types of skills. Some female as well as some male occupations require lengthy general training programs—nursing and architects, for example. Furthermore, some female as well as some male occupations require firm-specific training—executive secretaries and administrative assistants, for instance. Finally, some female as well as some male occupations require few skills and do not provide a potential for productivity increases through experience—for example, waitressing and janitorial work.[17]

The point is that men and women are in occupations of each skill type and that within each category certain occupations are "more" acceptable for women to enter than others. The human capital school's reliance on the primacy of the family in a woman's life could only explain a greater tendency of women to be in "low-skill" jobs. With this reasoning, they could not explain the concentration of women in a small number of female occupations within each skill category. To explain this concentration the school would have to rely on women's "tastes."

An elaboration of this point necessitates a brief description of their implicit theory of occupational choice, essentially a slightly modified version of the revealed preference theory of consumer behavior which states: "If their [two respective goods] price tags tell us that A is not cheaper than B, then there is only one plausible explanation of the consumer's choice—he bought A because he *likes* it better (italics added)."[18] We believe that an analogous description of a theory of occupational choice for women within the human capital framework would be: "If their [two respective occupations] wage tags tell us that A does not offer more than B, then there is only one explanation of the worker's choice—she entered A because she *likes* it better."

It is clear from our analogy that the model assumes freedom of choice. There is no acknowledgment or concern expressed over the constraints imposed by society which limit women's freedom to make their own decisions or influence the way in which others, such as employers, make decisions for them. Women's decisions to become secretaries and nurses rather than surveyors and pharmacists are seen as a matter of personal preferences. While human capital theorists do ac-

17. See Carol L. Jusenius, "The Influence of Work Experience and Typicality of Occupational Assignment on Women's Earnings," *Dual Careers*, Manpower Research Monograph no. 21, vol. 4 (Washington, D.C.: Department of Labor, 1976).

18. William J. Baumol, *Economic Theory and Operations Research*, 2d rev. ed. (Englewood Cliffs, N.J.: Prentice-Hall, Inc., 1965), p. 198.

knowledge that the extant set of tastes may reflect the socialization process of women's youth, they also note that attempts to understand this process are outside the scope of their analyses.[19]

In conclusion, the human capital model is subject to criticism on several grounds. It, too, relies on an elusive factor termed tastes to explain why women "choose" to enter a given occupation or to have a given preference for nonmarket work, without providing an underlying theory which would explain that choice. Moreover, it is not clear why *only* women should have such tastes nor is it clear why a large proportion of women should exhibit the same set of tastes—as demonstrated by their occupational distribution. An outcome of occupational segregation again requires an extreme distribution of tastes—only in this case it is the distribution of women's tastes which is relevant. Finally, just as the approach taken by Bergmann neglects supply-side considerations, the human capital school often fails to consider demand-side (employer) factors,[20] despite the elementary principle of economics that prices (wages) are determined by the intersection of both supply and demand curves.

The Monopsony Model

The theories discussed thus far have been based on models of perfect competition. In such a system a worker's wage equals the value of his or her marginal product and wage differentials between men and women reflect differing productivities—due either to women's lower level of accumulated human capital or to overcrowding with its associated implications of a relatively low capital-labor ratio. An important departure from this approach is the monopsony model, first presented by Robinson and more recently developed by Madden.[21]

As is well known in economic theory, a worker who faces a monopsonist receives a wage which is less than the value of his or her marginal product. The degree of divergence between wages and marginal value products depends upon the extent to which monopsony elements are present in a given labor market. Alternatively stated, the divergence is determined by the wage elasticity of the supply of labor to the firm.[22]

19. Victor R. Fuchs, "Differences in Hourly Earnings between Men and Women," *Monthly Labor Review* 94 (May 1971): 9–15; and Mincer and Polacheck.

20. They also neglect the possibility that wage differences associated with productivity differentials may be exacerbated by an overcrowding phenomenon. This point is made by Sawhill.

21. Janice Fanning Madden, *The Economics of Sex Discrimination* (Lexington, Mass.: Lexington Books, 1973); and Joan Robinson, *The Economics of Imperfect Competition* (1933; reprint ed., New York: St. Martin's Press, 1965).

22. For the case of a monopsonist selling his product in a competitive market, Madden's equation relating a worker's marginal value product to his/her wage is: $P(\delta Q/\delta L) = W(1 + 1/\theta)$, where θ is the elasticity of labor supply (see p. 71).

A crucial element of the monopsony model as developed by Madden is this relationship between elasticity of supply and wages. To explain, the less elastic the supply curve of labor, the lower will be the wage, assuming (1) a profit-maximizing firm and (2) an upward-sloping supply curve of labor to the firm. Thus, it is argued that women's wages are lower than those of men because the supply curve of women to the firm is less wage-elastic than that of men. In other words, a firm has greater monopsony power over women than over men.

Furthermore, this greater degree of power is caused by women's relative immobility—a lack of mobility which may be caused by the fixity of the woman's place of residence (a supply-side problem) or by a lack of demand for women in alternative occupations. In the first case, this is equivalent to the location of the husband's job, rather than that of the wife's, determining the family's place of residence; one possibility in the second case is occupational segregation.

While this model is intriguing, its general applicability may be limited. In the model, wage differences may be explained by women having a *less* elastic supply curve of labor to the firm; it is quite possible, however, that women's supply curve may, in fact, be more wage-elastic. An examination of the elements which underlie the supply curves of men and women helps to explain this possibility. First, since women have a socially acceptable occupation (housewife) outside the labor force, they have more mobility than men—in one sense at least. Their relative immobility within the labor force could be counterbalanced by their greater ability to move in and out of the labor market altogether. Second, offsetting men's greater possibilities for occupational and geographic mobility are the mobility-reducing factors of firm-specific training and pension rights which could be postulated to affect men more than women. Given these countervailing forces for both men and women, then, the wage-elasticity of women's supply curve of labor relative to that of men appears to be indeterminate a priori and may reasonably be expected to differ by occupational category. Thus, although the monopsony model (or better yet, an oligopsony model) would seem to offer some promise as a basis for future empirical analyses of the relationship between occupational segregation and wage differentials, at this point there appear to be a number of unresolved difficulties in its application to this problem.

An Assessment of the Neoclassical Models

In general, the neoclassical approach has generated a number of plausible explanations for the male-female pay differential. However, sex segregation is far from a necessary outcome in these models, and the factors which are identified as causes of pay differentials are not persuasive as causes of sex segregation *within* the neoclassical model.

A major problem is that the smooth marginal adjustments inherent in neoclassical models. particularly with respect to wage rates, make the extreme outcome of segregation highly unlikely. This also implies that segregation would be an unlikely outcome in a world for which the neoclassical models are a reasonably accurate description. This is the case regardless of the location of the postulated forces, that is, either on the demand or the supply side.

For example, as noted for the overcrowding model, complete exclusion of women from occupations (or firms) will occur only if the wage differential between male and female labor is not sufficiently large to compensate the employer for the disutility incurred by hiring women for "male" jobs. Here one needs to posit an extreme distribution of employer tastes to obtain the extreme outcome of segregation.

Supply-side factors, such as labor quality, are even less plausible explanations of the causes of segregation, since flexible wage rates can easily equalize per-unit labor costs among workers of different quality. The need for segregation is obviated, and its existence only emerges as an outcome of an extreme distribution of women's tastes.

On a purely theoretical level such difficulties can be relatively easily surmounted. One may simply postulate an extreme distribution of tastes or summon the necessary price or other rigidities.[23] However, it is our view that placing the issue within the context of a model which explicitly takes into account the institutions of the labor market is a more useful approach. Such an approach removes the need for an assumption of an *extreme* structure of tastes and enables one to specify more completely the rigidities within the system which provide the impetus toward segregation.

Thus, we turn to an institutional model to enhance our understanding of why the same set of factors which produce a male-female pay differential would also produce sex segregation. While such an analysis conducted solely at a theoretical level cannot finally determine whether demand- or supply-side factors are more important, by further elucidating the role which employers play in this process, it can strengthen the credibility of demand-side explanations.

An Institutional Approach

The particular institutional model which is presented here is derived from the internal labor market analysis.[24] The major application of

23. Madden does offer some reasons for a price-discriminating monopsonist to differentiate male and female labor markets. However, we believe her explanations would have been more satisfactory had they been firmly grounded in a more complete analysis of the institutional arrangements within the firm. A similar point can be raised regarding some of the rigidities to which Arrow alludes.

24. For early expositions of relevant concepts, see, e.g., John T. Dunlop, "The Task of Contemporary Wage Theory," in *New Concepts in Wage Determination*, ed. George W.

this model to pay differentials and employment distribution differences among groups has been the dual labor market formulation.²⁵ While the dual labor market analysis is relevant for understanding the causes and consequences of sex segregation, for a variety of reasons, we see it as an inadequate characterization of the total problem. Thus, what follows may be considered a more direct application of the internal labor market analysis to the problem of pay and employment distribution differences by sex, although it incorporates some of the insights of the dual labor market theorists. The intention is not to develop a rigorous formulation but to indicate the potential of this mode of analysis.²⁶

The Internal Labor Market Approach

The notion of an internal labor market focuses upon the division of the job structure of the enterprise into two categories of occupations. First are those job categories which are filled from sources external to the firm through the recruitment of new workers. Within clusters of related occupations, such entry jobs are generally restricted to lower-level positions. Second are those job categories which are filled from internal sources through the promotion and upgrading of presently employed workers. For the most part, access to this latter type of position occurs through advancement up well-defined promotion ladders. The process by which workers advance from entry-level positions to higher-level jobs is conceptualized within this approach as one in which they acquire, either formally or informally, added knowledge or skills which, for the most part, are specific or unique to the firm.

Within this framework the market forces delineated by neoclassical economic analysis are perceived as operating principally in occupations at the entry level. On the other hand, the requirement of enterprise-specific skills for the performance of internally allocated jobs

Taylor and Frank C. Pierson (New York: McGraw-Hill, Inc., 1957), pp. 117–39; E. Robert Livernash, "The Internal Wage Structure," in Taylor and Pierson, pp. 140–72; and Clark Kerr, "The Balkanization of Labor Markets," in *Labor Mobility and Economic Opportunity* (Cambridge, Mass.: M.I.T. Press, 1954), pp. 92–110. We have in this presentation drawn heavily on the synthesis of the human capital and institutional analyses provided by Peter B. Doeringer and Michael J. Piore, *Internal Labor Markets and Manpower Analysis* (Lexington, Mass.: D. C. Heath Co., 1971), and have also benefited from the recent clarification of a number of important issues by Michael L. Wachter, "Primary and Secondary Labor Markets: A Critique of the Dual Approach," vol. 3 in *Brookings Papers on Economic Activity*, ed. Arthur M. Okun and George L. Perry (Washington, D.C.: Brookings Institution, 1975) pp. 637–93. Since the internal labor market analysis has not been worked out with the rigor or even the consensus of the neoclassical approach, this presentation must be considered to some extent interpretive.

25. For elucidations of the dual labor market analysis, see, e.g., Doeringer and Piore; Michael J. Piore, "The Dual Labor Market: Theory and Implications" in *Problems in Political Economy*, ed. Gordon, pp. 90–94; and Gordon, *Theories of Poverty and Underemployment*.

26. See Blau, "Pay Differentials," for a rigorous development and application of such a model to the special case of intraoccupational pay and employment differences by sex.

works to prevent the development of a competitive market (in the traditional sense) for these categories of occupations. In the place of the direct operation of market forces, an internal labor market develops, that is, an administrative apparatus which allocates labor and determines wage rates within the firm.

With respect to the allocation of labor, administrative rules and customs define the boundaries of occupational "mobility clusters"—job categories within which horizontal and, more importantly, vertical mobility is possible. Stated somewhat differently, the advancement opportunities open to workers within the enterprise are generally determined by the original entry-level job the worker had obtained.[27]

With respect to wage determination, job evaluation plans and other administrative arrangements are frequently used to establish base pay rates for each occupational category and to specify wage relationships among occupations. Custom, as well as administrative arrangements, plays a role in maintaining interoccupational wage relationships. Within occupational categories, pay differentials among workers are generally based on seniority and merit considerations.

Thus, the internal labor market structure is seen as specifying a relatively rigid set of wage relationships and promotional possibilities, both of which are defined primarily in terms of job categories. The wage relationships among individuals and the promotional possibilities for any given individual are for the most part established as a consequence of their job assignment.[28]

Sex Segregation and Male-Female Pay Differentials

Two points in this theoretical framework are particularly relevant for an understanding of occupational segregation and its relationship to pay differentials by sex. First, within the internal labor market, group or categorical treatment of individuals is the norm. Such group treatment will be most efficient (result in the discarding of the least information), the greater the degree of intragroup homogeneity with respect to whatever characteristics are considered important.[29] Clearly, sex is an obvious basis for such differentiation, due to employers' distaste for hiring

27. This is not to say that *all* workers in a specific entry-job category will *automatically* be promoted to the related higher-level jobs but rather that the possibility of obtaining such promotions will be limited to that group of workers. The relative weight assigned to seniority and merit in promotion decisions varies by enterprise and by type of occupation, but sole reliance on seniority would be extremely rare.

28. Of course, as noted earlier, individual differentiation is possible; some individuals are promoted, and others are not; seniority and merit considerations result in intraoccupational pay differences. However, we see the scope for individual differentiation as narrow relative to the extent of categorical treatment.

29. At the limit, if all members of the group are identical, decision making on the basis of group characteristics would be equivalent to decision making based on the characteristics of each individual, and thus equally efficient.

women in male occupations and/or real or perceived quality differences between male and female labor.

Furthermore, while prejudice and stereotyping may cloud employers' decisions regarding occupational assignments for men and women, this does not prevent considerable differentiation *within* the group of female workers (i.e., on the basis of characteristics such as education, age, and marital status). Thus, we are postulating more than a simple dichotomy between male and female labor markets. This analysis is consistent with the observed range of characteristics of female jobs which was noted earlier.

Second, within the internal labor market framework, the "extreme" outcome of segregation is no longer surprising. Indeed, such segregation is the primary way in which employers can differentiate between men and women, *even* with respect to wage rates. Under the constraints imposed by the administered system of the internal labor market, the latitude of the employer to differentiate among individuals (or sex groups) is broadest with respect to the selection of new workers for entry jobs. It is somewhat less broad, but still considerable, with respect to the allocation of workers among job categories filled from internal sources. (Here the employer is constrained to select individuals only from job categories along "appropriate" promotion ladders and may be forced in some cases to give a greater than desired weight to seniority.)[30] It is narrowest with respect to wage differentiation among individuals within the same job category (such differentiation must be within the relatively narrow bounds determined by seniority and merit considerations), and with respect to the alteration of wage relationships among occupational categories.[31]

Indeed, within the internal labor market, wage rates might almost be considered the monetary (or value) dimension of the job structure. Once this conceptual linkage between occupational categories and wage rates has been established, it becomes clear that any factor that would tend to cause male-female pay differences would also tend to cause segregation along sex lines.

Illustrations of the Usefulness of the Internal Labor Market Analysis

The purpose of this section is to provide a few illustrations of the

---

30. Of course, these may not be onerous constraints, because workers in the designated job categories are presumably in the best position to obtain the requisite firm-specific training, while more experienced workers (those with greater seniority) may in general be the best qualified for promotion.

31. Two immediately testable hypotheses derived from this analysis are: (1) while it is unlikely that men and women will be employed in the same job in the same firm, when this does occur, sex pay differentiation should be close to zero, and (2) the relative wage position of the firm in comparison to others in the labor market should be consistent across related occupations. Support for these hypotheses is provided by Blau, "Pay Differentials," for selected white-collar occupations in three Northeastern cities.

way in which the institutional approach sheds light on the process of sex segregation and pay differentials between men and women. It also demonstrates the way in which this approach differs from the previously discussed neoclassical models.

Statistical discrimination.—One factor working to restrict the access of women to job categories (or firms) to which the internal labor market analysis calls attention is the possibility of what Piore[32] has termed "statistical discrimination," a situation in which decisions regarding individuals are based on group-derived probabilities. Thus, if employers perceive women as less stable workers (i.e., as having higher rates of turnover and/or absenteeism than men), then individual women may be excluded from certain types of employment on a probabilistic basis.[33] This is appropriately defined as a form of discrimination even if employers' perceptions of the average sex differential are correct, since it is a manifestation of stereotyping, the treatment of each individual member of a group as if he/she possessed the average characteristics of the group.

In a neoclassical world, such a consideration would be expected to result in pay differentials by sex, since employers would discount female wages in compensation for the higher fixed labor costs associated with the higher anticipated female turnover/absenteeism rates. However, given flexible wage rates, such labor costs differences would not necessarily result in segregation in these models.[34] In the internal labor market model, it becomes clear that segregation is the inevitable result, since higher labor costs are not an institutionally acceptable basis of intraoccupational pay differentiation.[35]

Occupational assignment versus occupational choice.—In the neoclassical world, and particularly within the framework of the human capital

32. See Piore.

33. In citing this view, we are in no way suggesting that it is correct. To our knowledge no evidence exists to support the proposition that, *other things being equal,* women have higher rates of turnover and/or absenteeism. See Weisskoff (n. 2 above), and Myra Strober, "Lower Pay for Women: A Case of Economic Discrimination?" *Industrial Relations* 2 (May 1972): 279–84, for a further discussion of the labor cost argument.

34. See Arrow (n. 9 above) for information costs; for statistical discrimination see Edwin S. Phelps, "The Statistical Theory of Racism and Sexism," *American Economic Review* 62 (September 1972): 659–61.

35. Some evidence that an assessment of probabilities may remain foremost in an employer's mind even when his own experience indicates that individual women can become long-term employees is provided in a local labor market study. One surveyed employer stated that if his present payroll supervisor (a woman) were to leave, he would replace her with a man—only because of the greater employment permanency for men. Yet this particular woman had been with the firm for 15 years. See Georgina M. Smith, *Help Wanted—Female: A Study of Demand and Supply in a Local Job Market for Women* (New Brunswick, N.J.: Institute of Management and Labor Relations, Rutgers University, 1965), p. 25.

analysis, individuals are expected to select an occupation on the basis of taste. While tastes are undoubtedly an important factor, they may be the critical variable for only a relatively small set of occupations, namely those in which the individual obtains some occupation-specific training prior to employment. For many jobs, the employer may determine the occupation of the worker within the broad limits set by the worker's tastes and alternative employment options.

Many jobs are unique to certain industries and even to certain enterprises. Individuals frequently come to a firm in search of work within a broad and rather vaguely defined category or cateogries of jobs. Employers (or those performing the personnel function within the firm) determine whether the individual is to be hired and for which entry-level job. If the worker remains with the firm, then this initial decision will determine the promotion opportunities open to him or her in succeeding years. Furthermore, management will decide whether such promotions occur and the speed with which the worker advances up the promotion ladder. Thus, in many cases a concept of occupational assignment may be more reflective of reality than the accepted notion of occupational choice. The occupational distribution differences between men and women may to some extent reflect employer decisions to exclude women from certain entry-level positions and their associated promotion ladders and/or to promote and upgrade women more slowly than men. Indeed, the very structure of the jobs typically open to women is likely to reflect employer perceptions regarding the average characteristics of female workers. Predominantly female occupations may be characterized by fewer possibilities for promotion and more numerous ports of entry than comparable male jobs—the common complaint that "women's jobs" are "dead-end jobs."[36]

Exogeneity of worker quality.—Proponents of the human capital school often seem to imply that individual productivity is uniquely and exogeneously determined by the characteristics of workers. On the other hand, while advocates of the overcrowding hypothesis do acknowledge productivity variations between men and women due to occupation or establishment of employment, they specify the capital-labor ratio as the underlying cause of productivity differences. An institutional approach calls attention to these and other factors.

Within an internal labor market framework, worker productivity is determined partly on the basis of individual characteristics but more importantly as a function of the attributes of each worker in combination with the characteristics of occupations and firms. The model suggests that a range of equal cost alternatives are open to the firm in terms of

36. For some evidence on these points, see Equal Employment Opportunity Commission, "A Unique Competence: A Study of Equal Employment Opportunity in the Bell System," in U.S. Congress, Senate, *Congressional Record: Extensions of Remarks* (February 17, 1972), 92d Cong., 2d sess., 1972, 118, 1243–72.

hiring practices, work organization, and wage policies. For example, the amount of labor turnover (and thus the average years of experience obtained by workers) in specific occupational categories or firms may be seen as the outcome of the personal characteristics of workers, the wage rate paid, the opportunities offered for advancement, working conditions, and the quality of management. Similarly, the skill levels of employees may reasonably be related to the existence and quality of training programs. Furthermore, the diligence and effort expended by workers in job-related tasks may be related to the wage standing of the firm and other personnel practices. Thus, denial of access to certain job categories or firms may mean not only that certain workers—for example, some women—receive lower wages but also that they are less productive. This further implies that reallocating individuals from one work environment to another could change their productivity, as well as their wage rate.

The Dual Labor Market Analysis[37]

As noted earlier, the dual labor market analysis has been the major application of the internal labor market approach to the set of wage and employment questions under consideration in this paper. The dual labor market analysis postulates that a dichotomy between "primary" and "secondary" employment characterizes the labor market position of disadvantaged groups like blacks. It has been suggested that the analysis may also be applied to women.

The primary market has the characteristics of a highly developed internal labor market. As noted earlier, entry is restricted to relatively few lower-level jobs; promotion ladders are long; worker stability is encouraged by high wages, opportunities for advancement, good working conditions, and provisions for job security. The administration of work rules is characterized by adherence to the principles of equity and due process.

At the other extreme, the secondary market more closely approximates a set of "unstructured markets." The occupational distribution is characterized by numerous ports of entry; promotion ladders are short or nonexistent; worker stability tends to be discouraged by low wages, little opportunity for advancement, poor working conditions, and little provision for job security. The administration of work rules may be characterized by arbitrary and even harsh discipline.

The desired long-term attachment between workers and firms in primary sector jobs leads employers to select new workers who have good future performance prospects, particularly with respect to job stability. Thus, statistical discrimination (as well as pure discrimination à la

37. For references for this section, see n. 24.

Becker) is seen to be a factor governing the access of workers to primary employment.

According to this theory, many job candidates who are excluded on such grounds do in fact possess the requisite behavioral characteristics for primary sector employment. While productivity (and/or labor cost) differences may account for a significant portion of the wage difference between these erroneously excluded individuals and those employed in the primary sector, such differences would be due to the way in which the work is structured in the secondary sector rather than to particular characteristics of these individuals.

It is likely that a higher proportion of women than men are in secondary jobs, and the dual labor market analysis is useful in understanding the causes and consequences of this distinction. However, this approach does not explain the further sex segregation which certainly exists in each sector. Nor does it do justice to the range of characteristics of predominantly female jobs, that is, the differentiation which occurs *within* the female sector. Further, in contrast to our formulation, it is not helpful in elucidating the differential treatment accorded to women and men *within* the primary sector, that is, within reasonably highly developed internal labor markets. Additional empirical research would be necessary to determine the relative importance of the primary-secondary distinction for women's labor market status.[38]

An Assessment of the Internal Labor Market Model

Some controversy among economists surrounds the question of whether the allocative and wage outcomes of the internal labor market do, in fact, diverge from those of a competitive market system, or whether the institutional arrangements emphasized by the internal labor market analysis are merely trappings which overlie, but do not alter, the outcomes predicted by neoclassical models.[39] Such a question is clearly of great importance to economists, since the necessity and usefulness of an institutional approach hinges upon its resolution. Although this paper has not fully examined this question, it has demonstrated that an institutional approach can help to explain why sex segregation and wage differentiation occur.

When a divergence of outcomes between the administered and competitive systems appears, it does not necessarily follow that the administered system is irrational or inefficient. Rather, it is precisely because the administered system does work relatively effectively on the whole, and because it is a reasonable adaptation to the conditions that

38. For additional and more general criticism of the dual labor market model see Wachter (n. 24 above).

39. For discussions of why the two models might result in different outcomes, see Doeringer and Piore and Wachter.

lead to the development of an internal market, that employers are willing to abide by institutional arrangements that might on the surface appear irrational.[40]

In a situation in which the market simply is not available, recourse must be had to other arrangements. Thus, while the institutional arrangements of the internal labor market do introduce a certain degree of rigidity and inflexibility into the processes of labor allocation and wage determination, they also serve to remove uncertainties which would hamper both the day-to-day operations and long-range planning needs of the individual firm. For example, where the firm-specific component of the skills necessary to perform internally allocated jobs is substantial, a situation of "bilateral monopoly" is created. On one side, the employer acquires a degree of monopsony power, since the worker's firm-specific skills are not transferable or valuable to other firms. On the other side, the worker acquires a degree of monopoly power over his or her job, since a supply of similarly qualified individuals is not available from outside the firm (and perhaps even from other sources within the firm) without considerable cost.

The wage outcome of such a situation is indeterminate within certain boundaries. Therefore, an administered system, despite its rigidities, may be preferable to both employers and workers than the alternative frequent haggling over wages and other working conditions—a constant test of the relative bargaining strength of each side. Similarly, where workers are not easily replaceable, employers may be more concerned about such factors as morale and are therefore more willing to adhere to the customs and traditions of the work place.[41]

While the internal labor market may be relatively efficient with respect to many aspects of its operation, it is not necessarily rational in its treatment of women and minorities—and it does not appear to produce socially satisfactory outcomes for these groups.

Conclusion

This paper has assessed the contributions made by neoclassical and institutional labor-market economists to the study of sex segregation and pay differentials between men and women. We have argued that the major contribution of the neoclassical school has been to suggest plausible reasons for male-female pay differences. However, the implications of these analyses for understanding the linkage between such pay

40. Economists will recognize that we make no claims here regarding the satisfaction of efficiency conditions. The internal labor market model simply has not been developed with sufficient rigor to permit a definitive statement regarding the efficiency of the system.

41. See Wachter for a lucid discussion of these and other issues relating to efficiency (see also Doeringer and Piore).

differentials and sex segregation have been found to be less satisfactory. Therefore, in an effort to understand this linkage better it became necessary to turn to an institutional approach. Although this particular institutional framework has clearly not been fully developed here, we have attempted to demonstrate that it is useful and thereby to show that it is deserving of further attention and elaboration. While the major points of the institutional analysis have not thus far been incorporated to any great extent into neoclassical models, it may well be possible, and indeed fruitful, for the profession to move in this direction.

University of Illinois at Urbana-Champaign (Blau)
Ohio State University (Jusenius)

Economic Dimensions of Occupational Segregation

Discrimination and Poverty among Women Who Head Families

Isabel Sawhill

Introduction

Attitudes toward working women and the wages they earn have long been influenced by the implicit assumption that men support families whereas women do not. Yet one out of every seven children in the United States lives in a family where the father is absent.[1] This paper is concerned with these families headed by women, with how and why they have been growing, their economic status, and the policy alternatives for dealing with the poverty they so often face. Data are presented which suggest that labor market discrimination and occupational segregation are factors which contribute to the lack of income which characterizes these families.

The Recent Growth of Families Headed by Women

Over the past decade, female-headed families with children[2] have grown almost ten times as fast as two-parent families. This unprec-

1. Even in husband-wife families, the wife's earnings are often essential to family well-being. In 1970, of those wives who worked full time during the entire year, 22 percent contributed over 50 percent of total family income. See Carolyn Shaw Bell, "Working Women's Contribution to Family Income," *Eastern Economic Journal* 1, no. 3 (July 1974): 185–201.

2. There are a large number of female-headed families *without* children (as when two

edented and rather surprising trend is depicted in figure 1. Moreover, it appears that this shift in family structure has accelerated in the last few years; there were one million more mothers heading families in 1973 than in 1970, an increase which exceeded the net growth over the entire previous decade.

In research being conducted at the Urban Institute during the past year or two, we have examined the reasons for this growth in some detail.[3] By far the most important factor contributing to such growth is increased marital instability, especially among relatively young women with children. Compared to their mothers' generation, young women today are two-and-a-half times as likely to be divorced by the time they reach their early thirties. Using somewhat conservative assumptions, demographers are predicting that almost one out of every three marriages among these younger couples will end in divorce at some time during their lives.[4] Other factors, such as higher illegitimacy rates and the decline of extended-family living arrangements, have also contributed to the increase in female-headed families, but they have played a decidedly minor role relative to marital instability.

What is causing this rise in divorce and separation rates? Our research suggests that an important factor is increasing economic opportunities for women outside marriage. There is now fairly convincing evidence that the higher a wife's earnings, other things being equal, the more likely it is that a couple will separate.[5] We suspect that changing attitudes about women's roles and the fact that more married women are participating in the labor market have combined to create new tensions within marriage while simultaneously decreasing the social and economic constraints which once bound many women to relatively unsatisfactory marriages.

Let me draw out the implications of this research even further. The ultimate form of occupational segregation would be a situation in which a culture dictated that all women be "housewives" with no access to any other occupation. Under these circumstances, women would have to marry, and remain married, for economic reasons. Social protections in the form of life insurance, alimony, child support, social security, and

---

sisters live together) and a still-larger number of female-headed *households*. Female-headed households include individuals living alone or with nonrelatives in addition to female-headed families. This paper focuses, then, on a subset of all female-headed households—i.e., those consisting of a mother and her children.

3. The results of much of this work are available in *Time of Transition: The Growth of Families Headed by Women* by Heather Ross and Isabel Sawhill, with the assistance of Anita MacIntosh (Washington, D.C.: Urban Institute, 1975).

4. Paul C. Glick and Arthur J. Norton, "Perspectives on the Recent Upturn in Divorce and Remarriage," *Demography* 10, no. 3 (August 1973): 301–14.

5. This finding is based on a regression analysis of the marital behavior of about 2,500 couples over the period 1968–72. The data are from the University of Michigan's "Panel Study of Income Dynamics."

**GROWTH OF FEMALE-HEADED FAMILIES WITH CHILDREN
(FHFCH) AND HUSBAND-WIFE FAMILIES WITH CHILDREN
(HWFCH) 1950-1974**
(1950 = 100)

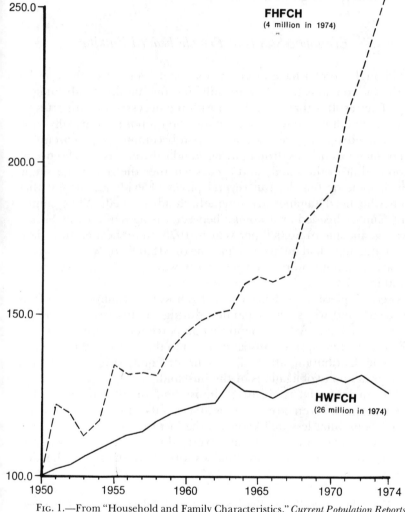

FIG. 1.—From "Household and Family Characteristics," *Current Population Reports,* ser. P-20 (Washington, D.C.: Bureau of the Census, 1974).

AFDC might be created to help those who became temporarily or permanently "unemployed." But most women would be reluctant to leave the security of married living especially if their age made it unlikely that they would be able to find a new "husband-employer." However, as other occupations opened up to women, they might be less reluctant to seek such a change. In addition, they could implicitly use these alternatives to bargain for better treatment within marriage. Just as the wages of secretaries can be expected to rise as more women move into the professions, so will the "rights" of all women (including housewives) increase as they gain access to new sources of employment generally and to the resources that go with them.

The Economic Status of Female-headed Families

Although women have more occupational alternatives than in the past, the fact remains that they are still an economically disadvantaged group. The result is that when faced with the necessity of supporting a family, many fall into poverty and those who do not must usually cope with a sharp drop in living standards upon becoming single parents.

To some extent, this drop in living standards reflects the absence of a second adult in the family and occurs whether the remaining single parent is male or female. But several pieces of evidence suggest that women who head families are uniquely disadvantaged. While single-parent families headed by a woman between the ages of 25 and 44 had an average income of $6,000 per year in 1973, those headed by a similarly situated man had an average income of $12,000, or twice as much. Two-parent families were even better off with an average income of $15,000 in 1973.[6]

A second piece of evidence comes from Robert Hampton's analysis of husbands and wives who separated during the first six years of the Michigan Panel Survey.[7] He found that 35 percent of ex-wives but only 19 percent of their former husbands fell into the bottom 30 percent of the income distribution, after adjustment for family size and any child support or alimony obligations of the husband.

Not surprisingly, therefore, almost half of all female-headed families with children are poor, and a similar proportion are on welfare.[8] Somewhat less well-known is the fact that many male-headed families were able to escape from poverty during the sixties with the result that a majority of all poor families with children are now headed by a woman.[9]

6. "Money Income in 1973 of Families and Persons in the U.S.," *Current Population Report,* ser. P-60, no. 97, table 29 (Washington, D.C.: Bureau of the Census, 1975).
7. Robert Hampton, "Marital Disruption: Some Social and Economic Consequences," in *Five Thousand American Families—Patterns of Economic Progress,* ed. Greg J. Duncan and James N. Morgan (Ann Arbor: Survey Research Center of the University of Michigan, 1975), 3:163–87.
8. "National Cross Tabulations," *Findings of the 1971 AFDC Study,* pt. 3 (Washington, D.C.: DHEW National Center for Social Statistics, 1973), table 34; and "Household and Family Characteristics: 1973," *Current Population Reports,* ser. P-20, no. 258 (Washington, D.C.: Bureau of the Census, 1974).
9. "Characteristics of the Low Income Population: 1973," *Current Population Reports,* ser. P-60, no. 98, table 4 (Washington, D.C.: Bureau of the Census, 1975).

Is this link between poverty and family structure inevitable? And if not, what kinds of changes in public policy or in social attitudes will be required to improve the economic status of these families?

The Role of Public Policy

The traditional response to the poverty of female-headed families has been income-conditioned transfers either in cash or in kind. But the increasing fragility of marital ties—perhaps exacerbated by the availability of these transfers[10]—together with changing attitudes about the economic dependency of women have led to the search for alternative solutions. One of these alternatives is to provide some combination of work incentives, market opportunities, and social services (such as child care) to enable low-income women to contribute more earned income to their families. Another alternative is to improve the flow of non-earned income to these families—to replace or supplement public transfers with private transfers in the form of child support from absent parents. Casual observation and some statistical evidence suggest that present state child-support laws have fallen far behind the needs of a rapidly growing population of one-parent homes and that enforcement of the existing inadequate laws is weakly and unevenly applied. In 1973, only 22 percent of court-ordered payments to AFDC families were being met in full, and in about half the cases there was no compliance at all.[11] Furthermore, data collected by the General Accounting Office in 1974 indicate that there is little relationship between a father's ability to pay and either the amount of the agreed-upon payment or his compliance with the law. Some low-income men are paying substantial proportions of their income to support their children while many who are more affluent have failed to comply at all.[12] Recent concern with this issue has produced new legislation (P.L. 94-88 signed August 9, 1975, 89 Stat. 433) establishing a separate organizational unit within HEW to monitor, evaluate, and assist the states in their child-support collection efforts. In addition, some research is being done on the costs and benefits of various kinds of administrative and enforcement procedures at the state level. But there has been no comprehensive assessment of the current system and no attempt to rethink and reformulate basic policy to meet the income needs of an ever-growing number of children living with only one parent.

Although greater attention needs to be given to improving the flow

10. Ross and Sawhill, *Time of Transition*, includes a detailed discussion of the extent to which AFDC contributes to family instability.

11. "Financial Circumstances," *Findings of the 1973 AFDC Study*, pt. 2-A (Washington, D.C.: DHEW National Center for Social Statistics, 1974), p. 4.

12. U.S. Congress, House, *Congressional Record*, 93d Cong., 2d sess., 1974, 120, pt. 168.

of both public and private transfers to female-headed families, such policies treat the symptoms rather than the basic causes of poverty for this group. The problem ultimately lies in the structure of the labor market and in social attitudes about women's position in society. The remainder of this paper focuses on the labor market handicaps facing low-income women and on the possibilities of moving this group toward greater independence from both private and public transfers.

Labor Market Opportunities

In recent years, much rhetoric has been heard on the subject of getting people "off the welfare rolls and onto payrolls," and much effort has been devoted to improving work incentives and providing supportive services (training, job placement, day care) for those on welfare. In spite of these efforts, only 16 percent of AFDC mothers were working in 1973.[13] Experience with WIN, as well as attitudinal surveys, has suggested that there is a very high motivation to work among welfare mothers. However, the low-paid jobs available to them are not very competitive with benefits available through AFDC and various in-kind programs, and the combined benefit-loss rates associated with these programs remain high. Although welfare reform which reduced the implicit tax on earned income could be expected to bring more welfare recipients into the labor force, there are well-known budgetary constraints associated with raising net wages in this manner.

More importantly, no amount of work effort on the part of female heads of families will go very far in reducing their poverty and dependence on welfare as long as these women face such low wages in the market. To illustrate the seriousness of this problem and its overwhelming importance in understanding the poverty and welfare dependence of female-headed families, three different analyses of female earnings are reviewed below. The first is based on an experiment with the Urban Institute's microsimulation model, the results of which have been presented in a paper by Richard Wertheimer.[14] The next is a secondary analysis of a set of findings from the 1960 Census, originally reported by Harold Guthrie and Gordon Sutton.[15] The final piece of evidence comes from some data I have tabulated from the University of Michigan's "Panel Study of Income Dynamics."

13. "Demographic and Program Characteristics," *Findings of the 1973 AFDC Study*, pt. 1 (Washington, D.C.: DHEW National Center for Social Statistics, 1974), p. 8.

14. Richard F. Wertheimer, "Earnings of Women: Implications of Equality in the Labor Market," Urban Institute Working Paper 980-1 (Washington, D.C.: Urban Institute, 1974).

15. Harold W. Guthrie and Gordon F. Sutton, "The Role of Earning Rates in Determining Poverty," Urban Institute Reprint 145-509-7 (Washington, D.C.: Urban Institute, 1973).

Evidence from the Urban Institute's Microsimulation Model

The Urban Institute's Microanalytic Model (UIMM) takes a sample representation of the United States population and simulates their behavior over time by applying a set of behavioral relationships (earnings functions, labor force participation functions, etc.) to microunits (families, persons) which modify their attributes each year as these units age, change their marital status, have children, migrate, participate in the labor force, earn, spend, save, and so forth. The behavioral relationships have been estimated from various bodies of data and are updated as new and better theory or information emerges from ongoing research in the social sciences.

In the microsimulation experiments reported here, the initial sample consisted of about 4,000 persons drawn from the 1960 Census 1-10,000 Public Use Sample. A base run of the model was used to produce a set of individual and family earnings figures by race and sex for the period 1960–69. Three experiments were then conducted with the model. In experiment 1, women were assigned the same wage rate function as men; that is, they were assumed to earn as much as men with the same characteristics (age, education, residence, etc.). In experiment 2, women were assumed to have the same labor force participation and hours-worked functions as men. Experiment 3 combined experiments 1 and 2 to give women the same wage, participation, and hours functions as men.

Table 1 presents the results of these experiments for white female heads of families with children.[16] The wage experiment (see column 3) increased average earnings by 36 percent while the participation and hours experiment increased them by only 13 percent. In other words, this group is handicapped not so much by an inability or unwillingness to work as by the fact that they earn much less than their male counterparts when they do work.

A number of caveats should be kept in mind in interpreting the above results. First, the sample sizes are small. Second, the earnings function does not include a good measure of labor force experience (age is used as a proxy), and the labor force and hours functions do not include an earnings variable (education is used as a proxy). As a result, the dynamic interdependence between earnings and labor force participation is not adequately captured in the model. Finally, the earnings function includes occupation, as an independent variable in four broadly defined categories, so that the wage experiment does not completely adjust for occupational segregation between men and women.

16. The results for nonwhites are not shown here because the sample size was much smaller. However, both their earnings and work participation are much lower initially— probably because they have larger families and face greater discrimination. The wage experiment has about the same effect as for white women but the participation-hours experiment has a greater impact than in the case of whites.

Table 1

DISTRIBUTION OF SIMULATED EARNINGS OF 57 WHITE FEMALE
FAMILY HEADS WITH CHILDREN IN 1969

Earnings Class* ($)	Base Run (%)	Experiment 1† (%)	Experiment 2‡ (%)	Experiment 3§ (%)
0–999	35	37	28	25
1,000–2,999	39	28	39	25
3,000–4,999	9	14	18	26
5,000–7,999	7	11	9	16
8,000–9,999	4	0	0	2
10,000–14,999	7	4	7	0
15,000+	0	7	0	7
Mean‖	$2,621	$3,567	$2,961	$3,871

SOURCE.—Wertheimer, "Earnings of Women," table 2, p. 8.
*Dollars deflated to a 1958 basis.
†In experiment 1, women were assigned the same wage rate function as men.
‡In experiment 2, women were assigned the same labor force participation and hours-worked function as men.
§In experiment 3, the women were assigned the same function as men in all three areas.
‖Includes those with zero earnings.

Some of the other limitations of the model have been discussed elsewhere and are less pertinent to the findings cited here.[17]

Evidence from the 1960 Census

In their paper "The Role of Earnings Rates in Determining Poverty," Harold Guthrie and Gordon Sutton estimated an earnings
regression[18] for each detailed (three-digit) occupation using data from
the 1960 Census on individuals 14 years of age or more who reported
they had worked 50–52 weeks in 1959. The authors then calculated
expected full-year earnings for different population subgroups defined
by sex, race, age, and education level. Drawing on this analysis I have
regrouped the occupations examined by Guthrie and Sutton into those
which are traditionally male occupations (80 percent or more of all
workers male), those which are traditionally female occupations (30 percent or less male), and mixed occupations (30–80 percent male). In each
category, I then tabulated the number of occupations in which a white
female high school graduate between the ages of 25 and 34 could be
expected to earn more than $3,000 per year (poverty-level wages). The
results are shown in table 2. Thirty-one percent of all occupations in-

17. See Wertheimer.
18. The independent variables used were age (quadratic form), race, sex, and education.

Table 2

CLASSIFICATION OF OCCUPATIONS BY MALE/FEMALE PREPONDERANCE IN 1960

Occupation	Occupations with Poverty-Level Wages*		Occupations with Non-Poverty-Level Wages*		Total Occupations	
	N	%	N	%	N	%
Traditionally male† ...	20	20	79	80	99	100
Traditionally female†	13	54	11	46	24	100
Mixed	15	48	16	52	31	100
Total	48	31	106	69	154	100

SOURCE.—Guthrie and Sutton, "The Role of Earnings Rates in Determining Poverty," pp. 471–500.

NOTE.—Calculations are based on data from the 1/1000 sample of the 1960 Census. An earnings regression was estimated for each three-digit occupation for persons 14 years of age or more who reported they had worked 50–52 weeks in 1959. Where there were fewer than 50 persons in an occupational category, groups were combined to obtain larger cells. In a few cases persons who worked less than a full year had to be included, but their earnings were weighted appropriately to measure full-year earnings.

*Occupations with poverty-level wages are defined as those in which a woman who worked 50–52 weeks per year would not be expected to earn more than $3,000 if she were a white high school graduate between the ages of 25 and 34.

†Traditionally male occupations are defined as those in which 80 percent or more of all workers were male, and traditionally female occupations as those in which 30 percent or less were male.

volved poverty-level wages for women. Only 20 percent of the traditionally male occupations would entail poverty-level wages for women, whereas 54 percent of the traditionally female occupations fall into this category. It appears, therefore, that a woman who must support a family has a much greater chance of successfully meeting this responsibility if she works in that sector of the labor market which has been traditionally reserved for men. Most occupations in the sector reserved for women do not pay enough to permit a family to subsist beyond the poverty line.

These data are suggestive rather than definitive, and an analysis of 1970 Census data might show a different set of results. However, table 2 tends to support the thesis that the crowding of women into a relatively small number of low-paid occupations is a major reason for the poverty of female-headed families.

Evidence from the Panel Study on Income Dynamics

The final piece of evidence on the earnings potential of female-headed families comes from data from the University of Michigan's Panel Study of Income Dynamics, which has collected information from a representative national sample of about 5,000 families since 1968.[19] From this sample, I selected all female heads of families with children

19. See Duncan and Morgan.

who were on welfare in 1968 and who were not working at that time. I then estimated two earnings functions, one based on data for all employed female heads of families with children, and one based on all employed male heads of families with children. I used these two earnings functions to calculate potential annual earnings for the mothers on welfare.[20] The final step involved comparing their potential earnings to the income they were receiving from AFDC.

The results of these calculations are shown in table 3. When the female earnings function is used to predict earnings, half the welfare mothers could not earn as much in the labor market as they were receiving on AFDC, and only a fourth of them could increase their income by as much as $1,000 by going to work full-time.[21] On the other hand, when the male earnings function is used to predict earnings, the results change quite dramatically. Only 17 percent are better off on welfare than from working, and slightly more than half could increase their income by $1,000 or more by entering the job market. This suggests that, if women could earn as much as men with similar characteristics, there would be far less welfare dependency among female-headed families.

Table 3

EARNINGS POTENTIAL OF FAMILIES ON WELFARE IN 1968

	Based on Earnings Function for Female Heads		Based on Earnings Function for Male Heads	
	N	%	N	%
Potential annual earnings less than AFDC income in 1967	56	51	19	17
Potential annual earnings greater than AFDC income in 1967:				
Difference <$500	17	15	15	14
Difference <$1,000	11	10	17	15
Difference ≥$1,000	26	24	59	54
Total..................	110	100	110	100

SOURCE.—University of Michigan "Panel Study of Income Dynamics."
NOTE.—Figures exclude women who were working as well as receiving welfare.

20. The dependent variable was average hourly earnings. The independent variables were age, education, parents' economic status, prevailing wages in the local labor market, and years of experience with present employer. Data on total labor force experience were not available. Separate regressions were run for whites and nonwhites. Potential annual earnings were calculated by multiplying expected average hourly earnings by 2,000 hours.

21. We assume, somewhat unrealistically, that the choice between welfare and work is an all or nothing one—i.e., that there is a 100 percent tax on earnings. On the other hand, we also ignore work-related expenses, positive taxes, and in-kind benefits which will also affect the choice between work and welfare.

Conclusions

The policy implications of the analyses presented in this paper are clear; if women earned as much income in the job market as men, there would be far less poverty and welfare dependency among women who head their own families. Many of these women face discrimination on the basis of both race and sex, but the elimination of sex discrimination alone would do much to improve their economic status.

It is easy to cite discrimination as the villain; it is much more difficult to define precisely what is meant by labor market discrimination, to describe the processes by which it operates, and to find specific remedies that will ameliorate the problem. Certainly occupational segregation is part of the process, and effective enforcement of affirmative action programs is part of the solution. Less tangible, but perhaps equally important, is the need to change attitudes about sex roles within the family. Women at all economic levels continue to marry and have children on the assumption that someone else will provide for the children. About one-third of these women are going to face the prospect of divorce at some point in their lives, and an even larger proportion will be divorced among those who are the least prepared to cope in terms of education and financial resources. If more young women were made aware of this risk, they might make a different set of decisions about their own education, work experience, and childbearing. They might become more aggressive about insisting on their fair share of the better-paid jobs which they have been led to believe they are not qualified for or not welcome to enter.

In the meantime, some social protections in the form of public and private transfers will be required to ease the transition to a new division of responsibility between men and women. As Margaret Mead suggests, "For women it will be essential to provide socially responsible protection during the period when the old forms, based on male responsibility, are becoming ineffective and new arrangements that will support women's freedom to earn and to function as independent individuals have not been realized on a very large scale. Without institutional protection of this kind the ever mounting number of mother-child homes will threaten (as the existence of such homes already does) the conscience of the community and lend tremendous support to arguments in favor of the superiority of older, traditionally sanctioned forms of social organization."[22]

The Urban Institute

22. Margaret Mead, "The Life Cycle and Its Variations: The Division of Roles," *Daedalus* 96, no. 3 (Summer 1967): 871–75.

ECONOMIC DIMENSIONS OF OCCUPATIONAL SEGREGATION

Women: The New Reserve Army of the Unemployed

Marianne A. Ferber and Helen M. Lowry

With unemployment at its highest level since World War II, and the rate among women significantly higher than among men, it is not surprising to find a growing amount of attention focused on female unemployment. Some researchers have suggested that the higher level of female unemployment reflects women's peculiar supply curve for their labor which also contributes to women's inferior economic position in the labor market. This paper will contend that women's labor market behavior may be an adaptation to their inferior position rather than a cause of it, and that, to a significant extent, discrimination is the cause of both. The term "discrimination" will be used as defined by Arrow to reflect the "concept that personal characteristics of the worker unrelated to productivity are also valued on the market."[1] Section I argues that the negative impact of the occupational distribution of women on their earnings cannot be completely explained except by postulating an important role for discrimination. Section II suggests that the same conclusion is true of the high unemployment rate of women. Section III discusses the policy implications of these findings.

---

1. Kenneth J. Arrow, "The Theory of Discrimination," in *Discrimination in Labor Markets,* ed. Orley Ashenfelter and Albert Rees (Princeton, N.J.: Princeton University Press, 1973), p. 3.

Occupational Distribution and Women's Earnings[2]

It is possible to determine the impact of occupational distribution on women's earnings by estimating the change that would occur in their annual average earnings if women were distributed among occupational categories in the same proportion as men with an equal number of years of education.[3]

Data on twelve major occupational categories and six educational classes were obtained from the 1970 Census.[4] Women's annual earnings were assumed to remain stable in all cases, but the proportion of the female labor force in each cell was made equal to the proportion of the male labor force in that cell, thereby raising the average level of women's earnings by $627 to $5,773 per year. Adjusting for the fact that women in the labor force have 0.1 years more schooling than men raises the earnings by $710.[5] It is reasonable to assume that this increase would be even greater if more detailed occupational categories were used (for example, if not only the same proportion of working women as men were professional workers, but the same proportion of women professional workers were doctors, lawyers, and engineers rather than nurses and schoolteachers) and if the fact were taken into account that earnings would rise in occupations women would leave and decline in those that they would enter.

More important than a precise estimate of the loss incurred by women because of their occupational distribution[6] is why earnings are lower in occupations in which women predominate, after controlling for differences in the number of hours worked, class of worker, and

2. This section is a summary of another article: Marianne Ferber and Helen M. Lowry, "The Sex Differential in Earnings: A Reappraisal," *Industrial and Labor Relations Review,* forthcoming.

3. At present, women and men are differentially educated by occupational group. In this analysis, the educational discrepancy should be removed.

4. U.S. Bureau of the Census, *Census of Population: 1970, Earnings by Occupation and Education,* Final Report PC(2)-8B (Washington, D.C.: Government Printing Office, 1973), tables 1 and 7.

5. This figure is based on an estimate of the value of additional education to women derived from the following regression equation: $Y_F = a + bM + cE_F$, where Y_F = median earnings of female workers, M = proportion of workers who are male, and E_F = median number of years of schooling of female workers. The observations were obtained from the detailed occupational categories.

6. Some authors have developed estimates of a greater loss in income (Sanborn, Fuchs) and other have developed lower less estimates (Polachek, and the Council of Economic Advisers). See Henry Sanborn, "Pay Differences between Men and Women," *Industrial and Labor Relations Review,* vol. 17, no. 4 (July 1964); Victor R. Fuchs, "Differences in Hourly Earnings between Men and Women," *Monthly Labor Review,* vol. 94, no. 5 (May 1971); Solomon Polachek, "Work Experience and the Difference between Male and Female Workers" (Ph.D. diss., Columbia University, 1973); and Council of Economic Advisers, *1973 Economic Report of the President* (Washington, D.C.: Government Printing Office, 1974).

number of years of experience. To explore this question, 1969 data for 260 occupations were used to estimate the coefficients of the regression equation shown in table 1.[7] The dependent variable is median earnings. The independent variables are the percentage of workers who were female in each occupation, the median number of years of schooling, sex, and all the possible combinations of these terms. Two observations were used from each occupation, one for men and one for women, according to the equation:

$$Y = b_0 + b_1F + b_2E + b_3S + b_4(F \times E) + b_5(F \times S) + b_6(E \times S) + b_7(F \times E \times S),$$

where Y = median earnings, F = proportion of workers who are female, E = median number of years of schooling, and S = sex (male = 1, female = 0).

Using a stepwise procedure, we arranged the estimates of the coefficients in the order in which the variables enter the regression (see table 1).

Since the sample size was so large, 520, the t-ratios corresponding to the estimated coefficients were all, technically, significantly large. The value of R^2 at each step represents the proportion of the variation in the dependent variable that is "explained" by those independent variables entered at that step and at all previous steps. The first three variables explain 84 percent of the variation in earnings by occupations. Not surprisingly, education is one of them. More interesting, however, is the importance of the interaction between education and sex, showing that

Table 1

Stepwise Regression of Earnings by Occupation

Variable	Final Unstandardized Regression Coefficient	Cumulative R^2
Constant	−1,634	...
$E \times S$	826*	.59
E	527*	.77
$F \times E \times S$	−1,416*	.84
$F \times E$	534***	.84
$F \times S$	13,792*	.84
S	−5,877**	.84
F	−7,949**	.84

*Significant at the .01 level.
**Significant at the .05 level.
***Significant at the .10 level.

7. U.S. Bureau of the Census, *Census of Population: 1970, Occupational Characteristics,* Final Report PC(2)-7A (Washington, D.C.: Government Printing Office, 1973), tables 1, 5, and 16.

education is considerably more rewarding for men than for women. One plausible interpretation of this phenomenon is that discrimination against women increases with the status of the occupation. But other explanations are possible. One would be that women lack the type of attributes that are necessary complements if higher education is to pay off, that they are naturally better suited to being nurses and grade school teachers than physicians and university professors.[8] Another is that "from school onward the career orientation of women differs strikingly from that of men. Most women do not have as strong a vocational emphasis in their schooling."[9]

The most interesting finding is that an increasing percentage of women in an occupation has a significant negative effect on the earnings of men in occupations of high educational level. The coefficient of the interaction term $F \times E \times S$ shows clearly that lower earnings in occupations with a higher proportion of women cannot be ascribed solely to the lower productivity of women, unless one is prepared to believe that men's productivity is somehow adversely affected by the mere presence of women.

A far more plausible hypothesis is that the virtual exclusion of women from many high-status jobs causes many educated women to crowd into the occupations to which they have access. This would be expected to result in relatively low wages for these educated women and for men in these occupations as well.

This hypothesis is confirmed by evidence that an increase in the percentage of women in an occupation over time has a negative effect on earnings. A simple correlation with the change in percentage of women in 260 occupations between 1949 and 1969 shows a correlation of $-.308$ for men's and $-.330$ for women's median earnings.

The Unemployment Rate of Women

Increasing attention has been devoted in recent years to the high unemployment rate for nonwhites, teenagers, and women[10] in comparison with that experienced by adult white men. Less attention has been paid to the fact that, except for nonwhites, the unemployment rate of the former groups has tended to increase relative to the latter in recent years. Furthermore, the female teenage unemployment rate has been

8. The fact that women constitute a far larger proportion of the high status professions in many other countries raises questions about this explanation. In the U.S., 12 percent of pharmacists are women, but this figure is 92 percent in Norway. In the U.S., 7 percent of physicians are women, but in the USSR, 65 percent are women. For dentists, the comparable U.S. figure is 2 percent; in Finland it is 77 percent.

9. Council of Economic Advisers, "The Economic Role of Women," in *1973 Economic Report of the President,* p. 101.

10. In this paper the term "the unemployment rate of women" refers to women 16 years and older unless otherwise specified.

increasing relative to that of male teenagers. Only Bergmann's crowding hypothesis[11] attempts to develop a common theoretical explanation for these differentials—and to explain the trend as well as the level of unemployment in the different groups.[12] The detailed examination below is concerned primarily with women's unemployment, but certain similarities among the three groups are also discussed. Anyone who doubts that they have much in common might find it a consciousness-raising experience to contemplate the question why white teenage males always grew up to be men, while black ones used to remain "boys," and females of either color still remain the "the girls in the office."

Three questions must be considered in addressing the problem of female unemployment: (1) Why is the unemployment rate for women higher than for men? (2) Why has the unemployment rate for women increased relative to the male rate? (3) Why are the cyclical variations in the unemployment rate smaller for women than for men? The aggregate male and female unemployment rates for the period 1947–74 are shown in figure 1.

Explaining the Higher Unemployment Rate for Women

The higher unemployment rate of women has been ascribed to differences in occupational distribution, the higher proportion of entrants and reentrants among adult women, higher turnover rates, less on-the-job training leading to placement in "dead-end" jobs which have higher layoff and turnover rates, less time spent looking for a job while unemployed, and a greater tendency to permit a spouse's job to determine location.

1. Occupational distribution.—The previous discussion on pay differentials would suggest that one explanation for the high unemployment rate of women might be their occupational distribution. However, when women are distributed across occupational categories in the same proportion as men, but with their own unemployment rates in each of the nine major occupational categories, the female unemployment rate for 1970 *increases* slightly, from 4.5 percent to 5.0 percent.[13]

Evidence that further corroborates the fact that under existing conditions women would not reduce their unemployment rate by moving into more predominantly "male" occupations is shown in table 2. Within

11. Barbara Bergmann, "The Effect on White Incomes of Discrimination in Employment," *Journal of Political Economy*, vol. 79, no. 2 (March/April 1971).

12. This discrimination hypothesis does not easily lend itself to explaining this trend since it would require assuming not only that discrimination exists but that it has become greater over time.

13. This confirms the findings of Nancy Barrett and Richard Morgenstern, "Why Do Blacks and Women Have High Unemployment Rates," *Journal of Human Resources*, vol. 9, no. 4 (Fall 1974). It is interesting to note that this relationship appears to have been similar for some time. In 1950, the unemployment rate was 3.4 percent and would have increased to 3.9 percent if women had had the same occupational distribution as men.

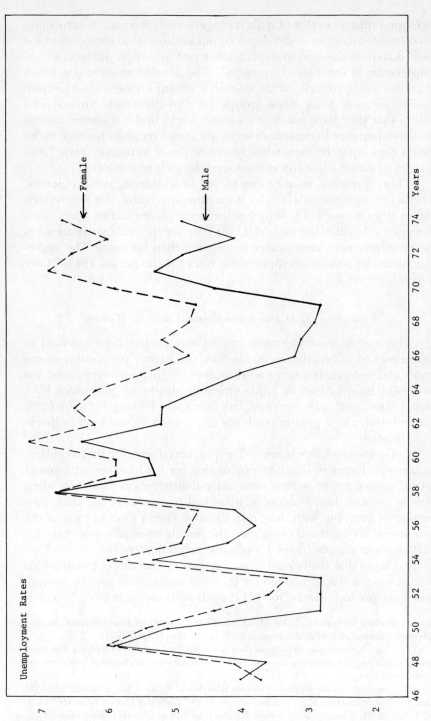

FIG. 1.—Male and female unemployment rates, 1947–74. Data for 1947–73 from *Handbook of Labor Statistics*, pp. 138–39; for 1973–74 from U.S. Dept. of Labor, *Employment Situation* (various issues), table A-6.

seven of the nine major occupational categories we find that the female unemployment rate declines as the percentage of women in the detailed occupational categories increases.

By way of contrast it should be noted that the male unemployment rate shows a positive correlation to the percentage of women in all major occupational categories where the percentage of women is 20 or higher, except in one case where the correlation is virtually zero. Although the occupational categories are so aggregated that higher correlation coefficients would not really be expected (for example, for sales workers, a more meaningful subgroup to compare would be commissioned workers, who are usually men, with noncommissioned workers, who are usually female), table 2 indicates that the female unemployment rate declines as the percentage of women in the detailed occupational categories increases.

2. *New entry and reentry.*—The relatively high proportion of new entrants and reentrants in the female labor force is a frequently suggested cause of the higher unemployment rate of women.[14] Data published in the *1975 Economic Report of the President* indicated that 0.3 percent of the female labor force in 1974 consisted of unemployed new entrants, a figure 0.2 percent higher than the rate for men. (Female unemployment in 1974 was at 5.5 percent.) Unemployed reentrants were a more significant factor, constituting 2.1 percent of the female labor force but only 0.7 percent of the male labor force during that year. Taken together, unemployed new entrants and reentrants could account for most (1.6 percent) of the unemployment differential of 1.9 percent between men and women in 1974.

The entry-reentry argument is not convincing, however, if the "discouraged worker" effect is taken into account. While a growing proportion of new entrants inflates the unemployment rate of women, since they are more likely to be unemployed during a period of job search, the larger proportion of discouraged workers who drop out of the labor market more than offsets the former effect. To illustrate, if both male and female new entrants are excluded from the unemployment statistics but discouraged workers are added in, then the differential between the unemployment rate of men and women in 1974 expands to 2.3 percent. In other words, although the inclusion of new entrants in the labor force has tended to increase the female unemployment rate as defined by the Bureau of Labor Statistics, the exclusion of workers who have dropped out of the labor force because they have been unable to find a job tends to understate female unemployment rates by an even larger amount.

14. See, e.g., Gertrude Bancroft, "Lessons from the Pattern of Unemployment in the Last Five Years," in *Prosperity and Unemployment,* ed. R. A. Gordon and M. S. Gordon (New York: John Wiley & Sons, 1966); K. D. Hoyle, "Why the Unemployed Look for Work," *Monthly Labor Review,* vol. 90, no. 2 (February 1967); and Beth Niemi, "The Female-Male Differential Unemployment Rates," *Industrial and Labor Relations Review,* vol. 27, no. 3 (April 1974).

Table 2

Relation of Female and Male Unemployment Rates to Percentage Female in Detailed Occupations within Major Occupational Categories in 1970

Major Occupational Category	% Female in Major Occupational Category	Detailed Occupational Categories	Correlation of % Female in Detailed Occupational Category to Unemployment Rate	
			Female	Male
Clerical and kindred workers	70	44	−.259	.222
Service workers	64	41	−.176	.005
Sales workers	40	13	.268	.747
Professional, technical, and kindred workers	37	26	−.327	−.043
Operatives	30	54	.166	.110
Farmers and farm managers, farm laborers, and farm foremen	18	6	−.212	.108
Managers and administrators (except farm)	16	23	−.507	−.248
Craftsmen and kindred workers	3	65	−.034	−.145
Laborers (except farm)	3	14	−.459	−.471

Moreover, reentrants represent both a decline and an addition to the unemployment rates. Although they are likely to be unemployed while looking for a job, in contrast with people who remain in the labor force while changing jobs, they previously left the labor force. If they left after a period of unemployment (the discouraged worker syndrome), their exit reduced the unemployment rate. (This may explain why married women have a lower unemployment rate than separated women.)[15] If they quit their jobs and leave the labor force, the vacancy is available for someone else who is looking for employment. Unless the job remains vacant, the unemployment rate is once again reduced. Thus, unless the labor market is exceedingly tight, it is unlikely that the net effect on women's unemployment from the reentry group would be great.

3. *Higher turnover rates.*—Some authors have cited higher turnover rates as an explanation for the higher female unemployment rate. Bergmann[16] has shown in a simulation model that the overall level of unemployment will not be affected by a high turnover rate except in times of a very tight labor market; the group with the high turnover rate will suffer a higher unemployment rate, while the more stable group will experience a comparable gain in employment. As Bergmann points out, this will be the case only when the two groups of workers are competing for the same jobs. And since substantial segmentation of the labor market exists, such a result is unlikely.[17]

There is evidence that tends to corroborate this argument. If high turnover does increase the unemployment rate for women, it would be expected to have a downward effect on the unemployment rate of men; when women quit their jobs, there are more vacancies for unemployed men to fill. Hence, men would be expected to have a lower unemployment rate in occupations with a larger proportion of women. In fact, the opposite relationship tends to exist as is shown in table 2.[18] While the

15. Waldman attributes the difference to the younger age of the children of separated women. Since no substantiating evidence is offered, we must regard this explanation as highly speculative. See E. K. Waldman, "Changes in the Labor Force Activity of Women," *Monthly Labor Review*, vol. 93, no. 6 (June 1970).

16. Fisher has found that very little teenage unemployment is caused by high turnover (see A. A. Fisher, "The Problem of Teenage Unemployment" [Ph.D. diss., University of California, Berkeley, 1968]).

17. Barbara Bergmann, "Labor Turnover, Segmentation and Rates of Unemployment: A Simulation-Theoretic Approach" (unpublished manuscript).

18. It has been suggested that since a large proportion of nonwhite men and a large proportion of women are frequently found in the same detailed occupational categories, the positive correlation of percentage female to the unemployment rates of men may be merely a reflection of the high unemployment rates of nonwhite men. While the effect of sex is undoubtedly confounded by the effect of race, the latter does not appear to be dominant in table 2. The two highest positive correlations of percentage female to the unemployment rates of men occur in major occupational categories (clerical and kindred workers and sales workers) in which women are 40 percent and 70 percent of the total, whereas nonwhite men constitute 2 and 3 percent, respectively.

positive correlation between the proportion of women in an occupational category and the unemployment rate of men does not prove that high turnover has no effect on female unemployment rates, it does show that the impact is not likely to be great.

4. *On-the-job training.*—The explanations we have considered so far involve variables that can be measured with reasonable accuracy and hence can be subjected to statistical tests. Other arguments are of a more speculative nature. The human capital school contends that women receive less on-the-job training, making them less valuable to employers and therefore more likely to be fired or not hired.[19] Blau and Jusenius (in this volume) have discussed the limited utility of this argument for understanding the causes of occupational segregation. Its usefulness for explaining the higher unemployment rates of women is equally limited.

5. *Job search time.*—Barnes and Jones,[20] as well as the *1975 Economic Report of the President,* have argued that the higher female unemployment rate can be partly explained by the fact that women spend less time searching for a job while unemployed. Although this may be the case, the data on time spent on job search, which are self-reported, are unreliable and prone to a sex bias.[21] It is reasonable to assume that men, under great pressure to be the chief breadwinners, would be more eager to convince themselves and others that they have worked very hard to find a job, while women have the acceptable alternative of spending more of their time as "bread makers." Also, it is difficult to estimate the effectiveness of the additional hours spent looking, after the best leads have been explored. Again, a man would have greater incentive to explore less-promising leads than a married woman.

6. *Geographic mobility.*—The greater willingness of men to move in order to find a job, and the greater likelihood that women will move even if it means giving up a job they presently have, could be a factor in the higher female unemployment rate.[22] Empirical evidence to test this hypothesis is extremely limited, since existing data show only that people moved, not the reasons for the move or their implications for unem-

19. The article most responsible for the acceptance of this approach is that by Jacob Mincer, "On-the-Job Training: Costs, Returns, and Some Implications" *Journal of Political Economy* 70, no. 5, pt. 2 (October 1962): 55. In this article Mincer states that "the age-earnings profiles . . . are the basic data used in deriving estimates of training costs" (see also Niemi, and Council of Economic Advisers, "Annual Report" in *1975 Economic Report of the President* [Washington, D.C.: Government Printing Office, 1975]). This approach ignores the fact that the purported deficiency of training is also widely used to explain the lower level of women's earnings. An appropriately lower wage should make the less experienced worker equally desirable.

20. W. F. Barnes and E. B. Jones, "Differences in Male and Female Quitting," *Journal of Human Resources,* vol. 9, no. 4 (Fall 1974).

21. R. D. Morgenstern and N. S. Barrett, "The Retrospective Bias in Unemployment Reporting by Sex, Race, and Age," *Journal of the American Statistical Association,* vol. 69, no. 346 (June 1974).

22. Niemi; and L. C. Hunter and G. L. Reid, *Urban Worker Mobility* (Paris: OECD, 1968).

ployment statistics. The *1975 Economic Report of the President* stated that "another factor that tends to increase the unemployment rate of married women is the migration of families. . . . Thus, in 1970, married women age 25 to 34 who had moved to a different county within the year had an unemployment rate of 11 percent, compared to 5 percent for non-migrants; among married men of the same age the rates for migrants and non-migrants were 4.8 percent and 2.1 percent, respectively."[23] The fact that, for both men and women, migrants had an unemployment rate somewhat more than double that of nonmigrants does not serve as an explanation of the higher unemployment rate for women than for men.

Explaining the Relative Increase in the Female Unemployment Rate

Although women have had a higher unemployment rate throughout the period studied, the differential in the male and female unemployment rates has been increasing, most notably since 1962. This development has been ascribed to several factors: a change in the definition of unemployment in 1967; a change in the labor force attachment of women; and, most plausibly, an increase in the number of women entering the labor force and crowding into relatively few occupations. Each of these explanations is discussed below.

1. Changing the unemployment definition in 1967.—The 1974 *Report of the Council of Economic Advisers* has offered another explanation of the growing gap between male and female unemployment. It points out that the definition of unemployment was changed in 1967 so as to include more women but to decrease the number of men who would be counted as unemployed.[24] There is limited evidence to support this contention. Barnes and Jones applied the 1967 definition to 1966 data and found that the unemployment rate of women became 0.4 percent higher and the unemployment rate for men, 0.3 percent lower. However, given the sampling error in the data, evidence for only one year is not adequate to support the argument. Furthermore, an examination of the data displayed in figure 1 shows no discontinuity in the time series between 1966 and 1967. On the contrary, the chart indicates a long-run increase in female relative to male unemployment throughout the period. The figure also shows that the relationship is affected by the level of unemployment—the gap tends to increase as the level of unemployment decreases—and an effort to control for that effect was made in order to

23. *1975 Economic Report of the President,* p. 105.
24. The definition was changed as follows: (1) People have always been classified as unemployed if they have not worked during the survey week but were available for work and made specific efforts to find a job. Prior to 1967 the period of active job search was not specified. Beginning in 1967 it was specified as the four-week period preceding the survey. (2) Before 1967, persons absent from work because of a vacation or a labor dispute who were at the same time looking for work were counted as unemployed. Since that time they have been counted as employed. (3) Persons stating that they had given up the search for work were counted as unemployed before, but not after, 1967.

isolate the impact of the definitional change. Although there was a large increase in the gap between male and female unemployment from 1966 to 1967, the gap was once again smaller in 1968. Furthermore, another large temporary peak was in 1951. In both 1951 and 1967, large numbers of men were absorbed into the military, resulting in an unusually low unemployment rate for men. Thus, it would appear that the change in definition of unemployment cannot be used to explain the increasing differential.

2. *Changes in labor force attachment.*—The proportion of women in the labor force who work part-time has been decreasing and, it is argued, full-time workers are less likely to drop out of the labor market when they are unemployed. Hence measured unemployment among women workers would presumably increase because women's labor force attachment has increased. On the other hand it is argued, for instance by Niemi, that the proportion of entrants and reentrants in, and the turnover of, the female labor force has increased as the proportion of married women who are working has increased. However, whereas the higher labor force participation rate of women 16 years and over—43.9 percent in 1972 as compared with 31.8 percent in 1947—is no doubt partly caused by the larger proportion of women who now enter, or reenter, the labor force after marriage and child rearing, there also appears to be an increasing proportion of women who never leave the labor force, or at least have a firm attachment to the labor market after one interruption. Mallan[25] has presented tentative findings which show that the labor force attachment of working women has, in fact, increased between 1961 and 1971. Women's unemployment may have increased because they are increasingly less willing to drop out of the labor force. This challenges Niemi's argument, and further accumulation of data with further analysis is needed before her hypothesis can be either confirmed or denied.[26]

3. *The crowding hypothesis.*—Only one of the explanations found in the literature can account for both the existence of the differential in female and male unemployment rates and its upward trend. This is the crowding hypothesis developed by Bergmann to explain both the low level of wages and the high level of unemployment of women.[27] The

25. Lucy B. Mallan, "Changes in Female Labor Force Experience, 1961–1971, and the Effect on Earnings" (presented at the annual meetings of the American Economists Association, San Francisco, December 1974).

26. Neither version helps to explain the relative increase in the unemployment of nonwhites or of teenagers. Our version, however, by pointing out the reduced willingness to drop out may help to explain the increasing ratio of the unemployment of female as compared to male teenagers.

27. Eckstein makes the argument in reverse, claiming that the low unemployment rate of men aged 25–54 is caused by the relative decline in their supply. See Otto Eckstein's comment on R. A. Gordon, "The Current Business Expansion in Perspective," in Gordon and Gordon (n. 4 above).

strength of this hypothesis is that it explains the disadvantaged status of women in the labor market in the presence or absence of market imperfections. According to this argument, women are crowded into a small number of women's occupations and, as more and more women enter the labor market, the crowding intensifies, leading to further female unemployment. Our finding that men experience lower wage rates and, often, higher unemployment rates in occupations with a large proportion of women supports the crowding hypothesis, since it suggests that everyone in an occupation is increasingly disadvantaged as more women move in, and that, furthermore, women would be more acceptable substitutes for men in occupations with a higher proportion of women. Women, on the other hand, suffer from crowding in female occupations but fare little better in male occupations, particularly as far as unemployment is concerned, because they are a less acceptable substitute for men in male occupations. This suggests that women's tendency to crowd into certain occupations is a rational response to their equally or more unfavorable situation in male occupations, rather than to any kind of lemming instinct.[28] This reasoning also helps to explain the findings in table 1 that men suffer more than women in detailed occupational groups where women are a large proportion of the total labor force.[29]

The following regression model was developed to test the hypothesis that the influx of women into the labor force can explain part of the increase in the male-female unemployment differential. The ratio of the unemployment rate of women to that of men was defined as a function of four independent variables: (1) the percentage of the labor force that is female, that is, the extent of crowding; (2) the annual change in the female civilian labor force, which might be expected to be significant because of the effect of entrants, reentrants, and discouraged workers on the unemployment rate of women; (3) the deviations of GNP in 1958 dollars around a trend line, representing a measure of the cyclical variations in labor market conditions; and (4) the annual change in the number of military personnel on active duty, which affects male unemployment.[30]

28. Similarly, the relatively unfavorable position of men in predominantly female occupations may explain the well-known tendency for occupations to become predominantly female after the percentage of women increases beyond a critical point.

29. The fact that no such relationship is found when comparing male unemployment rates between major occupational categories only shows that other factors are more important in determining their relative levels than the varying proportion of women.

30. See Beth Niemi in *Sex, Discrimination, and the Division of Labor*, ed. Cynthia B. Lloyd (New York: Columbia University Press, 1975). Niemi refers to an unpublished econometric study apparently using a similar approach which examines "the actual effect of the business cycle, the upward trend in female labor force participation, the military demand for manpower, and changes in school enrollment on the trend over time in the male-female unemployment differential." She also finds the growth in female labor force participation to be an important factor. (This book was published after this paper had been completed.)

The results of the regression analysis are displayed in table 3. All the coefficients of the independent variables were positive, as anticipated. The estimated coefficients of the percentage of the civilian labor force that is female, of the deviations of GNP around a trend line, and of the annual change in military personnel were all significantly different from zero at the 1-percent level; the coefficient of the annual change in the female civilian labor force at the 10-percent level. The "explanatory power," even when adjusted for the few degrees of freedom, was 82 percent. The Durbin-Watson statistic indicated the absence of negative serial correlation and was inconclusive in rejecting positive serial correlation. Multicollinearity was not a serious problem. The highest simple correlation between any two of the independent variables, $R^2 = 0.62$, was between the percentage of the civilian labor force that is female in year t and the change in the number of women in the civilian labor force from year $t - 1$ to year t.

Since the coefficient of F_t, the percentage of the labor force that is female, is positive, we can conclude that the long-run growth in the supply of women in the labor market has contributed to the unemployment rate of women relative to that of men. This evidence would seem to contradict the common contention that the increase in the employment of women has been primarily a response to increased demand. Without disputing the fact that demand has, in fact, increased, we note that the increase in the unemployment rate of women relative to that of men and the decline in earnings in female occupations relative to those in predominantly male occupations over time lead to the conclusion that it has been primarily the increase in supply that would explain women's em-

Table 3

Factors Explaining the Male-Female Differential in Unemployment Rates, 1948–72 [a]

Variable	Results of a Regression Analysis	
	Estimated Regression Coefficient	t-ratio
Constant	−0.068	−0.30
F_t	0.037*	4.89
$FCLF_t - FCLF_{t-1}$	0.130**	1.72
$DEV\ GNP_t$	0.003*	3.42
$MPOAD_t - MPOAD_{t-1}$ ...	0.222*	5.30

NOTE.—$URF_t/URM_t = b_0 + b_1 F_t + b_2 (FCLF_t - FCLF_{t-1}) + b_3\ (DEV\ \dot{GNP})_t + b_4\ (MPOAD_t - MPOAD_{t-1})$, where URF_t = the unemployment rate of women 16 years old and older in year t; URM_t = the unemployment rate of men 16 years old and older in year t; F_t = the percentage of the civilian labor force 16 years old and older that was female in year t; $FCLF_t$ = the number of women in the civilian labor force 16 years old and older, in year t, in millions of women; $DEV\ GNP_t$ = the deviation around a trend line of GNP in year t, in billions of 1958 dollars; $MPOAD_t$ = the military personnel on active duty in year t, in millions of personnel; and t = 1948, 1949, . . . , 1972.
[a] $N = 25$, $R^2 = 0.851$, adjusted $R^2 = 0.821$, Durbin-Watson statistic = 1.17.
*Significant at the 1% level.
**Significant at the 10% level.

ployment. In other words, it has not been the increased demand for typists that has made it possible for so many women to obtain jobs, but, rather, the increased supply of inexpensive women that has caused employers to hire so many typists.

That the estimated coefficient of the annual change in the number of women in the civilian labor force, $FCLF_t - FCLF_{t-1}$, is positive may mean that new entrants and reentrants tend to be unemployed for a time, while dropouts often come from the ranks of the unemployed. The positive, though small, coefficient of the deviations of GNP may indicate that cyclical variations in the economy are important to the relationship between male and female unemployment and that the ratio of female to male unemployment tends to rise in good years and fall in poorer ones.

The positive sign of the coefficient of the annual change in the number of military personnel on active duty is also significant. The effect represented by this variable is the sharp reduction in both the male civilian labor force and its unemployment rate, combined with a stable or only slightly reduced female unemployment rate, which occurred during national military buildups for the Korean and Vietnamese wars. When many young men are drafted, the unemployment rate of men is reduced, especially since unemployment rates tend to be high among people of draft age. Females are often not acceptable substitutes in the jobs these young men hold. When these men return to the civilian labor force as new entrants and reentrants, they would have high unemployment rates for some period of time, as shown in figure 1.

Explaining the Greater Cyclical Variations in the
Female Unemployment Rate

Since World War II (a period during which there has been no prolonged depression), women have fared relatively better during periods of high unemployment than in periods of low unemployment.[31] In other words, the gap between female and male unemployment has decreased as unemployment has increased. This is rather surprising in

31. There is evidence that a severe, prolonged depression, such as that of the thirties, might result in a much higher level of female unemployment relative to male unemployment than our regression model would predict. In 1940, the ratio of women's to men's unemployment rates was 1.08. As Kolachek suggests, the unemployment rate of men tends to increase during a recession because men experience a high rate of layoffs. But as the period of high unemployment continues, men may replace women and teenagers who have higher quit rates. Thus, differences in quit rates may become significant under these special conditions. It is also likely, as Reder points out, that during a period of high unemployment employers can exercise their preference for men without having to wait too long to fill a vacancy. Lastly, a severe scarcity of jobs may reinforce the notion that men should be given preference in hiring. See E. D. Kolachek, "The Composition of Unemployment and Public Policy," in Gordon and Gordon; and M. W. Reder, "Comments on Kenneth Arrow's 'The Theory of Discrimination,' " in Ashenfelter and Rees.

view of the fact that the opposite situation exists for a comparison of nonwhite and teenage unemployment rates with that of adult white men. It also appears to be in conflict with the generally accepted finding that "as unemployment increases, the relative rates for nonwhite workers, inexperienced workers, and the unskilled deteriorate more absolutely and possibly more than proportionately."[32]

1. *Female concentration in more stable sectors.*—Niemi has suggested that women are concentrated in less volatile sectors of the economy[33] in terms of the business cycle. If this were so, one would expect relatively small cyclical variations in the employment of women as compared to men. To determine whether this was so, trend lines were fitted for the employment of men and women in the civilian labor force for the period 1947–72. The sum of the squares of the deviations from the trend lines were compared, resulting in the sum for women being 1.04 times that for men. This minor difference cannot support the argument that the relatively modest variations in the unemployment rate of women can be explained by women's employment concentration in more stable occupational categories.

2. *Women's tendency to enter the labor market during prosperous periods.*—The generally accepted explanation for the relatively stable unemployment rate of women is their responsiveness to the conditions of the labor market; they tend to leave and remain out of the labor force during recessions and enter the labor force when unemployment is low. Thus, employment declines more sharply and unemployment increases to a lesser extent for women than for men during downswings. The opposite would be true during upswings.[34]

Although this pattern does not deny the existence of the "additional worker effect," in which women (and often teenagers) seek work when the husband becomes unemployed but leave the labor market when he finds a job, the net effect today is clearly in the opposite direction. One explanation for this may be that an increasingly larger proportion of wives of working husbands are in the labor market (45 percent in 1972 as compared to 28 percent in 1955),[35] leaving many fewer families in which the additional worker effect could occur.[36]

While no one questions that many women are willing to work when jobs are plentiful and drop out of the labor force when they cannot find

32. Eckstein, p. 49.

33. Niemi, "The Female-Male Differential Unemployment Rates."

34. A good review of the literature on this topic up to the mid-1960s is found in Jacob Mincer, "Labor Force Participation and Unemployment," in Gordon and Gordon.

35. U.S. Department of Labor, Bureau of Labor Statistics, *Handbook of Labor Statistics, 1973,* (Washington, D.C.: Government Printing Office).

36. The additional worker effect may be more important for teenagers, and it is known to be more important for black than for white women. This would account for greater cyclical variations in unemployment for these groups.

jobs, there are a number of different ways to interpret this situation. Mincer expresses the following view:

> It is no accident that the disguised unemployed are found mainly in the secondary labor force. ... Consider a population group whose average participation rate is 40 percent. ... Assume then that, on the average, an individual in such a group expects to spend 40 percent of his time in the labor force. The fact that 60 percent of his time is spent outside the labor force means that other than "gainful" activities are important. This implies that the opportunity costs of job-searching and job-holding are greater for secondary markets than for primary ones. ... Given some scope for timing of their activities, work in the labor market will be preferred at times when search costs are low and job conditions attractive. ... It is paradoxical that the optimization of timing labor-force activities creates the illusion of disguised unemployment.[37]

This statement deserves to be analyzed in some detail. Must we conclude that because secondary workers spend more time outside the labor market than primary ones, the costs of job holding and job searching are greater for the former? Underlying this line of reasoning is the assumption that only women have the alternative of productive work in the household. Such an assumption is unwarranted unless it can be shown that primary workers are not equally capable of doing this work. A far more reasonable assumption is that the opportunity cost of job holding and job searching is the same for both groups, but that the opportunity cost of household work is greater for that group which does better in the labor market, which, almost by definition, is the primary labor force group.

In addition, when a worker spends 60 percent of her time outside the labor force, does this constitute proof that she wants to be in the labor market only 40 percent of the time and that she prefers to devote herself to household work for the remainder? There is a good deal of evidence pointing in the opposite direction. The fact that women with more education and greater income potential are far more likely to be in the labor market, even though they also tend to have husbands who earn more, implies that women tend to leave the household when they can earn enough to justify their decision, rather than the assumption that women prefer household to other types of work.

Finally, we must question Mincer's suggestion that secondary workers can conveniently time their periods in and out of the labor market with the ups and downs in the economy. The opportunity cost of working is greatest when there are small children or illness in the family, and these cannot necessarily be timed to coincide with the business cycle.

37. Mincer, "Labor Force Participation and Unemployment," pp. 102–3.

Furthermore, prolonged recessions are associated with a lower, not a higher, birthrate.

We, therefore, conclude that the causes for the intermittent labor force participation of women are quite different from those suggested by Mincer. First, wives are unable to earn as much as their husbands, which makes them secondary wage earners, which in turn means that household responsibilities are relegated to them. When they cannot find a job that pays enough to enable them to replace their household services, they will not seek employment. When they perceive a realistic chance of finding such a job, they continue to search and hence are "unemployed." When they give up hope, they drop out and join that part of the "reserve army" that is not counted as part of the labor force. According to this interpretation, the appropriate measure of disguised unemployment is that proportion of women who would enter the labor force if we had genuinely full employment *and* if they were paid as much as men with comparable characteristics. Since the first condition has not been satisfied since World War II and the second condition has never been satisfied, there is no reasonable way to estimate the magnitude of disguised unemployment. It is, however, safe to say that the extent to which the gap between female and male unemployment declines in recessions is a minimal estimate of the amount by which the unemployment of women is understated during such times.[38]

Summary and Conclusions

The previous section has shown that to some extent, women's behavior contributes to their relatively high overt and disguised unemployment rate. They do have a higher turnover rate than men; they may spend less time on job search; they are less inclined to adjust their domicile to the availability of a job; they do tend to crowd into a few female occupations and to leave the labor market when conditions are unfavorable. But all these behavior patterns can be interpreted as a rational, and perhaps even inevitable, response to the existing discrimination in the labor market.

To the extent that the Becker-Arrow type of discrimination exists, women earn less than equally qualified men, even in the absence of occupational segregation. Workers who are underpaid relative to their capabilities tend to have higher turnover rates.[39] Furthermore, wives who tend to earn less than their husbands are relegated to a secondary

---

38. Another reason why this estimate is low is that it does not take account of those who have part-time jobs but would prefer to work full-time.

39. R. J. Flanagan, "Labor Turnover, Racial Unemployment Differentials, and the Dual Labor Market Hypothesis," National Technical Information Service, U.S. Department of Commerce, Springfield, Va. 1974.

status in the labor market and a primary status in the household. They, therefore, spend less time on job search, are more willing to stay with or follow their husband to the place where he has a job, and are less inclined to stay in the labor market during recessions.

Discrimination per se would not appear to explain why women tend to be segregated in occupational ghettos. But the fact that discrimination tends to cause career interruptions does help to channel women into those occupations where interruptions are not severely penalized.

Beyond this, a refinement of the Becker-Arrow discrimination hypothesis may be useful in explaining occupational segregation and crowding. The preference for male workers is greater in those sectors perceived, for whatever reasons, to be male preserves. The fact that men's wages and unemployment rates are more unfavorably affected by increasing numbers of women in an occupation than women's are suggests that the preference for men decreases as the occupation becomes less male. The fact that women tend to experience higher unemployment rates as the proportion of men in the occupation increases points in the same direction. Furthermore, casual observation tells us that there is less preference for male grade school teachers, nurses, and secretaries than for male superintendents of instruction, surgeons, and production engineers. The extent to which such differential discrimination causes women to avoid "male" occupations helps to explain crowding.

Most of the factors discussed above, except for the differential allocation of household responsibilities, are equally applicable to nonwhites, who also suffer from discrimination and crowding. The situation for teenagers, on the other hand, is substantially different. Teenagers frequently drop out of the labor market in order to improve their opportunity for more rewarding work later. (This is less true of black teenage men.) When they change jobs frequently, it is usually to find one better suited to their interests. However, teenage employment would gain if adult nonwhites and women would move out of the jobs where they compete against teenagers (the "crowded" occupations) and into those where they would compete with adult white men.

Thus, we reach the conclusion that discrimination—direct, indirect, and differential—causes some or even most of the disadvantaged situation of women in the labor market. Crowding in a severely segmented labor market is one of the most important factors in this situation. But advising women to move into more male occupations is not a realistic solution unless other changes take place as well.

Should a more equal distribution of unemployment rates between different groups occur, many would decry the higher incidence of unemployment among heads of households. But perhaps by then we shall have outgrown the view that a household with two adults has a "head" and a "dependent." It is nevertheless likely that a high unemployment rate among adult white males would be less politically acceptable than a high rate for the other groups and would lead to greater efforts to reduce overall unemployment. This might be done with less attendant inflationary pressure if the labor market were less segmented, for then we would no longer be confronted with full employment in one sector and high unemployment in others. Thus, the disappearance of the reserve army of the unemployed might not be such a painful experience after all.

University of Illinois at Urbana-Champaign (Ferber)
Oregon State University (Lowry)

Economic Dimensions of Occupational Segregation

Comment I

Kenneth Arrow

I will summarize these three interesting and useful papers of this section before commenting on the issues they raise.

Blau and Jusenius have attempted to survey the neoclassical and what they call the institutional or, more exactly, the internal labor market theories with regard to their implications for discrimination by sex. Within the neoclassical framework, they have concentrated on one particular possibility, the overcrowding hypothesis. They criticize the neoclassical viewpoint, because, to explain sex discrimination, it is necessary to bring in concepts of tastes, which are themselves unexplained.

Sawhill concentrates on the effects of sex discrimination in wages, particularly on female-headed households. The paper has two hypotheses. One is that divorces are made easier by increasing the alternative opportunities for females. The economic barrier is to some extent alleviated, although obviously not very much. Also, some support is given for the overcrowding hypothesis, at least in the form of the emphasis on differences in wages between predominantly female and predominantly male occupations.

Ferber and Lowry have concentrated primarily on employment. To put it very briefly and inaccurately, they have tried to refute the various explanations for potential unemployment rates which are based on some kind of intrinsic differences. Once more, there is an explanation in terms of the crowding hypothesis which Bergmann sponsored strongly some time ago, following the earlier work of Edgeworth. Again it is argued that the crowding hypothesis is, in effect, in need of explanation.

I should remark that there is nothing illegitimate in simply assuming crowding and drawing inferences. On the contrary, it is useful to take a hypothesis—for example, segregation by occupation—and draw the inferences from it. The fact that you are not explaining everything is no excuse for not explaining whatever you can explain on the basis of something else taken as a given. Science always does that. Nevertheless, it would obviously be useful, especially for policy purposes, to go beyond that.

Ferber and Lowry add an emphasis on the discouraged worker effect in explaining why the female unemployment rate does not rise more in recessions; female labor participants withdraw in disproportionately large numbers.

I would like to organize my remarks, not by the papers themselves but under five headings, which I read into the papers.

The first one is a model that I see semi-implicit, not fully spelled out, in some of the discussion of Ferber and Lowry and in the comments of Blau and Jusenius on the internal labor market. It might be called a model of perceptual equilibrium. This is a hypothesis which I have advanced as a partial explanation of segregation against blacks and which has not seemed to have received much attention, so I will take this opportunity to present it.

Rational adaptation by women to employer attitudes justifies employer attitudes to some extent. I am thinking particularly of high female mobility in and out of the labor force, an essential part of the mechanism Ferber and Lowry describe. It is correctly referred to as a rational adaptation to female job opportunities.

However, it is also true that employers are adapting rationally to this differential female reaction. Female workers perceive a lack of reward for certain kinds of accomplishments; therefore there is a lack of necessary accomplishments, and therefore employers do not expect these accomplishments to exist in women. It is essential to this argument that workers are being treated as groups and not as individuals. If employers would differentiate among individuals, all these phenomena would disappear.

Blau and Jusenius refer to this phenomenon under the heading of the internal labor market. This is a matter of terminology; it is certainly a real phenomenon of the world, however you want to label it. It occurs in many contexts, which include not only sex and race but also educational credentials, which serve a very similar function in providing an inexpensive source of information to employers and, for that matter, to employees too.

In the case of women who are perceived to go in and out of the market, the employer, not differentiating among women, lumps them together (Phelps has called this statistical discrimination); he gives less training to women and assigns them jobs in which the cost of turnover for him is minimized. Such a situation is a classic case for policy. This is a case of multiple equilibria; a concept sociologists as well as economists use in several contexts. A certain set of perceptions are mutually reinforcing. But we can have another stable situation with an entirely different set of perceptions where employers do not expect high female turnover and therefore hire females in positions which are sufficiently rewarding and stable to inhibit mobility out of the labor force. An analogous relationship is that between expectations by teachers and the performance of students. There is at least some evidence for the existence of mutually reinforcing equilibria at different levels.

The hypothesis of perceptual equilibrium does have the virtue of providing some explanation of crowding. Obviously, in this context, the different occupations do play different roles. In an occupation in which turnover is extremely easy and cheap, it does not matter what expectations the employer has, he can take chances. In other occupations, particularly with long specific training at stake, the employer's incentives are different.

I want to emphasize that I am certainly not claiming this is the whole story. There is clear evidence of just plain discrimination against women that could not be explained by actual or perceived behavior by them. I find myself in a rare state of agreement with our chair, that the basic explanation must lie outside the economic field. There is a certain amount of discriminatory behavior which is not going to be eliminated even when it is obviously not in the economic interest of the employer.

The second point that I want to make is a disagreement with one aspect of the Ferber-Lowry analysis—the relation of the high percentage of entrants and reentrants among female participants in the labor force relative to males and the differentials in the unemployment rate. They assert that there should be no connection. I think this is incorrect. Assume that everybody enters first into the pool of unemployed and then passes to the employed labor force. There will be some searching or waiting period. It is clear that, if there are two groups who are treated in every respect absolutely identically and have identical layoff rates, but one tends to withdraw and return frequently while the other does not, there will be differential unemployment rates.

My third point concerns the argument of Blau and Jusenius and many others that neoclassical theory has to bring in ad hoc hypotheses in order to draw any inferences relating either to differential unemployment, sexual segregation, or wage differences. The statement is correct, but actually the same ad hoc hypotheses are needed by the internal labor market theory. In fact, this is part of a large set of cases in which all competing theories thrown out by economists fail—Marxist and institutional theories, as well as neoclassical.

The basic root is outside the economic realm. For a parallel, the role of nationalism in economic behavior is inexplicable from a neoclassic point of view. Why should I, a consumer, care from whom I buy? Why should I therefore favor protection? Let me point out that the same is true of capitalists. Why should they be concerned with national interests? Why should they seek protection? A national boundary is, economically speaking, an arbitrary line. But notice that Marxian analysis exhibits exactly the same deficiencies. There is no more explanation there as to why nation should matter than there is in neoclassical economics. Why do not capitalists perceive their international unity in the class struggle? Economic arguments of all schools deal with anonymous individuals. The characteristics of sex, race, and nation are not incorporated. It may not be totally surprising that economic theories have nothing to say about the causes of sexual, racial, or national differences.

It is true that economic theories can say something about the effects, given that you have sexual discrimination or national identity. They are not in a position to explain why the phenomenon occurred in the first place.

Let us return to the internal labor market hypothesis. Jobs are classified, and somehow each job is assigned a wage. Well, why is the wage assigned to the job? Why don't we have females and males labeled the same but paid differently? There must be some ethical constraint somewhat outside the economic system itself which says you don't. Again, ad hoc hypotheses are needed.

Parenthetically, differential labeling of jobs by sex raises the question of the meaning of occupational segregation and crowding. Is segregation just a matter of titles, of calling a female a secretary and a man an executive assistant with more or less the same functions? Obviously, in fact women and men perform different functions. The occupations held by the two are really different in terms of duties and rights, and it is important to know why we have different sex proportions in these jobs.

A fourth observation is the neglect in the papers presented here of an argument advanced by theorists: that segregation is a response to the attitudes of fellow employees. We have a lot of evidence that the cause in many cases is resentment, for example, of having a female supervisor over male personnel. Whatever the cultural or other roots, it is important to realize that employer behavior is not the only controlling factor in discrimination.

Fifth, and finally, let me briefly discuss the relation of marriage and divorce to female wages. The quotation from Margaret Mead about the need for alternative social institutions to prevent revived defense of old institutions is clever enough. But let me say I do not know what the substitutes for the family might be. In my personal value judgment, the central purpose of a family is not the welfare of the father and mother but that of the children.

Children raised in single-headed families may possibly have a satis-factory environment, and I must admit that the outcomes of two-headed families have frequently been below reasonable standards. One cannot be dogmatic about the matter, but it seems clear there are obvious prob-lems in single-headed families as child-rearing institutions.

I must say that a world in which fathers throw off their respon-sibilities with regard to alimony payments, as Sawhill asserts, is a world I find very depressing. We have already gone through a period in which the family has largely shucked off its responsibility for its parents. I find that rather horrifying but, whatever it is, it seems to be a fact and no longer reversible. But I must say the idea that children are the next victims of the decay of the family does strike me as being completely possible. The home is an institution that has to be maintained as an economic unit and a nutritional unit for bringing up children, and it is hard to visualize how one-half the family, male or female, can be both parent and job holder. I realize there are a lot of issues here, such as child care, but its effects have to be rethought too.

Harvard University

ECONOMIC DIMENSIONS OF OCCUPATIONAL SEGREGATION

Comment II

David M. Gordon

Since we economists have a protean talent for missing the point altogether, I was pleased to discover that each of these three papers was helpful and very much to its point. Pursuing the implications of these papers more fully can bring us to some valuable conclusions about the economic dimensions of occupational segregation.

The Context in Economics

Orthodox economists have traditionally blamed the victims of segregation, but more and more of us are now beginning to realize that we must transform our systems of class and patriarchal domination to overcome the causes and consequences of occupational segregation. Economists did not discover the problem of occupational segregation by themselves, of course. They had neglected questions of discrimination for years. They were embarrassed into rediscovery by the determined protests of women and minority groups against their oppression. Many orthodox economists, trumpeting the "end of ideology," had become accomplished in their celebrations of the "market economy." Confronted with clear evidence of inequalities, most economists responded instinctively by trying to explain away those inequalities—effectively seeking to apologize for the system.

Their first response focused on pay differentials and occupational distributions. Economists sought to "explain" those differentials by accounting for inequalities in labor supply characteristics, such as years of schooling and age. If inequalities between men and women could be shown to reflect differences in productivity characteristics, then we could conclude that the market system was working and that women had simply erred by failing to acquire sufficiently productive individual attributes. (An easy way to blame the victim.)

However, these first studies proved frustrating. Careful efforts to "control" for individual attributes eliminated little of the differential in earnings between men and women. Perhaps there was discrimination after all.

Then came the human capital theorists. They argued that even if we cannot measure tangible differences, we can nonetheless be sure that more intangible, less measurable differences in productivity remain —differences in learning opportunities, in on-the-job experience and training, in preferences about risk. The possible explanations proliferated: the framework proved remarkably robust, principally because of the tautological tendencies of the analysis. If we assume that everything we cannot measure nonetheless reflects differences in productivity, then we can assume the problem away. As others have observed before me, we must allow the possibility of the null hypothesis that some variations in earnings do *not* reflect variations in marginal productivities if we are properly to test the alternative hypothesis that they do.

Soon enough, some orthodox economists—although regrettably few—began to regard the human capital explanations with skepticism. Many of these were drawn to the "occupational crowding" hypothesis. Women economists, in particular, inclined toward an analysis which charged openly that employers discriminated against women by blocking their access to a wide range of occupations. This new strand of analysis reflected a sharp reaction against the tendency to blame the victim.

But it did not cast aside any of the rest of the orthodox economic framework. As does other neoclassical analysis, the crowding framework presumes competition in general, employers as price takers, the equation of marginal rates of substitution, and so on. The world, bless its consistency, can be assumed to correspond to the premises of the neoclassical paradigm. Nearly everything about our economic system generates "optimality." There's just this little problem of employer discrimination, which we can use the government to overcome.

The Fatalism of Conventional Approaches

All these orthodox economic responses to the problem of occupational segregation have some important characteristics in common. The most important communality, in my view, is that each leads us to a kind of fatalism about the problem.

The first analyses of individual attributes induced fatalism because they explained so little about earnings differentials. Not knowing the causes, we could hardly know the cures.

Human capital explanations induce fatalism both because they suggest that the marvelous market is simply doing its thing and because they hide so much of their explanation behind the veil of intangible sources of human capital inequalities. Finding the real causes of earnings differences identified by human capital analyses has always seemed to me like an exercise in pillow punching.

From both these perspectives, finally, we can do little because the sources of segregation which they do identify reflect the operations of the market which, in the neoclassical tradition, we should not disturb.

I would also argue that a similar kind of fatalism grows out of the occupational crowding analysis. The crowding analysis accepts the existing *structure* of jobs and occupations because it accepts the neoclassical framework with its justifications of those structures. Given that acceptance, its singular policy prescription is that we must adjust the distribution of women and men (or other minorities) among those fixed occupational structures in order to equilibrate their representations. Necessarily, that prescription involves us in a zero-sum game. For every woman or black that we put into a higher-level occupation, we have to take a white male out of that same position. The sharp conflict over quotas and preferential hiring simply reflects this zero-sum aspect of the crowding perspective. Holding to that perspective involves us in policy battles which divide us into armed, opposing camps. Although the crowding hypothesis stamps the employer with the stigma of discrimination, it results in policies that penalize white male workers. Because it takes everything else about our economic system as untouchable, in my view, it proposes policies which permit employers to continue smiling all the way to the bank.

New Analytic Directions

Each paper in this section begins to contribute to some new directions in the economic analysis of occupational segregation—directions which can help break us out of that fatalism.

In identifying women as an essential brigade in the reserve army of the unemployed, Feber and Lowry provide a suggestive glimpse of the relationship between occupational segregation and the dynamics of capitalist economies. Their suggestions should be extended.

In the classic Marxian analysis of the reserve army, the economy itself tends continually to reinforce the ranks of the unemployed (or peripheral) workers. The dynamics of capital accumulation tend necessarily to bring new workers into that new reserve army both exogenously and endogenously—that is, both from outside and inside the prevailing wage labor force.

Exogenously, capitalism tends to break down precapitalist social relationships as it effects the progressive *extension* of the market exchange of commodities. As these precapitalist relationships dissolve, new groups of people are forced to enter the labor force. Classically, in England, the commercialization of agriculture pushed many workers off their subsistence plots into the labor market. More recently, among other tendencies, commodity exchange has been transforming household relationships in advanced capitalist economies. My colleague, Heidi Hartmann, has recently written a stimulating dissertation in which she analyzes the consequences of this transformation in its initial stages in this country, from 1900 to 1930.[1] Her analysis deepens our understanding of this more recent manifestation of the classical tendency. One (though not the only) consequence has been that many women have been forced out of the household into the labor force. The reserve army has been replenished.

Endogenously, in the classical analysis, the reserve army is continually replenished through the dynamics of surplus value accumulation in the production process. If unemployment diminishes, Marx argued, wages rise. Employers respond by substituting capital for labor, displacing workers. As workers are thrown off their jobs, the reserve army is reinforced once again.

In our modern economy, it seems to me that there are many parallel tendencies which both affect the occupational segregation of women and which replenish the reserve army from inside the economy. As workers unionize, for instance, their wages may rise. This often leads employers, others things being equal, to change their job structures away from the utilization of full-time unionized (or organizable) employees toward increasing reliance on part-time temporaries. (The examples proliferate; the increasing use of temporary clerical employees is the most dramatic.) This tendency, often operating in response to the previously secondary status of many women workers, tends to reinforce the reserve status of women as workers. Just as fast as men and women try to overcome their secondary status, employers take actions which tend to maintain that status.

These strands of analysis could be usefully pursued. Their application would lead us to a clearer appreciation, I think, of the ways in which capitalist economies tend to perpetuate the status of secondary working groups like women.

1. Heidi Hartmann, "Capitalism and Women's Work in the Home, 1900–1930" (Ph.D. diss., Yale University, 1974).

The Sawhill and Blau-Jusenius papers take us from these dynamic questions to a focus on the structure of jobs confronting women in the labor market. Sawhill emphasizes the dominant importance of the low wages facing women. Blau and Jusenius emphasize the structures of primary labor markets which reinforce the exclusion of women from those kinds of jobs. The two papers together help suggest the limited usefulness of the kinds of policy prescriptions which the overcrowding analysis implies. If government antidiscrimination policies were to increase the potential supply of women to higher-level occupations, do we have any reason to expect that wages in lower-level occupations would increase? Neither the competitiveness of those industries nor the elasticity of the supply of reserve workers seems likely to permit it. And would more jobs open up in the primary labor market because of new supplies of workers? The analyses of the structure of those labor markets suggest that they would not.

These analyses of labor market structure should also be pursued. They will help clarify for us the barriers to equality in capitalist economies where job structures evolve in such a way as to exacerbate divisions and hierarchies.

A Glimpse of the Structure of Female Occupations

Some of the work on labor market segmentation which a group of us have been pursuing can help provide a glimpse of the kinds of conclusions we may reach in pursuing these directions of analysis.[2] We have tried to develop some meaningful classifications of labor market structure. In my own provisional estimations, I have found that four main categories of jobs account for nearly 95 percent of all female employment in the United States:[3] (1) jobs in peripheral industries, including both peripheral manufacturing and retail trade; (2) the clerical occupations; (3) the health and education sectors; and (4) domestic service. Could anything be done to improve employment conditions for women in these job categories without thoroughly transforming our economic system?

It seems impossible to improve employment conditions in peripheral industries, first of all, because of their competitive industrial structures. Any efforts that unions or the government make to improve wages and working conditions in those industries are likely to erode

2. For a summary of some of the perspective of this work on labor market segmentation, with some interesting applications to occupational segregation by sex, see the papers in Richard C. Edwards, Michael Reich, and David M. Gordon, eds., *Labor Market Segmentation* (Lexington, Mass.: Lexington Books, 1975).

3. These estimates are being presented in my own paper, "Class and Segmentation in the United States: An Empirical and Methodological Review" (in preparation).

profit margins in those industries and force their collapse in this country.

Second, the clerical occupations cannot by themselves be upgraded without threatening the structure of hierarchies and specialization throughout the labor market. As Harry Braverman has shown in great detail in his recent classic, *Labor and Monopoly Capital*,[4] the hierarchy and division of the clerical occupations arose during the twentieth century partly as a consequence of the conscious application of scientific management techniques toward the control of labor. An attack on those divisions would seriously weaken capitalist control over the labor process, and the capitalist response to such an attack seems predictable.

Third, female concentration in the health and education sectors itself reflects the historic social division of labor between men and women in the production of labor power. Women have moved out of the household but continue to perform many of the same functions in the labor market. Attempts to upgrade women's roles in those sectors would involve a direct attack on the patriarchal systems of domination throughout society.

Fourth, domestic service, although declining, reflects many of those same strands of patriarchal domination.

The Terms of Struggle

These preliminary comments anticipate the kinds of conclusions I think we shall reach after much more detailed and sustained analyses. I agree entirely with Heidi Hartmann's paper (in this volume) that it is necessary to engage in two kinds of struggles to overcome the occupational segregation of women. The first struggle is to change family relationships—the relations between the sexes and the responsibility for child care—in order to begin attacking traditional patterns of patriarchal domination. The second struggle is to reverse a long standing historical tendency toward increasing inequality and hierarchical structure in the economic and social division of labor. In our present context, this requires changing, among other things, the structures of jobs. To accomplish that, in my view, we shall have to overturn capitalism, although such a transformation would not, by itself, be sufficient. (The Soviet Union is not adequate proof that socialism is incapable of accomplishing greater equality in the labor market.)

I have closed with an emphasis on the need for struggle. Since there is very little discussion about struggle in any of these papers or in the literature, it is not surprising that there has been little comment made about labor unions or about the organizing efforts now being made to

4. New York: Monthly Review Press, 1975.

expand the number of women who are, themselves, involved in labor union struggles. There is very little emphasis on what workers themselves have done to try to transform work structures and equalize job responsibilities. And, surprisingly enough, there is very little emphasis in these papers on what women have been doing as a part of their struggle to try to change those kinds of sexual relationships. These are the directions in which I think we need to go.

New School for Social Research

Economic Dimensions of Occupational Segregation

Comment III

Janice Fanning Madden

As Kenneth Arrow and David Gordon have done, I will discuss the general direction of research on occupational segregation in reference to the papers presented here with special attention to the questions which future research should address.

First, I want to define occupational segregation. For my purposes, the definition that Sandra Tangri gave is useful—that is, occupational segregation by sex occurs in the labor market whenever men and women are distributed over occupations in different ways.

The next logical question to ask is, Why is there a difference? There are three possibilities that are not mutually exclusive and probably occur simultaneously.

The first one is taste. The reason why women are employed in different ways than men could be that they choose different occupations; that is, they have different occupational preferences than men. The study of the way these preferences are formed is generally outside the range of economics. I suspect that occupational preferences are not independent of the opportunities, but that is a problem for psychological and sociological researchers to answer in their study of occupational segregation.

The second general explanation for occupational segregation is ability differences by sex. For example, Isabel Sawhill contends that "poor" women would not be as poor if they were in the same occupations as poor men, but I wonder how much of the variance in wages is explained by the wage equation used. Physical strength may well be an important worker characteristic of occupations employing this group and may explain the basis for occupational segregation at this level.

Skill differentials may also reflect different inherent preferences of men and women, different opportunities to acquire skills, or different opportunities to use skills. Ability differentials between men and women may be the result of discrimination which has taken place prior to entry into the labor market. The human capital argument that women enter the jobs they do because of the skills they have may be the other way around. Women may acquire the skills they do because of the job opportunities they perceive. Marianne Ferber takes issue with the technique of measuring differences in human capital through differences in wages. While she correctly perceives the circularity of this reasoning, she is unable actually to dispute the premise that women earn less because they invest less in human capital. The problem is that the empirical work is consistent with several alternative hypotheses. There is a desperate need to develop empirical methodology and data that can determine wage differentials based on human capital differences as opposed to those based solely on sex.

To the other extreme, Gordon has argued here that giving women more education and training will not improve their lot. My own empirical work on the Parnes data questions that conclusion.[1] I find very high returns for women relative to men in the younger age group with which I am working. The education problem that I see for women is not that the attainment of education does not help them, but rather it is the type of education they attain. Being trained as a history teacher at the secondary level or as an elementary school teacher is not comparable to being trained as an engineer, though the level of education attained is the same in each case.

The third reason for occupational segregation—occupational discrimination—is the one most within the province of economists. Occupational discrimination occurs whenever criteria other than productivity determine the number of men and women that have the opportunity to enter an occupation. Empirical studies have estimated the effect of occupational discrimination to be significant.[2]

The study of occupational discrimination involves two questions. The first is, What is the original cause of occupation allocation by sex?

1. J. Madden, "Evaluating the Returns to the Education of Women" (paper presented at the meeting of the Allied Social Science Associations, San Francisco, December 28, 1974).

2. See, e.g., V. R. Fuchs, "Differences in Hourly Earnings between Men and Women," *Monthly Labor Review* 94 (June 1971): 9–15; I. Sawhill, "The Economics of Discrimination against Women: Some New Findings," *Journal of Human Resources* 8 (Summer 1973): 383–96; B. G. Malkiel and J. A. Malkiel, "Male-Female Pay Differentials in Professional Employment," *American Economic Review* 63 (September 1973): 693–704.

This is for historians and anthropologists to answer. The second question, which may be entirely separate, is, What is maintaining occupational discrimination? The overcrowding hypothesis argues that women receive lower wages than men because an excess supply of workers in women's occupations lowers the equilibrium wage in those occupations relative to men's occupations. This hypothesis is only a description. It does not tell us why women do not enter higher-paying men's occupations. For example, why do women not move out of teaching and into engineering? The answer to this question requires more sophisticated economic models. The real problem is defining the *motivation* for sex discrimination in the labor market. The papers presented here suggest five different possibilities: the tastes or prejudices of economic agents, the power of male "oppressiveness;" the institution of a dual labor market, the profit in discrimination, and employer ignorance. Let's examine these in more detail.

First, there is the preference of the three economic agents —consumers, employees, and employers—that Gary Becker describes.[3] It is quite possible that a good number of occupations involve consumer contact, not only with a consumer directly, but also in terms of dealings within and outside the firm such as selling ideas or concepts. If clients do not want to deal with women, then women have to sell their products or ideas at lower prices than men if they are to be competitive with men. If that happens, occupational segregation should result since women move out of jobs that involve consumer contact. But if there are not enough jobs which involve no consumer contact so that all the women in the labor force could be hired in them, then we observe segregation of women out of consumer-contact occupations and also wage differentials between men and women in all occupations.

Discriminatory consumer preferences, then, should act to push women out of consumer-contact occupations, segregating them into noncontact occupations. Lower salaries result *only* if there are not enough noncontact occupations in which to employ the female labor force. It is common knowledge that consumer-contact occupations—that is, the services—employ disproportionately large numbers of women workers and pay them more poorly relative to men workers than do other occupations. Discrimination by consumers does not seem to provide the motivation for the occupational crowding patterns which are observed.

Arrow has already described how employee discrimination could account for some of the segregation. Men may not want to work with women and so employers find they cannot hire women—despite the profit motivation to do so—because they would lose their male labor

3. G. Becker, *The Economics of Discrimination* (Chicago: University of Chicago Press, 1957).

force or face a strike. Employers, then, could hire women only if they did not hire men. This behavior would certainly prompt job segregation but not wage differentials.

Finally, employers may discriminate against women in some occupations, forcing women to "overcrowd" in those occupations where there is less discrimination. This would clearly result in occupational segregation and wage differentials by sex. But this would be an unstable situation since any nondiscriminatory employer could profit by hiring women into the male occupation. Therefore, in the long run occupational segregation would disappear. Employer tastes, then, cannot provide the motivation for occupational segregation.

The second general area of motivation for discrimination is embedded in the radical approach, which is essentially a conspiratorial analysis. Men act as a group to discriminate against women in order to maintain their power in the society. Those who are arguing this approach are hard put to evidence this cartel, or even to evidence cooperation. How, exactly, have men gotten together as a group to exploit women? While one can argue that large groups of men might not work with women or might want to discriminate against women, if there are a few who have different attitudes, there should be a breakdown in the process for much the same reasons I have discussed above. Clearly the "cartel" does not break down, but the radical model does not tell us why.

The third general motivation for occupational discrimination comes from the dual labor market model, which Blau and Jusenius analyze a little too kindly. The dual labor market model has essentially the same problems that the overcrowding model and the radical model have. There is only a description of segregation. The model does not explain the motivation for *why* segregation continues. Why is the employer cooperating in discrimination against women as they enter the internal labor market?

One reason hypothesized by dual labor market theorists is statistical discrimination. On the one hand, there is evidence that statistical discrimination cannot explain the whole difference—that is, women do not turn over at a higher rate than men if they are in the same occupation. On the other hand, if statistical discrimination did account for the whole difference, the dual labor market model is not necessary to explain the differentials.

The assignment model mentioned by Blau and Jusenius is also unsatisfactory because it only argues that employers have tastes against hiring women and thus assign them to different sorts of jobs. Since it does not explain the basis for the assignment, this argument does not yield any new contribution.

Basically, the dual labor market is another version of an employer discrimination model. It does not explain why, if women are productive, they are not hired. Once again, why are there not some employers hiring women in order to increase their profits?

The fourth possible motivation for occupational discrimination is profit—simply, discriminatory actions occur because they are profitable. This model, on which I have based my research, is presented adequately in the Blau and Jusenius paper. While the motivation for occupational discrimination and wage differentials is clear in this model, there is the problem, cited by Jusenius, of demonstrating that female labor supply to the firm is less elastic than that of males. I believe this generally to be true for all occupations—mixed and segregated. While the available data shows that the elasticity of the aggregate female supply curve is greater than the male supply, these elasticity relationships are derived from aggregate labor supply curves which have been compiled by adding wage and hour data over a heterogeneous labor force at the existing wage levels. Since elasticity is the first derivative of hours worked with respect to the wage rate times the average wage divided by the average hours worked, and since the average women's wage is lower than the average men's wage, it is not surprising that women show greater wage elasticity than men. Points on the same linear labor supply curve closer to the origin are always more elastic than those points more distant from the origin (assuming a positive intercept). The empirical work has not provided any clue as to the relationship between the wage elasticities of men's and women's labor supply to the firm. Furthermore, casual observation of unionization of males and journey to work and job search patterns by sex support the notion of greater elasticity of labor supply among males than females. I am presently examining working commuting patterns in order to demonstrate this proposition more rigorously.[4] Nonetheless, it is true that the empirical verification of labor market imperfections, as assumed in this model, is still wanting.

The final motivation for occupational discrimination is one suggested by Thomas Schelling[5] and mentioned by Arrow at this conference. I choose to call this notion an ignorance model. Employers may not be aware of the capabilities of women and may have reached mistaken conclusions about the abilities of women. Once again we are back to the same problem of employer discrimination. If a few employers guess right about the ability of women, occupational discrimination would decrease over time. After surveying these explanations, I still have no definitive explanation of why occupational segregation is maintained, but I do think that that is the important economic issue.

4. J. Madden, "Spatial Considerations in the Economics of Sex Discrimination" (paper presented at the meeting of the Association of American Geographers, Milwaukee, April 21, 1975).

5. T. C. Schelling, "Discrimination without Prejudice: Some Innocuous Models" (Dis-

One alternative for future research is to take Arrow's notion of personnel investment[6]—that is, firms invest in personnel so that there is a cost attached to firing men employees and replacing them with women as women enter the labor force—and add some concept of scale economies. So, for example, a firm may require 200 workers to staff one occupational category. There are twenty women both qualified to be hired and also willing to work for lower wages than are comparably qualified men. But if the men employees dislike working with women, they will require a higher wage to do so. If equal pay is necessary either legally or morally, it would cost this firm more to mix the occupation than to maintain it as male. The firm does not have the alternative of creating a female occupation since there are not enough women to fill the entire category's requirements. Likewise, a firm operating at a smaller scale which requires only twenty such workers would hire the women but would pay them less if there are economies of scale such that smaller work forces are less efficient. This situation yields occupational discrimination against these twenty women.

While an understanding of the process by which occupational discrimination occurs is absolutely necessary to an analysis of the efficiency and equity effects of most government policies and programs, I believe that numerical goals and quotas would clearly work to break down segregation regardless of the discrimination model invoked. Equity considerations aside, the most efficient way to eliminate discrimination—social, educational, or economic—could well be to impose the costs of that discrimination on the American business community. Such action can be taken without determining where the blame actually lies. If employers are forced to hire women in traditionally male jobs, it is in their interest to develop a qualified female work force. If the costs are imposed on business, American enterprise could find ways to solve discrimination that government programs have not been able to touch.

University of Pennsylvania

---

cussion Paper no. 8, Public Policy Program, John F. Kennedy School of Government, Harvard University, May 1972).

6. K. Arrow, "Models of Job Discrimination," in *Racial Discrimination in Economic Life*, ed. A. Pascal (Lexington, Mass.: D. C. Heath Co., 1972).

THE POLICY ISSUES

Introduction

Phyllis A. Wallace

The policy statements in this chapter present several perspectives on how best to reduce the occupational segregation of women. Ruth Shaeffer indicates the primary problem in achieving occupational desegregation is changing the behavior of major institutional systems toward women. For example, employers in the private sector have become increasingly aware of the equal employment opportunity laws. However, Nira Long points out that as a bureaucrat in the federal government, she sees affirmative action goals frustrated by the Civil Service Commission's guidelines which, while ostensibly rewarding merit, frequently reward paper credentials and disregard the kinds of practical experience which many women have. Looking at industry, Winn Newman emphasizes better enforcement of existing laws. Since sex-segregated job structures lead to the establishment of discriminatory promotion systems and wage rates, implementation of the law will improve the economic status of many blue-collar women workers.

Bernice Sandler warns that sex discrimination will be much harder to eradicate than race discrimination and that investigation of policies and practices for their impact on women is critical. Janet Norwood's pessimism about long-range possibilities of improving the occupational profile of women workers is based on economic projections for 1985. An oversupply of educated people for the available jobs will require that more attention must be devoted now to techniques for restructuring job content and to ways of sustaining high levels of economic activity.

In the final presentation, Rosabeth Kanter focuses on models of research and intervention. The "social structural" model, directed at the nature of organizational structures and the organization of work, has great potential for reducing occupational segregation.

Alfred P. Sloan School of Management
Massachusetts Institute of Technology

THE POLICY ISSUES

Presentation I

Ruth G. Shaeffer

Thus far in this analysis of the occupational segregation of women, we have been talking about two topics: (1) how we got where we are and (2) some of the forces that are keeping us where we are. Now we are moving on to a third topic, readily distinguishable from the first two, even though they are all interrelated: how can our society move in the generally agreed-upon direction of less occupational segregation for women? This topic includes consideration of some new ideas, for there are some short-run adaptive approaches to take into account as well as considering how to correct all the long-run causes of our present dilemma.

I suspect not everyone is in agreement as to how best to define the goal toward which our society needs to move. At the moment this difference of opinion is probably not too important. To quibble about the goal definition now is rather like refusing to sail from New York until we decide whether the ship we are steering should dock at pier 1 or pier 5 in the port city that is our destination across the Atlantic Ocean. Right now we are so far away from that destination port that all we need to know is the general direction in which we should be heading.

Nonetheless, in talking about the goal, it is important not to try and foist our personal views and values on other women. Some women literally do not want to participate in the labor force—using that term to mean the paid labor force. Others are in the labor force, but, in terms of their own personal aspirations, would really like nothing more than to leave it. They regard women who are able to stay home with their children as having a sweet deal; it is exactly what they would like to do, too, if they could only afford it. So in talking about the goal, we probably want to talk about occupational desegregation only for those women who are participating in the paid labor force or would like to, rather than for the total female population.

Similarly, it is important to speak in terms of somewhat flexible goals for various occupations, rather than in terms of rigid, arbitrary quotas. Otherwise we may end up referring to women being forced into occupations they do not want to be in. I am not suggesting that the goals for female employment that employers are expected to meet for various occupational categories should not be demanding of affirmative action, but we do need to be willing to revise our ideas if, after a trial, those rigorous goals seem inappropriate both to the women who are directly involved and to their employers. Indeed, the goals that seem appropriate now might well change over time.

In order to decide how best to move toward less occupational segregation for women, it is important to have a better understanding of where we are now. We need to disaggregate the figures on where women are currently employed. Occupational patterns do vary enormously both by sector of the economy and by specific industry or type of employer. The overall, very general figures hide many forms of segregation. They also blur many of the barriers to correcting the present situation. For example, a woman who has been trained as a high school teacher of physics is not immediately perceived as having the necessary skills and knowledge to be employable by a business organization in some sort of a scientific, professional, or technical occupation. This is, perhaps, only a perceptual problem, but the barrier exists.

We live in a society shaped by its interrelated institutional systems. To achieve less occupational segregation for women, the primary problem is not to change the behavior of women nor even to change the behavior of men—although both of these things will happen. The primary problem is to change the behavior of our major institutional systems toward women.

What institutional behavior toward women needs to be changed? Those who have analyzed the problem in systems terms formulate a long list. First, of course, they point to the need to change the behavior of employers and of unions. But they also point to the need to change the behavior of our colleges and universities. And, working backward through the vocational preparation process, there is a demand for change in the behavior of our school systems, both in terms of their instruction and in terms of their guidance efforts for women. Other parts of the community must also change: the communications media, family pressures, and peer pressures.

In thinking through the problem of reducing occupational segregation for women by changing the behavior of all these complex social systems, one does indeed begin to see multiple interrelations. Virtually every institution in our society needs to change if we are to achieve less occupational segregation. And one of the key ideas that has come through in this interdisciplinary conference is: there probably is no one Archimedean point—no one single point where we can exert all the pressure and expect everything else to shift. We are dealing, instead, with a situation that might better be conceptualized as a series of simultaneous or, to some extent, lagged equations. If this is so, then the only way in which it is likely to be possible to change the overall outcome is to change virtually all of the terms in those equations simultaneously. For if we try to change just one factor, there will be too much resistance from other factors and there will not be any long-run effect.

Achieving less occupational segregation for women is, therefore, a stubborn, complex problem. It calls for many people working to change many kinds of institutional behavior simultaneously. In this way it may be possible to make a gradual shift from the existing vicious supply/demand equilibrium position to some other equally stable equilibrium position. (In his remarks, Kenneth Arrow has noted that there quite probably are other attainable equilibrium positions that have not yet been tried.)

Let me now narrow the focus of my remarks and talk only about how and why the behavior of employers in the private sector has been changing, the subject of my research at The Conference Board. Employers in the private sector have become increasingly aware of a very potent external tool that is being applied to force them to change the occupational patterns of the women they employ. It is Title VII of the Civil Rights Act of 1964. They emphasize the importance of this law, rather than of the executive order dealing with sex discrimination in employment because of the way the law is being interpreted by the federal courts.

Following a unanimous decision by the Supreme Court, the federal courts are defining discrimination in terms of the *consequences* of an employer's actions—the *effects,* and not the intent, of his actions. If any action that an employer takes has an adverse effect on the employment opportunities of any of the groups that are protected by the law—and women are one of the protected groups—then the employer must justify the necessity of continuing this discriminatory course of action. In other words, the employer is now on the defensive. The argument that it satisfies some business purpose or that it is acceptable to his customers or to his other employees is not enough, according to the Supreme Court. Rather, the employer must be able to prove that his discriminatory action is a matter of *business necessity*—that it is truly necessary to the safe and efficient operation of the business. And this, of course, is a very difficult thing to prove. There has been vigorous enforcement of Title VII by the federal courts, including some very substantial back-pay awards. The threat of potential class-action lawsuits is now sufficiently real to provide good reason for major employers to work to change their employment practices. Most are beginning to take actions that will change the occupational patterns of women by opening up the better-paying, more responsible jobs to them. Of course, most companies still have a long way to go, but it is clear from talking with them that they really are attempting to change. The law is proving to be a great teacher.

It has been surprising to the executives of many of our large, nationwide corporations to discover that their organizations are among the ones most needing to take action to comply with the federal nondis-crimination laws. They had honestly thought of their companies as being in the forefront of modern, scientific personnel administration. The discrimination against women and minorities was so "built into the woodwork" through superficially neutral policies and practices that most key business executives were totally unaware of it. The Supreme Court's results-oriented definition of discrimination has, therefore, been a reve-lation to many. It has called for a complete shift in their perspective.

The new judicial theory also requires businessmen to consider al-ternative actions. If there is some other action they could take that would accomplish their business purpose just as well but that would not have so much of a discriminatory effect on some protected group, then continu-ing to do what they have been doing is obviously not a matter of true necessity. Employers are thus required to search for less discriminatory action alternatives. When they do, they often discover that many of their selection standards and many of the procedures they have followed both in dealing with external labor markets for initial hiring and also in up-grading, transferring, and promoting existing employees are not really necessary. Indeed, many of their personnel policies and practices have turned out to be nothing more than convenient, well-established ways of doing business—not particularly effective, but unquestioned simply be-cause "things have always been done that way." Major employers now say the risk of class-action lawsuits has become so great that they must examine their existing practices and try to find less discriminatory alter-natives.

Business organizations are also learning much by watching the court decisions for analogies. What the courts have decided, for example, with respect to what constitutes race discrimination under Title VII is quite likely to be carried over by analogy to what would constitute sex dis-crimination under the same law. The same general rules may also be applied as to ways in which both kinds of discrimination might be avoided or overcome. The federal courts are much more conscious of the similarities than of the differences in the two situations because both categories of employment discrimination are forbidden by the very same provisions of the law. Similarly, the federal courts tend to draw analogies between what should be done to correct or avoid discrimination among blue-collar workers and what should be done for white-collar workers, because all employees are covered by the same provisions of the law.

The same provisions of Title VII also apply to all kinds of employers. There is not one section that deals with what business organizations should do, another section that deals with what municipal governments should do, and still another section dealing with what colleges and universities or some other kind of employer should do. And because precisely the same provisions do apply to all kinds of employers, the courts have been less prone to make the traditional distinctions among employing institutions that most of us make. They see all employers as being much alike, and they are requiring all of them to change their policies and practices in consistent ways.

Despite the obvious effectiveness of the law as a tool for pressuring major employers to change their ways, most observers agree that its enforcement has by no means been uniform. Indeed, they say this has been the primary deterrent to more rapid change efforts by employers.

Most equal employment opportunity coordinators and others who are committed to reducing the occupational segregation of women say that the primary need is not for new laws but, rather, for stronger and more consistent enforcement of the existing law. They also say it is now time for employers to share their experiences with respect to what does and does not work when it comes to reducing occupational discrimination against women. Thus far the federal government has given employers all sorts of prescriptions with respect to what they ought to do, but there is very little objective information available about what really happens if they do those things.

My next research project is to study what happens when companies try to take affirmative action to move women into nontraditional jobs. Subsequent projects may well deal with what is happening in other sectors of the economy. The reports of this research will undoubtedly serve to focus greater attention on the problem. But more than that, these reports may give employers some new and imaginative action alternatives to consider and also serve to warn them of some very real problems others have encountered. Employers may be able to act more appropriately to reduce the occupational segregation of women within their own organizations.

In the course of this research it may also become clear that it is not really appropriate to expect women to have proportional representation in all job categories at the present time—or perhaps ever. For example, part of the proposed supplement to the American Telephone and Telegraph consent agreement deals with moving women into outside craft jobs, such as those requiring telephone-pole climbing. The appendix to the proposed agreement includes a detailed definition of what the government will accept as being a good faith effort in this matter. Obviously, AT&T has been having severe problems finding enough women who will accept such jobs. There are many affirmative actions that the government and AT&T agree the company should take. If the company does all the specified things, then the government will acknowledge that a good faith effort has been made even though the specified goals have not been achieved. In other words, it simply may not be reasonable to expect that 40 percent of all AT&T's new pole climbers are going to be women because, at least at this particular time, even the women do not want that. This is precisely the kind of situation I had in mind when I mentioned the need to make realistic adjustments in hiring goals.

There is another thing that we at The Conference Board hope my research can accomplish—the reporting of some success stories. Thus far, very little positive reinforcement has been provided to employers who are reducing the occupational segregation of women. Recognition can be provided to those organizations that have learned how to make things happen in this very difficult area.

The Conference Board, New York City

THE POLICY ISSUES

Presentation II

Nira Long

Until December 1974, I was the contract compliance officer for AID (Agency for International Development), at which time the AID contract compliance responsibilities were transferred to the GSA (General Services Administration). There are other women involved in contract compliance in the federal government, but I was the only female director of a contract compliance program in an agency. We now have no women directors although there are some who are involved as regional directors.

I talk from the perspective of one who has had to implement affirmative action within a federal agency, one who has dealt with the merit principles of the civil service system, and one who has also tried to administer affirmative action by monitoring contractors' requirements for doing business with the federal government. It is from that perspective that I write because I have felt frustrated, as a bureaucrat, in reading these papers. Although a tremendous amount of brain power has been devoted to identifying the problem, very little has been devoted to identifying the solution. Thus, I leave with a sense of frustration, with many questions but few answers. I hope these questions can be re-addressed from the research point of view.

Also, there are several issues that have not been addressed that I think we now need to discuss. I agree with Ruth Shaeffer that we have a problem in defining goals at this time. In a sense, as researchers, we are too far removed from that to worry about it. However, our opponents worry about it all the time, and they get goals and quotas confused.

I define a goal as a "floor" and a quota as a "ceiling." Therefore, they are not the same thing at all. Without goals and timetables as an enforcement device in both the public and private sector, you simply cannot accomplish anything. However, when you try to address yourself to the problem of goals within the public sector, which is guided by a merit system, you become very frustrated. If I could even attain the right to establish goals in my own agency, I would not know what to do with that power. I am in an agency whose employees are constantly being terminated, and the news from Laos means they will continue to be terminated, right at the time when we have at last created an acceptable climate for bringing more women and minorities into the mainstream.

A lot of external pressure has contributed to the development of this climate. It is ridiculous to talk about implementing the Percy amendment when there are so few women in AID involved in meaningful program positions, especially in areas which are traditionally considered women's concerns—family planning, health, and nutrition. We are not even very well advanced in terms of traditional jobs for women.

Let me say a little about the difficulties of applying the principle of goals both within the public sector and within the private sector. We are not devoting enough time to these problems, and I fear that such opponents of affirmative action as Sidney Hook will win unless more resources are applied. I say this as a concerned bureaucrat.

Within the public sector we have devoted a tremendous amount of time attacking discrimination at the entry level positions, and we have finally convinced the Civil Service Commission that the Federal Service Entrance Examination (FSEE) needs to be revamped. But for those of us who are operating within the system, the real discrimination begins in the area of promotion. I wish that some of you could receive grants to do research about this system, at least for a year, to see what happens in terms of upward mobility. I am a college graduate with a law degree, and I find that there are very few times in which I need to apply that sort of training to the work I do. Yet I am the highest-ranking black woman in foreign affairs.

There may be one out of three weeks that I am called upon to make a decision that my secretaries could not make, since in government all that is needed for most decisions is common sense. Very little opportunity exists these days even to apply critical analysis for rational decision making. Most of the requirements for performing on the job are requirements that one can attain through on-the-job experience. If there is any place where we could really achieve parity, it would be in the public sector.

I have taken several informal polls of the number of people who are actually working in the areas in which they started out, in terms of their academic training, and I have discovered that there are very few of these people at the top. This was, of course, very informal polling, but sitting in senior staff meetings I often ask people where they started. Very few of them are working in areas in which they received academic training, demonstrating to me that on-the-job experience has a great deal to do with performance. I know that if I am able to perform better than someone else—because I remember we tried it this way last year and it did or did not work—I have had that opportunity for trial and error. I have mastered the jargon of the bureaucracy, the phrasing, the memowriting, and what-have-you.

Recognizing the fact that on-the-job training is an important learning experience, I simply set what I thought was a modest goal for the distribution of the present work force at AID in all the grade levels and positions. But this has never been accepted. If we had accomplished my goal, 19 percent of all our minorities would have been distributed throughout the various grades in the civil service system, and more than 50 percent of the women would have been redistributed. I think that this would have been attainable, because there are many people who are actually capable of performing on the job, except that they lack the academic credentials or the equivalent job experience for the promotion.

The fact that you have been a secretary and have trained your own boss to do what he is now doing does not count in the bureaucracy. Also, the Civil Service Commission does not encourage people to include unpaid experience in a resumé or application form. So what I am suggesting is that we need to develop a strategy which, while not attacking the merit principle, demonstrates how the present implementation of the merit system is hampering our efforts to bring more women and minorities into the public sector.

I have many examples of edicts on merit principles from the Civil Service Commission that work against equal opportunity. This would also be true at the local and state levels. Until we can convince the Congress, as well as the Civil Service Commission, that there must be some sort of flexibility within the merit principle or system to accommodate goals, we will not get very far in the public sector. And, at this time, the civil service commissions are not even advocating that agencies set goals. Moreover, in the public sector there is no accountability on the agencies' part if they fail to undertake affirmative action. There is accountability if, and only if, an agency is guilty of discrimination.

In the private sector, of course, there is much more accountability for failure to do something affirmative. At least under the executive order there is the threat of lost business with the federal government if affirmative actions are not taken.

However, as a bureaucrat who has tried to administer the executive order, I have encountered a number of problems. First, the cost of doing business with the federal government has become very high. If we insist that firms compile the necessary data to develop a meaningful affirmative action plan, then I am afraid that the contractors will want to pass that cost on to the federal government, and ultimately on to the consumer. This is a price that we, as a matter of public policy, should be willing to pay to assist a group that has been systematically left out of the mainstream, much in the same way we have underwritten a public policy for veterans. This point simply has not been made explicit.

Second, the article in the *New York Times* that described the problems involved in developing an acceptable affirmative action program, as illustrated at the University of California at Berkeley, has been repeated time after time in the federal agencies. I have been the contract compliance officer for all architect and engineering firms in the country, and for all nonprofit research institutions, as well as for auditors and accountants, so that, in effect, I have been the contract compliance officer for think tanks and white-collar firms. It has been a very frustrating assignment, and this leads me to talk a little about the Sidney Hook problem. Affirmative action guidelines and directions were given to bureaucrats to be applied within the context of blue-collar industries. I invested nearly nine months working with the Brookings Institution to get them to agree to hire one minority economist and two female economists. This happened despite the fact that Brookings has had grants to examine civil service legislation and practices within the federal government, while Brookings did not employ minorities in their professional work force. It was so frustrating that I often wished I had been responsible for the paper mills or for General Motors and could say, after all that effort, I had succeeded in getting General Motors to hire 600 truck drivers.

Similarly, a great deal of time was invested in trying to get Stanford Research Institute to devise a good affirmative action plan. Yet the availability of technically trained people within the work force meant that at the end of nearly nine months Stanford agreed to hire only a very limited number of people within certain disciplines. I did not have the data to demonstrate whether the people were or were not available in the disciplines where they were needed. Thus, I had to wait for the think tanks to supply the data before I could attack. Even then it was very difficult, because the data consisted of lists of minority people in graduate schools, from which only gross projections could be made regarding their availability to enter the work force. It was somewhat easier to set goals for nonprofessionals since community census data helped us define the possible population for hiring purposes. However, when you begin to talk about parity for minorities in professional positions, you find that less than 2 percent of engineers are from minority groups. I was able to rationalize some of this by simply saying that one black economist in Brookings is equivalent to sixteen truck drivers at General Motors because of the impact Brookings may have on public policy.

But what I am saying here is that I wish we had done a better job at this conference in defining solutions or figuring out how to apply these concepts to goals within certain industries and within the professions. Affirmative action works beautifully when you are dealing with blue-collar industry, but more time should have been devoted to the frustrations involved in implementing affirmative action guidelines in the academic and research communities so that we can come out with something far more meaningful than what we came out with at the University of California at Berkeley. As frustrated bureaucrats, some of us have begun to feel that maybe Sidney Hook is right and that affirmative action simply does not work when you deal with academia.

We also have not discussed the fact that the executive order does not apply to grantees of the federal government. I finally convinced my agency to agree not to provide a grant to a person or an entity that is not in compliance for a contract. But if you examine Title VI of the Civil Rights Act, it talks of discrimination in terms of recipients. The employment policies of grantees are discussed only in terms of college admissions and faculty. Similarly the executive order only talks about federally assisted construction grants, not about the whole area of grants. When you look to the Justice Department for solutions to the problems of grantees, there is no legislation or executive order that deals with the grantee discriminating in terms of employment.

It just so happens that in nine out of ten cases, grantees are also contractors or they qualify under Title VII of the Civil Rights Act so that you can get them for affirmative action. But we have added, as a matter of policy, that if a person or entity does not satisfy contractual compliance standards, then that person or entity should not qualify for a grant. Enforcement of that act, however, can be very difficult.

The other problem that we did not address at the conference is what kind of accountability you can expect from public agencies—what kind of clout or monitoring can be applied to public agencies to force affirmative action? The courts, of course, are taking care of the discrimination aspect, but there is no injunction handed down to public agencies on affirmative action. Finally, I do not think we can dismiss the fact that in many instances the whole affirmative action process was designed in a hiring climate, and although the courts are addressing the question of layoffs, we need more legislation, more deliberative thinking and research about affirmative action within a layoff climate, particularly when your opponents feel threatened by the competition moving into the work force at a time when the work force is shrinking.

Sociologists and psychologists need to spend more time figuring out how to cope with that fear. Concern about employment of the Vietnamese refugees is symptomatic of the fears in our own society about the job market. I hear it day after day about women as well. We also need to spend more time with psychologists and sociologists talking about the fear of success on the part of women. You can do all you want in parading success models for high school students, but I find that most high school girls want to know if a professional career precludes the chance to lead a normal life. Does success frighten off men? We tend to dismiss this as irrelevant on the grounds that the institutions could accommodate those women whose aspirations are already there and whose consciousness has already been raised, but I think concentrating on those women whose aspirations are already raised and are simply not accommodated is of critical importance before encouraging another group to knock on the doors. Some thought must be given to the fear many women have regarding success.

Finally, in a layoff situation, and particularly in the public sector, we need to develop a strategy to deal with the veterans' preference program. I can demonstrate to you that, during the last layoffs, it was not a problem of seniority for women but of veterans' preference. That is as difficult to attack as motherhood, but I think this question of veterans' preference lays the groundwork for an argument that will have to be fought and won in a few more years because its effect is discriminatory against women.

If I end on any point, I would hope that in the future we could adjust ourselves to the problems of finding goals, particularly in terms of parity. Then we could try to apply that concept within both the public and private sectors. This will require taking industry apart to see that the application of affirmative action in blue-collar industry is very different from the way you would apply affirmative action in an academic setting.

Agency for International Development

THE POLICY ISSUES

Presentation III

Winn Newman

Although I recognize the continuing need for new data, I am afraid I must disagree with the emphasis many of the previous speakers have given to the need for new studies of discrimination. We do not need more studies or new legislation nearly as much as we need to determine how best to bring about compliance with existing legislation. The discussion so far has emphasized the necessity of eliminating discrimination through the use of additional research, but little consideration has been given to the fact that the best and quickest way to get meaningful change is to enforce existing laws and compel compliance rather than to dream up new and original solutions which may require new legislation, or at best a period of long, protracted litigation before the results can be realized. I want to discuss how I believe we can get the most out of each dollar and each hour we spend to correct discrimination. I believe this can be best accomplished by concentrating on discrimination against blue-collar women and using existing laws to correct such discrimination. Unfortunately, most women's organizations have concentrated on the problems of the middle class and have devoted relatively little time and effort to the problems of women in blue-collar jobs.

Blatant sex discrimination exists today in virtually every industrial plant in the United States. I believe that the most effective way to combat discriminatory conditions is to file charges and lawsuits under Title VII, the Equal Pay Act, the federal executive order governing government contractors, and state and local equal opportunity laws. It is time

—eleven years after the effective date of the Equal Pay Act and ten years after the effective date of Title VII—to stop emphasizing the need to change attitudes and to educate people as to how badly women are treated. The best kind of education is the kind that results from success, the kind that results from making those who break the law give restitution to the discriminatees. The best way to do this, in my opinion, is to enforce the law by filing charges and lawsuits.

Let me back up and demonstrate. Until Title VII came along, and indeed until a few years ago when the courts made it clear that Title VII superseded state protective labor laws, most industrial employers had complied with these protective laws, resulting in a then legal, segregated job structure. Certain jobs or departments were occupied by only one sex, with women, of course, being assigned to the low-opportunity and low-pay jobs. Most seniority, promotional, and layoff systems had been built around the segregated hiring and assignment policies of employers, in compliance with state protective laws and/or their views of the jobs women were competent to perform. The courts have now made it clear that these systems are illegal if they have the effect of perpetuating past discrimination. Hence, if the departments had been segregated at one time—even if the segregation had occurred before the passage of Title VII—such a departmental seniority system is now considered illegal.

Thanks to the protective laws, sex-segregated jobs are far more common than race-segregated jobs, particularly in the North. Sex discrimination is, therefore, easier to prove and clean up by applying Title VII and other laws.

The remedies imposed by the courts require that women be allowed to achieve their "rightful place"—the job level they would have obtained on the basis of their total length of service with the employer if they had not been relegated to segregated, low-opportunity jobs. If vacancies are filled on the basis of "rightful place," women would skip over junior males who were hired for better jobs at a time when these jobs were denied to women. Proper application of the "rightful place" concept under Title VII would permit massive upgrading of women and would also guarantee equal treatment in the case of layoffs.

In most industrial plants where women and/or minorities have been hired but assigned to low-opportunity or low-paying jobs, the women and/or minorities have probably been laid off in violation of the "rightful place" doctrine. This is because most collective bargaining agreements do not permit employees to "bump" into a higher classification in order to avoid being laid off. The result is that women or minorities may be laid off, while junior white males who occupy a higher classification would remain or "bump" into the job of the laid-off minority or female worker. Clearly, the application of the "rightful place" principle would save hundreds of thousands of jobs for women and minorities who were discriminatorily assigned by the employer to lower classifications and who are now laid off.

In addition to the discriminatory promotion and layoff system, a sex-segregated job structure leads to the establishment of discriminatory wage rates. To demonstrate, in a case before the War Labor Board in 1945,[1] the board found, based on data provided by General Electric Co., that after GE professionally studied the jobs to determine the degree of skill, effort, and responsibility involved, it reduced the wage rate by one-third if the job was being performed by women. In the same case, Westinghouse Electric admitted following a similar practice, but it reduced the rate by 18–20 percent if the job was performed by women.

Although the actual wage rates have, of course, increased in the past thirty years, the general across-the-board increases applicable to all jobs have left the discriminatory pattern basically unchanged for those years (except for some changes in women's wage rates which have been effected as a result of litigation initiated by IUE [International Union of Electrical Workers] and others).

Let me demonstrate further. Some of the documents which are representative of practices in industry, for example, table 1, show the 1943 wage rates in a plant involved in a War Labor Board case. By following the fourth and fifth columns, you can see, for example, that female labor grade 5 and male labor grade 5 were assigned the same number of job evaluation points and were evaluated to be equal in skill, effort, and responsibility. However, the wage rates are different: $0.795 for women and $0.955 for men, or a differential of 20 percent. When the Equal Pay Act and Title VII were passed, it became illegal to have female and male rates. Therefore, the company struck the words "female" and "male" and changed the male grades 1 through 10 (see numbers in parentheses) to 6 through 15. Is that complying with the law? It means, of course, that on the fifteen-grade structure, the former grade 5 woman with 99–123 points has more skill than grades 6–9 (formerly male grades 1–4), but she is making less money than grades 6–9. That is one form of blatant discrimination that has continued.

Indeed, the policy of the U.S. Department of Labor aids employers who have a sexually discriminatory wage-rate policy. The department still publishes community wage surveys which spell out different rates for males and females in each classification. The surveys are used by employers who currently discriminate by paying different rates to males and females. Although the Labor Department clearly does not intend to have its data used for such illegal purposes, it would appear, regardless of the benefits of publishing such information, that such assistance should not be given to perpetuate discrimination.

In addition to wage-rate discrimination, at least until IUE filed a

1. General Electric Co. and Westinghouse Electric Corp., 28 War Labor Reports 666 (1945).

Table 1

Key Sheet to Day Work Base Rates

Labor Grade	Probationary Rate	Qualifying Rate	Standard Rate	Evaluation Point Range
		Female		
1	$0.615	$0.645	$0.675	0–49
2	0.645	0.675	0.705*	50–62*
3	0.675	0.705	0.735	63–78
4	0.705	0.735	0.765	79–98
5	0.735	0.765	0.795†	99–125†
		Male		
Common labor	...	...	$0.785	0–37
1 (6)	$0.785	$0.785	0.815	38–49
2 (7).............	0.785	0.815	0.845*	50–62*
3 (8)	0.815	0.845	0.875	63–78
4 (9)	0.845	0.875	0.905	79–98
5 (10)	0.875	0.905	0.955†	99–123†
6 (11)	0.905	0.955	1.055	124–154
7 (12)	0.955	1.055	1.055	155–199
8 (13)	1.055	1.055	1.155	199–239
9 (14)	1.055	1.155	1.255	240–299
10 (15)	1.155	1.255	1.405	300+

SOURCE.—Exhibit supplied by Westinghouse Electric Corporation in General Electric Co. and Westinghouse Electric Corp., 28 War Labor Reports 666 (1945).
*Note that evaluation point range is 50 to 62, while the standard wage rate for women is $0.705, for men $0.845.
†The evaluation point range of 99 to 123 shows a standard wage rate of $0.795 for women and $0.955 for men.

lawsuit at this plant, women were also denied access to grades 6–15. This is double-barreled discrimination: women get paid less for what they perform and also do not have access to the higher paying jobs. Women are working below common labor in many industries. (The War Labor Board decision referred to above suggests that any job rate below the rate paid common labor was probably discriminatory.) Note that the hiring policy of these large companies did not change, that is, women continued to be assigned only to those first five jobs until at least 1972. Hence, newly hired men were hired at grades 6 or above while women were hired at labor grades 1, 2, and sometimes 3. I emphasize this because the requirements for unskilled, entry-level, blue-collar jobs can be easily established to require approximately the same ability. On the other hand, individual qualifications for professional jobs are far more significant.

Contrary to statements made by other speakers, I do not think employers are interested in correcting wage-rate discrimination. From a monetary standpoint, why would they desire to correct wage-rate discrimination? Surely it does not cost any more to pay "front pay" than back pay. Except for the rarely used double back-pay provisions for willful violations of the Equal Pay Act, it costs no more to pay retroactively than it does to pay prospectively. Moreover, most employers have already saved money by not complying with Title VII for the past ten years and may continue to get away with violating the law. In addition, employers will try to stick unions with a half of the back pay, but this cannot be done for "front pay." (When unions have been found to be all or partially responsible for the discrimination, they have been required to share in the back-pay liability.) In addition, much is washed out and compromised during settlement discussion, and no discriminator pays 100 cents on a dollar when a lawsuit is settled.

It is time to take the profit out of discrimination. It is time to take the profit out of breaking the law. It is time to require immediate compliance with the law.

Table 2 shows what was done in an IUE settlement of a lawsuit. The suit was based on a comparison of forty-two job classifications. Some of the job titles we compared were the same, and others carried different titles. I think the typical employee erroneously assumes that, if a job has a different title, it is a different job.

As you can see from table 2, out of the twenty-one comparisons (forty-two job classifications) involved in the lawsuit, the settlement provided for three "women's" jobs to be raised to the level of the "men's" jobs (numbers 7, 11, and 12) and for two "women's" jobs to remain unchanged (numbers 15 and 21). In the remainder, the parties agreed that, although the "women's" jobs were not fully equal to the "men's" jobs, they were underrated and the rate differential was too great. Accordingly, the settlement provided for raising the rate of the remaining "women's" jobs and decreasing the differential. For example, in number 2, the parties raised the "female" grade 12 job to grade 15 because it was not actually equal to the "male" 16 job with which it was compared. We recognized that there was a difference between the grade 16 job and the grade 12 job but that the difference should be only one grade.

If you look down the last column, showing the number of males and females in each classification, there cannot be much question that this is purely and simply a segregated plant, in one of the largest companies in the United States. Job after job is limited to one sex.

This case points up an additional problem—that most women in this plant either do not recognize discrimination, do not understand that segregation constitutes discrimination, or are unwilling to complain. Although the local union president urged women to advise IUE of their complaints, and although IUE's associate general counsel, Ruth Weyand, who was interviewed extensively by the press and on television, asserted that IUE intended to file the lawsuit, only eighty of the 2,000 women in the plant authorized IUE to file a suit on their behalf. The settlement resulted in an average increase of about $0.35 per hour for 350 women, and about $350,000 in back pay. However, after the settle-

Table 2

Settlement

Job Title	Grade	Old Job Rate	New Grade	New Rate	Amount of Increase	Female/ Male
1. Surge test..............	11	$3.385	15	$3.725	$0.34	51/0
Surge test..............	16	3.865				3/23
2. Repair stator...........	12	3.465	15	3.725	0.26	25/0
Motor parts repair......	16	3.865				0/17
3. Lead maker............	7	3.14	9	3.255	0.155	10/0
Artos lead maker.......	13	3.55				0/3
4. Assembly	9	3.255	14	3.625	0.37	54/0
Assembly	16	3.835				0/43
5. Thermocouple test	12	3.465	14	3.63	0.165	2/0
Plotter test	19	4.40				0/2
6. Janitress	8	3.20	13	3.55	0.35	6/0
Janitor	13	3.55				1/7
7. Coil winder	10	3.305	14	3.625	0.32	33/0
Stator winder	14	3.625				0/15
8. Load coils	9	3.255	12	3.465	0.21	89/0
Insulate cores	13	3.55				0/10
9. Stator repair	12	3.465	15	3.725*		15/0
Motor repair	17	4.005	16	3.865*		0/5
10. Motor test	9	3.255	12	3.465	0.21	19/2
Motor test	18	4.20				0/32
11. Receiving insp.	12	3.465	18	4.20	0.735	3/0
Receiving insp.	18	4.20				0/9
12. Respooler..............	12	3.465	15	3.725	0.26	1/1
Salvage	15	3.725				0/6
13. Stacking	9	3.255	12†	3.465	0.21	8/1
Stacking	14	3.625	14	3.625		0/5
14. Compound pourer	9	3.255	12†	3.465	0.21	5/0
Pourer	14	3.725	14	3.625		0/2
15. Stockhelper	14	3.63	No change			9/14
Treater................	16	3.865				0/9
16. Back gear wind	10	3.385	14	3.625	0.32	9/0
Type I winding	16	3.825				1/3
17. Final motor insp.	11	3.385	15	3.785	0.34	6/0
Motor insp. parts	18	4.20				6/37
18. Motor assembly	10	3.385	14	3.625	0.32	3/0
Motor assembly	16	3.835				0/43
19. Stack rotor core	8	3.20	9	3.255	0.055	3/0
Stack rotor core	14	3.625				0/11
20. Lathe operator	8	3.20	11	3.385	0.185	5/0
Lathe operator	15	3.705				0/28
21. Packer egg crate........	14	3.63	No change			12/14
Pack & check	15	3.725				7/26

SOURCE.—Burry v. General Electric Company, USDC ND Ind. Ft. Wayne Division, C.A. No. 72F9.
NOTE.—Data as of November 11, 1972.
*Some grade 12 women raised to grade 15, others to grade 16.
†Some grade 9 employees were raised to grade 14.

ment was made and publicized among the employees, the union found itself in extreme disfavor with large numbers of women members. Charges of discrimination were now filed by women against the union. We thought we had done something decent and were surprised to be rapped over the head by women who did not get increases. They were not charging, however, that there was any sex discrimination in the plant. What they were charging was that, by giving certain women a wage increase, a wage inequity had been created with other women.

The psychology is interesting. "Jane," a grade 11, did not compare her job with "John's" grade 14 job; instead, she compared herself with "Sandra," a grade 8 who was a plaintiff in the lawsuit, as a result of which "Sandra" also became a grade 11. "Jane" was sure she was worth three grades more than "Sandra"—but she did not know she was worth as much as "John," who had been performing a "man's" job. This is a perfect example of the need to educate women to recognize simple, obvious sex discrimination so that they can begin to exercise their legal rights.

To settle this problem, we investigated and learned that there was, indeed, more sex discrimination than had been reported, and subsequently negotiated increases totaling another $700,000 annually for another 1,650 people. ("Jane's" grade 11 job was indeed equivalent to "John's" grade 14 job.)

These examples show the segregated work force. Other examples would show consistent patterns of women holding jobs below the level of common labor. For example, at one large multiplant company in the electrical industry, 75 percent of the women and 7 percent of the men are in the four lowest grades. In some large plants there are no women. In others, not a single woman had achieved a level as "high" as a janitor. Indeed, in one recent check of a large employer's hiring policy, it still hired women for entry-level jobs requiring no experience a full three grades below the hiring-in level for men. That practice still continues.

It is for these reasons that I stress the need to file charges and lawsuits and to make blue-collar and other women aware of how relatively easily they can correct wage-rate promotion and layoff discrimination which exists today in viritually every industrial plant, and thus reach their rightful place and proper wage rate. Let me make two additional points regarding wage rate discrimination:

1. In addition to the wage-rate discrimination which results from the deliberate assignment of lower rates to jobs occupied by women, there may also exist additional inadvertent discrimination in the job evaluation system itself. Industrial engineers, most of whom are males, generally value physical effort as being worth twice the value of mental effort. Does this reflect a male bias in basic job evaluation standards? If so, by the simple device of increasing the value given to mental effort, job evaluators would elevate the worth of a large number of traditionally

female jobs. Is there a valid basis for drawing an analogy between the socioeconomic bias that EEOC and the Supreme Court of the United States have determined illegally exists in many testing programs[2] and the assumptions of industrial engineers regarding the value they place upon physical effort as compared with job responsibility or skill? If so, should EEOC and the courts require that where there has been a history of a segregated job structure (practically every plant that traditionally employed women) the employer must validate the wage rates for former "female" jobs as it must now do for its testing program?

2. Is there a built-in sex bias in the way machinery is designed? Does an industrial engineer, generally a male, design a piece of machinery so that it can be handled by a person five feet three inches tall, or does he design it so that an employee has to be five feet eight inches tall? Does Title VII require that at least a minimal effort must be made to enable all persons to perform a job, for example, installation of a platform or box so that shorter persons can perform the work? This is not much different than the "frail male" doctrine that exists in much of industry—when a man cannot lift heavy weights, the other employees generally pitch in and help; but if a woman goes on the same job, the attitude frequently is "if she wants a man's job, let her do the work."

What these two points suggest is that EEOC should study whether there is a sex bias in the way blue-collar jobs are traditionally evaluated and designed in American industry, and whether there is a need to promulgate guidelines on these matters.

There is need for greater concentration in areas where the law is clearly established. The established legal doctrines can most effectively be applied at the unskilled or semi-skilled job levels where discrimination is easiest to prove. The simple application of the "rightful place" doctrine would bring about substantial gains in promotional opportunity and would protect substantial numbers of women against layoffs. Concentrated effort could also put an end to discriminatory hiring and assignment policies and bring about substantial increases in the wage rates which women receive for the work they presently perform.

International Union of Electrical Workers

2. Griggs v. Duke Power Company, 401, U.S. 424 (1971).

THE POLICY ISSUES

Presentation IV

Bernice Sandler

I want to talk a little about public policy and some of the things that we really need to work for. It is easier to change public policy than to change the actual behaviors of individuals in the real world, but public policy is a place to begin.

If you feel depressed about legislation and backlash, take a look at *A Matter of Simple Justice,* produced by the President's Task Force on Women's Rights and Responsibilities in 1970. It is amazing to see how many recommendations have actually been incorporated into law. Now we really need to build in a series of carrots and sticks with new legislation and begin to assess legislation in terms of its impact on women, employers, and the federal government.

I feel sex discrimination will be much harder to eradicate than race discrimination for several reasons. First, there is a lot less guilt about having been nasty to women and a lot less awareness of sex discrimination. But even more importantly, there is literally at least one woman in every house. I think that makes it much harder for the world at large, the male part of the world, really to look at some of the issues, since we are talking about relationships with the women with whom they live.

Nevertheless, there are many achievable goals, and I want to review a very quick "laundry list" of some of these. Obviously, the importance of existing laws is major. Although some of those laws were passed with virtually no opposition, we are now, however, faced with backlash that did not exist when they were enacted.

Women, along with minorities, do badly in a recession and tend to do well in a war. I am not, however, suggesting war as a public policy. We must keep existing legislation and close out the loopholes, while working to keep this legislation from being cut back, as the backlash increases.

Underpinning much of our existing legislation, particularly those laws which cover welfare, Social Security, and income tax, is the concept that men and women are very different—with different responsibilities, life styles, and options. Essentially, our legislation "punishes" women who work and have families. When my husband and I retire, not only will I get less from my TIAA pension plan than my husband will get from his, but I will also be penalized under our Social Security benefits. For example, a married couple, both earning a total of $500 a month, would get *less* Social Security benefits upon retirement than a couple composed of a nonworking wife and a man who earns $500 per month. That second family will get more when they retire because Social Security is based on the assumption that married women do not work.

Income tax discriminates enormously. If you are married, you are limited to one tax rebate per family. A couple gets the same, whether or not the wife works outside the home or within. If you have a husband you do not get as much as if you were *not* married and just living with the man. Then you each would have gotten your *own* rebate. The deduction for child care is the only income tax deduction that has an income limitation on it. You can deduct medical and other expenses in almost unlimited amounts, and they are considered legitimate deductions. In contrast, child-care deductions are limited after you have exceeded a certain income.

However, even women who follow traditional roles, such as staying at home to raise their children, are not exempt from indirect legislative discrimination. Social Security punishes both housewives and working wives. It does not matter which you are: if you are female, you are not going to get the best deal from Social Security. If I hire someone and pay them a salary to take care of my children, that employee can be covered by disability insurance. But if I stay home with my children and stay out of the paid labor force, I cannot be covered under disability insurance through Social Security, and it is almost impossible to obtain such coverage through a private insurer.

The Equal Rights Amendment (ERA) when we get it, and *we will* get it, will take care of some of the legal inequities. The ERA will force some of the laws to be changed, but there is still a lot that needs to be done. Insurance, pensions, and other benefits need to be examined. These are covered under Title VII of the Civil Rights Act and several cases are already working their way through the courts.

We need to develop legislative incentives to break the lockstep of discrimination. Some of these already exist, but more are needed. One that I would like to see is a legislative incentive to encourage a four-day work week during a recession, rather than laying off the last hired. This would also encourage employers to avoid firing some people. Instead, employers are now penalized in a variety of ways when they put people on a part-time basis (e.g., they pay more in matching Social Security benefits).

Policies can also be changed without legislation. A few years ago, HEW (Department of Health, Education, and Welfare) had a good basic model, although they did not implement it satisfactorily. They set up the Women's Action Program, including task forces to look at the impact of HEW programs. Discrimination is often covert rather than deliberate, and nothing is done until someone points this out. The Women's Action Program task forces uncovered many discriminatory policies and practices, some of which could be changed very easily, although many were not changed. Still, this model could be used in virtually every federal agency to provide a mechanism to examine the effect of policies and practices on women.

Another example of policy change is the regulation for apprentice-ship training. It already states that there shall be no discrimination in apprenticeship training programs on the basis of race *or sex*. Then the regulation details how to develop an apprenticeship training program for minorities only. Indeed, they really do not mean minorities; they mean only minority *men*. Much of our federal policy concerning minorities, in terms of equal opportunity, poverty, retraining, and so forth, has been geared to minority men only.

We are watching very closely to insure that policies aimed at ending sex discrimination will indeed recognize that women are represented in all races. We are extremely concerned that all data collected at the federal level should be collected by race and by sex simultaneously, so that we can evaluate what happens to minority women.

The Women's Equity Action League (WEAL) looked at a study of sex discrimination in public schools to see if there were differences for minority girls. While all girls were unable to take air-conditioning mechanics, or to learn radio mechanics, etc., minority girls found it difficult to enroll in the clerical courses at this school. They were enrolled in food-handling courses and were encouraged to enter even lower-paying jobs than nonminority women.

We need to recognize that women are the fastest growing and potentially the largest advocacy group in the country. We are going to act as an advocacy and pressure group. Moral pressure is simply not enough. With the "exception" of the people at this meeting, who I know act morally, the rest of the world usually does not act morally. They react to pressure, including legal pressure, which is very effective. We are going to have to use the tactics that other groups have used. We are going to have to form coalitions. One of the exciting developments, and one of the few good things that is coming out of the recession, is that we are getting stronger coalitions between minority and women's groups.

Even the leadership conference in Washington now has a task force on women's rights, and they have begun to be very helpful in a variety of issues with Congress. The recent Minimum Wage Act is a good example of coalitions. For years the minority groups have been trying, unsuccessfully, to get the minimum wage to cover domestic workers. This past year, the so-called middle-class professional women joined the struggle with minorities. This coalition provided enough extra pressure to get the act over the top so that legislation now covers domestic workers.

More than anything, we need to increase the discontent of women. Nobody changes anything unless they are uncomfortable. This is one of the major things we need to do because many women are simply unaware that there is discrimination, and are unaware that women are being hurt. Women are often unaware that many of the gains they are making are related to the women's movement. I am a little annoyed when some women gets a breakthrough job, the first woman in construction, etc., for in fact she may not be the first; but the newspapers play it up as if she is, and she thinks she is. Inevitably a reporter asks, "Are you for women's lib?" (a remark that tells you the reporter does not know that few women in the women's movement call it "women's lib"). Then the "first woman" says, "No I am not for women's lib; I am against it." She is unaware of how the movement helped her to get her job.

Increasing awareness, developing specific solutions, watching to see that they get implemented, monitoring policies and practices—these are things that need to be done. Research itself, in a sense, needs to be politicized. I realize that is a dirty word in research, but I am not talking about a bias in doing the research but in *choosing* the research, in *disseminating* it, and in *using* it. To do research that has a payoff is critical. It can have an impact on public policy, particularly if it is designed with that effect in mind.

We also need more women in leadership positions all across the board. We need to infiltrate the power structure. We need to continue to work at getting better federal enforcement. Thomas Jefferson said that eternal vigilance is the price of liberty, and I am finally aware of what this really means. We have to watch the Congress and other federal agencies. HEW is a good example. The General Accounting Office, the investigative arm of the Congress, has found that HEW has been grossly incompetent, and I do mean grossly. Women's groups such as WEAL, NOW, the Federation of Organizations of Professional Women, Association of Women in Science, and NEA have joined together and are suing HEW for lack of enforcement.

Title IX already has been cut back legislatively, and HEW has a work plan whereby there will be no new investigations of either race or sex bias in academic institutions until September 1976. There is also a new proposal whereby HEW seeks to get rid of its responsibility to respond to individual complaints. This could give HEW the power to do only what they want and not respond to any complaints that anyone would file.

Women's work has just begun. We have much to do. I used to think it would take five years to get it all taken care of. Now I think it will take hundreds of years. We are talking about something that will have as profound an impact on the lives of men and women as the Industrial Revolution.

I would like to close with a new "revelation" from the Bible that was "discovered" by a woman archaeologist about a year ago which says,

And they shall beat their pots and pans into printing presses,
And weave their cloth into protest banners.
Nations of women shall lift up their voices with nations of other women,
Neither shall they accept discrimination any more.

It may sound apocryphal, but I think it may yet prove to come from the Book of Prophets, for women are indeed learning the politics of power. They are learning that the hand that rocks the cradle can indeed rock the boat.

Project on the Status and Education of Women
Association of American Colleges

THE POLICY ISSUES

Presentation V

Janet L. Norwood

I want to talk to you as an economist rather than as a bureaucrat. Some of the points in the previous discussion give me cause for concern. We cannot look at women as one group. Women, by age groups, have very different labor force experience.

The expansion in our economy over the past few decades has been accompanied by a significant increase in the participation of women in the labor force. Since 1965, nearly 60 percent of the net growth in the labor force has been due to women, who now account for 40 percent of the country's entire work force. In spite of these changes in the labor force composition, current figures on the employment of women in this country bear a striking resemblance to those of 10, 20, even 30 years ago. Women still account for more than one-half of all workers in the service industries, especially in education, health, hotels, restaurants, and private households. In other major industrial categories, women are still concentrated in large numbers in some subgroups such as clothing manufacturing and general merchandise. The BLS data show that in 1974 close to 70 percent of all salesworkers and almost 78 percent of all clerical staff were women. Women represented 82 percent of all librarians; 93 percent of all nurses, dieticians, and therapists; 60 percent of all social workers; 70 percent of all elementary and secondary school teachers. Three-quarters of all ironers and pressers were women, and women represented two-thirds of all laundry and dry cleaning workers. Unfortunately, the female-intensive occupations and industries all tend to fall at the low end of the wage scale. In spite of the landmark legislation and some judicial actions of recent years to prohibit employment discrimination based on sex, the median earnings of women are still only 60 percent of the earnings of men. More important, there has been no real change in this ratio in the last seven years. So long as women remain concentrated in low-wage occupations in low-wage industries, there is little likelihood that the situation will improve.

Where do we go from here? The largest proportion of women is in clerical occupations. Thirty-five percent of all employed women are clerical workers, compared to 6 percent of men. It seems to me that the goal is to move this cluster of women out of the category in which they are now located into occupations which are higher paying, which are perhaps more challenging, and which offer more possibilities for women to realize their potential. In general, this means moving them into some of the managerial classifications in which they are now underrepresented or into the professional and technical occupational group. Of course, there is room for change *within* an occupational group: the nurses could be physicians, and the laboratory workers, scientists. But if we really want to improve the situation, we must move some of this large group of women who are in the clerical occupations into other occupations.

Now, in order to do that, to improve the occupational profile of women workers, we really need more jobs. I assume that we can agree that our basic goal is not to replace men with women and put the men in the unemployed group. What we want to do is to improve the occupational profile of women by putting them into better jobs. So we need, first and foremost, a growing and expanding economy which will, over the long run, add new jobs to the labor force.

Where will these jobs be? In the 1960s women responded to the demand created by new jobs in really amazing proportions. Where were those jobs? Those jobs were largely, in the expanding economy of the sixties, not entirely but substantially in service industries. Where do we find women today? We find women in service industries and in service occupations.

Certainly no one has a crystal ball about the future. BLS has prepared projections of the economy through 1985, but they should be used with care. We have some problems in developing the basic assumptions and the particular models. All that we can say is that certain things can happen if we rely upon some of the conditions assumed and on the data of the past. Projections into the future are based upon the data of the past. That is a very important point to keep in mind in doing research on women since the labor force status of women has changed significantly in recent years.

The bureau's projections to 1985 indicate an expansion in the number of jobs to about 100 million. In general, there will be more people who are educated to hold jobs than there are jobs requiring people with an education. That is not to say that education does not have a value in and of itself. However, looked at in terms of the labor market, our projections indicate that by 1985, there will be an oversupply of educated people compared with job requirements. This will hamper our ability to reduce or eliminate occupational segregation.

If we are to make any significant inroad in the reduction of occupational segregation, we must somehow create and sustain an economy which continues to grow and which produces more job opportunities for both men and women. We must give considerably more attention than we have in the past to techniques for restructuring job content and to methods for improving job satisfaction for workers.

Now, I would like to answer the questions that have been raised about BLS data. Two points were made. Let me start first with Bernice Sandler's comment that all data should be collected by race and by sex. I agree with you. However, when data are provided with a sex breakdown or a race breakdown, subgroups of the population are represented, and the sample sizes have to be considerably larger. What does that mean? It does not mean that the Bureau of Labor Statistics does not want to do it. Rather, it means that the Bureau of Labor Statistics does not have enough money to collect the amount of data required by that decision.

So I would like to suggest that you add to your list of issues for women to advocate—advocacy at budget time, when we really need it. Women should come out and support strongly the need for funds to provide more and better data. We are publishing more than we have published in the past, and next month we will be publishing new occupational data. Some of these data are drawn from small samples, but I keep remembering when I worry about the possibility of people like Winn Newman using them in lawsuits, that Carolyn Bell once told me that I should remember always that it was men who taught me about sampling error.

Now, Winn Newman's point. We do publish area wage-survey data with a sex breakdown. I think we have here a conflict in the suggestions that were made. It is the kind of conflict that the Bureau of Labor Statistics frequently faces. People come to us insisting that more data be published with sex breakdowns. Other people come to us and say: "Don't you realize that the data can be misused? You should not be producing them; you are not doing the public a service."

The data which Winn Newman is complaining about are averages that are not necessarily indications of discrimination. There is an industry mix in these data. Women are concentrated in particular industries, and there is, as you all know, a high correlation between earnings and industry; we should, therefore, expect differences in these averages for men and for women. But let me say that even if the data were to show deliberate and overt discrimination in a plant, it is the responsibility of a public agency and the Bureau of Labor Statistics to "tell it like it is." We are a data-producing and analyzing agency. Our responsibility is to indicate what has happened and to provide that information in as unbiased a way as possible to the public.

If we started to worry all the time about how our data might be used rather than worrying about some of the large sampling errors on household heads—females with relatives present, without relatives present, and the number of ironers and pressers—we would never publish anything.

Bureau of Labor Statistics

The Policy Issues

Presentation VI

Rosabeth Moss Kanter

In any area of social science inquiry that corresponds to major public policy concerns, models of research and intervention are closely intertwined. The connection found by intellectual historians and sociologists of knowledge between "objective" science and its political context must be even firmer in areas such as the "woman question," in which research findings are likely to be quickly seized by policymakers and activists as a guide to their efforts in making or resisting change. The kinds of research social scientists do determine the kinds of interventions that they make when they translate their own research into action, and research types may also determine the kinds of interventions other people make when they take the latest social science findings and translate them into action programs.

In my experience both as a researcher and as a consultant to companies implementing affirmative action programs and reorganizing opportunities for women, I have identified three major research styles that are connected with very different kinds of interventions. Each model has radically different implications for the level of intervention, the assumptions about women, the scope of change, and the effectiveness of change. They also differ greatly in the amount of backlash they permit—that is, in the amount of ammunition they present to the opponents of change in the position of women.

The three models may be called "temperamental," "role related," and "social structural." They correspond, roughly, to concern with the individual, role, and organizational levels as determinants of social life. While each may have validity as descriptions of pieces of reality, their consequences for the issue of occupational segregation make one model—the social structural—preferable to the other two as a research strategy with the potential to promote change.

The first model, the temperamental, involves the study of women's character and personality. A large number of studies of female socialization, of sex differences, and indeed, perhaps half of the recent investigations in the sex roles field, fall into this category. This may reflect the American tendency to seek explanations for social phenomena in the individual, as well as the dominance of psychology as a science and therapy in the United States. The assumption behind this model can be overstated as follows: women differ from men in their character, temperament, attitudes, self-esteem, language, gestures, and interpersonal orientations, whether by nature, early socialization, or accumulated learning as a result of coping with an inferior position. Despite recent criticisms of the reification of sex differences, and recent findings that question whether there *are* many significant sex differences stemming from childhood socialization, this model remains popular, particularly in its applications.

When translated into intervention, particularly in industry, the temperamental model implies the need for remedial programs for women. The intervention style is one of compensation for deficiencies. The assumption here is that women enter the work force, come into leadership roles, or compete for managerial and professional positions, socialized not quite correctly for the demands of the organizational-occupation worlds. It is thus important to have compensatory programs that will help women overcome the character defects interfering with their work effectiveness and entry into male-dominated occupations. These programs are not necessarily oriented toward making women more like men, but they identify skills or knowledge areas in which women are considered less competent, and they assume that women's motivation and temperament are the major reinforcers of occupational segregation. Examples of these kinds of programs include assertiveness-training workshops, management-assessment programs for women, and short (e.g., two to three day) sessions of consciousness raising and career planning for women in a particular company, with such titles as "Women in Management."

I do not want to discount the positive aspects of these programs, especially those on management skills and self-assertion. Besides the support and ego boost they give to the women attending, a major benefit is that they have employed a wide range of female consultants, often the first women hired by a corporation as an outside consultant. Short-term training programs in this tradition, based on the temperamental research model and offering remedial learning for women, have served as an outlet for entrepreneurial activity on the part of women who have started their own firms in response to the growing market for these kinds of services. Given a declining economy and a need to generate new jobs, the fact that the women's movement has generated entrepreneurial and creative activity—even activity "selling" the movement—is a benefit.

But there are also dangers to the temperamental model of research when translated into intervention. First, it is not yet clear that compensatory training programs or consciousness-raising efforts have any long-term impact on the nature of the occupational world, just as it is not yet clear that changing the consciousness of individuals is the most effective strategy for social change. One could argue that increasing the number of "properly socialized" and appropriately motivated women does not, by itself, affect the structure of the organizational world. The danger of too much energy committed in this direction is that it too easily takes on the appearance of progress (and give companies something to point to in their affirmative action reviews) but allows the structure of the organization to remain intact.

The second danger is that of stereotyping. Even the new feminist research on sex-role socialization and sex differences has sometimes had the unfortunate consequence of creating a new set of stereotypes about what women feel and how women behave. Despite the large amount of overlap between the sexes in most research, the tendency to label and polarize and thus to exaggerate differences remains in much reporting of data, which may, for example, report the mean scores of male and female populations but not the degree of overlap. Those women in industry, particularly those pioneering in male fields, who avoid identification with the women's movement are often responding to their fear of being stereotyped. They may resist being singled out for special attention or argue against the implementation of special programs for women because they do not want the differences of behavior or attitudes between them and their male colleagues exaggerated—when indeed there may be few differences. Because the women who are succeeding in higher-status occupations are probably a special group anyway, it is likely, in fact, that many of the generalizations about women's character and socialization will not apply to them. (Interviews with women selling industrial chemicals offered indications in this direction.)

The third danger of the temperamental model of research and intervention is that it reinforces several traditional attitudes: that men set the standards for occupational success and that women are deficient, requiring remedial and compensatory attention. Thus, people in power are supported in their view that women are deficient.

There is also an opposing viewpoint within the temperamental model. Some feminists hold that women are different (by virtue of biology or socialization) but that these differences make them superior to men, not inferior. This perspective stresses the existence of a women's culture of nurturance, support, and expressiveness. The suggested intervention, then, is to get more women into positions of power, for the assumption (again, stated in an oversimplified fashion) is that women will handle power in a more benign, more egalitarian, more humane fashion. While this view arouses sympathetic echoes in most feminists, it unfortunately has little empirical evidence to back its claims, and it too promotes stereotypes, even though the images are positively rather than negatively valued.

The second research model is role related. In conjunction with research on character and temperament, it accounts for the large majority of all efforts in the sex roles field. This model focuses on the division of labor between men and women, beginning with the family, as the key to women's position and the foundation of occupational segregation. Research in this area centers on role dichotomies and role dilemmas, and it considers change in conceptions of family roles the major issue to be addressed. Often, in this research style, the larger social world tends to be seen as a reflection or projection of basic male-female roles derived from the family—that is, that both the segregation of occupations within the world of work and the segregation of housework from labor market work find their origin in the family and continue to be reinforced by family patterns and attitudes toward family roles. Thus, it is considered legitimate, in research in this tradition, to turn attention away from the world of work per se and toward the constraints the family division of labor puts on male and female roles. Attention is concentrated on the smaller space around the individual, rather than the larger social structure.

Research that locates the important issues in the division of family roles tends to encourage intervention strategies oriented toward the individual's role conceptions. Interventions in the educational system are primary among these. Especially on the upper levels, but increasingly in early childhood education, programs are mounted to help women conceive of their roles differently, to see that they can manage dual roles and to prepare them to deal with the conflicts assumed to result. Consciousness raising for men might also be a related strategy: to encourage men to see enlarged possibilities for women and perhaps to take a larger share of the family responsibilities. Structural solutions are also proposed, such as child-care arrangements and part-time work. These again are seen as permitting women to carry out more easily their multiple roles, with the necessity for women to balance labor market work with family work implicit. Thus, the possibilities for women in the occupational world, as seen in this model, are dominated by the family and role conceptions, and interventions focus on the management of family and role-related problems.

The virtues of this model resemble that of the first. Many individuals do come to view themselves differently, and reexamination of messages about roles conveyed by the educational system is all to the good. A loosening of traditional attitudes toward the family division of labor, continuing a long-term secular trend, makes more flexibility possible for husband and wife and provides the next generation with an enlarged choice of life-styles. But there is too often a conservative thrust in the assumptions informing research and intervention in this tradition. The traditional nuclear family model is generally assumed, leaving a heavy burden on each husband and wife to work out role-related issues by themselves. Alternatives, such as cooperative neighborhood arrangements, extended family networks, or communal households, all of which reduce the family role-related conflicts experienced by women and help them enter the labor market as somewhat-freer agents, ought to be considered as well.

Role-related research and intervention focuses too much attention on the family and not enough on the workplace. A large number of women enter the labor market without family responsibilities, yet their situation is not necessarily better than that of married women or mothers (though it appears that successful women executives often remain single during the early stages of their careers). Because so much attention is directed toward family-related roles, employers are handed a set of stereotypes to add to those about women's temperament that permit convenient excuses for women's segregated occupational roles and generally inferior status. Even single women and proven career women in one professional unit of a large corporation reported that concern about their current (or imagined future) family responsibilities was raised by managers in their career reviews.

At the same time, the nature of the work world itself is virtually ignored in this research style. The occupational world enters analysis as though it were homogeneous, as though the *fact* of working is all that is important for a woman and not the kind of work, its organizational context, or its relation to other occupations. The notion that one can talk about career-family conflicts without specifying the kind of career and its attendant rewards and constraints is ludicrous. Yet too often in sex-role research either the work situations or the family situations of women remain indifferentiated, and interventions thus have an overly global quality.

If the first model unintentionally supports an image of women as deficient, the second supports an image of women as overcommitted, or torn between obligations, or most appropriately performing roles resembling those they play in the family. In both cases, opponents of change in the occupational situation of women may be receiving, again unintentionally, fuel for their resistance to change.

There is a third model of research and intervention, the social structural, that has greater potential for reducing occupational segregation.

This model makes fewer assumptions about the nature or roles of women (and thus avoids statements that stereotype women or that could be read negatively), and it attacks the work situation directly. Compared with the amount of research and analysis done in the first two styles, investigation and intervention in this third area is minimal.

Social structural research is directed at the nature of organizational structures and the organization of work. Occupations do not exist in a vacuum; they occur within institutions. Those institutions' structures —who works with whom, who dominates whom, how members of occupations come into contact with one another—are the topics of analysis and explanation. I suggest (and I am marshaling the evidence for this assertion elsewhere)[1] that a number of structural and situational variables are more important determinants of the organizational behavior of women (and men) than sex differences or global social roles. These variables include: opportunity structures, internal labor markets, dominance structures, and sex ratios within and across hierarchical levels. These determine or highly influence the likelihood that women on the job will have high motivation, will be able to demonstrate competence and confidence, will be seen as promotable, will be productive, and will be effective in leadership roles. At the same time, these structural-situational variables also have impact on the individual's attitudes and family roles, that is, on those issues considered important in the first two models. For example, as women gain power in work situations, roles within the family are affected; organizational structural changes do feed back into those very systems that have been seen, in the second model, as the root of women's inferior position in the workplace.

There are a large number of action research possibilities and intervention strategies that ought to be explored in this area. Some of them are currently underway both in the United States and other countries, but they have not yet received widespread research attention or policy interest. Perhaps this is in part because researcher-activists have easier access to individuals, to low-status systems such as education, and to small groups such as families than they do to large organizational entities such as corporations.

First, as part of the reorganization of work itself, it is important to consider the modification of hierarchy. Many schemes for increasing participation and leveling power differences have been proposed, but often they have failed to go beyond the level of the small group or to have much structural impact on tasks, although organization development strategies could operate in the long run to benefit women. At the present time, one of the most promising structural interventions is "flex time" or flexible working hours. Flex time not only rearranges working

1. In *Women and Organizations* (Englewood Cliffs, N.J.: Prentice Hall, Inc., 1976).

hours and can thus help women with family responsibilities (feeding into issues of the second model),[2] but it also brings with it, as researchers in Europe are discovering, many other modifications of the organization of work. It is difficult to maintain certain kinds of hierarchical structures when people have to be able to act as replacements for absentees, and if workers have a greater degree of autonomy and control over their work situations. Flex time also promotes sharing of jobs, members of work teams training one another, and participation—all conditions that ought to improve the prospects for women to gain self-esteem, work satisfaction, motivation, and learning.

Europe is far ahead of the United States in theorizing about and implementing flexible working hours, although there are a number of American experiments currently underway (e.g., the First National Bank of Boston). The potential of flex time to encourage major work reorganizations is dramatically illustrated by the case of Interflex, a German firm with a large share of the responsibility for promoting the concept internationally. Interflex is a profit-making business firm that sells electronic time-recording devices and helps organizations implement flex time. Despite its conventional business trappings, it is run as a work collective or cooperative, in which wages are decided by consensus, and profit sharing is based on a combination of job-rank and peer-performance evaluations. Interflex has gone beyond working hours per se to experiment with change in many of the structural conditions that have traditionally operated as barriers to women's upward mobility at work.

Another structural issue is how women are introduced to new positions. The government sets down guidelines, and the company hires the requisite number of female bodies. What do they do then? What happens next? What sorts of training are offered, introductions to the company made? What kinds of networks are created?—an issue of special concern for women in fields where they are still numerically scarce. How are the women integrated with their male peers? This issue was faced by a team in which I participated charged with designing a management-training program for a large New England company, to put women into a first-line supervisor job (foreman), a position never before occupied by a woman, with responsibility for a largely male work force in craft jobs. In our design we tried to be concerned about all the structural issues which often defeat women entering "male jobs." The issues included building a team out of the men and women being trained, so that the women in the group would be more closely attached to their male peers. Higher-level supervisors were involved in the program, and lines of communication opened. Other managers in the field (especially men) were involved and made to feel part of the project. A rhythm of training

2. It should come as no surprise that one piece of research found married women to be more favorable to flex time than any other group.

activities and field involvement was developed. Some of these strategies are part of routine training programs in industry, but routine programs were adapted with an eye toward dealing with organization structure, especially communication, as well as the teaching of skills to individuals. We hoped to develop a structural context conducive to the women's success as foremen that would help regardless of their own individual skills.

Clerical work is another major area for structural intervention. In many companies, lines of mobility out of the clerical hierarchy simply do not exist—and the clerical ranks *do* constitute a hierarchy in the fullest sense of the word. In large companies, many levels and statuses of clerical workers are recognized, and women can be promoted through the clerical ranks all the way up to executive secretary. But lines of mobility into other jobs and other functions must be recognized and used. Large corporations are often so large and so complex that they cannot even be called "bureaucracies" in the classical sense any longer. For example, while each division or department may be hierarchically organized and have an organization chart, it is often very difficult to discern what is a promotion or what is a comparable job across departments, particularly on the nonexempt levels to which clerical workers belong. Career paths are much better known on the exempt, or salaried, employee levels and are best known for management jobs.

The secretary-boss relationship could also be changed to benefit women.[3] One large New York company is working on this problem, but change is very slow in an area so fraught with tradition. One part of their effort is to change the job from a personal relationship (like a traditional patrimony) to a rationalized task (like other jobs in the company) that has a job description (many companies do not have these for certain clerical workers) and performance appraisals (even rarer). Both of these systems create a work contract for clerical workers that enables them to be evaluated for the work they actually do, rather than for an idiosyncratic relationship with a particular man. At the same time, performance appraisals serve as an educational device for the women and a way for the company to identify high-potential employees. Many companies do not even know the capabilities of the women working for them, particularly women buried in the clerical ranks. These sorts of minimal changes—to extend to clerical women systems that already exist for management men—can often be very effective in changing the opportunity structure in the organization over time. First, of course, one has to convince a company that they should even pay attention to secretaries and clerical workers.

Sex ratios, finally, represent a major unexplored structural issue for both research and intervention. In fact, I am now trying to prove that a number of generalizations about women at work are really a function of

---

3. See *Women and Organizations*, chap. 3.

the proportions of women found in a particular work group or work setting.[4] Many of us have probably experienced the issues of tokenism first hand—that is, being an only woman or one of very few women in a group of men. The token woman faces a variety of issues that are now being specified rigorously by social-psychological experiments. She is likely to be isolated from the mainstream of group life, to suffer self-doubt and lowered self-esteem, or to fall into one of a variety of stereotyped roles (such as mother, sex object, pet, or iron maiden). The fact of numerical minority rather than aspects of the woman herself create these tendencies. If there are *two* women in a group rather than one, other dynamics may result: for example, group members forcing them together or setting one up against the other.

Further research on the effects of sex ratios, such as identification of the "tipping point" at which minority member dynamics no longer occur, can have important intervention consequences. Again, this issue directs attention to the structural context surrounding a woman and not just her own behavioral tendencies. In placing women, one would look at the numerical balance that will result when women are put into particular groups or offices. At present when many companies hire women (particularly those companies facing government pressure to place women in every function and on every level), they are immediately dispersed so that every unit will have *its* woman. But there are significant policy issues here. Perhaps women should be clustered rather than spread and dispersed. And if they cannot be clustered, perhaps networks should be formed that bring women together and help compensate for minority status.

However, if networks of women are formed, they should be job related and task related rather than female-concerns related. Personal networks for sociability in the context of a work organization would tend to promote the image of women contained in the temperamental model—that companies must compensate for women's deficiencies and bring them together for support because they could not make it on their own. But job-related task forces serve the social-psychological functions while reinforcing a more positive image of women. If women in the organization have some legitimate task-related purpose for getting together, then they can be clustered in a meaningful way. It is interesting to note that more flexible and more participatory organization structures can also serve this end, for they tend to force a great deal of interaction across work group boundaries.

Paying attention to the kinds of structural issues outlined here, and

4. See "Women and the Structure of Organizations," *Another Voice*, ed. M. Millman and R. M. Kanter (New York: Doubleday Anchor Books, 1975), and "Some Effects of Proportions on Group Life: Skewed Sex Ratios and Responses to Token Women," in press, available from Center for Research on Women in Higher Education and the Professions, Wellesley College.

others that could be identified through an organizational perspective, has a great deal of potential for changing women's relationship to the work place and affecting occupational segregation. In order to effect long-term social change, we need much more research on the implications for women of the arrangement of work in a variety of organizational settings.

Brandeis University and
Harvard Law School

SUMMARY STATEMENT

Toward Dimorphics: A Summary Statement to the Conference on Occupational Segregation

Myra H. Strober

My task is to summarize the proceedings of this conference. It is, however, impossible to provide an "objective" account of an event such as this. A number of ideas have been presented, and for each of us their selection, absorption, and integration must progress in accordance with previous training and predilection. My summary is, perforce, a personal one.

First, I will discuss Kenneth Boulding's fascinating view that this conference marks the birth of a new science, dimorphics. Second, I will examine a major theme of the conference, the importance of interaction mechanisms among societal systems, and I will elaborate a "systems interaction model" of occupational segregation. Third, I will address the issue of goals and analyze participants' views of some of the characteristics of the "good," occupationally integrated society. Fourth, I will summarize some of the policy issues discussed at the conference and, in the final section, outline some unanswered questions of dimorphics.

The Birth of Dimorphics

Let us begin with the birth of a new science, dimorphics. It may be defined as the study of the differences between male and female roles, or the study of occupational segregation, occupation being defined broadly. With what questions does this new science deal? Kenneth

Boulding has suggested three: What is it? What can it be? What should it be? Let me expand and recommend some additional ones: (1) What is the distribution of men and women among different occupations, or, how do male and female roles differ in our society and how are these role differences changing over time?—What is it? (2) How did this particular set of roles or occupations come to be differentiated or segregated? (3) How is the system of segregation maintained? (4) What are the possible alternatives to the segregated system?—What can it be? (5) What are the most desirable alternatives?—What should it be? and (6) How can we best achieve the desired alternatives?

The paradigm of dimorphics has not yet been clearly articulated, and perhaps until it is we should follow Adam Smith's precedent and call our new subject an inquiry. Yet, in several other respects dimorphics clearly meets the test of a new science. For example, the questions being addressed by dimorphics are sufficiently intriguing to "attract an enduring group of adherents away from competing modes of scientific activity"[1] so that an invisible college of dimorphists is now emerging.

Perhaps one of the key attributes of dimorphics is its interdisciplinary nature; one of the principle components in the materialization of the inquiry was, no doubt, the identification of a problem cutting across so many areas. Anthropology, art, economics, history, law, literature, political science, and sociology all contribute to dimorphics. In turn, the interdisciplinary nature of dimorphics has contributed to what has so far been the inquiry's most significant insight: the importance of the relatedness or feedback among societal systems, a theme that appears in virtually all of the conference papers and comments.

Systems Interaction Mechanisms and Occupational Segregation: A Model

Harold Leavitt notes that at one time male-female roles were in an equilibrium supported by all societal systems: legal, economic, social, and cultural. However, something perturbed that equilibrium (precisely what it was is a matter of some disagreement), and now, in Kenneth Arrow's terms, we are in search of a new one.

The papers by Heidi Hartmann and Elise Boulding consistently make the point that the origin and maintenance of occupational segregation are the result of interactions among several societal institutions. In particular, Hartmann discusses the roles of the state, the family, employers, and unions. Francine Blau and Carol Jusenius point out that

---

1. Thomas S. Kuhn, *The Structure of Scientific Revolutions*, 2d ed. (Chicago: University of Chicago Press, 1970), p. 10.

when systems interactions are taken into account, the notion that the victims of occupational segregation are themselves responsible for their plight is seen as incorrect. Finally, Constantina Safilios-Rothschild emphasizes the importance of the interrelation of the family and occupational systems, an emphasis echoed in the papers by Isabel Sawhill and Marianne Ferber and Helen Lowry.

The interrelatedness of societal systems and the strength of established traditions are important in answering a serious question for economists: since individual employers could increase profits by hiring women into male occupations and paying them lower wages than those paid to males, why have these profit opportunities not served to break down the system of occupational segregation? Why is occupational segregation or crowding maintained? Using other phraseology, how is the conspiracy maintained? Or why does the cartel not break up? Or, in the language of the dual labor market theorists, why do employers not hire women into traditional male ports of entry?

There are obviously several important elements in the answer to this question. However, based on this conference, the major answer is that occupational segregation at the workplace has been maintained because all other systems in the society have so strongly supported it. Social, legal, cultural, and other economic pressures have simply been too great to allow individual employers to break the occupational cartel. The economist might respond to this incredulously, asking, "Can you mean that employers have been affected by forces greater than profit maximization?" The dimorphist would answer the economist affirmatively, noting that the strength of social, legal, cultural, and economic conventions has tended to cement the status quo on both the supply and demand sides of the labor market.

On the supply side, young women generally have been unwilling to apply for men's jobs. Historically, society's goal for women has been marriage. Women who internalized this goal found it distasteful to contemplate taking male jobs, since doing so might diminish their sexual attractiveness and hence their marriage prospects. Literature, school curricula, the media, and the absence of role models in nontraditional occupations have all buttressed women's desire to enter female-typed pursuits. Moreover, during periods of job scarcity women no doubt have feared that taking a male (*read* breadwinner's) job, especially at a lower rate of pay, might be cause for community ostracism.

On the demand side, again, social convention has played an important role. Employers as well as women were appropriately socialized to respect the traditional sex division of labor. Subtle pressures from family, employees, customers, and "the community" no doubt continuously reenforced certain hiring taboos. I have often been intrigued in this respect by the behavior of late nineteenth-century steel mill owners who, rather than employ women, preferred to incur the costs of recruiting male labor from Eastern Europe.[2] It may have been permissible to employ women in textile factories, but it was simply unthinkable to put them into steel mills, although there is some evidence that, at least in Pennsylvania prior to 1885, wives of foreign workers (who, presumably, were not covered by the niceties of community propriety) did assist their husbands in piecework labor in the coke yards. These wives, however, were *not* on the company payrolls; they merely helped their husbands to earn higher wages.[3]

The multitude of supports for the status quo on both the supply and demand sides of the labor market created what is known in the economic development literature as a vicious circle. The question which then arises, of course, is how is the vicious circle broken? How does occupational segregation change? A systems interaction model would explain changes in occupational segregation as follows.

As portrayed in figure 1, the vicious circle is broken by some outside change agent, some systemic jolt,[4] such as a war, the invention of a new machine (e.g., the typewriter), the appearance of a new method of organizing work (e.g., the common school), or simply the growth of large-scale business. The jolt need not necessarily be sudden; it can also build slowly over time. Moreover, although the jolt is pictured in figure 1 as coming from outside the system, it can also arise from within the system. The important point is that *the systemic jolt must act upon both the demand for labor and the mind-set of the community* (the media, legal institutions, literature, the family, etc). The arrows labeled (1) in the figure indicate that the change agent affects both labor demand and societal values and goals.

Once societal values and goals are changed by the jolt, employers begin to think it acceptable to meet their increased labor demand with female workers. This is indicated by arrow (2) portraying the influence of societal changes on employer thinking. At the same time changes in societal values are affecting the thinking of women. This, too, is indicated by an arrow labeled (2). Employers now begin actively to seek women workers. This is represented by arrow (3). Finally, once *both* changes in societal values and employer demand have impinged upon women, women begin to supply their labor to nontraditional occupa-

2. See, e.g., John A. Fitch, *The Steel Workers* (New York: Russell Sage Foundation, 1911), pp. 139–49. Many Slavs were brought in as strikebreakers. But they were also hired in nonstrike years. Not only were Slavs preferred to women. As Fitch points out, because they were willing to work for lower wages than native boys or sons of already established immigrants, Slav were also preferred to these groups.

3. H. C. Frick, U.S. Congress, Senate, *Investigation of Labor Troubles*, 52d Congress, 2d Sess., Report no. 1280 (February 10, 1893), pp. 158–59.

4. The role of crisis in facilitating role de-differentiation has been discussed in Jean Lipman-Blumen, "Role De-differentiation as a System Response to Crisis: Occupational and Political Roles for Women," *Sociological Inquiry* 43, no. 2 (1973): 105–29.

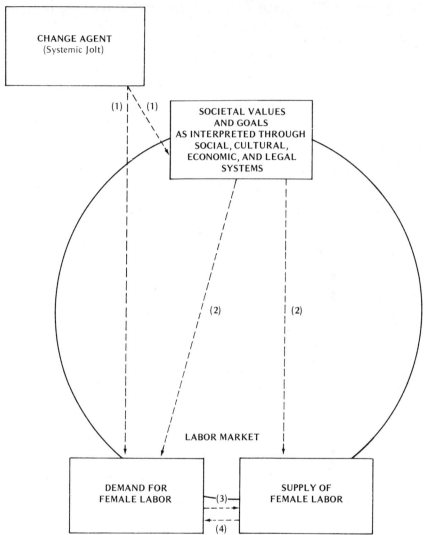

FIG. 1.—A system interaction model of changes in occupational segregation

tions, either paid work per se or particular paid jobs which have heretofore been reserved for men. This is represented by arrow (4).

It must be noted that systemic jolts which do not affect both the demand for labor and societal values will not break the vicious circle. Changes in labor demand alone, unless they somehow engineer changes in societal values, will not result in increased occupational integration. Moreover, systemic jolts that have exceedingly important effects on societal values but no immediate effects on labor demand—as, for example, the pasteurization of milk or the invention of effective birth control devices—will have no immediate effects on employment or occupational integration. It is important to understand that, as a result of changes affecting values but not labor demand, women may be ready to enter certain occupations long before employers receive the necessary impetus to hire them.

There is, of course, no guarantee that the labor supply forthcoming in response to a change in labor demand and system values will be such as just to clear the market at the original wage rate. If women begin to realize that employers are willing to hire them into a particular occupation and at the same time societal codes are encouraging them to work in that occupation, it is certainly possible for the increase in female labor supply to that occupation to be greater than the increase in the demand. And, if women are crowded into that occupation (i.e., employers refuse to hire them into other occupations, and/or women are reluctant to enter other occupations), then decreases in wages in the occupation and increases in female unemployment rates will result.

Further insight into occupational segregation may be obtained by applying our model to the Soviet experience. Gail Lapidus's paper on the Soviet Union may be interpreted to provide some interesting lessons with respect to system perturbation. The Soviets have consciously and successfully perturbed their system so as to bring women into the paid work force. The requirements of economic development and the exigencies of war and wartime destruction provided a powerful systemic jolt which affected labor demand, societal values and mores, and, ultimately, labor supply. However, the initial series of jolts did not affect male-female roles in the family. Nor did subsequent government policy seek to affect these roles. Thus, while some occupational integration has been achieved, Soviet women now experience both tremendous role conflict and occupational segregation at the workplace.

In Arrow's terms, the Soviet Union has not yet achieved a new equilibrium with respect to male-female work roles. The interrelatedness of the labor market and other societal systems does *not* mean that changes in the labor market will automatically cause appropriate adjustments in the other systems to attain a new equilibrium. It appears, instead that established traditions are extremely potent in maintaining occupational segregation. Some changes at the workplace can result from an initial systemic jolt. But unless a conscious effort is made to further affect other societal systems, neither occupational integration at the workplace nor a new systems equilibrium can be successfully achieved.

Some Likely Characteristics of the "Good" Occupationally Integrated Society

Let us turn now to the question of the likely characteristics of the "good," occupationally integrated society. Conference participants appear to concur on the definition of occupational segregation: the inequality of the distribution of men and women among occupations. We also all seem to take as a matter of faith the possibility of an "equal" distribution of the sexes among jobs in a modern society. However, what is less agreed upon is the definition of "equality" in such a society. For many this question appears to be relatively unimportant; we are so far from equality, their reasoning goes, that we ought to spend our efforts moving toward it and worry later about when and whether we have achieved it. Others *are* concerned about ultimate goals and ask, how do we know when occupational segregation no longer exists?

Several answers have been offered to this question. Some of us would say that in an equal society women would represent precisely 50 percent of the job holders in each paid and unpaid occupation not requiring sexual characteristics. Others would argue that the definition of occupational integration should be linked to women's labor force participation, so that, for example, if women represent 40 percent of the labor force, equality would require that they represent 40 percent of all jobholders in each occupation. Finally, a much looser definition, and the one to which I subscribe, has been put forth. It specifies that occupational integration can be said to exist when people make choices about their occupational goal based on their own tastes and talents, unfettered by societal notions of occupational sex appropriateness. The criteria for equality are thus shifted from outcome to opportunity.

What attributes in particular would a nonoccupationally segregated society have? Dimorphics, it should be noted, has a far different value system from neoclassical economics. Dimorphics is willing, where necessary, to sacrifice neoclassical economics' god, efficiency, in order to achieve other goals. Indeed, an important characteristic of an occupationally integrated society would be its emphasis on a multiplicity of societal desiderata. Thus, an occupationally integrated society would adopt, in Safilios-Rothschild's terms, more than one salient status line, so that it would be possible for individuals to be considered successful for many different reasons, with each route to success open to all, regardless of sex. The decrease in exclusive emphasis on efficiency combined with the availability of multiple salient status lines would both facilitate and reenforce occupational integration. We might expect that in an occupationally integrated society, or in one striving to achieve such integration, there would be far less importance attached to unbroken labor force participation through time, far more opportunities for part-time work, many more fathers participating intensively in child rearing, and much more interest in experimentation with family and community support systems.

There is one important question about the "good," occupationally integrated society which has produced some discord among conference participants. Mary Rowe raises the possibility that intense participation

in child rearing by fathers would provide psychological benefits not only
to the particular men performing such work, but also to the society as a
whole. Her thesis is that individuals who care for children develop ministrant behavior toward people in general and that if men spent a substantial part of their time raising children, our society would become more
nurturant and less competitive. Several people question whether
women, who now raise children, are any more ministrant than men.
Others willing to grant that child rearing fosters proclivities for general
nurturance, wondered whether such proclivities might not be swamped
by the necessity to compete in the world of work. The thesis that so-
called feminine values (nurturance, noncompetitiveness, etc.) can be
made to prevail in society has recently also been put forth by Herbert
Marcuse.[5] In his view, women's liberation would result in feminine
characteristics being universalized in (socialist) society. Even granting for
the moment the concept of "feminine characteristics," there remain
questions about the durability of these characteristics as women move
into traditionally male pursuits. The achievement of a more ministrant
society merely as a byproduct of occupational integration appears uncer-
tain.

Policy Strategies

The question of policy strategies has, I believe, been shortchanged
at this conference. In those policy discussions which were held, considerable emphasis was placed on affirmative action. Important issues were
raised. The difference between a goal and a quota has been analyzed by
Nira Long. Her distinction between the two, that a goal is a floor while a
quota is a ceiling, is useful. Long also examines the problem of applying
affirmative action policies to white-collar workers, and particularly to
professionals. Several conference participants point out the necessity of
disaggregating, by age, race, class, etc., when designing policy strategies.

Janet Norwood raises the question of the precise job categories into
which we hope to move people in order to achieve occcupational integration. Her view of the exceedingly few possibilities for movement is sober-
ing. Martha Griffiths echoes Norwood's concerns when she discusses
impending labor-saving changes in the clerical field. While the decrease
of jobs in this heavily female occupation makes it *possible* to move women
into other occupations, unless women are trained to operate the new
technological equipment and unless these other occupations require increases in labor, occupational integration will not be facilitated.

The necessity to go beyond present affirmative action policies was a
frequent conference theme. During several discussions the point was

5. Herbert Marcuse, "Feminism and Marxism," in *City Lights Anthology,* ed. Lawrence
Ferlinghetti (City Lights, 1974).

made that women should be given "credit" in the job market for their service to society and their accumulated experience during child rearing. Some suggested that a child-rearing preference, similar to the current veteran's preference, be adopted. The likely economic and social consequences of such a policy need to be explored.

A second area for policy consideration which was raised in one of the discussion sessions concerned women in less-developed countries. Elise Boulding and Hanna Papanek cited evidence of increasing occupational segregation and a worsening of women's relative position in societies in the initial stages of industrialization. Conference participants were exhorted to design policy strategies for preventing further development of this trend.

Some Unanswered Questions for Dimorphics

Dimorphics has just begun. Thomas Kuhn, in his book, *The Structure of Scientific Revolutions,* suggests that a new science leaves "all sorts of problems for the redefined group of practitioners to resolve."[6] In addition to elaborating a paradigm, expanding the systems interaction model proposed here, and providing general answers to the questions raised in the first section of this summary, dimorphics must deal with some specific theoretical and policy questions not analyzed by this conference. Some of these unanswered questions are:

First, the origin of occupational segregation (regardless of its particular pattern) remains unclear. How did men get to be heads of states and families? Why did women come to be dominated by men? Hartmann and Elise Boulding's contentions that the sexes were once equal is interesting, but their evidence merely changes the questions somewhat; it does not eliminate them.

A second unanswered question was raised by Barbara Bergmann. How does "the system" determine which sex gets which jobs? Will the emerging physician assistant occupation be male or female? Why? Will it vary by the sex composition of physicians in the various medical specialties? Why?

Third, why is it likely that one sex or another will tend to dominate a particular occupation? Why, even if both sexes initially engage in a particular occupation, does the occupation eventually "tip" toward one sex or the other? Are there tipping points? How are they determined?

In the policy areas, the conference, unfortunately, did not discuss the use of the tax system to provide incentives to business and individuals to move toward occupational integration.[7] Nor was the issue of in-

6. Kuhn, p. 10.
7. Some innovative possibilities for tax incentives are suggested in Carolyn S. Bell, "Alternatives for Social Change: The Future Status of Women" (paper prepared for the

come distribution in the occupationally integrated society adequately analyzed.

Another important point which was not addressed was whether tokenism is a stable equilibrium. Harriet Zellner, in a 1970 article,[8] made the distinction between erroneous and deliberate employer discrimination. If discrimination is erroneous, then an initial "application" of affirmative action is likely to be effective. For, as employers hire women into previously all-male occupations, they come to realize that women are productive "appropriate" workers, and so they hire more women. In other words, tokenism may be an unstable equilibrium. In this case, affirmative action is a far more effective technique for achieving occupational integration than in the case where employer discrimination is deliberate.

Undoubtedly conference participants and readers of this volume could list numerous additional theoretical and policy questions that ought to be pursued. Not only must dimorphics begin to deal with these unanswered questions; it must also develop techniques of interdisciplinary research. So far there has been little dimorphic research that could be called truly interdisciplinary. For the most part, we have been content with looking at common problems separately, each of us writing solely from the point of view of one's own discipline. True interdisciplinary research, of course, can sometimes be troublesome. There are conceptual and semantic differences to be overcome. Concepts of verification must be agreed upon. Yet, although it may be difficult to work in this emerging field, the rewards are likely to be numerous. For as Judith Long Laws noted, the way we study a system can influence the system itself.

Graduate School of Business
Stanford University

Mr. and Mrs. Spencer T. Olin Conference and the Status of Women in Higher Education and the Professions at Washington University, St. Louis, April 16–17, 1975), pp. 17–24.

8. Harriet Zellner, "Discrimination against Women, Occupational Segregation, and the Relative Wage," *American Economic Review* 62 (May 1972): 157–60.

APPENDIX

Sex Differences in Economists' Fields of Specialization

Myra H. Strober and Barbara B. Reagan

Most discussions of occupational segregation center around rather broad occupational definitions. Thus, social scientists frequently note the proportion of the female labor force who are clerical workers, or the proportion of all female professional and technical workers who are elementary and high school teachers. However, occupational segregation can also be analyzed within more narrowly defined occupations.

For example, while it is interesting to know why so few women choose to enter medicine or why so few are permitted to enter, it is also interesting to determine why those women who do become physicians are disproportionately found in pediatrics and psychiatry. Many of the factors involved in answering the second question are also involved in answering the first. Moreover, because of the reduced variability of career-choice determinants and the smaller variety of barriers to career-choice fulfillment, analysis of narrowly defined occupations can be particularly fruitful in yielding answers to questions about occupational segregation.

This paper looks at sex differences in the field specializations of economists. Section I proposes a path model of field choice. Section II describes the data base with which the model is tested. In the third section, empirical tests are presented and discussed. Section IV consid-

We wish to thank Patti Osborne, Lynn Rosener, and Patricia Kirby for research assistance, and the Carnegie Foundation for financial support.

ers some implications of our work and provides suggestions for further research.

I. A Path Model of Field Choice

For an occupation as a whole, a female-male occupational index (FMOI) may be computed as follows:

$$FMOI = \frac{number\ of\ women\ in\ occupation}{number\ of\ men\ in\ occupation} \times 100 .$$

For each specialty within an occupation, a similar index, a female-male specialty index (FMSI) may be computed in the same way.

Where women in an occupation are distributed among specialties in different proportions from men, the values of the several FMSIs will differ from the value of FMOI. Where an FMSI is greater than FMOI, that specialty may be considered relatively female intensive; where an FMSI is less than FMOI, relatively few females are found in the specialty. The degree of relative female intensity of a specialty may be calculated by subtracting its FMSI from FMOI. In this study, the vector of FMSIs in economics is the dependent variable. Our aim is to examine the determinants of the degree of female intensity of women economists' choice of field specialty.

The decision to enter a particular field, with a particular degree of female intensity, may be viewed as the culmination of a series of earlier decisions. At each decision point the individual may be viewed as having a set of career aspirations or goals. These aspirations are related to the individual's tastes, capabilities, personality, energy level, etc. In addition, at each decision point the individual faces a series of opportunities (or barriers). Those gatekeepers who open opportunities to women (or close them off) are conditioned to think certain opportunities are far more suitable for one sex or the other.

Aspirations and opportunities are not, however, independent. A prolonged absence of opportunity may reduce aspirations. Moreover, sex-role socialization, by teaching women that certain jobs are "inappropriate," can have a powerful influence on women's career aspirations.[1] The so-called inherent attraction of women to certain fields is probably much less inherent than the result of a long process of socialization. Because aspiration and opportunity are so interrelated, it is difficult to find variables which measure or affect one but not the other. The variables in our model clearly measure and affect both.

1. Judith Long Laws, "Work Aspiration of Women: False Leads and New Starts," in this volume.

Our model is a path model[2] with three phases; background, high school, and college/graduate school, leading to the decision to enter, at the Ph.D. level or in subsequent applications, a specialty with a particular FMSI. The phases of the path are depicted in table 1. The path model assumes the following causal ordering: high school variables are affected by background variables. In turn, college and graduate school variables are affected directly by high school variables and both directly and indirectly by background variables. Finally, the decision to enter a specialty with a particular FMSI is affected directly by college and graduate school variables and both directly and indirectly by background and high school variables.

With respect to the effects of background variables on high school variables, we hypothesize that, *ceteris paribus,* the later the date of birth, the more urban the home town, and the higher the level of parents' education, the higher are the woman's career aspirations and the greater are her career opportunities. Thus, the more likely she is to take more than the required number of years of high school mathematics and to make an early (precollege) decision to enter the predominantly male field of economics.

It also seems that older women economists might have been pushed or encouraged to go into fields of specialization considered to be more appropriate for women (e.g., consumer economics, labor economics, population, welfare programs) more often than younger women, and thus we hypothesize that later date of birth would have a direct negative effect on female-intensive-field choice.

With respect to the effect of high school variables on college and graduate school variables, we expect again that, *ceteris paribus,* the more years a woman has studied high school mathematics and the earlier her decision to become an economist, the more likely she is to have higher career aspirations. Her earlier decision to study more than the required amount of mathematics is particularly important in creating career opportunities.[3] Thus, we hypothesize that such a woman is likely to (1) choose B.A. and Ph.D. schools with high-quality economics programs, (2) major in economics as an undergraduate, and (3) study more than the average amount of college-level mathematics. We also postulate that such a woman has had less than the usual amount of pressure to conform to norms of female behavior and/or has disregarded these norms, so that she is less likely to pursue economics as a field of study in order to help people, a motive often deemed stereotypically female. When people are asked to

---

2. For an analysis of path models and a bibliography on the subject, see Duane F. Alwin and Robert M. Hauser, "The Decomposition of Effects in Path Analysis," *American Sociological Review* 40 (February 1975): 37–47.

3. For a discussion of this point, see Lucy W. Sells, "The Mathematics Filter and the Education of Women and Minorities" (paper presented to the annual meeting of the American Association for the Advancement of Science, Boston, February 18, 1976).

Table 1

Variables Included in Path Model of Field Choice by Ph.D. Economists

Phase 1: Background Variables	Phase 2: High School Variables	Phase 3: College/Graduate School Variables	Dependent Variable: Field Decision
Date of birth (BDATEBKTD)	Early decision to be an economist (EDEC)	Number of years of college mathematics (CMATH)	Female-male specialty index (FMSI)
Size of hometown (URBHOME)	Number of years of high school math (MATH)	Majored in economics as undergraduate (MAJ)	...
Level of parents' education (PARED)	...	Primary reason for becoming an economist was to help people (HELPING)	...
...	...	Quality of B.A. school (QBASCHL)	
...	...	Quality of Ph.D. school (QPHDSCHL)	

NOTES.—The variables were coded as follows: (1) BDATEBKTD: 1 = earlier than 1900; 2 = 1900–1909; 3 = 1910–19; 4 = 1920–29; 5 = 1930–39; 6 = 1940–49; 7 = 1950–59. (2) URBHOME: 1 = lived, at age fourteen, in a metropolitan area with a population of more than 50,000; 0 = did not live in such an area at age fourteen. (3) PARED: Parents' educational level was obtained by adding mother's and father's levels. For *one* parent these levels were coded as: 1 = grammar school or less; 2 = some high school; 3 = high school graduate; 4 = some college or other school; 5 = college graduate; 6 = some graduate school; 7 = graduate degree or professional degree. Thus the variable parents' educational level ranges in value from 2 to 14. (4) EDEC: 1 = decided to become an economist before entering college; 0 = decided to become an economist after entering college. (5) MATH: number of years of high school math; e.g., 2.5, 3.0, etc. (6) CMATH: number of years of college math; e.g., 2.5, 3.0, etc. (7) MAJ: 1 = majored in economics in college; 0 = did not major in economics in college. (8) HELPING: 1 = at time individual decided to be an economist, primary reason for decision was in order to help people; 0 = primary reason was something other than wanting to help people. (9) QBASCHL and QPHDSCHL: 5 = the seven schools which, according to the Cartter Report, have the top economics departments in the country: M.I.T., Harvard; Yale; Stanford; University of California, Berkeley; Princeton; and University of Chicago; 4 = schools in the so-called Chairman's Group, except for the seven included in the first category: Oxford, Cambridge, the London School of Economics, and the University of Paris are also included in category 2. Thus, there is a total of forty schools in this category; 3 = thirteen small undergraduate colleges to which the AAUP in 1973 gave its highest or second-highest ranking for full professors' salaries: Amherst, Antioch, Barnard, Goucher, Grinnell, Oberlin, Pomona, Smith, Swarthmore, Vassar, Wellesley, Wesleyan, and Williams; 2 = 132 other schools not in one of the four other categories. (10) FMSI: See table 2 for derivation of this variable.

express motives, it may be that women who have been conditioned that certain motives are unfeminine will not express or even recognize those motives. Men, on the other hand, will express them. Thus, the desire to help others may not be less prevalent for men, but may appear to be so because of more frequent expression of other motives.

As noted earlier, background variables are related to college and graduate school variables indirectly through their effects on high school variables. But background variables may also be related directly to college and graduate school variables. For example, more highly educated parents may create aspirations by steering their children toward better schools or create opportunities by being willing to make the higher undergraduate tuition payments required at many of the higher quality schools. In such instances, level of parents' education will be directly positively related to quality of B.A. school.

The hypothesized relationships between college graduate school variables and the FMSI are as follows: we postulate a negative coefficient between the number of years of college mathematics and the FMSI, that is, *ceteris paribus*, women who are more quantitatively oriented are presumed to be less traditionally female in their aspirations and therefore less likely to choose female-intensive specialties. The relationship between majoring in economics as an undergraduate and later choosing or finding the only opportunities are in a female-intensive specialty is hypothesized to be negative. We are speculating that women with a strong enough interest in economics at the undergraduate level to major in economics would be less likely to confine their later choice of specialty to a field with a high FMSI. (About 30 percent of the Ph.D. or A.B.D. economists surveyed, male or female, did not major in economics as undergraduates.) On the other hand, the relationship between choosing economics as an occupation in order to help people and choosing a relatively female-intensive specialty is presumed to be positive. This is because several of the female-intensive specialties tend to deal with people and the reduction of poverty and suffering (e.g., labor economics, medical economics, economics of welfare programs and economic development).

Somewhat more problematical are the expected signs on the coefficients relating quality of the B.A. and the Ph.D. schools attended with the female intensity of the specialty chosen. On the one hand, women who have later dates of birth, highly educated parents, urban hometowns, more high school mathematics, and a precollege decision to be an economist are, for reasons discussed earlier, both less likely to choose female-intensive specialties and more likely to attend high-quality B.A. or Ph.D. programs. Thus we might expect a negative relationship between quality of schools attended and the FMSI. On the other hand, women who attend high-quality B.A. or Ph.D. programs may find the highly prestigious professors at these institutions particularly difficult to emulate. Women students in high-quality programs may therefore be particularly

motivated to move into those specialties in which women have traditionally worked and succeeded. Which of these effects, if any, will predominate is unclear, and we cannot easily predict the signs of the coefficients
relating FMSI to the quality of the economics program at B.A. and Ph.D.
schools attended.

It should be noted, of course, that a specialty has many attributes in
addition to its degree of relative female intensity. While we expect that
women's choice of specialty is influenced significantly by the variables we
have discussed, we also expect that our model will explain only a small
fraction of the variance in the vector of FMSIs.

II. The Data Base

In December 1971, at its annual meeting, the American Economic
Association (AEA) took steps to create the Committee on the Status of
Women in the Economics Profession (CSWEP). In 1972 CSWEP came
into being and began to develop a roster of women economists and
embarked upon a campaign to "register" such women. Women registered
with CSWEP in order to receive its newsletter, keep up with current job
information, and be included in lists of women sent by CSWEP in response to inquiries by prospective employers and groups looking for
speakers. By the summer of 1974 CSWEP had names and addresses for
1,363 women economists. In August 1974 a questionnaire asking for
information on education, employment, job-market experience,
affirmative-action experience, and background was sent to these 1,363
women. We obtained a matched male sample in two stages. First, we
requested each woman economist to supply the names and addresses of
three male economists who were in her class when the woman did her
highest level of academic work in economics. Three names were requested, but only one was selected in order to try to reduce bias stemming
from the tendency to supply, in the first instance, the name of a fellow
student who had achieved eminence. As the female questionnaires came
in, the number of the male matched for educational institution who was to
be selected was rotated, so that for the first female respondent the first
male listed was chosen, for the second respondent the second male listed
was chosen, and so on.

The second method of obtaining matches was numerically much
more important. In early 1975 printouts by sex based on the October
1974 AEA *Directory of Members* were made available to us. Three
hundred and thirteen women economists not previously registered with
CSWEP were located in the *Directory* printouts and were sent questionnaires. In addition, the male economists were classified by school and
year of degree, and then one was selected at random from among those
who had gone to the same graduate school in the same class as a woman

economist. Men matched in this manner were sent questionnaires. By May 1975, after appropriate follow-up procedures,[4] we had completed questionnaires from 949 women, a response rate of 56 percent. We also had 782 completed questionnaires from male economists, a response rate of 47 percent. Of the male matches, 130 were obtained from names supplied by female respondents; the remainder, 652, were selected at random from the AEA printouts of males matched by school and class.

After screening questionnaires for inappropriate respondents (e.g., a few respondents who were not economists) and for respondents who had no match, we obtained a matched sample of 1,240 (620 men and 620 women).

Calculation of the dependent variable, FMSI, was based on a sample size of 1,032 (516 men and 516 women), including only those in the matched sample who either had a Ph.D. or were completing a Ph.D. thesis (see table 2). The sample size for testing the path model was somewhat smaller, 780 (391 men and 389 women), as respondents with missing data on relevant independent variables were excluded from the computer runs.

III. Empirical Tests

A review of preliminary data from the CSWEP 1974–75 Survey of Economists indicated the presence of sex differences in the field specialization of economists.[5] For example, we found that while 19 percent of the female economists in our sample are in the labor field, only 10 percent of the profession as a whole (which is about 88 percent male) is in that field. Sex differences by field of specialization are also present in our sample of 1,032 Ph.D. and A.B.D. (all but dissertation) economists, as may be seen in table 2. Differences in field distributions by sex are statistically significant ($\chi^2 = 33.16$; $P < .0001$). In the final column of table 2 we have calculated the FMSI for each specialty. It should be noted that the numbers of men and women in the sample are the same so that FMOI is equal to 100. The FMSI values range from a low of 48 in business and finance, marketing, and accounting (group 500) and in agriculture and natural resources (group 700) to a high of 153 in manpower, labor, and population (group 800) and 135 in welfare

4. In October 1974 those who had not responded to the August mailing received a postcard requesting that they complete their questionnaire and asking for some basic data if they did not plan to do so. In November a second copy of the questionnaire was sent to those from whom responses had not been received. In March 1975, a reminder postcard was sent to those women economists, and their male matches, whose names and addresses had been obtained from the AEA printouts.

5. See Myra H. Strober, "Women Economists: Career Aspirations, Education and Training," *American Economic Review* 65 (May 1975): 96.

Table 2

Male and Female Economists by Specialty* Ph.D.'s and A.B.D.'s†

Specialty	Ph.D. Female (N)	+ A.B.D. Female (N)	= Total Female (F) (N)	Ph.D. Male (N)	+ A.B.D. Male (N)	= Total Male (M) (N)	Female/Male Specialty Index (F/M [×100])
General economics; theory; history; systems (000)	68	26	94	58	24	82	114.6
Economic growth; development; planning; fluctuations (100)	27	20	47	32	9	41	114.6
Economic statistics (200)	18	8	26	16	19	35	74.3
Domestic monetary and fiscal theory and institutions (300)	36	30	66	56	36	92	71.7
International economics (400)	25	13	38	20	11	31	122.6
Business and finance; marketing; accounting (500)	8	2	10	16	5	21	47.6
Industrial organization; technological change; industry studies (600)	19	14	33	31	25	56	58.9
Agriculture; natural resources (700)	7	8	15	22	9	31	48.4
Manpower; labor; population (800)	65	39	104	48	20	68	152.9
Welfare programs; consumer economics; urban and regional economics (900)	44	25	69	22	29	51	135.3
Total	326	190	516	326	190	516	100.0

*These specialties and associated codes are those used by the *Journal of Economic Literature*.
†All but dissertation. These are graduate students currently writing their theses.

programs, consumer economics, and urban and regional sciences (group 900).

When the economists in the sample who have not yet completed their dissertations are considered separately as an indication of possible new trends in relative female or male intensity of fields within economics, little change can be seen. The two most male-intensive fields in economics for the sample as a whole (noted above) appear to be staying that way. Of the two most female-intensive fields, manpower, labor, and population (group 800) appears to be getting even more female intensive; whereas welfare programs, consumer economics, and urban and regional economics (group 900) is becoming less female intensive in the last few years. This latter change may be related to the current demand for urban economists. Among young women A.B.D.'s, the important change not also seen among young men A.B.D.'s is the relative increase in the number of women going into monetary and fiscal economics (group 300).

A. Regression for Female Economists

To test the path model described earlier, we ran eight stepwise regressions in the following order. First, the three background variables were regressed separately on each of the high school variables. Second, the five background and high school variables were regressed separately on each of the five college/graduate school variables. Finally, the ten background, high school and college/graduate school variables were regressed against the FMSI. The means and standard deviations of the variables used in the regressions are given in table 3.

In order to trace the relevant paths, we looked first at the regression with FMSI as the dependent variable. Any variable significantly ($F \geq 2.0$) related to FMSI was considered to be part of the path. For the 389 women Ph.D.'s and A.B.D.'s with the necessary information to be included in the regressions,[6] the only variable significantly related to relative female intensity of specialty field was the dummy variable, MAJ, which takes a value = 1 if the woman majored in economics as an undergraduate. As hypothesized, this relationship is negative. If no other variables are included in the equation we have the following result:

$$\text{FMSI} = 116.67 - 8.37 \text{ MAJ} \ (R^2 = .012).$$
$$(4.84)$$

Numbers in parentheses below the b values are F values. If we allow variables with an $F \geq 1.0$ to also be included in the equation, we raise the

---

6. Regressions were also run using a pairwise deletion of cases. The results were similar to those reported here.

Table 3

Mean and Standard Deviations of Variables Included
in Path Analysis

Variables	Male Sample ($N = 391$)	Female Sample ($N = 389$)
Background variables:		
Date of birth	5.47	5.43
	(1.05)	(1.03)
Size of hometown at age fourteen	0.54	0.58
	(0.50)	(0.50)
Parents' educational level	7.57	8.84
	(3.24)	(3.35)
High school variables:		
Early decision to be an economist (i.e., before college)	0.04	0.04
	(0.20)	(0.19)
Number of years of high school mathematics	3.59	3.49
	(1.07)	(0.89)
College and graduate school variables:		
Quality of B.A. school	2.28	2.44
	(1.47)	(1.46)
Majored in economics	0.69	0.71
	(0.46)	(0.46)
Number of years of college mathematics	1.28	1.15
	(1.44)	(1.58)
Quality of Ph.D. school	3.45	3.48
	(1.47)	(1.46)
Primary reason for becoming an economist was to help people	0.14	0.15
	(0.35)	(0.36)
Dependent variable:		
Female/male specialty index (FMSI)	98.6	109.73
	(35.3)	(34.24)

NOTE.—See table 1 for definition of variables, table 2 for derivation of FMSI. S.D. shown in parentheses.

coefficient on MAJ slightly, and have the following result:

$$FMSI = 117.26 - 8.94 \text{ MAJ} - 1.41 \text{ QPHDSCHL}$$
$$(5.48) \qquad (1.36)$$
$$+ 3.92 \text{ URBHOME} \ (R^2 = .019),$$
$$(1.25)$$

where QPHDSCHL is the quality of the Ph.D. school attended and UR-BHOME is a dummy variable $= 1$ if at age fourteen the woman lived in a metropolitan area with a population $>50,000$.

To continue tracing out our path, we now look at the equation in which MAJ is the dependent variable and note the following result:

$$MAJ = 0.54 + 0.296 \text{ EDEC} + 0.04 \text{ MATH} \ (R^2 = .024),$$
$$(6.20) \qquad (2.88)$$

where EDEC is a dummy $= 1$ if the individual made an early decision (before starting college) to be an economist and MATH is equal to the number of years of high school mathematics. As hypothesized, an early decision to be an economist and number of years of high school math are positively related to the decision to major in economics.

Looking at the regressions in which EDEC and MATH are, respectively, the dependent variables, we note the following: In the EDEC equation, none of the background variables is significant at the $F = 2.0$ level. For the MATH equation, as hypothesized, date of birth is significantly positively related to number of years of high school math:

$$\text{MATH} = 1.82 + 0.307 \text{ BDATEBKTD } (R^2 = .126) ,$$
$$(55.7)$$

where BDATEBKTD takes on a value from 1 to 7, representing birth dates from before 1900 to the 1950s.

In figure 1, a summary of the relationships is presented in a path diagram. The number in brackets next to the path coefficient, β, is the regression coefficient. From the path diagram, we can see the interrelationships among date of birth, an early decision to study economics, the number of years of high school math, the decision to major in economics, and the decision to choose a specialty field with a particular FMSI.

While the path analysis provides support for several of the hypotheses in our decision model, it should be noted that, as expected, there is a

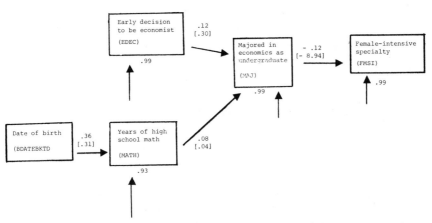

FIG. 1.—A path model of field choice for women economists. See table 1 for definition of variables. Bracketed coefficients are regression coefficients, b; unbracketed coefficients are normalized regression coefficients, β, also called path coefficients. Path coefficients are conditional upon those variables shown on the chart plus others included in the regression in order to optimize the included parameters according to the mean square error criterion. Coefficients along arrows from the outside of the path are the unexplained variance equal to $\sqrt{1 - R^2}$.

high unexplained variance in all phases of the path. It should also be noted that several of our hypotheses are *not* supported. In particular, while the number of years of high school mathematics is indirectly related to the FMSI variable, neither number of years of high school math (MATH) nor number of years of college math (CMATH) is directly related to FMSI. And even in the equation for major in economics as an undergraduate (MAJ), the effect of high school math is relatively small. We also tested for, but did not find, a significant relationship between FMSI and the desire to study economics primarily because it provided an opportunity to apply mathematics. The hypothesis that more quantitatively oriented women are less likely to choose female-intensive specialties receives only partial support from our analyses. Nor is the desire to study economics primarily in order to help people, HELPING, significantly related to the choice by women of a relatively female-intensive specialty.

B. Regressions for Male Economists

Although our model was designed to predict the degree of female intensity of specialty choice of women, we also used the model to test for sex differences in such choices by running the series of regressions already described for our male sample. The path model of field choice for the male sample is presented in figure 2. The two variables significantly related to FMSI are HELPING, the desire to study economics primarily in order to help people, and QBASCHL, quality of B.A. school attended.

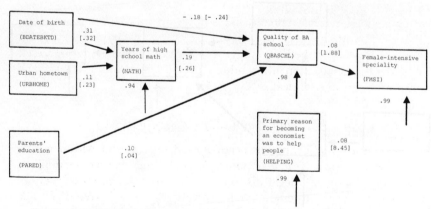

Fig. 2.—A path model of field choice for men economists. See table 1 for definition of variables. Bracketed coefficients are regression coefficients, *b;* unbracketed coefficients are normalized regression coefficients, β, also called path coefficients. Path coefficients are conditional upon those variables shown on the chart plus others included in the regression in order to optimize the included parameters according to the mean square error criterion. Coefficients along arrows from the outside of the path are the unexplained variance equal to $\sqrt{1 - R^2}$.

The reason why men who attend high-quality schools for their B.A. degree should be more likely than other men to pursue relatively female-intensive fields is not readily apparent.

Three other aspects of the male regressions are noteworthy. First, it is interesting that while the desire to study economics primarily in order to help people is not a statistically significant determinant of female field choice, it is significantly related to male economists' decisions to enter relatively female-intensive specialties. Second, as in the female regressions, MATH in high school has an indirect but not a direct relationship to FMSI. However, while in the female regressions having more math in high school was likely to lead to specialization in relatively less female-intensive fields, the opposite is the case in the male regressions. For men, more high school math is associated with attending a higher quality B.A. school, which is then associated with being more likely to choose a female-intensive speciality. Finally, while urbanness of hometown does not appear to significantly influence the number of years of high school math for women economists, relative urbanness of hometown is statistically significant in determining the quantity of mathematics studied by men economists.

C. Regressions for Male and Female Economists

When the male and female economists are pooled for the regressions and sex (F = 1, M = 0) is added as an independent variable, the relative importance of sex and the other variables can be seen from the β coefficients. Even after all the other variables in the model are held constant, sex is still the most important of the factors explaining choice of female-intensive specialties or male-intensive specialties.[7] Thus, there probably are other aspects of social conditioning or barriers to entry for women not yet identified. (To suggest genetic reasons for this difference in field of specialization after other variables in the model are held constant seems nonsensical.)

IV. Conclusion and Implications

This study has examined occupational segregation within a narrowly defined occupation, economics, by analyzing several determinants of women economists' decisions to enter various fields of specialization. A woman's decision to enter a field with a particular degree of female intensity was viewed as the culmination of a series of earlier decisions, and path analysis was used to model this decision-making process. Variables measuring both career aspirations and career opportunities were

---

7. Betas are .15 for SEX (F = 1, M = 0), .07 for HELPING, .06 for MAJ, and .06 for OBASCHL in regression with female-intensive specialty as the dependent variable.

utilized in the model. The model was tested on data collected by the American Economic Association Committee on the Status of Women in the Economics Profession (CSWEP) in the 1974–75 Survey of Economists.

We found that the most important determinant of the degree of relative female intensity of field choice was whether or not a woman economist majored in economics in undergraduate college. Women who did not major in economics as undergraduates were more likely to choose relatively female-intensive fields for specialization in Ph.D. study or subsequent applications. In addition, we found that women who majored in economics as undergraduates were likely to have made an early (precollege) decision to be an economist and to have taken more years of high school math than the average student. This latter finding again underlines the importance of intervention at the high school level if we wish to increase the number of women economists. Clearly, both introduction of economics as a possible field for women and the encouragement of math skills are needed to increase the number of women majoring in economics as undergraduates. Although later date of birth indirectly is negatively associated with choice of a female-intensive specialty, it was not found to be directly so as expected. Younger women still are specializing disproportionately in female-intensive fields. The amount of math in college was expected to be negatively related to a choice by women of female-intensive fields, but was not found to be a significant factor after the amount of high school math was held constant (the amounts of high school and college math are correlated; $R = .38$).

Our model, though designed to predict women's field choice, was also tested on a sample of male economists matched, for school and year of degree, to the female sample. For men we found that the decision to choose a relatively female-intensive specialty was related to the quality of B.A. school attended and to the desire to study economics primarily in order to help people. Even more unexpected was the finding that, for men, the number of years of mathematics studied in high school was indirectly related to the decision to pursue a relatively female-intensive specialty. While in the female regressions having more math in high school was likely to lead to specialization in relatively less female-intensive fields, the opposite was the case in the male regressions.

Our results pose interesting questions regarding perceptions of field differences in prestige, intellectual challenge, and mathematical ability required. In addition, although we have tacitly assumed here that the various specialties are not associated with differences in financial rewards, the validity of this assumption is by no means clear and needs to be tested. Since this paper is one of the first to be prepared using the matched sample of the 1974–75 Survey of Economists, it is hoped that further exploration of the differences in salaries of women and men economists from that survey will shed more light on factors which influence choice of specialized field. Also, differences in explicit barriers to entry and advancement for women need to be studied further, both with these survey data and with other available information.[8] It may be that influences bearing on choice of dissertation research or allocation of postdoctorate research programs to women and/or to specific fields of specialization involve the most subtle forms of occupational segregation and sexism—differential encouragement on the part of male mentors.

It is clear from this volume that disaggregation to the occupational level is necessary to analyze sexism. It also seems clear from this paper that disaggregation to the field of specialization within an occupation provides further evidence of the pervasiveness of occupational segregation by sex.

Finally, our study demonstrates the fruitfulness of using path analysis to examine the determinants of occupational segregation and to highlight critical decision points along the decision path. It also indicates that the critical points along men's decision paths may be different from those along women's paths. The determination of critical choice points is useful for designing social policies to permit individuals to make career choices in accordance with taste and talent, unfettered by subtle or explicit societal barriers.

Stanford University (Strober)
Southern Methodist University (Reagan)

8. For a discussion of explicit barriers to entry into particular specialties, see Michelle Patterson, "Sex and Specialization in Academe and the Professions," in *Academic Women on the Move,* ed. Alice S. Rossi and Ann Calderwood (New York: Russell Sage Foundation, 1973), esp. pp. 323–24 on barriers in anthropology.

Index

Abbott, Edith, 159

Ables, B., 29

Achievement syndrome, components of, 45

Affirmative action, 86, 257–58, 259; accountability in public sector, 261, 263; backlash, 282; difficulties in academic communities, 262–63; implementation of, 282; role-related research model, 285–86; social structural research model, 286–91; temperamental research model, 283–85; tokenism, 302

Agency for International Development (AID), 259, 260, 261

Agrovillage, 97

Alimony and child support, 8

American Council on Education, 85

American Economic Association Committee on the Status of Women in the Economics Profession (CSWEP), viii, 3, 90, 308; Survey of Economists, 309, 316

American Telephone and Telegraph (AT&T), employment practices of, 66, 69, 257–58

Anthony, Susan B., 163

Arrow, Kenneth J., 213, 230, 245, 247, 249; equilibrium, 255, 294, 298; personal investment, 250

Aspiration, as psychological event, 33; effect of sex discrimination, 44; fluctuation in, 33–34; increased level of, 78; limited achievement, 54; research on formation of, 37; role relationships, 3

Association of Women in Science, 276

Athletic contests, female exclusion from, 23

Bailey, M., 45

Baker, Elizabeth F., 159

Ban, P. L., 28

Barnes, W. F., 222, 223

Bartending, restrictive laws, 64–65

Becker, Gary S., 184, 230, 247

Beecher, Catharine, 87, 88

Bell, Carolyn, 280

Bergmann, Barbara R., 184, 185, 217, 221, 224, 233

Blau, Francine, 4, 222, 233, 234, 235, 242, 248, 249, 294

Blumenfield, W. S., 29

Bona fide occupational qualification (BFOQ), 69–70, 84

Boserup, Ester, *Woman's Role in Economic Development*, 143

Boulding, Elise, 4, 173, 175, 294, 301

Boulding, Kenneth, 2, 293, 294

Bradwell v. *Illinois*, 61

Brandeis, 165

Brandt, E. M., 27

Tangri, Sandra, 245
Tax legislation, 13
Tiger, Lionel, 25, 91
Time, as critical issue, 78
Time magazine, 10
Tully, Judy Corder, 19
Turnover rates, 221

Unemployment, definition change, 223; female ration of, 9; rate, 216
UNESCO Time Budget Series, 111
Unions, and protective legislation, 159, 164–65; regulations of, 10; wage rate differences, 10
United Nation's World Conference of International Women's Year, 2–3, 4
Urban Institute, 202, 206; Microanalytic Model (UIMM), 207–8
Urban middle-class women, Middle Ages, 105
USSR, 4, 243, 298; authoritarian paternalism, 136; female employment patterns, 124–32; income differentials, 132–34; occupational segregation, 134; sexual equality and employment, 122–24; social transformation, 119–20; structural changes, 54

Veterans' preference program, 264
Vicarious achievement patterns, 19

Wage differentials, 11; Middle Ages, 104–5
Wage-rate discrimination, 268
Waldrop, M. R., 27
Walker, Kathryn, 35
War Labor Board, 267, 268
Welfare mothers, motivation to work, 206
Wellesley College Center for Research on Women in Higher Education and Professions, vii
Wertheimer, Richard, 206
Whiting, Beatrice, 27
Wirtz, Willard, 9
Woman's Role in Economic Development, Boserup, Ester, 143
Women and Madness, Chesler, Phyllis, 7
"Women, Bread and Babies," 176
Women heads of household, 2, 14; care of children, 103
Women's Christian Temperance Union, 173
Women's Equity Action League (WEAL), 72, 275, 276
Women's role, as childbearer, 20
Women's Trade Union League, 155
Women workers, economic need of, 9
Work, social structure of, 86; upgrading status of, 94
Workloads, 98
Work motivation, incentives, 41–42, 48; misconceptions, 34–37; social comparison, 42–43; studies of, 40–41
World Plan of Action, 3

Zellner, Harriet, 302